Lecture Notes in Artificial Intell

Subseries of Lecture Notes in Computer Sci
Edited by J. G. Carbonell and J. Siekmann

Lecture Notes in Computer Science
Edited by G. Goos, J. Hartmanis, and J. van Leeuwen

Springer

Berlin
Heidelberg
New York
Barcelona
Hong Kong
London
Milan
Paris
Tokyo

Pier Luca Lanzi Wolfgang Stolzmann
Stewart W. Wilson (Eds.)

Advances in Learning Classifier Systems

Third International Workshop, IWLCS 2000
Paris, France, September 15-16, 2000
Revised Papers

 Springer

Series Editors

Jaime G. Carbonell,Carnegie Mellon University, Pittsburgh, PA, USA
Jörg Siekmann, University of Saarland, Saarbrücken, Germany

Volume Editors

Pier Luca Lanzi
Politecnico di Milano
Dipartimento di Elettronica e Informazione
Artificial Intelligence and Robotics Laboratory
Piazza Leonardo da Vinci 32, 20133 Milan, Italy
E-mail: pierluca.lanzi@polimi.it

Wolfgang Stolzmann
DaimlerChrysler AG
Research and Technology, Cognition and Robotics
Alt-Moabit 96A, 10559 Berlin, Germany
E-mail: wolfgang.stolzmann@daimlerchrysler.com

Stewart W. Wilson
Prediction Dynamics, Concord, MA 01742, USA, and
The University of Illinois
Department of General Engineering
Urbana-Champaign, IL 61801, USA
E-mail: wilson@prediction-dynamics.com

Cataloging-in-Publication Data applied for

Die Deutsche Bibliothek - CIP-Einheitsaufnahme

Advances in learning classifier systems : third international workshop ;
revised papers / IWLCS 2000, Paris, France, September 15 - 16, 2000.
Pier Luca Lanzi . . . (ed.). - Berlin ; Heidelberg ; New York ; Barcelona ;
Hong Kong ; London ; Milan ; Paris ; Singapore ; Tokyo : Springer, 2001
   (Lecture notes in computer science ; Vol. 1996 : Lecture notes in
   artificial intelligence)
   ISBN 3-540-42437-7

CR Subject Classification (1998): I.2, F.4.1, F.1.1

ISBN 3-540-42437-7 Springer-Verlag Berlin Heidelberg New York

Springer-Verlag Berlin Heidelberg New York
a member of BertelsmannSpringer Science+Business Media GmbH

http://www.springer.de

© Springer-Verlag Berlin Heidelberg 2001

Typesetting: Camera-ready by author, data conversion by PTP Berlin, Stefan Sossna
Printed on acid-free paper   SPIN 10782167   06/3142   5 4 3 2 1 0

Preface

Learning classifier systems are rule-based systems that exploit evolutionary computation and reinforcement learning to solve difficult problems. They were introduced in 1978 by John H. Holland, the father of genetic algorithms, and since then they have been applied to domains as diverse as autonomous robotics, trading agents, and data mining.

At the Second International Workshop on Learning Classifier Systems (IWLCS 99), held July 13, 1999, in Orlando, Florida, active researchers reported on the then current state of learning classifier system research and highlighted some of the most promising research directions. The most interesting contributions to the meeting are included in the book *Learning Classifier Systems: From Foundations to Applications*, published as LNAI 1813 by Springer-Verlag.

The following year, the Third International Workshop on Learning Classifier Systems (IWLCS 2000), held September 15–16 in Paris, gave participants the opportunity to discuss further advances in learning classifier systems. We have included in this volume revised and extended versions of thirteen of the papers presented at the workshop.

The volume has been organized into four parts. Part I is dedicated to important theoretical issues of learning classifier systems research including formal models for studying convergence properties and analysis of performance. Part II contains papers discussing applications of learning classifier systems such as medical data analysis, market analysis, data mining, and control. Part III presents some advanced architectures in which classifier systems interact to achieve common goals. Part IV contains the most updated learning classifier systems bibliography with more than 600 references. An appendix contains a paper presenting a formal description of XCS, currently the most intensively studied learning classifier system model.

We believe this volume will be the ideal companion for researchers interested in learning classifier systems and will provide useful insights into the most relevant topics and the most interesting open issues.

April 2001

Pier Luca Lanzi
Wolfgang Stolzmann
Stewart W. Wilson

Organization

The Third International Workshop on Learning Classifier Systems (IWLCS 2000) was held September 15–16, 2000 in Paris, France, between the Sixth International Conference on the Simulation of Adaptive Behavior (SAB 2000) and the The Sixth International Conference on Parallel Problem Solving from Nature (PPSN VI).

Organizing Committee

Pier Luca Lanzi	Politecnico di Milano, Italy
Wolfgang Stolzmann	DaimlerChrysler AG, Germany
Stewart W. Wilson	The University of Illinois at Urbana-Champaign, USA
	Prediction Dynamics, USA

Program Committee

Andrea Bonarini	Politecnico di Milano, Italy
Lashon B. Booker	The MITRE Corporation, USA
Marco Dorigo	Université Libre de Bruxelles, Belgium
David E. Goldberg	The University of Illinois at Urbana-Champaign, USA
John H. Holmes	University of Pennsylvania, USA
Tim Kovacs	University of Birmingham, UK
Pier Luca Lanzi	Politecnico di Milano, Italy
Rick L. Riolo	University of Michigan, USA
Robert E. Smith	The University of The West of England, UK
Wolfgang Stolzmann	DaimlerChrysler AG, Germany
Stewart W. Wilson	The University of Illinois at Urbana-Champaign, USA
	Prediction Dynamics, USA

Table of Contents

III   Advanced Architectures

IV   The Bibliography

V   Appendix

Part I

Theory

An Artificial Economy of Post Production Systems

Eric B. Baum and Igor Durdanovic

NEC Research Institute
4 Independence Way
Princeton, NJ 08540, USA
{eric,igord}@research.nj.nec.com

Abstract. We study the problem of how a computer program can learn, by interacting with an environment, to return an algorithm for solving a class of problems. The two example domains studied in this paper are Blocks World stacking problems and Rubik's Cube. Our approach is to simulate the evolution of an artificial economy of computer programs called "agents". Simple rules imposed on the economy result in credit assignment, factoring the problem of evolving an overall program for the class of problems into simpler problems of evolving agents that specialize on aspects of the problem and collaborate to solve the overall class. In this paper our agents are Post Production Systems. Our system, called Hayek4, has learned from random examples a program that solves arbitrary block stacking problems. The program essentially consists of about 5 learned rules and some learned control information. Solution of an instance with n blocks in its goal stack requires the automatic chaining of the rules in correct sequence about $2n$ deep. Hayek4 has also learned to correct Rubik's cubes scrambled with up to about 7 random rotations. These results can also be seen in the automatic theorem proving context as a way to learn domain knowledge allowing one to automatically generate compact proofs.

1   Introduction

We study the problem of how a computer program can learn, by interacting with an environment, to return an algorithm for solving a class of problems. This is a problem that humans are often good at. An example can be seen in Blocks World, c.f. Fig. 1. Humans easily describe a procedure that can solve arbitrary size instances. Rubik's cube is a harder, well known example. Humans, after playing with the cube and thinking for a week, often learn so as to be able to solve a randomly-scrambled cube quickly.

This problem is formalized as reinforcement learning(RL) [1]. In RL the learner interacts with an environment that it can sense and take actions on, and that makes "money" payments when a series of correct actions puts it in the right state. The learner's goal is to discover a strategy that earns money efficiently. The literature discusses two approaches to RL. The first, called "value

P.L. Lanzi, W. Stolzmann, and S.W. Wilson (Eds.): IWLCS 2000, LNAI 1996, pp. 3–20, 2001.
© Springer-Verlag Berlin Heidelberg 2001

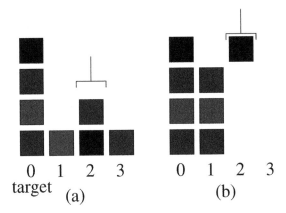

Fig. 1. We present a series of randomly chosen Blocks World instances, gradually increasing the size as the system learns. Each instance contains 4 stacks of colored blocks, with $2n$ total blocks and k colors. The leftmost stack, stack 0, serves as a template only and is of height n. The other three stacks contain, between them, the same multi-set of colored blocks as stack 0. The learner can pick up the top block on any but stack 0 and place the block on top of any stack but 0. The learner takes actions until it asserts "*Done*", or exceeds $10n \log_3(k)$ actions. If the learner copies stack 0 to stack 1 and states *Done*, it receives a reward of n. If it uses $10n \log_3(k)$ actions or states *Done* without copying stack 0, it terminates activity with no reward. Figure (a) shows the initial state for an example with $n = 4$ and $k = 3$. Figure (b) shows the position just before solution. The instance ends with the blue block on stack 1. Note the goal is to discover an *algorithm* capable of solving random new instances. The best human-generated algorithm of which we are aware uses $4n \log_2(k)$ actions.

iteration", attempts to learn an evaluation function mapping each state to an estimate of its value, and then returns the algorithm: take the action leading to the state of highest value. This approach has had one striking success in Backgammon, but this is apparently due to the fact that a linear evaluation function is effective in this domain [2]. Value iteration appears essentially hopeless in domains that have huge state spaces unless they also have an extremely simple and learnable evaluation function [3]. Blocks World has a huge state space and no simple evaluation function. Without hand coded features, but with algorithmic improvements designed to grapple with the problem, TD learning could only learn to find a specific block if under no more than 2 other blocks [3]. Given a useful hand coded feature, TD learning succeeds in training a neural net to solve problems with up to about 8 blocks [4]. Rubik's cube also apparently has no simple evaluation function: it takes a long series of moves in the right direction to reach a state at which progress is easily apparent.

The second approach (known in the RL literature as "policy iteration") attempts to learn a program directly. Evolutionary programming methods can be applied here. However, the space of programs is huge, and its fitness landscape is typically rough, so such methods are of limited applicability. Koza [5] applied

GP to the far simpler problem of solving a single instance of Blocks World, rather than producing an algorithm to solve arbitrary Blocks World instances . Given hand coded features including "next block needed", GP succeeded in solving a single 9 block problem. Asked to produce an algorithm for solving random problems, and given a powerful hand coded feature, GP succeeded in producing a program capable of solving only instances with about 5 blocks [4]. Similarly, Inductive Logic Programming solved only about 2 block instances [6]. On Rubik's cube as well we are unaware of pure learning or program evolution work, most of the work being concerned with planning from a given position, rather than reinforcement learning or developing an algorithm. The work most closely related to ours on Rubik's cube appears to be that of Korf [7], who fed in a series of subgoals (getting the cubies right one by one in a specified order) and then found, by a combination of search and cleverly tailored tricks, a program that is able to tabulate sequences of actions achieving each subgoal from the previous, eventually unscrambling an arbitrarily scrambled Rubik's cube.

We view Holland's Classifier systems [8] as a seminal approach to deal with searching the huge program space. By using an economic model to assign credit to modules, it might be possible to factor the search. By finding modules instead of whole programs, the combinatorial explosion might be mitigated. However, Holland Classifiers have not been successful at solving complex problems either [9].

In a series of previous papers [10,11,4], we have reported results on why Classifiers fail and how their problems can be corrected. In our view, there are two basic problems. First, their economic model is flawed, which leads to misallocation of credit. We have corrected this by imposing an economic model based on two general principles, conservation of money and strong property rights, which prevent these misallocations. Second, the representation language used by classifiers seems insufficiently powerful. Many useful classifier programs are unstable, since useful rules will go broke and be removed unless high bidding classifiers tend to follow low bidding classifiers [10,12], the exact opposite of what would be needed for Holland's intuition [8] of "default hierarchies". Although classifiers are in principle Turing complete [13], it is unclear whether classifier systems remain computationally universal when one restricts consideration to configurations which are dynamically stable. We address this representation problem by using more powerful agent language.

Our first economic model, Hayek1, used simple agents, and because of the dynamic stability problem could only solve large Blocks World problems when given intermediate reward for partial progress [10]. Our last economic model, Hayek3, used agents that compute S-expressions [4]. This model of computation was not Turing-complete, and so the system could not produce a program capable of solving arbitrary instances. It did, however, produce systems capable of solving random instances with hundreds of blocks given only end reward. The stark contrast between standard classifier systems, which have trouble forming chains more than a few classifiers deep [9], and Hayek1 and Hayek3's ability to learn systems with stable chains several hundred agents deep showed the critical importance of imposing an economic framework respecting property rights and conservation of money.

Here we report experiments with Hayek4. Hayek4 uses agents that are written in a Post Production System. This language is Turing complete. Although Post proved computational completeness of his Production systems almost as long ago as Turing and Church [14,15], we are unaware of any previous papers studying the automatic or evolutionary programming of Post systems. The system we describe here, Hayek4, evolves collections of agents that solve arbitrary Blocks World Problems. It has also learned to solve essentially all instances of Rubik's cube scrambled with up to 7 rotations, but has not succeeded in learning larger Rubik's cube problems because the search space for new useful agents was too large.

One can also look at Hayek4's accomplishment here in the framework of theorem proving. The Post Production system can be seen as an axiom and a set of productions from which one can deduce theorems. The key problem in theorem proving is how to decide which productions to use in which order, in order to efficiently prove theorems. Hayek has solved this problem for Blocks World, generating extremely concise proofs.

Section 2 will briefly review Post Production Systems. Section 3 will briefly review our economic construction. Section 4 will describe our experimental results on Blocks World. Section 5 discusses how this can be viewed from a theorem proving context. Section 6 will describe our results on Rubik's cube. Section 7 is a conclusion.

2   Post Systems

A Post System consists of an axiom and a sequence of productions (also called rules). The axiom consists of a string of symbols. The productions are of form $L \to R$ where L is the antecedent and R is the consequent. R and L are each strings of symbols and variables, such that any variable appearing in the consequent also appears in the antecedent. Computation proceeds by looking through the productions in order, until a production is found whose antecedent matches the axiom, that is there is some instantiation of the variables as strings of symbols making the antecedent identical to the axiom. This instantiation of the variables is then substituted in the consequent, which replaces the axiom. One iterates this procedure, looking through the productions in order to find a legal substitution, making the substitution, and replacing the axiom, until no production matches, at which time computation halts.

Post proved that any formal system (e.g. any Turing machine) can be reduced to a Post system and indeed even a Post system in canonical form, i.e. having a single axiom and productions only of the form $g\$ \to \$h$, where the $ are variables [15,14]. The tape of the Turing machine corresponds to a string fed into the Post system as its axiom, and appropriate productions represent the Turing Machine's transition table. (Since the tape of the Turing Machine is usually called its *Input*, it might be clearer to refer to the axiom of the Post system as an Input, but we will stay with the terminology of [16].)

In this paper we discuss programs composed of a number of agents, organized into an artificial economy as described in the following section. The agents are each composed of a number of productions. The world is presented to the agent as the axiom, and the agent then computes as a Post system, iteratively applying its productions that match.

For example, in the Blocks World problem, the world is encoded as a string: $a(b)(c)(d)(e)$ where a is either not there or a single symbol chosen from the set $C = \{c_1...c_k\}$ of colors, and b, c, d, and e are each strings of symbols chosen from the set C. Here a represents the block in the hand (or is missing if there is no block in hand), b, c, d, e represent respectively the stacks 0,1,2,3.

Our productions are strings over $\{x_i$ for $i = 1, ..., 8$, y, $g1$, $g2$, $g3$, $d1$, $d2$, $d3$, $*$, $(,)\}$. Here $g1...g3$ (resp. $d1, ..., d3$) mean grab (drop) from stack 1,2,3; $*$ denotes "done" ending the instance, variables x_i match a string and variable y matches only a single character. We use a greedy variable match where the largest string that allows a match is chosen.

It is, of course, essential to allow only changes to the world corresponding to physical actions. If we allowed it to, our system might readily evolve a set of string rewrites that resulted in a string representing a solved world, but using intermediate states not respecting the physics of Blocks World, e.g. that a grab picks up one block off the top of one stack. We don't want to reward agents for such fantasies. The way we imposed the restriction of physicality was to consider the string manipulations that the agents compute as pure internal thought, not affecting the world. At the end of an agent's computation, we look at the string it generates and extract the physical actions: grabs, drops, and dones. We then execute these actions on the world (but if and only if the agent wins the auction, as discussed in the next section).

Examples of rules that have evolved include $(x0)(x0)(x7)(x1) \rightarrow * * g1$ and $(x0y0x1)(x0)(x7)(x3y0x5) \rightarrow g3g2d1$. For more such, and explanations of how they work, see section 4. Assuming the latter rule matches it generates a sequence of actions $g3g2d1$ that would then (if it wins the auction) be executed on the world.

An alternative, equivalent view of the Post Production system as a Theorem Proving system is discussed in section 5.

3   Economic Model

Our system, which we call Hayek4, consists of a collection of rules, and a collection of agents. Each agent is composed of a sequence of rules from the collection, a wealth, and a numerical bid.

Computation proceeds in a series of auctions. In each auction, each agent computes its next action by executing a Post-system with the world as initial axiom. The actions of the highest bidder are applied on the world leading it to the new state.

The winning agent in each auction pays its bid to the winner of the previous auction. If it solves the instance and says done, it collects reward from the world.

After each instance, all agents are assessed a tax proportional to the amount of computation they have done, in order to promote evolution of efficient agents. Also, any agent with less money than it was initiated with is removed and its money returned to its creator. Any rule not used in some living agent, and any rule that has not been applicable in the last 1000 instances is removed.

A number W is initiated as 0, and then raised as larger instances are solved, to be slightly larger than the reward for solving the largest instances being presented. Each auction, any agent with wealth at least $10W$ creates a child, giving it an initial endowment of W. The system is initiated with a single special agent called "Root". Root does not bid but simply creates random agents. The random creation process is discussed more below. At the end of each instance, each agent passes .25 fraction of its profit in that instance, plus an additional increment of 10^{-4} to its parent.

This structure of payments and capital allocations is based on simple principles. The system is set up so that everything is owned by some agent, property rights are respected, and money is conserved. Under those circumstances, if agents are rational in that they choose to make only profitable transactions, a new agent can earn money only by increasing payment to the system from the world. The agents are not initially rational, indeed they are random, but less rational agents are exploited and go broke.

We ensure that everything is owned by auctioning the world to a single agent. The guideline for all *ad hoc* choices, e.g. the one quarter fraction of profit passed to one's creator, is that the property holder might reasonably make a similar choice if given the option. Creators are viewed as investors-in, (or alternatively owners-of) their children. For example, endowing one's child with W is reasonable since it will need about this amount of money to bid rationally. We did not experiment with these various choices. Our experience with past experimentation in related models is that within reasonable ranges performance is not very sensitive to parameter values, and since runs are stochastic and take a day or more it is impossible to optimize.

By contrast, such property rights are not enforced in most multi-agent systems. For example, Holland's classifiers have multiple agents active at once, so there is no clear title to payments from the world, which are then typically divided among active agents. This is a recipe for "Tragedy of the Commons", since all agents want to be active when payment is expected, whether or not their actions harm the system. Zero Based Classifier Systems, sometimes known as ZCS, [17] have only one action active, but decide which action wins the auction probabilistically, with probability proportional to bid. This violates property rights by forcing agents to accept low bids for their property. When we modify our system to choose the winning bidder probabilistically in this fashion, it immediately breaks and can no longer form long chains of agents or learn to solve Blocks World instances larger than a handful of blocks.

When property rights and conservation of money are not enforced, agents can profit at the expense of the system. Evolution maximizes the interests of the agents. But a local optimum of the system will **not** be a local optimum for the agents. Thus the system can **not** converge to a local optimum. No wonder you can't form long chains of agents. The problems with Holland Classifiers and related models and the necessity for imposing property rights and conservation of money are discussed in more detail in [10,11,4].

Our creation process for new agents/rules is as follows.

```
Root:
    creates agent with randomly between 1..4 rules
    where each rule with p=0.5 is random (new rule)
    or with p=0.5 is a randomly picked existing rule.

Wealthy Agent:
    creates agent that is a modification of itself. To modify
    repeat with exiting p=0.25 the following:
    with p=0.3  it inserts a new rule
    with p=0.3  it deletes an old rule
    with p=0.15 it reshuffles rules
    with p=0.15 it replaces an old rule with new rule
    with p=0.10 it mutates an old rule.

insertion of a new rule:
    with p = 0.25 a new random rule is created
    with p = 0.75 an existing rule is picked

replacement of a rule:
    with p = 0.5 a new random rule is created
    with p = 0.5 an existing rule is picked

mutation of a rule
    left side:
     repeats with exiting p=0.25:
      with p = 1/3 delete a symbol
      with p = 1/3 insert a symbol
      with p = 1/3 replace a symbol
    right side:
     repeats with exitting p=0.25
        with p=0.25 delete a symbol
        with p=0.25 insert a symbol
        with p=0.25 replace a symbol
        with p=0.25 reshuffle symbols.
    Brackets, i.e ''('' and '')'', are being used for structuring
    purposes only and are neither inserted nor deleted.

Any new rule so created is inserted in the rule population.
```

This rule creation process was also not experimented with, simply picked *ad hoc*.

New agents are assigned a numeric bid using the "bid-epsilon" procedure [10]: the first time a new agent has a production that matches, the agent is assigned a bid ϵ higher than the currently winning bid, with new agents bidding last. A new agent thus wins that auction, and its bid is then fixed. ϵ was .01 in these experiments.

We initially tried running using a Root that produced random productions. Unfortunately, the system could not get started. The search space for productions is so huge that randomly produced strings rarely do anything useful. Moreover, they can match themselves and generate loops that are slow to simulate, and also rarely do anything useful. The upshot is that when we used the pure Post system with a Root that created purely random strings, the system never succeeded in solving even 1 block examples. Until it starts solving small examples, it gets no feedback, and thus is engaged in purely random search for a working program, which is essentially hopeless.

The solution we used in this paper is to write a Root that created initial productions which respected the syntax of the problem. That is, our root agent created only productions that had the brackets in the appropriate places to match the syntax we were using for the world. That is, Root produced rules that had antecedents of form $S_0(S_1)(S_2)(S_3)(S_4)$ where the S_i were random strings of variables. Moreover, the rules Root produced had consequents that were simply strings of actions. Then, at the end of the auction, we applied the string of actions generated by the winning agent to the world. New rules were then produced by mutations of the rules produced by root, as described above.

We are continuing research in how to get a purer Post production system to initialize itself effectively.

4   Experimental Results on Blocks World

Hayek4 was trained by presenting random Blocks World instances, with size chosen according to a distribution that presented increasingly larger instances as Hayek4 learned to solve smaller ones. The distribution was as follows. We present instances of size 1 until one instance is solved. Then we initiate $c = 1$, and present instances of size i with probability chosen from a Gaussian distribution around instances of size c. To be precise, we let $\sigma = c/10 + 2$ and choose i with probability $p(i)$ proportional to $exp(-(c - i)^2 * 0.5/\sigma^2)$. We maintain a running estimate $solved(c)$ of the fraction of the last 100 instances of size c that have been solved. When $solved(c) > 0.75$ we increase c by 1, and when $solved(c) < .25$ we decrease it by 1. This presents larger instances as we learn.

After a day of computation on a 300 MHz Pentium II processor, Hayek4 learns a program capable of solving arbitrary Blocks World instances. The learned program solves random, new, 100-block instances in several seconds. Figure 2 shows evolution of such a run. In this case, among the over 1000 agents present, agents 1134, 1147, 1154, and 1161 are currently winning all bids, and serve together as a program solving arbitrary instances. The program is simple and intuitive. It first clears blocks off stack 1, putting them on stack 3, until only

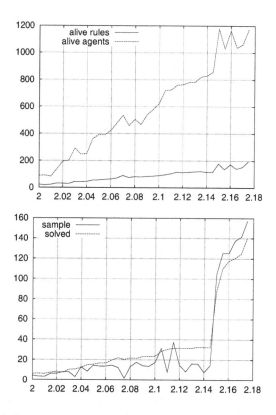

Fig. 2. Figure (a) shows the number of alive rules and alive agents. Figure (b) shows the moving average, over the last 100 instances, of the score, computed as $\sqrt{2 \sum_i p(i) i}$ for $p(i)$ = fraction instances of size i solved. "Solved" gives score as the system is running, "sampled" gives score on periodic samples where we turn off new agent creation. In sampled mode, Hayek4 is solving *all* instances presented (which are up to size about 158) and is using a program that would solve arbitrary instances. The horizontal axis is in millions of instances. We are showing the period between 2 and 2.18 million instances where it discovered how to solve arbitray instances.

correctly colored blocks remain on stack 1. Then, if the next block it needs is on stack 3, it digs down in 3 to find it, putting all the blocks it removes on 2. Alternatively, if the next block it needs is on 2, it digs down in 2 to find it, putting all blocks removed on 3.

This program is embodied in the following rules. The respective agents contain other rules that don't fire. We have cleaned some semantically unimportant symbols from the rules for pedagogical clarity.

(1) $(x5)(x6)(x1)(x7) \rightarrow g1d3$ in agent 1147, which bids 7.78.

(2) $(x6y0x2)(x6)(x5y0)(x3) \rightarrow g2d1$ in agent 1154, which bids 8.07.

(3) $(x2y0x5)(x2)(x3)(x7y0x0) \rightarrow g3d2$ also in agent 1154.

(4) $(x3y0x5)(x3y0)(x0)(x1) \rightarrow g2d3$ in agent 1134, which bids 8.05.
(5) $(x4y0)(x4)(x7y0)(x1) \rightarrow g2d1*$ in agent 1161, which bids 35.8.

These agents work together as follows. Rule 1 always matches. All rules contained by higher bidding agents in the population match only when stack 1 contains no incorrect blocks, i.e. when every block in stack 1 is the same color as the corresponding block in stack 0. Thus, whenever there are incorrect blocks on stack 1, agent 1147 wins and clears a block from stack 1. This will occur as many auctions in a row as necessary to clear all incorrect blocks from stack 1. Once stack 1 contains no incorrect blocks, the next block needed to extend it must be on stack 2 or stack 3. If the next needed block is on top of stack 2, rule 2 matches (matching y0 to the color of the next block needed) and moves this block to stack 1. Otherwise, if the next needed block is on stack 3, rule 3 matches, and moves the top block from from stack 3 to stack 2. As long as the next need block is on stack 3, 1154 wins successive auctions and digs down 3 to find the correct block. When the next needed block is not on 3 or on top of 2, 1134 wins the auction, and uses rule (4) to move blocks from stack 2 to stack 3, until it uncovers the next needed block on stack 2. Finally, when stack 1 and stack 0 are identical except for the last needed block, which is on stack 2, agent 1161 wins with a bid of 35.8 and applies rule (5), which moves the last block to 1 and says "done".

Note: (a) this program will solve arbitrary instances. (b) All the agents are profitable: 1147 comes earliest and bids least, 1134 is always followed by itself or 1154. 1154 loses tiny amounts of money when it is followed by 1134, but more than makes up for it by being eventually followed by 1161. 1161 is profitable for any instances with final reward over 35, and so is wealthy in the distribution the system was seeing at the time this set of agents was winning bids. (c) This particular set of agents is winning auctions at the moment, but new agents are continually created and the set of agents winning auctions is thus changing as time goes on. It continues, however, to stably solve instances, sometimes briefly disrupting the universal solver, but soon reassembling it from available rules. (d) Solution of instances depends on all of the more than 1000 agents in the population having bids in appropriate ranges (so that they don't interfere). (e) Solution involves chaining roughly $2n$ agents to solve an instance with n blocks on the goal stack. (g) The solution is intuitive and reasonably efficient. For the distribution of instances presented, it is unclear whether any strategy would be substantially more efficient. To use substantially fewer actions in worst case requires a sophisticated strategy that temporarily stacks incorrect blocks on stack 1.

We have done a few comparison experiments. First, we used the exact same scheme except that we chose the winning bidder in each auction with probability proportional to bid, as advocated in Zeroth level Classifier Systems [17] (a widely studied CS variant). This breaks property rights, and immediately broke performance. Such systems solved only problems with about 4 blocks.

Second, we attempted to learn a Post system by a stochastic hill climbing search. We initiated a CBS (current best solution) as an agent containing the rule

$(x1)(x2)(x3)(x4) \rightarrow g3g2d1*$ which solves 1 block instances. We then iteratively modified the CBS (exactly as described in §3), tested the modified solution, and replaced the CBS with the modified solution whenever the new solution performed better. We used an instance distribution calculated to work well with this hill climber, presenting instances of a fixed size and increasing the size by one when the CBS succeeded in solving 80% of the current size. This approach built a single Post Production agent, without use of the economic framework. The best this approach could do, after testing several hundred million Post systems, was to produce a Post system that solved about 40% of 10 block problems.

5 Theorem Proving

There is an alternative way to look at what Hayek4 is doing here: namely as theorem proving. In this formalism, Blocks World is defined by an axiom:

$$Axiom: \ A1 \ (x0)(x0)()().$$

and a series of productions:

$$Grab1: \ (x0)(x1y0)(x2)(x3) \rightarrow y0(x0)(x1)(x2)(x3)$$

$$Grab2: \ (x0)(x1)(x2y0)(x3) \rightarrow y0(x0)(x1)(x2)(x3)$$

$$Grab3: \ (x0)(x1)(x2)(x3y0) \rightarrow y0(x0)(x1)(x2)(x3)$$

$$Drop1: \ y0(x0)(x1)(x2)(x3) \rightarrow (x0)(x1y0)(x2)(x3)$$

$$Drop2: \ y0(x0)(x1)(x2)(x3) \rightarrow (x0)(x1)(x2y0)(x3)$$

$$Drop3: \ y0(x0)(x1)(x2)(x3) \rightarrow (x0)(x1)(x2)(x3y0)$$

where again xi match strings and $y0$ matches a single variable. Now, given any conjecture, i.e. potential Blocks World

$$C1: \ S0(S1)(S2)(S3)(S4),$$

where again $S0$ is a single color or empty, and $S1, S2, S3$, and $S4$ are strings of colors or empty, one's goal is to prove $C1$. In order to prove that $C1$ is a statement in Blocks World one has to find sequence of rules $R_1 \ldots R_N$, for each $R_i \in \{Grab1, Grab2, \ldots, Drop3\}$, that reduce statement $C1$ down to the axiom $A1$:

$$C \xrightarrow{R_1} S_1 \xrightarrow{R_2} S_2 \xrightarrow{R_3} \cdots \xrightarrow{R_{n-1}} S_{N-1} \xrightarrow{R_N} A1$$

where the first $\rightarrow$ comes from the application of R_1 etc. and the S_i are some intermediate states reached by sequential application of the rules R_i. Note that $Grab1$ and $Drop1$ are inverses.

If we were to make an attempt to find such a proof by brute force for an arbitrary Blocks World statement, say an instance of size n using k colors, we would have to search $2^{4*n*\log_2(k)}$ different states (since the best human generated algorithm needs $4*n*\log_2(k)$ actions).

Hayek4 however, has learned control rules, so it finds a proof in less than $10 * n * \log_3(k)$ steps! Finding control rules that allow rapid theorem proving is the central problem in automatic theorem proving. Hayek4 has solved it well in this case.

6   Rubik's Cube

We also did experiments training Hayek4 to solve Rubik's cube. We tried a variety of presentation and reward schemes and encodings, which had roughly similar results. We will briefly describe one such here.

Hayek4 was presented with training instances formed by taking a solved cube and applying a sequence of random rotations to it. Initial instances were formed with one quarter rotation (on a randomly chosen face), and as Hayek learned we supplied instances generated using longer sequences of random rotations. Each instance ended when Hayek said *done* or timed out. If Hayek said done, and the cube was correct it was given reward 1, else it was given reward 0.

Agents consisted of several productions as in the Blocks World system, each production having a condition and an action. The action consisted of a sequence of rotations, and possibly a *done*. We allowed 12 possible rotations: a quarter turn of each of the 6 faces in either direction. The condition consisted of a sequence of 54 variables: $(a1, a2, \ldots, a54)$. The condition matched the cube if there was some assignment of colors to the variables that matched the colors of the 54 faces on the cube. Again we faced the problem of getting the system started. This problem was even worse in Rubik's cube than in Blocks World because the productions are so long: the world is represented by a string 54 elements long, plus syntax markers. This is an enormous search space. We dealt with this again by introducing productions respecting the syntax of the world. The best performance occured when we used a method that initiated new agents based on the state of the world as follows. If at the beginning of a new instance no agent matched, then we added a new production to the system and a new agent using it. The condition of the new production was given by taking the exact position of the cube, expressed in 6 variables (corresponding to the 6 colors on the cube) and generalizing it by replacing up to 10% of the variables with new variables. The action of the new production was given by taking the known sequence that would solve the instance, and using the first few actions of it. Thus this new agent could immediately bid, and would earn money, and would advance the current instance towards solution. Again, at the end of the auction, we applied the action sequence of the winning agent to the world. We also introduced new agents as before as mutations of existing agents. An example instance and its solution is shown in the Appendix.

As can be seen from Fig. 3, Hayek then learned to solve instances with up to about 7 random rotations. At this point we had so many agents in the population (about 20,000) that the simulation was very slow, and so didn't improve much over a week of running. At this final point, Hayek is using about 20,000 agents to solve about 35 million states– all the states reachable with up to 7 rotations.

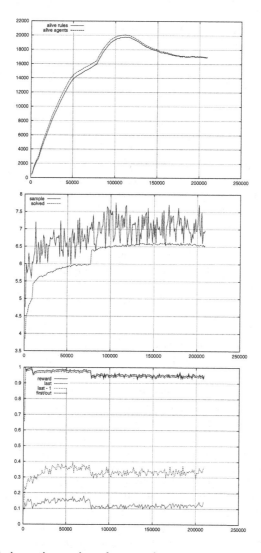

Fig. 3. Figure (a) shows the number of agents alive vs instance. Figure (b) shows the sampled and solved scores. Solved gives score as we are running. Sampled gives score on periodic samples where we turn off new agent creation and present 10 examples of each rotation length from 1 to 30. Score in each case is computed as $\sqrt{2 \sum_i p(i) i}$ for $p(i) =$ fraction instances of i rotations solved. Hayek is solving almost all instances with up to 7 rotations and few beyond that. Figure (c) shows the bids in the final, next to last, and first auction, as well as the reward. Bid rises smoothly starting low and rising till the final bid accurately estimates the reward.

Solution of each instance utilized approximately 3 auctions– that is we had three (or sometimes up to 5) agents following each other. Bids rose as the instance came closer to solution, with Hayek's agents learning to accurately estimate the proximity to solution.

7   Discussion

The success of Hayek4 on Blocks World, coupled with the success of previous Hayek versions using radically different representations, shows that our economic model is consistently able to assign credit and achieve deep chaining of agents and solution of hard Blocks World Problems. Control experiments where property rights are broken, or where no economic structure is used at all, indicate the importance of the property rights in promoting the evolution of cooperation among modules, dividing and conquering problems that are far too complex to solve by alternative means. This is the first Hayek version for which the agents are potentially Turing universal, and accordingly the first to evolve universal solvers from end reward only. The Rubik's cube results again show that the economic model is capable of building stable chains, and that it can divide and conquer hard problems.

In both the Blocks World and the Rubik's Cube problems, the size of the search space was initially a problem. The economic model seems to be capable of stably assigning credit to collections of agents and organizing them to collaborate. However, we have to be able to generate useful agents in order to progress. The search space in Blocks World was prohibitive until we imposed the syntax, and after that random mutation was able to find useful agents. The search space in Rubik's cube was even bigger, with a state of the world being represented by a 54 symbol string. This prevented Hayek from learning a general solver. It worked best when we introduced agents that matched the world and made progress, but we did not find a small collection of agents capable of generalizing to all instances. One reason for this may have been simply the number of instances we were able to process. Because of the much bigger search space, involving 54 symbol strings, Hayek evolved more agents, and thus ran much slower than in Blocks World. For this reason, after a week or so of running we have only seen a few hundred thousand instances. For Blocks World we evolved programs that solve arbitrary instances, but only after a few million or so instances. Hayek has not had the time to discover such sophisticated programs for Rubik's cube.

The economic model greatly reduces the search for a program to solve hard problems by factoring the problem. Instead of finding a whole program to solve the problem, one can make progress as long as it is possible to find useful modules. But for very complex problems, finding useful modules is still a difficult problem. Future work is needed in automatic extraction of the syntax of the problem, and in whether some sort of meta-level learning is capable of suggesting useful new agents.

The present work is the first of which we are aware where a Post system has been trained. This is the first Hayek version for which the agents are potentially Turing universal, and accordingly the first to evolve universal solvers from end reward only. This is also the first theorem Prover we are aware of where the proof strategy has been learned. The pattern matching ability of the Post system appears powerful and potentially of wide application. Post rules appear to have a very different quality from the S-expression representation of Hayek3. S-expression and many other representations perform numerical computations. The Post system is evolving to match structural properties of the system that may be difficult to express numerically.

References

1. Sutton, R. S. & Barto, A. G. *Reinforcement Learning, an introduction.* MIT Press, Cambridge, (1998).
2. Tesauro, G. Temporal difference learning and td-gammon. *CACM* **38**(3), 58 (1995).
3. Whitehead, S. & Ballard, D. Learning to perceive and act. *Machine Learning* **7**(1), 45 (1991).
4. Baum, E. & Durdanovic, I. Evolution of cooperative problem-soving in an artificial economy. *Neural Computation* **12**(12) (2000).
5. Koza, J. *Genetic Programming.* MIT Press, Cambridge, (1992).
6. Dzeroski, S., Blockeel, H. & De Raedt, L. Relational reinforcement learning. in *Proc. 12th ICML,* (Shavlik, J., ed) (Morgan Kaufman, San Mateo, CA, 1998).
7. Korf, R. E. Planning as search: A quantitative approach. *AIJ* **33**, 65 (1987).
8. Holland, J. H. Escaping brittleness: the possibilities of general purpose learning algorithms applied to parallel rule-based systems. in *Machine Learning, vol.2 p.593,* (Michalski, R. S., Carbonell, J. G. & Mitchell, T. M., eds). Morgan Kauffman, Los Altos, CA (1986).
9. Wilson, S. & Goldberg, D. A critical review of classifier systems. in *Proc. 3rd ICGA, p 244* (Morgan Kauffman, San Mateo, CA, 1989).
10. Baum, E. B. Toward a model of mind as a laissez-faire economy of idiots, extended abstract. in *Proc. 13th ICML '96, p28,* (Saitta, L., ed) (Morgan Kaufman, San Francisco, CA, 1996). and in Machine Learning (1999)v35n2.
11. Baum, E. B. Manifesto for an evolutionary economics of intelligence. in *Neural Networks and Machine Learning,p.285,* (Bishop, C. M., ed). Springer-Verlag (1998).
12. Lettau, M. & Uhlig, H. Rule of thumb and dynamic programming. *American Economic Review* , (1999). in press.
13. Forrest, S. Implementing semantic network structures using the classifiersystem. in *Proc. First International Conference on Genetic Algorithms,* 188–196 (Lawrence Erlbaum Associates, Hillsdale, NJ, 1985).
14. Minsky, M. *Computation: Finite and Infinite Machines.* Prentice-Hall Inc, Englewood Cliffs, NJ, (1967).
15. Post, E. L. Formal reductions of the general combinatorial decision problem. *American Journal of Math* **52**, 264–268 (1943).
16. Minsky, M. *The Society of Mind.* Simon and Schuster, New York, (1986).
17. Wilson, S. Zcs: a zeroth level classifier system. *Evolutionary Computation* **2**(1), 1–18 (1994).

8   Appendix: A Rubik Example

Below is shown some of the data from an instance. First we see a sequence of Rubik positions as an instance is solved. The first instance was generated by the randomly generated 7 rotation sequence FRfkKtK. (Each of these letters corresponds to a 1/4 rotation of one face.) No agent matched the initial position, so a new rule was added, as pictured, that matched (in this case exactly) and took the action k, which undoes the last rotation, K, with which the instance was generated. (The six possible clockwise rotations are denoted F, K, R, L, T, B, and the corresponding six possible counterclockwise rotations are denoted f,k,r,l,t,b.) Agent 14566 was added that incorporated this rule. It won the first auction with bid 0.

Below is pictured the sequence of positions, the winning agent in each position, and the actions it took. The letters w,y,b,r,g,o stand for the six colors of the cube facelets. Below that we see the listing of the auctions, showing the auction number, the cumulative number of moves done to the cube, the number of the agent that won the auction, its ID number, the reward it received, and its winning bid.

Below that are pictured 6 rules used by winning agents, and below that a listing of the 4 agents that won auctions in this instance. This final listing shows which rules are part of which agent. (There are of course many more agents and rules in the system, not shown here.)

Note that the system solved this instance using 5 auctions. It accurately estimates as it is nearing solution, with the winning bid in each auction higher than in the last, so all the agents that participated made money. Agent 472 (which has ID number 4374) contains 3 different productions, and won the last two auctions, using different productions. Its final action was *, indicating *done*.

```
Task: 0/35.7/40
wwyyyyyyy
brgbbrbbr
oogggoggo
bggywwyww
rbboobooo
rrrrrgwww
'.FRfkKtK'
add: y1y1y4y4y4y4y4y4y4y0y3y5y0y0y3y0y0y3y2y2y5y5y5y2y5y5y2
     y0y5y5y4y1y1y4y1y1y3y0y0y2y2y0y2y2y2y3y3y3y3y3y5y1y1y1 -> k
405214 bid:  0.0000000 k
Task: 2/35.8/40
wwyyyyyyy
brrbbbbbb
goooggogg
wggwwwwww
yyboobooo
rrrrrgrrg
'FRfkKtK.k'
1396 bid:  0.0100000 KT
```

```
Task: 3/35.10/40
bbgrrgrrg
bbobbobbo
ywwyooyoo
rrrwwwwww
yybyyryyr
ggoggoggw
'FRfkKtKk.XKT'
40420 bid:  0.9800000 f
Task: 4/35.11/40
obbobbobb
ggggggggg
wwrwwrwwr
yyyyyyyyy
woowoowoo
brrbrrbrr
'FRfkKtKkXKT.Yzf'
4374 bid:  0.9900000 k
Task: 5/35.12/40
ggggggggg
wwwwwwwww
yyyyyyyyy
bbbbbbbbb
ooooooooo
rrrrrrrrr
'FRfkKtKkXKTYzf.Yk'
4374 bid:  0.9900000 *
Task: 6/35.12/40
ggggggggg
wwwwwwwww
yyyyyyyyy
bbbbbbbbb
ooooooooo
rrrrrrrrr
'FRfkKtKkXKTYzfYk.'
Time:11.491000, 11.500000
Size:7 307999.6 success
  a# move#    A#     A_ID#    reward       bid
  0.    8 14566    405214  0.0000000  0.0000000
  1.   10   218      1396  0.0000000  0.0100000
  2.   11  1664     40420  0.0000000  0.9800000
  3.   12   472      4374  0.0000000  0.9900000
  4.   12   472      4374  1.0000000  0.9900000

Rules:    14461 Total R/A: 402806/405215
  R#
    0 y4y4y4y4y4y4y4y4y4y0y0y0y0y0y0y0y0y0y5y5y5y5y5y5y5y5y5
      y1y1y1y1y1y1y1y1y1y2y2y2y2y2y2y2y2y2y3y3y3y3y3y3y3y3y3 -> *
    2 y4y4y4y4y4y4y4y4y4y0y0y3y0y0y3y0y0y3y5y5y5y5y5y5y5y5y5
      y2y1y1y2y1y1y2y1y1y0y0y0y2y2y2y2y2y2y3y3y3y3y3y3y1y1y1 -> k
```

```
    5 y2y2y2y4y4y4y4y4y4y5y0y0y2y0y0y2y0y0y5y5y3y5y5y3y5y5y3
      y1y1y4y1y1y3y1y1y3y5y2y2y5y2y2y1y1y1y0y0y0y4y3y3y4y3y3 -> f
   10 y4y4y4y4y4y4y4y4y2y0y3y2y0y3y2y0y3y5y5y5y5y5y5y5y5y5y5
      y2y1y3y2y1y3y2y1y3y0y0y0y2y2y2y1y1y1y0y0y0y3y3y3y1y1y1 -> fk
  291 y4y4y4y4y4y3y4y4y3y0y0y0y0y4y0y0y4y5y5y5y0y5y5y0y2y2
      y3y1y1y3y1y1y1y1y1y1y2y2y2y2y2y2y3y3y5y3y3y5y5y5y3 -> KT
14460 y1y1y4y4y4y4y4y4y0y3y5y0y0y3y0y0y3y2y2y5y5y5y2y5y5y2
      y0y5y5y4y1y1y4y1y1y3y0y0y2y2y0y2y2y2y3y3y3y3y3y5y1y1y1 -> k
```

```
Agents:    14567
  A#       ID#   BID_eps Rules
 218      1396   +0.010 R291
 472      4374   +0.990 R2 R10 R0
1664     40420   +0.980 R5
14566   405214   +0.010 R14460
```

Simple Markov Models of the Genetic Algorithm in Classifier Systems: Accuracy-Based Fitness

Larry Bull

Intelligent Computer Systems Centre
Faculty of Computer Studies & Mathematics
University of the West of England
Bristol BS16 1QY, U.K.
larry.bull@uwe.ac.uk

Abstract. Michigan-style Classifier Systems use Genetic Algorithms to facilitate rule-discovery, where rule fitness has traditionally been prediction-based. Current research has shifted to the use of accuracy-based fitness. This paper presents a simple Markov model of the algorithm in such systems, allowing comparison between the two forms of rule utility measure. Using a single-step task the previously discussed benefits of accuracy over prediction are clearly shown with regard to overgeneral rules. The effects of a niche-based algorithm (maximal generality) are also briefly examined, as are the effects of mutation under the two fitness schemes.

1 Introduction

Learning Classifier Systems (LCSs) [Holland et al. 1986] use Genetic Algorithms (GAs) [Holland 1975] to discover new rules/generalizations for a given problem space. In the original formalism rule fitness is prediction-based, i.e. fitness (strength) serves as a predictor of future payoff. Current research has shifted to the use of the accuracy in such rule predictions as the fitness measure, after [Wilson 1995] (see also [Frey & Slate 1991]). Under this scheme the problems due to overgeneral rules which receive a high average payoff but are sub-optimal in numerous situations can be avoided, as highlighted in [Wilson 1995] and developed in [Kovacs 1996].

In this paper results from developing a simple Markov model of the GA in LCSs are presented, where the model is based on that introduced by Goldberg and Segrest [1987]. Using a single-step task it is shown that the current shift in fitness scheme has significant effects on the resulting transition matrices of the GA's Markov chain and hence on expected system behaviour. That is, as has been discussed in the literature, results show the use of rule prediction accuracy as the fitness measure for the GA greatly improves the ability of LCSs to produce effective mappings of the problem space through a bias against overgeneral rules.

The paper is arranged as follows: the next section introduces the model. Section 3 presents the task considered here and Sect. 4 the results from its use in the model. The formation of maximally general rule-sets and the use of a niche-based GA are then briefly examined. Finally, the behaviour of mutation is explored.

P.L. Lanzi, W. Stolzmann, and S.W. Wilson (Eds.): IWLCS 2000, LNAI 1996, pp. 21–28, 2001.
© Springer-Verlag Berlin Heidelberg 2001

2 The Model

Goldberg and Segrest [1987] introduced a simple Markov model of a one-bit two-class (binary), generational genetic algorithm. Using a population of size N, they note that there are $N+1$ possible states i, where i is the population with exactly i individuals of class A, and hence $N-i$ individuals of class B. The model defines an $(N+1)\times(N+1)$ transition matrix $P(i,j)$ mapping the current state i to the state j, a population containing exactly j individuals of class A. Horn et al. [1994] used the model to examine niching in a single-step task LCS.

The simple GA model uses fitness-proportional selection. If f_A denotes the fitness of class A and f_B of class B, the probability of selecting an individual from A (p_A) is :

$$p_A = \frac{f_A\,i}{f_A\,i + f_B\,(N\text{-}i)} \tag{1}$$

Hence the probability of selecting an individual of class B is $p_B = 1 - p_A$.

This has been used to define a simple steady-state GA model, assuming one rule reproduces and one rule is replaced randomly per GA invocation [Bull 2000]:

$$P(i,j) = \begin{cases} 1 & i \in \{0,N\},\, j=i \\ p_A\,((N\text{-}i)/N) & i = 1,....,N\text{-}1,\, j=i+1 \\ p_B\,(i/N) & i = 1,....,N\text{-}1,\, j=i\text{-}1 \\ 1 - p_A\,((N\text{-}i)/N) - p_B(i/N) & i = 1,....,N\text{-}1,\, j=i \\ 0 & \text{otherwise} \end{cases} \tag{2}$$

where the first term corresponds to the absorbing states of the selection only model, the second term says that the number of individuals of class A will increase if one is selected as a parent and a class B individual is replaced, the third is the opposite case, and the last terms cover all other possibilities.

In this paper a simple single-step task is used. The single bit of the above model is taken as a rule type such that the behaviour of an accurate rule which matches just one situation and an overgeneral rule which matches a number of situations can be considered under the two fitness schemes. Hence this is similar to the afore mentioned work of Horn et al. [1994].

Under the traditional prediction-based scheme, with the accurate rule represented by individuals of class A and the overgeneral by class B :

$$f_A = \text{reward}(\,[A]_A\,) \tag{3}$$

$$f_B = \frac{1}{n} \sum_{[A]_B \,\in\, [A]_r}^{R} \text{reward}([A]_r) \tag{4}$$

where $[A]_x$ denotes an action set to which a rule of class X belongs and reward($[A]_x$)

is the payoff obtained by a rule in action set X. Note f_B is in n action sets and $[A]_A$ O $[A]_B$.

For the accuracy-based case, simplified functions of those presented in [Lanzi & Wilson 1999] are used in conjunction with Equations 3 and 4, i.e. :

$$\text{prediction error, } \varepsilon = |\text{ reward}([A]_x - f_x)|$$
$$\text{accuracy, } k = 0.1(\varepsilon/\varepsilon_0)^{-3}, \quad \text{where } \varepsilon < \varepsilon_0 \text{ then } k = 1 \text{ and } \varepsilon_0 = 0.01$$
$$\text{relative accuracy, } k' = k / \Sigma k, \quad \text{where } k' \text{ replaces } f_x \text{ in Eq. 1}$$

(5)

In all cases the implication is that sufficient time passes between GA invocations for parameter convergence (as in the related [Bull 2000]).

3 The Task

This paper considers a simple single-step task as defined by the following table:

Input	Action	Payoff		
1	1	1000		
1	0	0		
0	1	1000		
0	0	3000	2000	1000

The extra entries in the payoff for input 0:output 0 will be used to examine effects in reward variance.

The rule of class A considered here (the specific rule) is 1:1 and the rule of class B (the overgeneral) is #:0, where the first bit corresponds to the condition and the second to the action.

Hence, under the traditional prediction-based fitness scheme the fitness of A $f_A =$ 1000 (Eq. 3) and the fitness of B in the first case (0:0 = 3000) is $f_B = 1500$ (Eq. 4). Conversely, under the accuracy-based scheme $f_A \cong$ and $f_B \cong 0$ (both Eq. 5).

These fitnesses can then be used in conjunction with the Markov model derived in Equation 2 to examine the behaviour of the GA under the two schemes.

4 Results

Due to the simplicity of the model it is possible to visualise the resulting transition matrix $P(i,j)$. Figure 1 shows graphs of the resulting probabilities from varying the payoff of the last entry in the reward table given above, with rule-base size $N=50$.

In the first case of prediction-based fitness (Fig. 1a) it can be seen that, as discussed in the literature [e.g. Kovacs 1996], there is a greater selection pressure to increase the number of overgeneral rules (B) when they receive a higher average payoff than the accurate rules (A), i.e. when 0:0 = 3000 here. Hence in this case, the action of the GA will cause the LCS to lose the appropriate rule for input 1 (i-> 0). As the size of the average payoff of the overgeneral decreases, the selection pressure towards increasing the number of overgenerals decreases: when 0:0 = 2000, the selective pressure is the same (random drift), i.e. $P(i,i+1) = P(i,i-1)$ since $f_A = f_B$; and when 0:0 = 1000, $P(i,i+1) > P(i,i-1)$. Therefore these results clearly show how an LCS using the prediction-based fitness scheme is sensitive to the reward scheme with regard to the generation of an effective rule-set for the problem domain; the model shows prediction-based fitness promoting incorrect rules.

Figure 1b shows the resulting transition matrices for the accuracy-based case. Here it can be seen that there is no significant selective pressure for the overgeneral rule $(P(i,i+1) >> P(i,i-1))$ and that as the number of instances of the accurate rule increases $(>i)$ its selective pressure decreases from a maximum due to the use of relative accuracy. Also, again unlike the prediction-based scheme, the GA using accuracy as the fitness measure has no noticeable change in selective pressure as the reward function is changed here. Hence, as simulations have shown, accuracy-based fitness promotes appropriate rules in the generation of an accurate mapping of the input/output space (see [Kovacs 1999] for discussion of other issues).

A second aspect of the use of accuracy-based fitness is now examined with the presented model.

5   Maximal Generality and a Niche-Based GA

Wilson's "generalization hypothesis" [1995] suggests that in the accuracy-based XCS, given two rules of equal accuracy with one more general than the other, the former will become dominant due to its increased chance of being involved in a reproduction event (since it is a member of more match sets).

The model can be used to (simply) demonstrate the prerequisite of this hypothesis by considering the progress of the previous accurate rule 1:1 and the more general rule #:1 (class B) on the task described above. For the two inputs of the rule #:1 the predicted payoff is 1000 and so both rules are equally accurate. Therefore the selective pressure for either should be equal (random drift) under the panmictic GA of the model. Figure 2a shows this to be the case.

If a further term is added to Equation 2 to consider the effects of a niche GA, p_{nga}, the generalization hypothesis can be shown in principle. That is, $p_{nga} > 1$ implies more chances of reproduction per LCS cycle. Hence, if the reproductive bias of the maximally general rule is assumed:

$$P(i,j) = \begin{cases} 1 & i \in \{0,N\}, j=i \\ p_A\,((N-i)/N) & i = 1,....,N\text{-}1, j=i+1 \\ p_B\,(i/N)\;p_{nga} & i = 1,....,N\text{-}1, j=i\text{-}1 \\ 1 - p_A\,((N-i)/N) - p_B(i/N)\,p_{nga} & i = 1,....,N\text{-}1, j=i \\ 0 & \text{otherwise} \end{cases} \qquad (6)$$

Figure 2b shows the effect of $p_{nga} = 2$. It can be seen, as expected, that there is now a greater selective pressure for the maximally general rule $(P(i,i-1) > P(i,i+1))$.

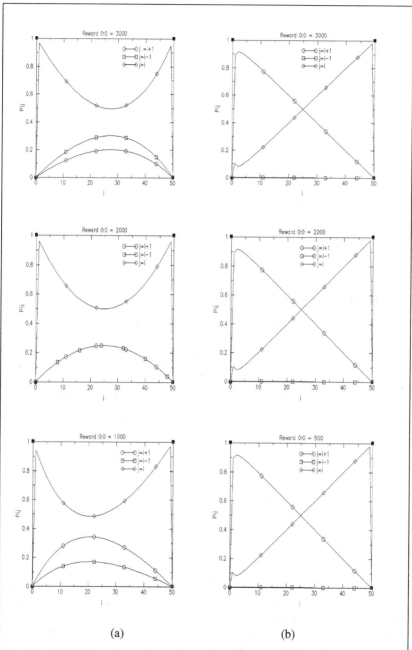

(a)   (b)

Fig. 1. Probabilities for the single-step task under the different reward levels. For clarity, the absorbing states are not shown here.

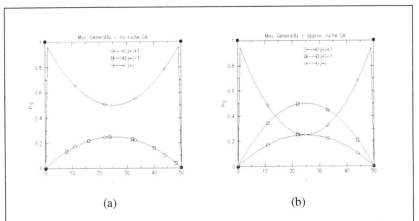

Fig. 2. Comparison of probabilities under the generalization hypothesis. (a) shows the pan-mictic GA and (b) approximates a niche GA.

6 Mutation

It has recently been suggested that self-adaptive mutation techniques, such as those used in Meta-Evolutionary Programming [Fogel 1992], can be used in LCSs [Bull et al. 2000]. Results showed that it is possible to allow the mutation rate to evolve over time in LCSs which make use of either prediction-based fitness or accuracy-based fitness. However, in the latter case the LCS (XCS) showed a greater sensitivity to the mutation rate p_m, with a significant drop in comparative performance until the average rate dropped closer to that typically used; XCS appeared much less robust to changes in the mutation rate.

The above model derived in Equation 2 can be extended to consider mutation:

$$P(i,j) = \begin{cases} p_A \left((N-i)/N \right) (1 - p_m) + p_B ((N-i)/N) p_m & i = 0,....,N, j=i+1 \\ p_B (i/N) (1 - p_m) + p_A (i/N) p_m & i = 0,....,N, j=i-1 \\ 1 - (p_A ((N-i)/N)(1 - p_m) + p_B ((N-i)/N) p_m) - \\ \quad (p_B (i/N) (1 - p_m) + p_A (i/N) p_m) & i = 0,....,N, j=i \\ 0 & \text{otherwise} \end{cases}$$

(7)

where, for example, the first term corresponds to the case where a class A individual is selected, survives mutation and a class B individual is replaced, or a class B individual is selected, altered by mutation to class A and a class B individual is replaced. Note the chain is now ergodic under mutation, rather than absorbing.

Figure 3 shows the magnitude of effects on the resulting transition matrix when the mutation rate is varied under the two reward schemes ($p_m = 0.02$ and 0.2). Here the worst case is considered, that of the overgeneralist rule (class B) having fitness 1500, i.e. 0:0 = 3000. It can be seen (Figure 3a) that under the prediction-based scheme, the probability of increasing the number of accurate rules is actually greater than that of the overgeneralist $(P(i,i+1) > P(i,i-1))$ whilst the former's proportion of the rule-base is low, roughly $i<20$. Thereafter the probability of increasing the number of overgeneralists remains significantly higher than that for the accurate rule (as before), with an increase as i increases under higher mutation.

The accuracy-based system (Fig. 3b) experiences a steadily increasing (almost linear) probability for increasing the number of overgeneralists as the number of accurate rules increases, i.e. $>i$. With the increase in mutation rate it can be seen that this becomes significant. Rough calculation of the area under $j=i-1$ with $p_m = 0.2$ shows a ten-fold increase in probability over the case with $p_m = 0.02$. That is, a direct correlation is seen between the increase in probability of increasing the number of overgeneralists and the magnitude of increase in p_m.

This result therefore appears to support the findings of Bull et al. [2000] in that the change in behaviour under a raised mutation rate seems more marked under accuracy-based fitness than prediction. Of course, fitness inheritance and rule reinforcement are also very different in XCS than a standard LCS and these aspects may also be contributing to the change in behaviour - this is currently under investigation. The model is also being used to examine the sensitivity of other accuracy functions to the underlying mutation rate, in combination with empirical experiments. The use of different selection schemes for the GA is also being investigated.

7 Conclusions

Learning Classifier Systems use GAs to discover appropriate rules. This paper has presented a simple Markov model of the GA in LCSs, with the aim of examining the effects of different types of fitness scheme in a single-step task. It has been shown that the traditional prediction-based scheme is sensitive to the reward levels of the task and

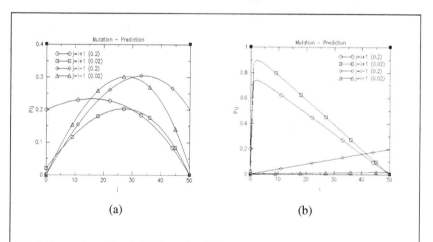

Fig. 3. Comparison of probabilities under different mutation rates. (a) shows the prediction-based system and (b) the accuracy-based. Equalising pressure $i=j$ not shown for clarity.

hence can promote overgeneral rules at the expense of more specific/appropriate rules. In contrast, it has been shown that accuracy-based fitness, as in XCS for example, is not sensitive to reward levels and does not promote higher average prediction rules.

The effects of a niche-based GA and varying mutation rates have also been examined.

The results from this model are now being extended to more complex Markov models of GAs in LCSs, as well as to examine the effects of accuracy functions in general.

References

Bull, L. (2000) Simple Markov Models of the Genetic Algorithm in Classifier Systems: Multi-step Tasks. *Submitted to IWLCS-2000*.

Bull, L., Hurst, J. & Tomlinson, A. (2000) Self-Adaptive Mutation in Classifier System Controllers. In J-A. Meyer, A. Berthor, D. Floreano, H. Roitblatt & S.W. Wilson (eds) *From Animals to Animats 6 - The Sixth International Conference on the Simulation of Adaptive Behaviour*, MIT Press.

Frey, P.W. & Slate, D.J. (1991) Letter Recognition using Holland-style Adaptive Classifiers. *Machine Learning* 6:161-182.

Goldberg, D. & Segrest, P. (1987) Finite Markov Chain Analysis of Genetic Algorithms. In J.J. Grefenstette (ed.) *Proceedings of the Second International Conference on Genetic Algorithms*, Lawrence Erlbaum, pp1-7.

Holland, J.H. (1975) *Adaptation in Natural and Artificial Systems*, University of Michigan Press.

Holland, J.H., Holyoak, K.J., Nisbett, R.E. & Thagard, P.R. (1986) *Induction: Processes of Inference, Learning and Discovery*. MIT Press.

Horn, J., Goldberg, D. & Deb, K. (1994) Implicit Niching in a Learning Classifier System: Nature's Way. *Evolutionary Computation*, 2(1):37-65.

Kovacs, T. (1996) XCS Classifier System Reliably Evolves Accurate, Complete, and Minimal Representations for Bollean Functions. Technical Report CSR-96-17 School of Computer Science, University of Birmingham, UK.

Kovacs, T. (1999) Strength or Accuracy ? A Comparison of Two Approaches to Fitness Calculation in Learning Classifier Systems. In A.S. Wu (ed.) *Proceedings of the 1999 Genetic and Evolutionary Computation Conference Workshop Program*, Gecco, pp290-297.

Lanzi, P-L. & Wilson, S.W. (1999) Optimal Classifier System Performance in Non-Markov Environments. Tech. Report N99.36 Dipartmento di Eletronica e Infromazione. Politecnico di Milano.

Wilson, S.W. (1995) Classifier Fitness Based on Accuracy. *Evolutionary Computation* 3(2):149-177.

Simple Markov Models of the Genetic Algorithm in Classifier Systems: Multi-step Tasks

Larry Bull

Intelligent Computer Systems Centre
Faculty of Computer Studies & Mathematics
University of the West of England
Bristol BS16 1QY, U.K.
larry.bull@uwe.ac.uk

Abstract. Michigan-style Classifier Systems use Genetic Algorithms to facilitate rule-discovery. This paper presents a simple Markov model of the algorithm in such systems, with the aim of examining the effects of different types of interdependence between niches in multi-step tasks. Using the model it is shown that the existence of, what is here termed, partner rule variance can have significant and detrimental effects on the Genetic Algorithm's expected behaviour. Suggestions are made as to how to reduce these effects, making connections with other recent work in the area.

1 Introduction

Learning Classifier Systems (LCSs) [Holland et al. 1986] use Genetic Algorithms (GAs) [Holland 1975] to discover new rules/generalizations for a given problem space. Booker [1985] suggested a restricted mating scheme to improve the maintenance of niches in LCSs whereby rules active on one given time-step do not necessarily compete and interbreed with rules active on another step. That is, rules in an individual niche can be seen to "coevolve" with the rules in other niches. This is particularly relevant for delayed reward tasks in which multiple niches must be maintained for the LCS to function effectively; a number of appropriate rules must be learnt which lead the system, in a piecemeal and highly interdependent way, from an initial stimulus to the goal.

In this paper results from developing a simple Markov model of a niched-GA LCS are presented, where the model is based on that introduced by Goldberg and Segrest [1987]. It is shown that the *type* of relationship between the coevolving niches - "match-sets" [Wilson 1994] - of a multi-step task can have significant effects on the resulting transition matrices of the GA's Markov chain and hence on expected system behaviour. That is, the existence of partner rule variance (see later) is shown to severely affect the expected behaviour of the rule-discovery process.

The paper is arranged as follows: the next section introduces the model. Section 3 presents the payoff landscapes considered here and Section 4 the results from their use in the model. Finally, all findings are discussed.

P.L. Lanzi, W. Stolzmann, and S.W. Wilson (Eds.): IWLCS 2000, LNAI 1996, pp. 29–36, 2001.
© Springer-Verlag Berlin Heidelberg 2001

2 The Model

Goldberg and Segrest [1987] introduced a simple Markov model of a one-bit two-class (binary), generational genetic algorithm. Using a population of size N, they note that there are $N+1$ possible states i, where i is the population with exactly i individuals of class A, and hence $N-i$ individuals of class B. The model defines an $(N+1)\times(N+1)$ transition matrix $P(i,j)$ mapping the current state i to the state j, a population containing exactly j individuals of class A.

The simple GA model uses fitness-proportional selection. If f_A denotes the fitness of class A and f_B of class B, the probability of selecting an individual from A (p_A) is :

$$p_A \;=\; \frac{f_A\, i}{f_A\, i + f_B\,(N\text{-}i)} \tag{1}$$

Hence the probability of selecting an individual of class B is $p_B = 1 - p_A$.

Further, the probability of going from a state with i A's to a state with j A's is:

$$P(i,j) \;=\; \binom{N}{j}\,(p_A)^j\,(p_B)^{N-j} \tag{2}$$

Substituting for p_A and p_B :

$$P(i,j) \;=\; \binom{N}{j}\left(\frac{f_A\, i}{f_A\, i + f_B\,(N\text{-}i)}\right)^{j}\left(1 - \frac{f_A\, i}{f_A\, i + f_B\,(N\text{-}i)}\right)^{N-j} \tag{3}$$

Thus Equation 3 defines the transition matrix for a population of size N under a simple generational GA using selection only. Goldberg and Segrest note this is an *absorbing* Markov chain, in that $P(0,0) = P(N,N) = 1$, rather than ergodic.

To create a simple steady-state GA version of this model (note the above model was used by [Horn et al. 1994] to examine niching in a single-step LCS), assuming one rule reproduces and one rule is replaced randomly per GA invocation the following transition probabilities can be used:

$$P(i,j) \;=\; \begin{cases} 1 & i \in \{0,N\},\, j=i \\ p_A\,((N\text{-}i)/N) & i = 1,.....,N\text{-}1,\, j=i+1 \\ p_B\,(i/N) & i = 1,.....,N\text{-}1,\, j=i\text{-}1 \\ 1 - p_A\,((N\text{-}i)/N) - p_B(i/N) & i = 1,.....,N\text{-}1,\, j=i \\ 0 & \text{otherwise} \end{cases} \tag{4}$$

where the first term corresponds to the absorbing states, the second term says that the number of individuals of class A will increase if one is selected as a parent and a class B individual is replaced, the third is the opposite case, and the last terms cover all other possibilities.

In this paper the simplest form of multi-step task is used: a two-step task is examined in which a rule from one niche/match-set is partnered with a rule from a second match-set before payoff is received. The behaviour of the last of these match-sets will be considered, to avoid/reduce reinforcement issues, with the genetic constituency of the other being altered manually to examine effects; one Markov chain is used. The single bit of the above model will be taken as the action of the rules and all rules in a match-set are assumed to have the same, and appropriate, condition; generalization (#) is not included.

Further, for simplicity, it is assumed that the offspring rule generated on each GA invocation is evaluated with a random individual from the other match-set (similar to an "explore" cycle in XCS [Wilson 1995]) and that there is no internal memory, i.e. :

$$f_1 = f_{10} \frac{N-i'}{N} + f_{11} \frac{i'}{N}$$

$$f_0 = f_{00} \frac{N-i'}{N} + f_{01} \frac{i'}{N} \tag{5}$$

where $f_A = f_1$, $f_B = f_0$, f_{10} denotes the fitness/payoff obtained by an individual whose action is a one and whose partner's action was a zero, and so on, and where i' is the number of individuals in the other match-set with an action value of one. The size of both niches is assumed to be both equal and constant here (N, hence rule-base = $2N$).

Substituting into Equation 1:

$$p_A = \frac{i \ (f_{10} \ ((N-i')/N) + f_{11} \ (i'/N) \ )}{i \ (f_{10} \ ((N-i')/N) + f_{11} \ (i'/N) \ ) + (N-i') \ (f_{00} \ ((N-i')/N) + f_{01} \ (i'/N) \ )} \tag{6}$$

It is noted that this implies sufficient time passes between GA invocations for strength/fitness convergence.

3 Task Landscapes

In coevolutionary systems two general classes of inter-entity relationship can be identified with regard to an entity's fitness/payoff landscape: in the first, the higher possible rewards are reachable from one configuration, regardless of the configuration of the entity's evaluation partner; and in the second, the opposite is true in that the best configuration of an entity changes depending upon the configuration of its partner. This (epistasis) is here termed as "partner rule variance" for the match-sets of an LCS. For example, without partner rule variance, in a two-step maze task, the higher payoffs may always be received by going left on the last step, regardless of whether a left or right move is made on the first step. Figure 1 shows the example payoff landscapes used in this paper for each of these two classes of interdependence. It is noted that absolute values are not important, as long as there is some noticeable difference between configurations, e.g. in (a) $f_{11} = f_{01}$, as will be seen.

partner rule variance

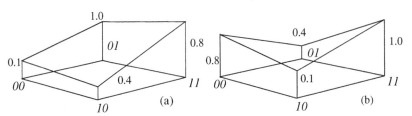

(a)   (b)

Fig. 1. The two payoff landscapes used throughout. The first bit corresponds to the rule action value action value of the evaluating individual, the second to that of its partner from the other match-set. E.g. in (a) action 0 followed by 1 leads to reward 1.0.

4 Results

Due to the simplicity of the model it is possible to visualise the resulting transition matrix $P(i,j)$. Figure 2 shows graphs of the resulting probabilities from varying the constituency of the partnering match-sets with $N=50$. In both cases, as the number of ones increases (i'), the "part" of the given payoff landscape the evolving match-set experiences *changes*. For example, without partner rule variance (2(a)), when $i'=0$, $f_1=1.0$ and $f_0=0.1$ (Figure 1). Similarly, when $i'=N$ $f_1=0.8$ and $f_0=0.4$. Under these two (extreme) conditions the selective pressure *varies* since $0.1/1.0 < 0.4/0.8$. This can be seen in the graphs since the relative difference in the possible changes in population ($j=i$) is much less in the latter case; the probability of increasing the number of ones ($j=i+1$) is significantly lower when $i'=N$ than when $i'=0$. However, in all cases $P(i,i+1) > P(i,i-1)$. That is, regardless of whether the evaluating rule's partner from the first match-set has action one or zero, its best action value is a one and the simple GA identifies this fact.

The same general behaviour occurs under partner rule variance. However, here the selection pressure can actually *disappear* depending on the constituency of the other match-set. Figure 2(b) shows the probabilities of $j=i+1$ and $j=i-1$ become roughly equal thus representing the case of genetic drift (around $i'=N/2$); a change in either direction, increasing or decreasing i, is equally likely. Hence, under normal rule discovery in an LCS, *the effective selection pressure can vary over time*, possibly dramatically, until an equilibrium is reached and the constituency of the coevolving match-sets stops changing.

5 Conclusions

Learning Classifier Systems use GAs to discover appropriate rules. This paper has presented a simple Markov model of the GA in LCSs, with the aim of examining the

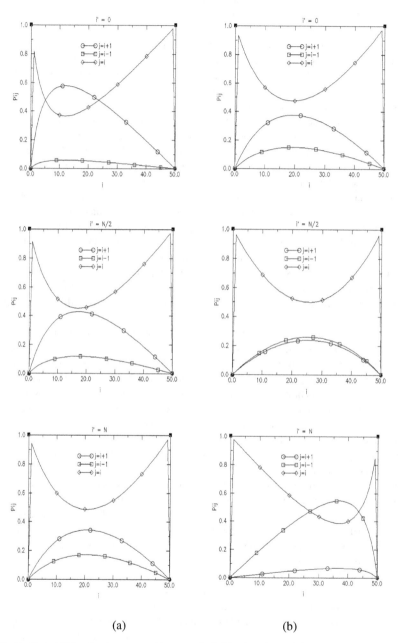

(a)   (b)

Fig. 2. Probabilities for the two multi-step tasks in Fig. 1 under a niche scheme. For clarity, the absorbing states are not shown here.

effects of different types of interdependence between niches in multi-step tasks. It has been shown that the existence of partner rule variance, whereby optimal behaviour in one niche changes with a change in behaviour in another niche of the task, can have significant and detrimental effects on expected behaviour. This is due to varying selection pressure caused by changes in the relative differences between action payoffs; for a given degree of interdependence between LCS match-sets, as the constituency of those match-sets changes under the GA, the selection pressure of the GA is dynamic, possibly passing through periods of random drift.

In the model presented here the simplest possible action selection strategy was used - random, as under XCS's explore trials. Traditionally, LCS have used a fitness proportionate scheme [Holland et al. 1986] which would slightly reduce the effects of partner variance discussed here. Wilson [1995] proposed an equal bias between stochastic and deterministic action selection, however consecutive explore trials during the majority (early part) of a run is not uncommon [e.g. Lanzi & Wilson 1999]. Conversely, with Q-learning [Watkins 1989], due to its use of max$Q(cond., action)$, variance on all but the last time step during exploit trials would show little variance (depending on the number of null entries in the Q-table) which may help to counter effects. These issues are currently under examination.

Similarly, the use of selective pressure in the replacement strategy of the GA would reduce the effects of partner variance. Related to this, the use of a rank-based reproduction selection scheme is currently under investigation both within the model and experimentally.

It is noted that although payoff and fitness are synonymous in the model used, as in the traditional LCS formalism, the classification of the type of relationship between niches applies equally to fitness based on accuracy (e.g. [Frey & Slate 1991][Wilson 1995]). However, it is predicted that such a system, i.e. XCS, will not suffer from partner rule variance as much since a significant change in a partnering match-set will cause a significant change in accuracy, thereby causing a faster response (change) locally (see [Kovacs 1999] for related discussions). That is, the transitory periods are predicted to be much shorter in an accuracy-based LCS. This is now being examined experimentally and shares similar features to Lanzi and Colombetti's [1999] work in stochastic environments.

Since selection pressure for the rule-discovery component is not constant in LCS during exploration, this implies that the effects of the genetic search operators also vary over time. That is, with a traditionally fixed mutation rate decreasing/increasing search (or drift) is obtained with increasing/decreasing selection pressure. In light of this, and the general benefits reported in the literature, self-adaptive mutation operators based on those used in Evolution Strategies [Rechenberg 1973] and later forms of Evolutionary Programming [Fogel 1992] have recently been added to LCS. Initial results indicate that self-adaptation is possible and that improvements in performance can be obtained [Bull & Hurst 2000].

The use of fixed genetic and activation links between rules in succeeding match-sets - Corporate Classifier Systems [e.g. Tomlinson & Bull 1998] - may also reduce this effect by reducing the chance of partner variance. Again, this is being examined.

Finally, the results from this model are now being extended to more complex Markov models of GAs in LCSs, based on the work of Nix and Vose [1992]. More complex models of the reward component are also being incorporated (after [Westerdale 1999]).

References

Booker, L. (1985) Improving the Performance of Genetic Algorithms in Classifier Systems. In J.J. Grefenstette (ed.) *Proceedings of the First International Conference on Genetic Algorithms and their Applications*, Lawrence Erlbaum Associates, pp80-93.

Bull, L. & Hurst, J. (2000) Self-Adaptive Mutation in ZCS Controllers. In S. Cagnoni, R.Poli, G. Smith, D. Corne, M. Oates, E. Hart, P-L. Lanzi, E. Willem, Y. Li, B. Paechter & T.C Fogarty (eds) *Real-World Applications of Evolutionary Computing: Proceedings of the EvoNet Workshops - EvoRob 2000*, Springer, pp339-346.

Fogel, D.B. (1992) *Evolving Artificial Intelligence*. PhD dissertation, University of California.

Frey, P.W. & Slate, D.J. (1991) Letter Recognition using Holland-style Adaptive Classifiers. *Machine Learning* 6:161-182.

Goldberg, D. & Segrest, P. (1987) Finite Markov Chain Analysis of Genetic Algorithms. In J.J. Grefenstette (ed.) *Proceedings of the Second International Conference on Genetic Algorithms*, Lawrence Erlbaum, pp1-7.

Holland, J.H. (1975) *Adaptation in Natural and Artificial Systems*, University of Michigan Press.

Holland, J.H., Holyoak, K.J., Nisbett, R.E. & Thagard, P.R. (1986) *Induction: Processes of Inference, Learning and Discovery*. MIT Press.

Horn, J., Goldberg, D. & Deb, K. (1994) Implicit Niching in a Learning Classifier System: Nature's Way. *Evolutionary Computation*, 2(1):37-65.

Kovacs, T. (1999) Strength or Accuracy ? A Comparison of Two Approaches to Fitness Calculation in Learning Classifier Systems. In A.S. Wu (ed.) *Proceedings of the 1999 Genetic and Evolutionary Computation Conference Workshop Program*, Gecco, pp290-297.

Lanzi, P-L. & Colombetti, M. (1999) An Extension to the XCS Classifier System for Stochastic Environments. In W.Banzhaf, J.Daida, A.E.Eiben, M.H.Garzon, V.Honavar, M.Jakiela & R.E.Smith (eds) *Proceedings of the Genetic and Evolutionary Computation Conference - Gecco '99*, Morgan Kauffman, pp353-360.

Lanzi, P-L. & Wilson, S.W. (1999) Optimal Classifier System Performance in Non-Markov Environments. Tech. Report N99.36 Dipartmento di Eletronica e Infromazione. Politecnico di Milano.

Nix, A.E. & Vose, M.D. (1992) Modelling Genetic Algorithms with Markov Chains. *Annals of Mathematics and Artificial Intelligence*, 5(1):79-88.

Rechenberg, I. (1973) *Evolutionsstrategie; Optimierung technischer Systeme nach Prinzipen der biologischen Evolution*. Frommann-Holzboog Verlag.

Tomlinson, A. & Bull, L. (1998) A Corporate Classifier System. In A.E. Eiben, T. Bäck, M. Schoenauer & H-P. Schwefel (eds.) *Parallel Problem Solving from Nature - PPSN V*, Springer, pp. 550-559.

Watkins, C. (1989) *Learning from Delayed Rewards*. PhD Dissertation, Cambridge.

Westerdale, T.H. (1999) An Approach to Credit Assignment in Classifier Systems. *Complexity* 4(2):

Wilson, S.W. (1994) ZCS: A Zeroth-level Classifier System. *Evolutionary Computation* 2(1):1-18.

Wilson, S.W. (1995) Classifier Fitness Based on Accuracy. *Evolutionary Computation* 3(2):149-177.

Probability-Enhanced Predictions in the Anticipatory Classifier System

Martin V. Butz[1], David E. Goldberg[2], and Wolfgang Stolzmann[3]

[1] Institute for Psychology III & Department of Computer Science
University of Würzburg, Germany
butz@psychologie.uni-wuerzburg.de
[2] Illinois Genetic Algorithms Laboratory
Department of General Engineering
University of Illinois at Urbana-Champaign, IL, USA
deg@illigal.ge.uiuc.edu
[3] DaimlerChrysler AG
Research and Technology
Berlin, Germany
wolfgang.stolzmann@daimlerchrysler.com

Abstract. The Anticipatory Classifier System (ACS) recently showed many capabilities new to the Learning Classifier System field. Due to its enhanced rule structure with an effect part, it forms an internal environmental representation, learns latently besides the common reward learning, and can use many cognitive processes. This paper introduces a probability-enhancement in the predictions of the ACS which enables the system to handle different kinds of non-determinism in an environment. Experiments in two different mazes will show that the ACS is now able to handle action-noise and irrelevant random attributes in the perceptions. Furthermore, applications with a recently introduced GA will reveal the general independence of the two new mechanism as well as the ability of the GA to substantially decrease the population size.

1 Introduction

In contrast to the condition-action-payoff structure of classifiers in other Learning Classifier Systems (LCSs), the Anticipatory Classifier System (ACS) has a condition-action-effect-payoff structure (Stolzmann, 1997, Stolzmann, 1998). Furthermore, the learning is based on the accuracy of the predicted effects (i.e. the anticipations) rather than on the payoff predictions, as in original LCSs, or the accuracy of the payoff predictions, as in XCS (Wilson, 1995).

The anticipation based learning enables the ACS to learn latently (i.e. learning an environmental model without getting any reward) which was already investigated in Stolzmann (1997). In combination with the enhanced classifier structure, the learning mechanism results in a complete internal model of the environment rather than a condition-action-payoff model. This model enables the ACS to use more sophisticated processes (i.e. cognitive processes).

P.L. Lanzi, W. Stolzmann, and S.W. Wilson (Eds.): IWLCS 2000, LNAI 1996, pp. 37–51, 2001.

Stolzmann, Butz, Hoffmann, and Goldberg (2000) investigated the present cognitive capabilities, introduced two new ones and outlined possible future applications.

Until now, the ACS considered all changing attributes as results from its actions. Butz, Goldberg, and Stolzmann (1999) revealed the limits of such an approach. It was shown that the ACS relies on a *perceptual causality* in the environment and that any *non-determinism* challenges the learning mechanism. In particular, an environment was investigated where randomly changing attributes or noise in the actions challenged the ACS. Stolzmann (1997) already proposed the formation of an attention spot in the ACS by introducing an additional 'don't care' symbol in the effect part (rule right-hand side). However, an attention spot cannot solve tasks where an action in a particular situation can lead to different results. Thus, this paper introduces probability-enhanced effects (PEEs) in the right-hand side of a rule, that can form an attention spot as well as can consider different possible changes in the environment.

The next section gives an overview of the ACS with all its current mechanisms. Next, Sect. 3 introduces the PEEs of a classifier and the associated mechanism. Section 4 gives results in mazes with disturbing random attributes as well as noise in the actions. Finally, a discussion is provided.

2   Overview of the ACS

In Stolzmann (1997) the basic structure of the ACS with its anticipatory learning process (ALP) was introduced. Stolzmann (2000) published the additional mark in the ALP. Finally, Butz, Goldberg, and Stolzmann (2000) introduced an enhancement of the application of the ALP and a genetic algorithm (GA) to the ACS. This section gives an overview of the current state-of-the-art. Further details of the mechanisms in the ACS can be found in the cited papers.

2.1   The Basic Structure

An ACS always interacts with an environment. In order to be able to learn, it relies on a perceptual causality in successive states. At each time step t it perceives a state $\sigma(t) \in \mathcal{I} = \{\iota_1, \iota_2, ..., \iota_m\}^L$, executes an action $\alpha(t) \in \mathcal{A} = \{\alpha_1, \alpha_2, ..., \alpha_n\}$ and receives payoff $\rho(t) \in \Re$, where m represents the number of different possible detector values, ι_i the different detector values, L the number of detectors, n the number of different executable actions, and α_i the different actions.

The ACS stores its knowledge in rules, which are called classifiers. A classifier consists of a condition part C, an action part A, an effect part E and a mark M ($C, E \in \{\iota_1, ..., \iota_m, \#\}^L$, $A \in \{\alpha_1, ..., \alpha_m\}$ and $M = (m_1, ..., m_L)$ with $m_i \subseteq \{\iota_1, ..., \iota_m\}$). A '#'-symbol in C (i.e. a 'don't-care' symbol) matches any detector information in the attribute while a '#'-symbol in E (i.e. a 'pass-through' symbol) predicts that the corresponding detector value does not change after the execution of the action A. Furthermore, each classifier cl has got the following parameters:

- The quality $q \in [0, 1]$ measures the accuracy of the anticipations.
- The reward measure $r \in \Re$ predicts the payoff from an environment.
- The time stamp t_s specifies the time when last the GA was applied in a set where cl was in.
- The experience measure exp counts how often the classifier's quality was updated.
- The numerosity measure num measures the number of traditional or micro-classifiers the *macroclassifier cl* represents (identical to the *macroclassifiers* in XCS, Wilson, 1995).

Learning in the ACS starts always with a completely general knowledge (i.e. classifiers for each action with only '#'-symbols in C and E). A behavioral act (see Fig. 1) forms at first a match set out of the current population considering the current state $\sigma(t)$. Next, the ACS decides with a probability of ϵ whether to choose an action randomly or whether to choose a classifier by roulette-wheel selection with the bid $q * r$ in the match set and choose its action. Considering the action, an action set is formed. After the execution of the action, first the ALP (with respect to the resulting state $\sigma(t+1)$) and then the GA modify the action set and produce the learning set. Finally, the reward measure r is updated considering the perceived payoff $\rho(t)$ and the maximal reward prediction $q * r$ in the next match set $M_{set}(t+1)$.

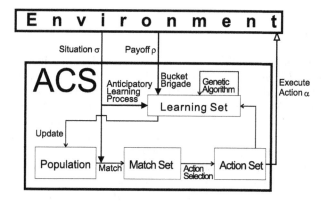

Fig. 1. A behavioral act in the ACS with all the involved learning procedures

2.2 The ALP

The ALP modifies the action set with respect to the resulting state $\sigma(t+1)$. In the ALP new, more specialized classifiers are formed out of inaccurate, more general ones considering the mark M, the anticipation of the classifier, and $\sigma(t+1)$. Furthermore, the quality q of each classifier is updated with learning rate b_q.

$$\text{increase} : q = (1 - b_q) * q + b_q \qquad (1)$$

$$\text{decrease} : q = (1 - b_q) * q \tag{2}$$

If q decreases under $\theta_i = 0.1$, the classifier is considered as *inadequate* and is deleted. If q is greater than $\theta_r = 0.9$, ACS considers the classifier as *reliable* and uses it in the internal environmental model.

The ALP distinguishes between a perceived change or non-change. If a change was perceived, it further distinguishes between correct and incorrect anticipation of each classifier in the action set.

In the case where no change occurred, the so called *useless case*, each classifier in the set is marked ($M'_{cl} = (m'_1, ..., m'_L)$ with $m'_i = m_i \cup \{\iota_i\}$) and its quality is decreased (Eq. 2).

If a change occurred, each classifier is considered separately. If a classifier anticipates the effects of the action incorrectly, the so called *unexpected case*, its quality is decreased (Eq. 2) and it is marked. Moreover, if the classifier can be specialized in the effect part (resulting in a classifier that predicts the encountered changes correctly), then a new classifier will be formed. On the other hand, if a classifier anticipates the effects correctly, the so called *expected case*, its quality is increased (Eq. 1). Moreover, if the classifier is marked and the difference between mark and previous state reveal a possibility to specialize the condition part to prevent the encountered error(s), a new classifier is generated.

A more detailed description of the ALP can be found in Butz, Goldberg, & Stolzmann (2000).

2.3   The GA

While the ALP only specializes rules and thus resembles a specialization pressure in the ACS, the GA generalizes. It is applied, after the ALP modified the learning set. It is only applied, if the average time since the last GA in the set is greater than the threshold θ_{ga}. Two classifiers are then selected with roulette wheel selection where the bid of each classifier is the cube of its quality (q^3). With a probability μ a non-#-symbol in the condition part of the selected classifiers is changed to a #-symbol (i.e. mutated). Crossover is applied only in the conditions with a probability of χ. The resulting classifiers are inserted into the population if they are not completely general. If a produced classifier already exists, its numerosity is increased. Finally, classifiers are deleted in the action set, if the size of the resulting set is greater than the action set size threshold θ_{as}.

2.4   Subsumption

In order to balance the specialization due to the ALP and the generalization due to the GA, subsumption (similar to XCS (Wilson, 1998)) was introduced to the ACS (Butz, Goldberg, & Stolzmann, 2000). When a new classifier is generated and there is an accurate, more general, unmarked classifier with a sufficient experience ($exp > \theta exp$), then the new classifier is not inserted into the population but q or num of the old classifier is increased dependent if the ALP or the GA generated the new classifier, respectively. Although subsumption was introduced together with the GA it works independent from the GA and is applied in all the experiments presented here.

2.5   Reinforcement Learning

In order to realize reward learning, the reward measure r of the classifiers in the resulting learning set is updated similar to Q-learning (Watkins & Dayan, 1992) and the Bucket-Brigade (Holland, 1985) idea:

$$r = r + b_r * (\gamma * \max_{cl \in M_{set}(t+1)} (q_{cl} * r_{cl}) + \rho(t) - r) \tag{3}$$

b_r is the learning rate and γ the discount factor. However, this paper investigates only the latent learning abilities of the ACS and thus, the formation of an environmental representation. The reinforcement learning abilities are not investigated herein.

3   The Probability-Enhanced Effects (PEEs)

In Butz, Goldberg, and Stolzmann (1999) two particular problems of *non-determinism* were identified that challenged the ACS mechanism. (1) Violated Relevance: When an environment sends additional randomly changing attributes, each classifier predicts the outcome of a random attribute with a probability of 50%. Thus, no classifier gets reliable and no environmental model is formed. (2) Action-Noise: When the result of an action is not deterministic (identical to the stochastic environments in Lanzi, 1999), the environmental model can only be built, if the probability of a successful execution is greater than 0.9 (otherwise, most classifiers do not get reliable). This section introduces the PEEs that will solve both challenges.

3.1   The New Structure of the Effect Part E

To be able to generate classifiers that predict all possible effects correctly and thus become reliable in these environments, the effect part E can be enhanced. Each attribute in E is no longer a symbol, but instead is replaced by a set of symbols with respective probabilities for the occurrence of each symbol, where the probabilities in each attribute always sum to one. Thus, for example the not enhanced effect part $E = [0, 1, \#, 2]$ is now coded as $E = [\{(0, 1.0)\}, \{(1, 1.0)\}, \{(\#, 1.0)\}, \{(2, 1.0)\}]$. We will write a not enhanced attribute in E simply as x rather than $\{(x, 1.0)\}$ to allow the old notation for not enhanced effects and to simplify the notation of PEEs. Enhancing the first attribute of E predicting a 60 to 40 percent change of 0 or 1, respectively, changes E to $[\{(0, 0.6), (1, 0.4)\}, 1, \#, 2]$.

A classifier with PEEs is treated identical to a normal classifier in the GA. However, in the ALP application we need to make further distinctions.

We need to redefine when a classifier made a correct anticipations since the new classifiers do not predict certain states anymore, but rather give a probability distribution over the possible attributes in the next state. A classifier in our method anticipates correctly if in each attribute one particular value corresponds to the value of the attribute in the resulting state. For now, the respective probabilities of the particular symbols are not considered in the learning process. However, when a classifier with PEEs anticipates correctly, the respective probability values in the PEEs are increased with the update parameter $b_p = 0.05$: $p = p + b_p(1 - p)$ and next, the relative probability of each value in an attribute is recalculated dividing each probability by the sum of the probabilities in one attribute. A closer observation of the evolving classifier lists (not shown here) showed that the probabilities in the PEEs reflect the environmental settings accurately.

Moreover, the *useless case* needs to be modified. If an enhanced classifier anticipates that no change occurs, the quality of the classifier will be increased. This is necessary to enable the learning of cases where an action only sometimes causes an actual change. The next section explains when an enhancement of an effect part occurs.

3.2 How and When to Enhance an Effect Part E

The enhancement in E can easily lead to an over-generalized rule. What about a classifier that is fairly general in C and predicts that basically anything can happen? Such a classifier would become reliable, since it always predicts correct changes. Right now, there is no mechanism that detects such an over-generalized effect part. Thus, an enhancement in E may only occur if it is really necessary.

Consequently, each classifier gets an additional boolean parameter ee (the 'enhance effects' parameter) which specifies if the classifier should be enhanced in E. The idea is that when a classifier cannot be further differentiated in the conditions and still does not predict the correct effects all the time, it sets ee to true indicating that in the specified situation the execution of the specified action results in different effects. When a classifier is generated, ee is always set to $false$. Moreover, ee is set back to $false$ when the classifier gets an additional mark that differs from the current M (indicating that the classifier can be differentiated from this state). The parameter ee is set to $true$, when the classifier cl is (1) in the expected case, (2) it has a mark M, and (3) C cannot be further differentiated from M.

An enhancement can occur in two cases. If the criterions for setting ee are true and there is another classifier cl_j in the current learning set that is ready to be joined, a new, effect-enhanced classifier will be generated. It must be assured that $ee_{cl_j} = true$, M_{cl_j} is not enhanced, and $M_{cl_j} = M_{cl}$. In the new classifier the two effect parts E of the parental classifiers are merged into one part E with the above structure. The C parts are combined so that the resulting C has #-symbols only in the attributes in that both parents have #-symbols. Moreover, to allow the representation of state-action pairs where a change occurs only sometimes, a new, enhanced classifier is also generated, if a classifier with $ee = true$ takes part in the *useless case* (and the marking in this process does not alter the current mark). In this case the condition part C of the new classifier stays the same, and E is enhanced in the attributes with non-#-symbols.

An example of the enhancement process is given in Sect. 4.1.

4   The Resulting Performance in Different Mazes

This section presents results from experiments using the ACS with PEEs in two two-dimensional mazes with additional misleading properties. The Woods1 environment was previously investigated with ZCS and XCS (Wilson, 1994, Wilson, 1995). The Maze4 environment was introduced by (Lanzi, 1997) for XCS. In the presented results we use the following parameters: $\rho = 1$, $b_q = b_r = 0.05$, $\gamma = 0.95$ and $\epsilon = 0.8$. The parameters for the GA were set to $\theta_{ga} = 100$, $theta_{as} = 20$, $\mu = 0.3$, $\chi = 0.0$, and $\theta_{exp} = 20$. Perceptions in the two mazes are coded as a string with eight attributes for the eight adjacent cells. $\sigma \in \{., O, F\}^8$ where a '.' represents an empty position, an 'O' an obstacle, and an 'F' a position with food. Executable actions are movements in the eight directions, $\alpha \in \{N, NE, E, SE, S, SW, W, NW\}$. All results are averaged over ten runs. After examining an example of the new mechanism in Woods1, we will give results without GA and in Sect. 4.4 with GA application in both environments violating relevance as well as adding action-noise.

4.1   Performance in Woods1

Fig. 2. Woods1

Woods1 is very suitable to examine the behavior of a learning agent. It is a Markov environment where the accessibility of all states is equal. Figure 2 shows Woods1 with an animat indicated by the '*'. This section gives first an example of the mechanism associated with the PEEs. Next, it presents first results.

The animat at the indicated position perceives the situation $\sigma = (.....OOF)$. When adding an additional random attribute, the animat either perceives $\sigma = (.....OOF0)$ or $\sigma = (.....OOF1)$. At a particular time t the ACS may perceive $\sigma(t) = (.....OOF0)$ and move one step north ($\alpha(t) = N$). The consequent state is either $\sigma(t+1) = (.....OF.0)$ or $\sigma(t+1) = (.....OF.1)$. Both results will be experienced sometimes resulting in two classifiers
$cl_1 = [\#\#\#\#\#\#OF\#] - N - [\#\#\#\#\#\#\#F.\#]$ and
$cl_2 = [\#\#\#\#\#\#OF0] - N - [\#\#\#\#\#\#\#F.1]$
(showing $C - A - E$). cl_1 can still be applied in $\sigma = (.....OOF1)$. Thus, applying the marking mechanism a new classifier cl_3 will be formed where the #-symbol in the last attribute is specialized to 0
$cl_3 = [\#\#\#\#\#\#OF0] - N - [\#\#\#\#\#\#\#F.\#]$.
Now, cl_2 and cl_3 can only be applied in $\sigma = (.....OOF0)$ and will be eventually marked by the state itself, since they predict a result which occurs at a

50% chance. Thus, *ee* of both classifiers will be set to *true* since there is no difference between the mark and the indicated state when applied successfully. Consequently, a new, effect-enhanced classifier will be formed that has the structure

$$cl_4 = [\#\#\#\#\#\#OF0] - N - [\#\#\#\#\#\#F.\{(0, 0.5), (1, 0.5)\}].$$

This classifier now predicts correctly the deterministic changes due to the execution of N and further predicts that the last attribute will change to 1 with a 50% chance. Since this classifier always anticipates correctly, its quality q will increase over 90% and will consequently become part of the internal environmental representation.

The left-hand side of Fig. 3 shows the resulting performance in Woods1. As a comparison, also the learning curve without any non-determinism in the environment is shown. The correct anticipations measure is evaluated by considering in each situation in the environment each possible movement and checking if there is a reliable classifier that matches in the conditions and predicts the correct effects of the movement. The population size is the number of distinct classifiers in the population. When adding randomly changing attributes, the evolution of the whole internal environmental representation takes longer, but the ACS is able to build it completely. The population size grows to a relatively high level, when adding the random attributes as should be expected. In a maze with i random attributes one situation looks like 2^i different situations. Although the ACS is able to solve the effect-problem, it still needs to solve the puzzle for all possible situations, which can also be observed in the above example. Classifiers with different stages of PEEs increase the population size further.

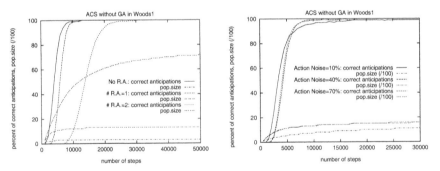

Fig. 3. The ACS is able to learn the Woods1 environment with additional randomly changing attributes on the left hand side and action-noise on the right hand side due to the PEEs.

The right-hand side of Fig. 3 shows results in Woods1 with action-noise p_n. With a probability of p_n an executed action does not lead to the intended position but to the position on the left or right. If a position is blocked, the action does not cause any effect. The figure reveals that the ACS is able to learn the relations. Interestingly, the best performance is not reached when the action-noise is on the lowest level but on the highest level. This is because when p_n is high, all three outcomes of the action have approximately the same probability. Thus, all three necessary classifiers evolve with the same probability and get joined quickly. When p_n is low, the classifiers that predict the improbable changes take longer to evolve and often get inadequate and thus deleted. Consequently, it takes longer to form classifiers with adequate PEEs.

4.2   Performance in Maze4

O	O	O	O	O	O	O	O
O			O			F	O
O	O			O			O
O	O		O			O	O
O							O
O	O		O				O
O				O			O
O	O	O	O	O	O	O	O

Fig. 4. Maze4

The Maze4 environment (Fig. 4) is a different challenge for the ACS. While in the Woods1 environment every position is equally probable to access, in Maze4 the probabilities are distributed unequally. The whole area in the North-West quadrant of the maze is much less likely to be explored than the eastern area (because of the additional obstacles barring access to the North-West quadrant). Figure 5 shows the resulting performance in Maze4. The comparison of different numbers of random attributes shows again how the size of the population grows when additional random attributes are added. Furthermore, it shows how much longer it takes until a complete internal model is formed. As predicted, it is harder to achieve a complete knowledge since it takes much longer until all parts of the maze are experienced often enough. When adding action-noise to the environment, the same effect as in Woods1 can be observed. When p_n is low, the knowledge in the beginning increases faster but a 100% knowledge is hardly reached as the merging of classifiers is much more unlikely. When the noise level is on 70% the performance is the best, but also the population grows the most.

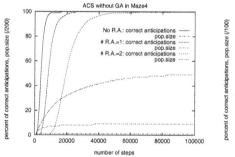 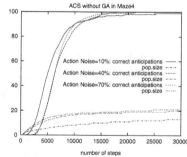

Fig. 5. Also in Maze4 with additional random attributes on the left hand side and action-noise on the right hand side, the ACS is able to learn the internal environmental representation due to the PEEs.

4.3   Action-Noise Combined with Random Attributes

So far, we have shown that the PEEs and the associated mechanism are able to detect attributes that change independently from their own actions as well as detect that an action can cause different effects with a certain probability. However, it still needs to be shown if the combination of the two sources of non-determinism can be detected. Is the mechanism able to focus on the relevant eight attributes and realize in the mean time that an action can cause three different effects? Figure 6 shows that this is indeed possible. The ACS is able to form a complete internal model of the environment. It is forming classifiers that predict that after an action, the random attribute is going to change with an approximately 50% probability and furthermore that the action can cause three different effects. Maze4 again takes longer to be learned completely. However, as in all experiments with additional random attributes, the population size grows to a high level. In the next section we will show that the GA is able to decrease this population growth.

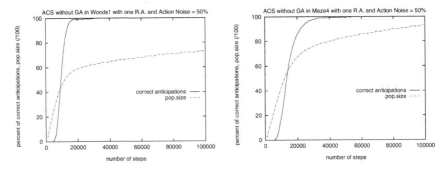

Fig. 6. The ACS is also able to handle the combination of a random attribute and action-noise.

4.4   Combining the PEEs with the GA

In the experiments with random attributes, the population size increases with the number of random attributes. We claimed that there are two reasons for this behavior: (1) classifiers evolve that predict a part of the possible changes and stay as suboptimal classifiers in the population, and (2) classifiers that predict all possible changes specify one specific constellation of the random attributes in the conditions. Consequently, a classifier is needed for each combination of random attributes.

Overcoming this difficulty is exactly what the GA is meant for. The genetic generalization pressure can form an attention spot on those attributes which are relevant in the conditions. The ALP cannot realize that the result does not depend on the random attributes but the GA can. Generalizing the good classifiers by mutation leads to classifiers that match more often in each situation. Eventually, classifiers will evolve that completely ignore the random attributes in the conditions and predict that they will either change or stay the same.

Figure 7 shows that the ACS with GA is really able to generate the intended classifiers. The change in the population size shows that the ACS with GA is exploring early in the run. Once the knowledge increases, the population size starts to decrease and converges to the above-mentioned classifiers. In Woods1 with two additional random attributes, this results in a complete environmental representation with a ten times smaller population size. In Woods1 with three additional random attributes the population size in the ACS without GA increases to a level of 25000 classifiers while with GA the size of the population never reaches a size of 5000 and converges in the end to less than 600 classifiers – more than 40 times less than without GA. Also in Maze4 the population size decreases substantially. However, we can observe that the knowledge does not reach a 100% knowledge level permanently. This is the case because of the unequal frequencies of experiencing each of the states in Maze4. Since the ACS experiences part of the states much more often, the GA generalizes over this subset of states and sometimes drives out part of the classifiers necessary for the seldom experienced states. Nevertheless, the environmental representation is still near perfect.

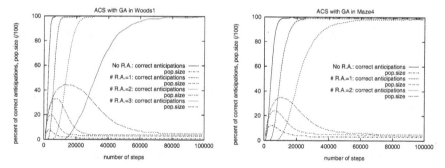

Fig. 7. When the ACS with PEEs and GA is applied in Woods1 and Maze4 with additional random attributes, the result is a great decrease in the size of the classifier list and in no decrease in the performance.

When we add the GA in the mazes with action-noise the knowledge does not completely stay at 100% (Fig. 8). A closer look at the classifier list in this case shows that classifiers evolve that match in different situations and predict all possible changes in those situations. The GA generalizes classifiers that have PEEs. Accidently, such a classifier can now also predict a part or even all possible changes in another situation. If it predicts a part of another situation, the ALP will generate a more specialized classifier that suddenly only matches in the new situation but actually predicts more changes than are possible in this situation. However, for now, the GA works completely independently from the

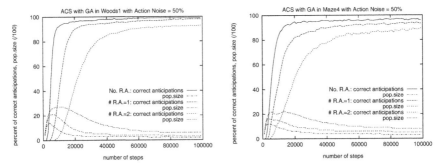

Fig. 8. Applying the ACS with PEEs and GA in Woods1 and Maze4 with additional noise results again in a decrease in size but also a slight decrease in the performance.

PEEs. We have shown that the GA is able to substantially decrease the size of the population while the formation of the environmental representation stays very close to perfect.

5   Discussion

Although a detailed observation of the evolving classifier lists (not shown herein) revealed that the probability distribution in the PEEs accurately reflect the current environmental settings, the usefulness of this distribution was not further investigated as yet. Enhancements in the reinforcement learning mechanisms as well as in the cognitive capabilities of the ACS are imaginable. The update rule of the reward prediction (Eq. 3) could for example be modified to consider the transition probability reflected by the probabilities in the enhanced effect parts. In planning applications, the probabilities of the enhanced effects could be used as a measure for the probability of actually reaching the aimed position. The advantages and limits of such approaches need to be investigated in detail.

Moreover, as already mentioned in Butz, Goldberg, and Stolzmann (1999), there are other possibilities of representing PEEs. One other possibility is to allow different effect strings in one classifier concretely specifying the distinct possible changes. Especially, a hybrid of the two approaches sounds reasonable, which consequently should form classifiers that predict a 50/50 chance in the random attributes in each effect-string. In the example of Section 4.1 with one additional attribute and 50% noise the perfect classifier would look like this:

$$0.25 : [\#\#\#\#O\#\#.\{(0, 0.5), (1, 0.5)\}]$$
$$[\#\#\#\#\#\#\#F\#] - N - 0.50 : [\#\#\#\#\#\#\#F.\{(0, 0.5), (1, 0.5)\}]$$
$$0.25 : [\#\#OO\#...\{(0, 0.5), (1, 0.5)\}]$$

Future research will show if the ACS is able to form such classifiers reliably.

Nonetheless, this paper has demonstrated a first approach in the ACS to handle non-determinism in an environment with PEEs. The resulting ACS was able to handle randomly changing attributes as well as action-noise. Due to the carful detection of *non-determinism* and the consequent effect-enhancement, an accurate and complete environmental model evolved. When additionally applying a GA, the ACS was able to solve the tasks with a substantial decrease in the population size. However, a slight problem of over-generalization was observed.

In order to prevent the over-generalization of PEEs in the application of the ACS with GA in an environment with action-noise, the GA could consider the amount of enhancement in the PEEs in some way. It should prefer the classifiers that are accurate, maximally general but not over-general in the effect parts for reproduction and the over-general classifiers in the effect parts for deletion.

Considering the observed over-generalization of conditions in environments with an unequal probability distribution of experiencing states, we first need to reconsider what is our main goal. When we want to build a system which behaves similar to real animals, then this observation should actually not bother us too much. The loss of knowledge is similar to the process of forgetting special exceptions that occur seldom. Moreover, the present near-complete internal environmental representation could directly be used to overcome the loss of knowledge. By introducing a new cognitive process, the ACS could directly explore regions in an environment that it did not experience for a long time (a first approach is given in Stolzmann & Butz, 2000). On the other hand, if we view the ACS as a traditional LCS, we could approach the problem with default hierarchies (Holland, Holyoak, Nisbett, & Thagard, 1986). This should result in an implicit formation of more specialized exception rules that overrule more general rules in the special cases. A modification of the GA as well as a hierarchy in the usage of the environmental representation would be necessary to realize such an approach.

Nevertheless, without any enhancement in the GA and thus a complete independence from the PEEs, the ACS was still able to form a near-optimal representation of the environment with a much smaller population size. In the application with only additional randomly changing attributes the environmental representation even got perfect and the population size decreased enormously. Thus, the ACS is now able to handle non-deterministic environments generating classifiers that are accurate and maximally general. More research is needed to reveal in what other types of environments the PEEs are useful as well as where they are limited.

Acknowledgments. The authors would like to thank Dimitri Knjazew, Martin Pelikan, and Stewart Wilson for valuable discussions and useful comments as well as the Automated Learning Group of NCSA at the University of Illinois in Urbana-Champaign for their support.

The work was sponsored by the Air Force Office of Scientific Research, Air Force Materiel Command, USAF, under grant F49620-97-1-0050. Research funding for this work was also provided by the National Science Foundation under grant DMI-9908252. Support was also provided by a grant from the U. S. Army Research Laboratory under the Federated Laboratory Program, Cooperative Agreement DAAL01-96-2-0003. The U. S. Government is authorized to reproduce and distribute reprints for Government purposes notwithstanding any copyright notation thereon. Additionally, research funding was provided by the German Research Foundation DFG.

The views and conclusions contained herein are those of the authors and should not be interpreted as necessarily representing the official policies or endorsements, either expressed or implied, of the Air Force Office of Scientific Research, the National Science Foundation, the U. S. Army, or the U. S. Government.

References

Butz, M. V., Goldberg, D. E., & Stolzmann, W. (1999). *New challenges for an Anticipatory Classifier System: Hard problems and possible solutions* (IlliGAL report 99019). University of Illinois at Urbana-Champaign: Illinois Genetic Algorithms Laboratory.

Butz, M. V., Goldberg, D. E., & Stolzmann, W. (2000). Introducing a genetic generalization pressure to the anticipatory classifier system: Part 1 - theoretical approach. In Whitely, D., Goldberg, D. E., Cantu-Paz, E., Spector, L., Parmee, I., & Beyer, H.-G. (Eds.), *Proceedings of the Genetic and Evolutionary Computation Conference (GECCO-2000)* pp. 34–41. San Francisco, CA: Morgan Kaufmann.

Holland, J. H. (1985). Properties of the bucket brigade algorithm. In *Proceedings of an International Conference on Genetic Algorithms and their Applications* pp. 1–7. Carnegie-Mellon University, Pittsburgh, PA: John J. Grefenstette.

Holland, J. H., Holyoak, K. J., Nisbett, R. E., & Thagard, P. R. (1986). *Induction: Processes of inference, learning, and discovery.* Cambridge, MA: MIT Press.

Lanzi, P. L. (1997). A study of the generalization capabilities of XCS. In Baeck, T. (Ed.), *Proceedings of the Seventh International Conference on Genetic Algorithm* pp. 418–425. San Francisco, California: Morgan Kaufmann.

Lanzi, P. L. (1999). An extension to the XCS classifier system for stochastic environments. In Banzhaf, W., Daida, J., Eiben, A. E., Garzon, M. H., Honavar, V., Jakiela, M., & Smith, R. E. (Eds.), *Proceedings of the Genetic and Evolutionary Computation Conference (GECCO-99)* pp. 353–360. San Francisco, CA: Morgan Kaufmann.

Stolzmann, W. (1997). *Antizipative Classifier Systeme [Anticipatory classifier systems].* Osnabrueck, Germany: Shaker Verlag, Aachen, Germany.

Stolzmann, W. (1998). Anticipatory classifier systems. In Koza, J. R., Banzhaf, W., Chellapilla, K., Deb, K., Dorigo, M., Fogel, D. B., Garzon, M. H., Goldberg, D. E., Iba, H., & Riolo, R. (Eds.), *Genetic Programming '98* pp. 658–664. San Francisco: Morgan Kaufmann.

Stolzmann, W. (2000). An introduction to anticipatory classifier systems. In Lanzi, P. L., Stolzmann, W., & Wilson, S. W. (Eds.), *Learning Classifier Systems: From Foundations to Applications, LNAI 1813* pp. 175–194. Berlin: Springer-Verlag.

Stolzmann, W., & Butz, M. V. (2000). Latent learning and action-planning in robots with Anticipatory Classifier Systems. In Lanzi, P. L., Stolzmann, W., & Wilson, S. W. (Eds.), *Learning Classifier Systems: From Foundations to Applications, LNAI 1813* pp. 301–317. Berlin: Springer-Verlag.

Stolzmann, W., Butz, M. V., Hoffmann, J., & Goldberg, D. E. (2000). First cognitive capabilities in the anticipatory classifier system. In Meyer, J.-A., Berthoz, A., Floreano, D., Roitblat, H., & Wilson, S. W. (Eds.), *From Animals to Animats 6: Proceedings of the Sixth International Conference on Simulation of Adaptive Behavior* pp. 287–296. Cambridge, MA: MIT press.

Watkins, C. J. C. H., & Dayan, P. (1992). Q-learning. *Machine Learning, 8*(3), 272–292.

Wilson, S. W. (1994). ZCS: A zeroth level classifier system. *Evolutionary Computation, 2*(1), 1–18.

Wilson, S. W. (1995). Classifier fitness based on accuracy. *Evolutionary Computation, 3*(2), 149–175.

Wilson, S. W. (1998). Generalization in the XCS classifier system. In Koza, J. R., Banzhaf, W., Chellapilla, K., Deb, K., Dorigo, M., Fogel, D. B., Garzon, M. H., Goldberg, D. E., Iba, H., & Riolo, R. (Eds.), *Genetic Programming 1998: Proceedings of the Third Annual Conference* pp. 665–674. San Francisco: Morgan Kaufmann.

YACS: Combining Dynamic Programming with Generalization in Classifier Systems

Pierre Gérard[1,2] and Olivier Sigaud[1]

[1] Dassault Aviation, DGT/DPR/ESA
78, Quai Marcel Dassault, 92552 St-Cloud Cedex
[2] AnimatLab (LIP6), 8, rue du capitaine Scott, 75015 PARIS
pierre.gerard@lip6.fr, olivier.sigaud@dassault-aviation.fr

Abstract. This paper describes our work on the use of anticipation in Learning Classifier Systems (LCS) applied to Markov problems. We present YACS[1], a new kind of Anticipatory Classifier System. It calls upon classifiers with a [*Condition*], an [*Action*] and an [*Effect*] part.

As in the traditional LCS framework, the classifier discovery process relies on a selection and a creation mechanism. As in the Anticipatory Classifier System (ACS), YACS looks for classifiers which anticipate well rather than for classifiers which propose an optimal action. The creation mechanism does not rely on classical genetic operators but on a specialization operator, which is explicitly driven by experience. Likewise, the action qualities of the classifiers are not computed by a classical bucket-brigade algorithm, but by a variety of the value iteration algorithm that takes advantage of the effect part of the classifiers.

This paper presents the latent learning process of YACS. The description of the reinforcement learning process is focussed on the problem induced by the joint use of generalization and dynamic programming methods.

1 Introduction

Our work takes place in the *reinforcement learning* framework. We model an agent which acts on this environment and receives a reward and a new perception. More precisely, we use the Learning Classifier Systems (LCS) framework whose principles have been set down by [Holland et al., 1986], [Goldberg, 1989] and [Booker et al., 1989].

More recent achievements in this framework are due to [Wilson, 1994] and [Wilson, 1995], [Dorigo, 1994], [Stolzmann, 1998] and [Lanzi, 2000] among others. Most of these research efforts deal with Markov problems, *i.e.* problems in which the distribution of probability for getting a perception only depends on the previous perception and action. The system we present here is designed to solve such problems, although we envision extending our work to non-Markov problems in the future, as [Cliff and Ross, 1994] and [Lanzi, 1998] do.

In this framework, our basic assumptions are the following:

---

[1] YACS stands for "Yet Another Classifier System"

P.L. Lanzi, W. Stolzmann, and S.W. Wilson (Eds.): IWLCS 2000, LNAI 1996, pp. 52–69, 2001.
© Springer-Verlag Berlin Heidelberg 2001

- rather than generating new classifiers with random genetic operators and evaluating them afterwards, we drive the classifier discovery process by experience, slightly improving what [Dorigo, 1994] did;
- rather than using a plain reinforcement learning process, the agent performs *latent learning*[2] to use its anticipation capabilities. This latent learning process can take place even if no reward is given by the environment. The joint use of latent learning and dynamic programming algorithms speeds up the convergence towards an optimal behavior once reward sources are identified. It has already been exploited in DynaQ+ [Sutton and Barto, 1998];
- we want to reduce the number of classifiers as much as possible. So, we never have two classifiers such that one is strictly more general than another.

In the next section, we present the components of YACS. As both our system and Stolzmann's ACS[3] [Stolzmann, 1998] deal with classifiers with an effect part, we will highlight how the learning process detailed in Sect. 3 differs in both systems. In this section, we pay a particular attention to the joint use of generalization and dynamic programming. In Sect. 4, we present the preliminary results obtained on a very simple application.

2   Features of the System

The system we designed uses a set of different classifiers[4]. Each *classifier* is a set of ordered *messages*. Each message is a set of ordered *tokens*. All classifiers share the same structure and message lengths.

Tokens may take discrete values in a range $[0,\ NbPossibleValues - 1]$, in which case they are specialized token, or they may take a # value. We have two kinds of tokens: *action tokens* and *perception tokens*. Action tokens are symbols representing elementary actions, for example the activation level of a particular engine in a robot. Perception tokens are symbols representing elementary perceptions, for example the value given by a particular sensor.

The system deals with two kinds of messages: *action* and *perception* messages, containing respectively action and perception tokens. The range of all tokens at the same place are the same for all messages of the same kind.

Two tokens are said to *match* if at least one is a # token, or if both have the same value. Two messages of the same kind are said to *match* if all their tokens match the corresponding token in the other message.

If every token of a perception message is less general or equal to the corresponding tokens of a second message, and if at least two corresponding tokens are different, the first message is *more specialized* than the second one. Specialized/general token ratios do not make sense in YACS. If a message is neither

---

[2] The term *latent learning* comes from the psychology field and was first used by [Riolo, 1991] in the LCS framework..-+

[3] Anticipatory Classifier System

[4] A classifier is never added to the classifier set if another one in the set has the same [*Condition*], [*Action*] and [*Effect*] parts.

more nor less general than another one, then YACS does not draw any relation between their specialization level.

As in ACS [Stolzmann, 1998], a classifier is composed of three parts: the [Condition] and the [Effect] parts are perception messages, the [Action] part is an action message.

The tokens of an [Effect] part act as a filter: a # in the [Effect] part is a *don't change* token and means "the elementary perception represented by the token will remain unchanged at the next time step if the classifier is fired"; any other value is interpreted straight-forwardly. When the condition of a classifier matches a perception, we use the *passthrough* operator to predict the next perception if the action of the classifier is chosen: The *passthrough* operator works on perception tokens [5] as follows :

$$passthrough(t_p, t_e) = \begin{cases} t_p \ if \ t_e = \# \\ t_e \ otherwise \end{cases}$$

Applying the *passthrough* operator on perception messages consists in applying the operator on their tokens.

Let C be a classifier with a [Condition] part matching the [Perception] message. Then C anticipates the perception $[Perception].passthrough(C.[Effect])$[6] when the action $C.[Action]$ is performed just after [Perception] occurs. r We also use the reverse operator of *passthrough* – the *difference* operator – which works on perception tokens[7] as follows:

$$difference(t_2, t_1) = \begin{cases} \# \ if \ t_2 = t_1 \\ t_2 \ otherwise \end{cases}$$

Given two successive perceptions, this operator allows to compute what an [Effect] part should have been to predict correctly the second one if given the first.

An immediate reward estimate R is associated to each classifier. R reflects the expected *immediate reward* if the classifier is fired[8]. It is estimated from direct experience. Dynamic programming algorithms like value iteration take advantage of immediate reward estimates and information provided by the [Effect] part to compute an optimal policy.

Each classifier also keeps a trace T of *good* and *bad* markers memorizing past anticipation mistakes and successes. The length of this trace is bounded by a fixed memory size m.

When two classifiers share the same [Action] part and if a [Condition] part is more specialized than the other one, the first classifier is more specialized than

---

[5] t_p is the token of a [Perception] and t_e is the token of an [Effect] part.

[6] We use the dot symbol (.) to identify a part of a composed item. For example, $C.[Condition]$ means "the [Condition] part of the classifier C"; $C.R$ means "the R estimate of the classifier C" (its immediate reward estimate); $t.S$ means "the S estimate of the token t". Hence, we always use the "×" symbol for multiplication.

[7] t_2 is a token of a perception occuring just after the perception containing t_1

[8] The default R is 0.

the other. We do not consider the [*Effect*] part of a classifier to determine its specialization level because a # in the [*Effect*] is a *don't change* token and not a *don't care* token as in a [*Condition*] part.

For every classifier, each general token of the [*Condition*] part keeps an *expected improvement by specialization* estimate S[9] which helps to drive the specialization process (see Sect. 3.3)

The system also uses a set of every perception encountered during the lifetime of the agent. This set only contains one instance of each perception. It is not ordered.

3   The Algorithm

Like [Stolzmann, 1998] and [Witkowski, 1999], we have an [*Effect*] part in the classifiers. The classifier discovery process builds a set of classifiers which anticipate well rather than classifiers which act optimally. This knowledge about state transitions allows the system to plan its actions or to use a variety of the value iteration algorithm. It becomes able to adjust his policy very fast when a new reward source is discovered.

As in many other works, we divide the life-time of the agent into discrete time steps. During a time step, the agent acts as follows:

1. It gets a reward and a perception from the environment;
2. It learns about the dynamics of its environment and the optimality of actions;
3. It selects an action according to what it learned;
4. It acts correspondingly in the environment.

The *latent learning* process is in charge of discovering adequate classifiers which model the dynamics of the environment. In ACS [Stolzmann, 1998] the ALP[10] modifies at the same time [*Condition*] and [*Effect*] parts in order to reflect the changes in the dynamic of the environment. In YACS the [*Effect*] part alone provides all the information about changes in the environment. A specialized token in the [*Effect*] part always indicates a change in the environment, regardless of the corresponding token in the [*Condition*] part. In YACS, the latent learning process can be divided into two simple and separate processes:

– adjusting the [*Effect*] parts (Sect. 3.2);
– discovering relevant [*Condition*] parts (Sect. 3.3).

A [*Condition*] part may specify a state of the environment even if it is not fully specialized. Furthermore, the minimal set of tokens necessary to specify a state does not necessarily correspond to the changing tokens of the perceptions when the classifier is fired. However, in ACS [Stolzmann, 1998], the ALP always specializes the [*Condition*] part and the [*Effect*] part at the same time, and only when the corresponding token in the perceptions is changing. As a result (see

---

[9] The default S is 0.5.
[10] Anticipation Learning Process

[Butz et al., 2000a]), some [*Condition*] parts may be over-specialized. Splitting the anticipatory learning process into two separate processes helps to overcome this problem.

The *reinforcement learning* process takes advantage of the model of the dynamics of the environment computed by the latent learning process. In Sect. 3.5 we present a problem induced when we jointly want to take advantage of generalization and use dynamic programming algorithms like value iteration, and we propose a solution.

The *action selection* uses a winner-take-all strategy (see Sect. 3.6).

3.1   Getting a Reward and a New Perception

When the system comes to time step t, it gets from the environment the new perception [*Perception*]$_t$ and the reward value $Reward_t$ resulting from the last selected action.

If the new perception is not present in the set of encountered perceptions, it is added. YACS only keeps one instance of every encountered perception. One may argue that this set can become very large in huge environments. But in Sect. 3.5 we show that anyway, the system must deal with information about specific situations in order to use dynamic programming. So this list is also in a part of the algorithm which would not work if it was not available.

As the system learns from one step temporal differences, the latent learning process relies on a memory of the last perception. So the system stores the last perception [*Perception*]$_{t-1}$ and forgets [*Perception*]$_{t-2}$.

If the [*Condition*] part of no classifier matches it for a particular [*Action*] message, one is added to the classifier set. The [*Effect*] part of the new classifier is set to *difference*([*Perception*]$_t$, [*Perception*]$_{t-1}$). The [*Condition*] part is such that:

- it matches [*Perception*]$_t$;
- it is neither more general nor more specialized than any [*Condition*] part of the [*Condition*] part of any other classifier with the same [*Action*] part.
- it is as general as possible, considering the previous constraints.

These conditions allow to add maximally general classifiers without introducing redundancies with already specialized ones.

3.2   Learning to Anticipate

This process is the part of the latent learning process which is in charge of discovering accurate [*Effect*] parts. When the system learns to anticipate, it may create some new classifiers, with suitable [*Effect*] parts straight-forwardly settled according to experience. As [Witkowski, 1999] and [Butz and Stolzmann, 1999] do, the algorithm does not only evaluate the classifiers which have been fired, but also takes advantage of experience to evaluate all the classifiers which could have been fired.

At each time step, the [Desired Effect] message is computed according to the formula:

$$[Desired\ Effect] \leftarrow difference([Perception]_t, [Perception]_{t-1})$$

This message corresponds to the anticipation of a classifier that would have anticipated well at the last time step and whose selection (see Sect. 3.6) would have driven the system to act as it actually did. Classifiers can be involved in the anticipation learning process even if they were not actually selected. These classifiers C are such that $C.[Condition]$ matches $[Perception]_{t-1}$ and $C.[Action]$ matches $[Action]_{t-1}$.

Let us consider such a classifier C.

- If $C.[Prediction]$ equals [Desired Anticipation], the classifier would have anticipated well, and we add a *good* marker to its trace T of anticipation mistakes and successes.
- In either case, the classifier C would have made an anticipation mistake and we add a a *bad* marker to its trace. Moreover, if no classifier did anticipate correctly, we add a new classifier which anticipates well. As in [Stolzmann, 1998], the anticipation is *covered* and we add a new classifier which is the same as the initial one but its [Effect] part which is set to the [Desired Effect]. Its trace T only contains a single *good* marker.

Our *anticipation covering* mechanism creates classifiers with relevant [Effect] parts by taking advantage of direct experience rather than genetic algorithms (GA). It differs from the ACS anticipation covering since it does only modify the [Effect] part. The anticipation covering mechanism allows to learn straightforwardly when an action does not change the perceptions of the system.

3.3   Learning Relevant Conditions

In Sect. 3.2 we have explained how, while learning to anticipate, the system adds new classifiers to adjust [Effect] parts. This section explains how [Condition] parts are adjusted.

The MutSpec Operator. The classifier discovery problem is usually solved by a GA using a creation process driven by mutation and crossover on classifiers selected by their quality. operators. These blind operators do not explicitly take advantage of the experience of the agent. Dorigo's *MutSpec* operator [Dorigo, 1994] improves the classifier discovery process by driving the specialization of the classifiers according to its experience. Our purpose is to build a classifier system without mutation nor crossover operators. Like McCallum's U-TREE algorithm [McCallum, 1996], our system starts without making any distinction between world states, and incrementally introduces experience driven specializations in [Condition] parts.

At the first time step, the classifier set contains one general classifier for each possible action. The [Condition] and [Effect] parts only contain # tokens.

At each time step, we add *good* and *bad* markers in the trace T of anticipation mistakes and sucesses (see Sect. 3.2) of several classifiers. This trace works as a FIFO list with a finite length m. When the trace is full -*i.e.* its size equals m-, we assume that the anticipation accuracy of the classifier has been checked enough and

- if the trace of the classifier only contains *good* markers, it always anticipated well and it does not need to be more specialized;
- if the trace of the classifier only contains *bad* markers, and if it is not the only one matching a particular perception of the encountered perception set for a particular action, it is discarded;
- if the trace of the classifier contains *good* and *bad* makers, it sometimes anticipates well and sometimes not. The classifier *oscillates* and its [*Condition*] part needs to be specialized.

The specialization process is designed to discover relevant [*Condition*] parts, it uses the *MutSpec* operator introduced by [Dorigo, 1994]. The *MutSpec* operator selects a joker token of the classifier and produces one new classifier for each possible specialized value of the selected token. The original classifier is discarded.

For instance, when the first token is selected, and assuming that it only may take two values (0 or 1) the classifier [#|#|#|#] [0] [#|#|#|#] produces two classifiers:

- [0|#|#|#] [0] [#|#|#|#];
- [1|#|#|#] [0] [#|#|#|#].

So, if the [*Condition*] part of the original classifier was matching several states of the environment, each resulting [*Condition*] part will match a subset of these states. We want YACS to be able to choose the token to specialize in such a way that the two resulting subsets have an equal cardinality, in order to reduce the number of specializations and thus the over-specialization.

The Expected Improvement by Specialization Estimate. Choosing at random the token to specialize as in Dorigo's original work would lead to an over-specialization of the [*Condition*] parts and thus to a sub-optimal number of classifiers. We improve this selection by using the *expected improvement by specialization* estimate S associated to each general token of each [*Condition*] part. This value estimates how much the specialization of the token would help to split the state set covered by the [*Condition*] part into several sub-sets of equal cardinality.

Let us consider a classifier which tries to anticipate the consequences of an action in several situations. If the value of a particular feature of the perception when the classifier anticipates well is always different from the value when it makes anticipation mistakes, then the [*Condition*] part must be specialized according to this particular feature, and the estimate S will get a high value.

In order to compute the estimates S, each classifier memorizes the perception preceeding the last anticipation mistake [BadPerception] and the last perception preceeding the last anticipation success [GoodPerception]. Each time the [Action] part of a classifier matches [Action$_{t-1}$] and its [Condition] part matches [Perception$_{t-1}$], the [Perception$_t$] allows to check the accuracy of the [Effect] part.

- If the [Effect] part is *correct*, for each feature of the environment:
    - if a particular token of [BadPerception] equals the corresponding feature of [Perception$_{t-1}$], then the corresponding estimate S is *decreased* using a Widrow-Hoff delta rule;
    - if a particular token of [BadPerception] differs from the corresponding feature of [Perception$_{t-1}$], then the corresponding estimate S is *increased* using a Widrow-Hoff delta rule;
- If the [Effect] part is *incorrect*, for each feature of the environment:
    - if a particular token of [GoodPerception] equals the corresponding feature of [Perception$_{t-1}$], then the corresponding estimate S is *decreased* using a Widrow-Hoff delta rule;
    - if a particular token of [GoodPerception] differs from the corresponding feature of [Perception$_{t-1}$], then the corresponding estimate S is *increased* using a Widrow-Hoff delta rule;

This process allows every classifier to identify which general token should be first specialized in order to improve the relevance of the [Condition] part. These estimates allow to specialize unchanging features without requiering a dedicated mechanism like the *specification of unchanging components* in ACS [Stolzmann, 1999].

3.4   The Specialization Process

The *expected improvement by specialization estimates* allow the classifier specialization mechanism to be driven by experience and are used in the [Condition] specialization process.

When a classifier sometimes anticipate well and sometimes not - *ie* when its anticipation trace contains *good* and *bad* markers – it oscillates and its [Condition] part needs to be specialized. If such a classifier is oscillating, thanks to the *anticipation covering* mechanism, the classifier set contains at least one other classifier with the same [Condition] and [Action] parts and with a different [Effect] part.

The specialization process is very careful: YACS waits that every classifier with the same [Condition] and [Action] parts has been identified as an *oscillating* classifier, and that its anticipation trace is full. At this point, these classifiers elect together the feature to specialize. The estimates S corresponding to each feature of the environment are summed among the classifiers, and the feature with the highest sum is chosen to get specialized. The *MutSpec* operator is then applied to every classifier.

MutSpec may create classifiers that will never be used nor evaluated because their [*Condition*] part matches no possible perception. To avoid such classifiers, we remove every classifier which does not match any perception in the set of already encountered perceptions.

In this section, we described how YACS performs latent learning in two separate processes:

- learning accurate [*Effect*] parts by temporal difference learning;
- carefuly specializing the [*Condition*] parts.

The set of classifiers discovered by the latent learning process is a model of the dynamics of the environment which provides information about the state transitions. It takes advantage of the generalization to discover regularities and keep the model small.

3.5 Learning to Act

In this section, we will describe how YACS takes advantage of the model of the environment to speed up the reinforcement learning process. We first introduce the value iteration algorithm and the way YACS identifies the reward sources. Then we explain how the use of generalization forbids to compute one single quality for each classifier. We finally present two strategies that may be used and our reasons to propose a different one.

Value Iteration. To back-propagate the reward, we use a simplified variety of value iteration: a dynamic programming algorithm which solves the Bellmann equations [Bellman, 1957] by iteratively refining qualities for (state, action) pairs by using the formula:

$$Q(s, a) = R(s, a) + \gamma \sum_{s'} T(s, a, s')V(s') \tag{1}$$

where

$$V(s) = max_a Q(s, a) \tag{2}$$

$Q(s, a)$ is the quality of action a in state s. γ is the temporal discount factor. $V(s)$ is the desirability value of the state s. $R(s, a)$ is the immediate expected reward when the agent performs action a in state s. T(s,a,s') is the probability for reaching state s' when performing action a in state s.

As our system is designed to deal with deterministic environment, we do not use the transition probabilities and replace the expected future cumulative reward $\sum_{s'} T(s, a, s')V(s')$ by $max_{s'} V(s')$ where s' is a state anticipated when the system performs the action a in state s.

Learning about Immediate Reward. The latent learning provides the information about state transitions. In order to use a dynamic programming algorithm, the system computes the immediate expected rewards corresponding to $R(s, a)$. At each time step, the immediate reward estimates R of every classifier such that $C.[Condition]$ matches $[Perception]_{t-1}$ and $C.[Action]$ matches $[Action]_{t-1}$ are updated according to the formula:

$$R \leftarrow (1 - \beta) \times R + \beta \times CurrentReward$$

Here again, the algorithm updates values of classifiers which have not been actually fired.

The Generalization Problem. If YACS would not use generalization, it would be easy to compute a single quality of action for each classifier by using the formula:

$$C.Q \leftarrow C.R + \gamma \times max_{C'} C'.Q$$

In classifier systems without an $[Effect]$ part, a classifier is kept when it helps maximizing reward on the long run, or when it is able to predict the reward. When we use classifiers with an $[Effect]$ part, the decision to keep or remove a classifier ony relies on its ability to predict the next perceptions. It does not take the reward into account.

This way of considering the fitness of a classifier gives rise to a new way of considering generalization. A classifier is too general when a joker token prevents the anticipation to be accurate, regardless of the payoff. It is too specialized if its anticipation ability would remain accurate if some joker were added in its $[Condition]$ part, regardless of the payoff.

For example, let us consider a classifier which could be interpreted in a maze environment as "when the agent percieves a wall on the north, if it tries to move north, nothing will change in its perceptions: it will remain in the same square". Such a classifier is accurate, since it would not anticipate better if a joker token of its $[Condition]$ part was specialized. It is kept and will not be further specialized. The problem is that such an accurate classifier is not too general with respect to anticipation, but it introduces a kind of perceptual aliasing since it matches in several different situations.

Because of the discount factor (γ in formula 1), the qualities associated to the states which are close to the goal are much higher than the qualities associated to the states which are far from the goal. So one can not compute a single quality for a classifier whose $[Condition]$ part matches a several perception recieved at different distances from the goal.

So, as the generalization helps to discover regularities in the environment instead of simply providing a kind of selective attention, some classifier may be fired in several states and thus it becomes impossible to compute a single quality for each general classifier.

Possible Solutions. In order to avoid this problem, one solution could be to introduce the detection of over-general classifiers with respect to payoff and to specialize such classifiers. But this solution is not coherent with our approach: the latent learning process, which provides a model of the dynamics of the environment, must take place even in the absence of rewards. We want to model dynamics of the environment with as few classifiers as possible in order to reduce computation time. Thus the model must take advantage of every regularities of the environment. So, classifiers which do not anticipate well should be further specialized.

Another solution is the use of a lookahead planning algorithm rather than a variety of the value iteration algorithm. At each time step, the system would have to build a plan starting with the current perception. [Butz and Stolzmann, 1999] proposes an enhancement to ACS which uses explicit goals to perform bidirectional planning, but comes out of the reinforcemnt learning framework. A general classifier used at different levels of the planning process is interpreted in different contexts and this should solve the problem of perceptual aliasing introduced by over-general classifiers with respect to payoff but accurate with respect to anticipation. But as a result, the system may suffer from a lack of reactivity.

Storing Values for Every Already Encountered Perception. The solution we propose is to associate a desirability value to each specialized [Perception] in the already encountered perception list. YACS stores values corresponding to $V(s)$ in the formula 2 – one for each [Perception] – instead of storing qualities corresponding to $Q(s, a)$ – one for each [Perception]/[Action] pair – as it is the case for Q-Learning [Watkins, 1989] and DynaQ+ [Sutton and Barto, 1998].

To compute the quality associated to a [Perception], we first identify all the classifiers C such that $C.[Condition]$ matches [Perception]. If such a classifier was fired, the immediate reward would be $C.R$ and the expected cumulative reward would be the value of the perception anticipated by the classifier. In a more formal way, the quality Q associated to a [Perception] can be updated by using the formula:

$$[Perception].Q \leftarrow max_C C.R + \gamma \times [Perception].passthrough(C.[Effect]).Q$$

where $C.[Condition]$ matches [Perception]

So the system computes values for each perception and takes advantage of the model provided by the latent learning process to update these values without actually experiencing every transition. When the classifier system anticipates well in every situation, the agent may adapt its behavior quickly to new reward sources.

3.6   Selecting an Action

When the system gets a [Perception] from the environment, it selects all the classifiers C whose [Condition] part matches it. These classifiers anticipate the following perception by computing $[Perception].passthrough(C.[Effect])$. Then they compute a quality by adding the immediate reward estimate $C.R$ and the discounted expected reward which is the value of the following perception mutiplied by the discount factor γ. The selected action is the action of the classifier with the highest quality.

4   Preliminary Results

4.1   A Simple Maze Problem

We use the maze problem described in Fig. 1 in order to evaluate our algorithm. This maze illustrates a state transition diagram with nine states and four possible transitions starting from each state.

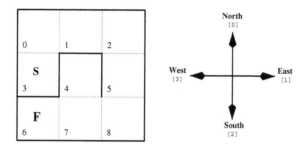

Fig. 1. A simple maze problem

The agent is always situated in a square. It can perceive the abscence or presence of walls in each cardinal direction (N, E, S and W). For instance, the agent percieves [1|0|0|1] in square 0 and [1|1|0|0] in square 2. The agent is given four possible actions: to move in any of the four cardinal directions.

An experience is divided into several trials. For each trial, the agent starts in square S. At each time step, it can make every possible action, including dumb actions like hitting a wall. When it comes to square 6, it gets a reward of 1 and it is given the opportunity to learn about the state transition. Then a new trial starts in square 3.

This goal can be reached optimaly in 8 successive time steps. The number of time steps is one more than the number of actions, because we let the agent perceive the walls arround the square 6 when it is rewarded.

4.2   Presentation of the Results

The results we present here have been obtained with a learning rate β of 0.1 and a memory size m of 3.

Latent Learning. We let the system move in the maze for 1000 time steps without any reward. During this time, it moves randomly and performs latent learning to model the dynamics of the environment. Figure 2 shows the evolution of the average number of classifiers over 1000 experiments.

Figure 3 shows the evolution of the number of classifiers on a representative single experiment.

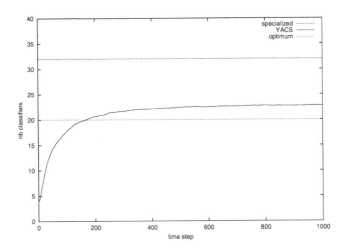

Fig. 2. Average evolution of the number of classifiers

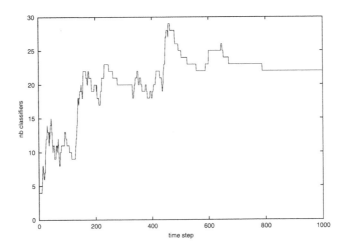

Fig. 3. Evolution of the number of classifiers for one experiment

The minimal number of classifiers to accurately model the whole environment is 20. The number of fully specialized classifiers needed to model the dynamics of the environment is 32. The number of classifiers produced by YACS converges arround 23.

YACS finds very accurately regularities like "when there is a wall on the north, moving north does not produce any changes in the perceptions", but sometimes specializes the classifiers in a non optimal way in early time steps, because of some partially representative samples of experience. As a result, the number of classifiers may be sub-optimal.

Reinforcement Learning. After these 1000 time steps of exploration, the system is given a reward when it reaches the goal. Figure 4 shows the average number of time steps the system needed to achieve successsive trials with reward, over 1000 experiments. Figure 5 shows the number of time steps the system needed to achieve successive trials for the same single experiment as for Fig. 3. The number of time steps of the first trial is high because the system has not already been rewarded yet and thus has no way to find the optimal way to the goal.

After this first trial, the system has identified a reward source and takes advantage of its model of the environment to quickly find the optimal path to the goal. The agent does not immediately behave optimaly because the system does not perform a complete value iteration each time step. In order to get a

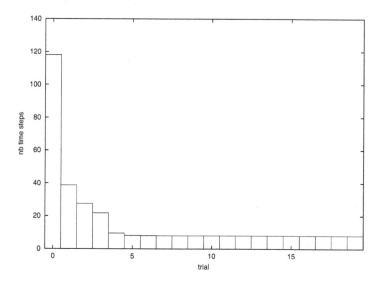

Fig. 4. Average number of time step to reach goal in successive trials

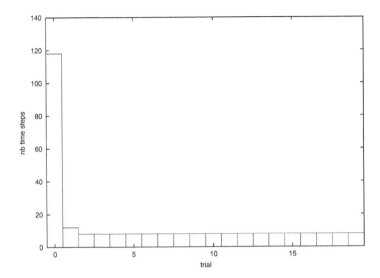

Fig. 5. Number of time steps to reach the goal in successive trials for one experiment. YACS was able to build an accurate model of the environment within the 1000 exploration time steps

good reactivity/planning tradeoff, only one step of value iteration is performed each time step. As a result, the agent needs several time steps to adjust its policy.

In Fig. 4, the average convergence looks slower because the average values take into account several experiments like the one shown in Fig. 6. In such experiments, the model of the environment was not perfectly accurate after the 1000 time steps of exploration. The system needed some more sub-optimal trials to adjust the model.

5   Discussion

The results presented in Sect. 4 are encouraging but YACS still suffers two major drawbacks.

5.1   The Exploration/Exploitation Tradeoff

In YACS, the reinforcement learning process works fine only if the model provided by the latent learning is complete and accurate. If the classifiers are not specialized enough, the system may "imagine" transitions which are incorrect in the actual environment, and which may prevent the system to find the way to the goal. Over 1000 experiments, the system was 17 times unable to reach the goal within 1000 time step after the exploration steps and the first trial leading

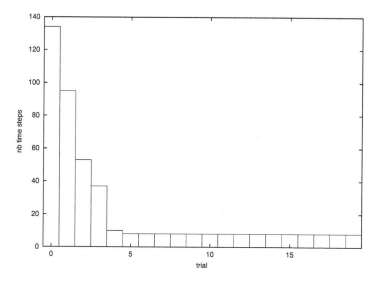

Fig. 6. Number of time steps to reach goal in successive trials for one experiment. YACS was not able to build an accurate model of the environment within the 1000 exploration time steps

to the identification of the reward source. These experiments are not taken into account in Figs. 2 and 4. This drawback forbids YACS to simultaneously build the model while exploiting safely a partial model of the environment.

5.2   The Need for a Generalization Mechanism

Having an efficient generalization mechanism is important in the LCS approach since generalization is one of the most original features of LCS with respect to basic reinforcement learning algorithms. Even if YACS is able to stop the specialization process when there is no more need for more specialized classifiers, it still lacks a specific generalization process. This leads our system to sub-optimality problems:

– choosing to specialize a bad token in early time steps may lead to a sub-optimal number of classifiers;
– in a changing environment, the adaptation of YACS relies on the condition covering mechanism, and leads to over-specialized classifiers and a sub-optimal number of classifiers.

A generalization mechanism should offer the opportunity for the system to reconsider early choices of tokens to specialize, and to discover reliable and accurate classifiers.

6   Conclusion and Future Work

Our work takes place in a recent trend on LCS research which focuses on the use of anticipation in order to improve the quality of classifiers and increase the learning speed. As most researchers in this trend [Stolzmann, 1998] and [Witkowski, 1999], we have designed YACS, a system which combines latent learning and reinforcement learning. We have highlighted difficulties due to generalization when we use latent learning through dynamic programming algorithms. We also presented some experimental results which were dealing with YACS involved in a simple maze environment, but YACS is also used for bigger applications as in [Sigaud, 2000].

But YACS still lacks a generalization process. Recent works like [Lanzi, 1999] and [Butz et al., 2000b] has shown that this generalization concern is shared by other researchers. [Butz et al., 2000b] proposes a solution using the selection pressure of a GA to favor the emergence of reliable and general classifiers in ACS. Since we are reluctant to use the blind search mechanisms of GAs, we will investigate alternative solutions in the short term future.

References

[Bellman, 1957] Bellman, R. E. (1957). *Dynamic Programming*. Princeton University Press, Princeton, NJ.

[Booker et al., 1989] Booker, L., Goldberg, D. E., and Holland, J. H. (1989). Classifier systems and genetic algorithms. *Artificial Intelligence*, 40(1-3):235–282.

[Butz et al., 2000a] Butz, M. V., Goldberg, D. E., and Stolzmann, W. (2000a). Introducing a genetic generalization pressure to the anticipatory classifier system part i: Theoretical approach. In *Proceedings of the 2000 Genetic and Evolutionary Computation Conference (GECCO 2000)*.

[Butz et al., 2000b] Butz, M. V., Goldberg, D. E., and Stolzmann, W. (2000b). Investigating generalization in the anticipatory classifier system. In *Proceedings of the Sixth International Conference on Parallel Problem Solving from Nature*.

[Butz and Stolzmann, 1999] Butz, M. V. and Stolzmann, W. (1999). Action-planning in anticipatory classifier sytems. In *Proceedings of the 1999 Genetic and Evolutionary Computation Conference Workshop Program*.

[Cliff and Ross, 1994] Cliff, D. and Ross, S. (1994). Adding memory to ZCS. *Adaptive Behavior*, 3(2):101–150.

[Dorigo, 1994] Dorigo, M. (1994). Genetic and non-genetic operators in ALECSYS. *Evolutionary Computation*, 1(2):151–164.

[Goldberg, 1989] Goldberg, D. E. (1989). *Genetic Algorithms in Search, Optimization, and Machine Learning*. Addison Wesley.

[Holland et al., 1986] Holland, J. H., Holyoak, K. J., Nisbett, R. E., and Thagard, P. R. (1986). *Induction*. MIT Press.

[Lanzi, 1998] Lanzi, P. L. (1998). Adding memory to XCS. In *Proceedings of the IEEE Conference on Evolutionary Computation (ICEC98)*. IEEE Press.

[Lanzi, 1999] Lanzi, P. L. (1999). An analysis of generalization in the XCS classifier system. *Evolutionary Computation*, 2(7):125–149.

[Lanzi, 2000] Lanzi, P. L. (2000). Toward optimal performance in classifier systems. *Evolutionary Computation Journal*. in print.

[McCallum, 1996] McCallum, R. A. (1996). Learning to use selective attention and short-term memory. In Maes, P., Mataric, M., Meyer, J.-A., Pollack, J., and Wilson, S. W., (Eds.), *Proceedings of the Fourth International Conference on Simulation of Adaptive Behavior*, pages 315–324, Cambridge, MA. MIT Press.

[Riolo, 1991] Riolo, R. L. (1991). Lookahead planning and latent learning in a classifier system. In Meyer, J.-A. and Wilson, S. W., (Eds.), *From animals to animats: Proceedings of the First International Conference on Simulation of Adaptative Behavior*, pages 316–326, Cambridge, MA. MIT Press.

[Sigaud, 2000] Sigaud, O. (2000). Using classifier systems as adaptive expert systems for control. In Stolzmann, W., Lanzi, P.-L., and Wilson, S. W., (Eds.), *LNCS : New trends in Classifier Systems*. Springer-Verlag.

[Stolzmann, 1998] Stolzmann, W. (1998). Anticipatory classifier systems. In Koza, J., Banzhaf, W., Chellapilla, K., Deb, K., Dorigo, M., Fogel, D., Garzon, M., Goldberg, D., Iba, H., and Riolo, R., (Eds.), *Genetic Programming*. Morgan Kaufmann Publishers, Inc., San Francisco, CA.

[Stolzmann, 1999] Stolzmann, W. (1999). Latent learning in khepera robots with anticipatory classifier systems. In *Proceedings of the 1999 Genetic and Evolutionary Computation Conference Workshop Program*.

[Sutton and Barto, 1998] Sutton, R. S. and Barto, A. (1998). *Reinforcement Learning: An Introduction*. MIT Press.

[Watkins, 1989] Watkins, C. J. (1989). *Learning with delayed rewards*. PhD thesis, Psychology Department, University of Cambridge, England.

[Wilson, 1994] Wilson, S. W. (1994). ZCS, a zeroth level classifier system. *Evolutionary Computation*, 2(1):1–18.

[Wilson, 1995] Wilson, S. W. (1995). Classifier fitness based on accuracy. *Evolutionary Computation*, 3(2):149–175.

[Witkowski, 1999] Witkowski, C. M. (1999). Integrating unsupervised learning, motivation and action selection in an a-life agent. In Floreano, D., Mondada, F., and Nicoud, J.-D., (Eds.), *5th European Conference on Artificial Life (ECAL-99)*, pages 355–364, Lausanne. Springer.

A Self-Adaptive Classifier System

Jacob Hurst and Larry Bull

Intelligent Computer Systems Centre
Faculty of Computer Studies & Mathematics
University of the West of England
Bristol BS16 1QY, U.K.
jacob.hurst@uwe.ac.uk

Abstract. The use and benefits of self-adaptive parameters, particularly mutation, are well-known within evolutionary computing. In this paper we examine the use of parameter self-adaptation in Michigan-style Classifier Systems with the aim of improving their performance and ease of use. We implement a fully self-adaptive ZCS classifier and examine its performance in a multi-step environment. It is shown that the mutation rate, learning rate, discount factor and tax rate can be developed along with an appropriate solution/rule-base, resulting in improved performance over results using fixed rate parameters. We go on to show that the benefits of self-adaptation are particularly marked in non-stationary environments.

1 Introduction

Within Genetic Algorithms (GAs) [Holland 1975] and Genetic Programming [Koza 1991] the parameters controlling the algorithm are traditionally global and remain constant over time. However, in Evolutionary Strategies [Rechenberg 1973] and later forms of Evolutionary Programming (Meta-EP) [Fogel 1992], the mutation rate is a locally evolving entity in itself, i.e. it adapts during the search process. This "self-adaptive" form of mutation not only reduces the number of hand-tunable parameters of the evolutionary algorithm, it has also been shown to improve performance (e.g. see [Bäck 1992] for results with a self-adaptive GA). In this paper we examine the use of self-adaptive parameters within Michigan-style Classifier Systems (CSs) [Holland et al. 1986], more specifically in Wilson's ZCS [Wilson 1994] system.

The performance of self-adapting *all* learning parameters simultaneously within ZCS is examined using the "animat" [Wilson 1985] task Woods 14-06. This environment was originally used by Ross and Cliff [1995] to investigate rule chaining and the addition of temporary memory in ZCS. This paper demonstrates that when using adaptive parameters, the same performance is produced as when using the parameters suggested by the system designer.

One of the claims of using adaptive parameters is that they are particularly useful in changing environments. We present a non-stationary version of the Woods 14-06 environment and show that the use of self-adaptation significantly improves performance over the traditional approach. Previous work [Bull & Hurst 2000] has concentrated on just using an adaptive mutation rate in ZCS. Experiments within the

P.L. Lanzi, W. Stolzmann, and S.W. Wilson (Eds.): IWLCS 2000, LNAI 1996, pp. 70–79, 2001.
© Springer-Verlag Berlin Heidelberg 2001

changing environments illustrate the advantage of adapting the other parameters in the system and not just the mutation rate.

The paper is arranged as follows: the next section briefly introduces ZCS, Section 3 describes how self-adaptation is implemented, Section 4 describes the task and examines the effects of the self-adaptation. Section 5 presents results from a non-stationary Woods 14-06 environment. Section 6 examines the level of adaptation within each niche of the Woods 14-06 environment.

2   ZCS

ZCS is a "Zeroth-level" Michigan-style Classifier System without internal memory, where the rule-base consists of a number (N) of condition/action rules in which the condition is a string of characters from the usual ternary alphabet {0,1,#} and the action is represented by a binary string. Associated with each rule is a strength scalar which acts as an indication of the perceived utility of that rule within the system. This strength of each rule is initialised to a predetermined value termed S_0.

Reinforcement in ZCS consists of redistributing strength between subsequent "action sets", or the matched rules from the previous time step which asserted the chosen output or "action". A fixed fraction (β) of the strength of each member of the action set ([A]) at each time-step is placed in a "common bucket". A record is kept of the previous action set $[A]_{-1}$ and if this is not empty then the members of this action set each receive an equal share of the contents of the current bucket, once this has been reduced by a pre-determined discount factor (γ). If a reward is received from the environment then a fixed fraction (β) of this value is distributed evenly amongst the members of [A]. Finally, a tax (τ) is imposed on all matched rules that do not belong to [A] on each time-step in order to encourage exploitation of the stronger classifiers.

ZCS employs two discovery mechanisms, a panmictic GA and a covering operator. On each time-step there is a probability p of GA invocation. When called, the GA uses roulette wheel selection to determine two parent rules based on strength. Two offspring are produced via mutation (probability μ) and crossover (single point with probability χ). The parents then donate half of their strengths to their offspring who replace existing members of the rule-base. The deleted rules are chosen using roulette wheel selection based on the reciprocal of rule strength. If on some time-step, no rules match or all matched rules have a combined strength of less than ϕ times the rule-base average, then a covering operator is invoked.

The default parameters presented for ZCS, and unless otherwise stated for this paper, are: $N = 400$, $S_0=20$, $\beta = 0.2$, $\gamma = 0.71$, $\tau = 0.1$, $\chi = 0.5$, $\mu = 0.002$, $p = 0.25$, $\phi = 0.5$

Thus ZCS represents a "basic classifier system for reinforcement learning that retains much of Holland's original framework while simplifying it so as to increase ease of understanding and performance" [Wilson 1994]. For this reason the ZCS architecture has been chosen to examine the basic behaviour of classifier systems with self-adaptive parameters. The reader is referred to [Wilson 1994] for full details of ZCS.

3 Self-Adaptation in Classifier Systems

3.1 Mutation

Previously [e.g. Bull & Hurst 2000], we have shown that it is possible to self-adapt the mutation rate within learning classifier systems using the same form of self-adaptive mutation as in Meta-EP. That is, each rule has its own mutation rate μ, stored as a real number. This parameter is passed to its offspring either under recombination or directly (depending upon the satisfaction of χ). The offspring then applies its mutation rate to itself using a Gaussian distribution, i.e. $\mu_i' = \mu_i + N(0,\mu_i)$, before mutating the rest of the rule at the resulting rate. It is noted that this form of self-adaptation is simpler than that typically used in Evolutionary Strategies, where a Lognormal is applied to μ. However, the simpler form was shown to be effective and has been suggested to work better in noisy environments [Angeline et al. 1996].

Results showed that suitable mutation rates could be evolved and that a positional bias occurred in the inductive chains formed. It is usual for the mutation rate to go to zero as the population converges to a solution to maintain fitness [Bäck 1992]. The same effect was found in the CSs, but the time taken for a rule's mutation rate to drop was dependent upon its position; rules for environmental stimuli closest to reward lost their mutation rate first and vice versa.

We also note that this is in contrast to the adaptive form of genetic search (crossover) introduced by Wilson [1987] for CSs, under which a system entropy measure was used to alter the operator rate; Wilson showed benefits from increasing crossover as entropy dropped using predetermined rules of adjustment to a global rate.

3.2 Learning Rate, Tax Rate, and Discount Factor

We have examined the effects of self-adapting the learning rate parameter [Hurst & Bull 2000]. Initial results from using the same mechanism as for mutation showed unpredictable behaviour. After the initial learning of the problem sporadic loss in performance occurred. This behaviour is explained by the selfish adaptation of the parameter. When the problem has been learnt there is little utility for the individual classifier to continue to increase the fitness of other classifiers. As a result the learning rate is turned down as the run proceeds. This is fine when the system remains unperturbed by the genetic operators. When this disruption occurs the system exhibits a loss of performance. To overcome this effective loss of co-operation the learning rate used at each reinforcement cycle is chosen from the rules in the previous action set. The choice is made by roulette wheel selection based on the fitness of the classifiers. In this way co-operation is maintained and enforced between action sets and suitable learning rates are seen to develop. Note that mutation is via a creep operator at the rate specified by μ, i.e. $\beta' = \beta + N(0,1)$.

The performance of a Michigan-style classifier system - ZCS - with the simultaneous self-adaptation of the mutation rate, learning rate, discount factor and tax rate is now examined. To maintain co-operation within the system the tax rate has to be treated in the same way as the learning rate, i.e. the tax rate at each step is obtained from the previous action set. The discount factor's linkage is in the opposite direction. The discount factor is obtained from the current action set and applied to the previous action set. Therefore, each classifier holds a parameter for mutation rate, learning rate, discount factor and tax. These parameters are altered and changed by the genetic operators of the classifier system.

4 Self-Adaptive ZCS in the Wood 14-06 Environment

4.1 The Task

Wilson [1994] introduced the simple multi-step Woods 1 environment to examine the performance of ZCS. Woods 1 is a two dimensional rectilinear 5x5 toroidal grid. Sixteen cells are blank, eight contain rocks and one contains food. ZCS is used to develop the controller of a robot/animat which must traverse the map in search of food. On each time step the animat receives a sensory message which describes the eight surrounding cells. The message is encoded as a 16-bit binary string with two bits representing each cardinal direction. A blank cell is represented by 00, food (F) by 11 and trees (T) by 10 (01 has no meaning). The message is ordered with the cell directly above the animat represented by the first bit-pair, and then proceeding clockwise around the animat. Experiments using self-adaptive parameters in Woods 1 failed to give informative results (not shown). It was found that the parameter settings appeared to have no negative effect on performance.

A variation on this environment, Woods 14-06, is used in the experiments described in this paper. This is shown in Fig. 1. This is a more difficult problem for ZCS to solve than the Woods 1 environment. It is a harder problem as it requires the formation of longer chains of rules to solve the problem. At each cell there is a unique sense vector, and only one action which takes the animat closer to the food F. This makes the environment particularly useful for experiments involving environmental change. If the food is moved as in Fig. 1b to form Woods 14-06b the optimal action for each cell will have to change. The numbering in Fig. 1b, is used in the niche analysis described in Section 6. Using the Woods 14-06 environment rather then the Woods 1 environment allows ZCS to demonstrate the potential of parameter adaptation.

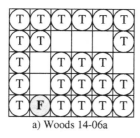
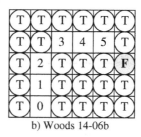
a) Woods 14-06a   b) Woods 14-06b

Fig. 1. The environment Woods 14-06. a) The original configuration. b) The configuration after the food has been moved

The performance of ZCS is evaluated by indicating how many steps the "animat" takes to obtain food after being randomly positioned in the environment. This is displayed as a running average of the last 50 problems and is averaged over ten runs (as in [Ross & Cliff 1995]).

4.2 Results

Fig. 2a illustrates the performance of ZCS with fixed and adaptive parameters. It shows the results of three experiments:

1) ZCS run with adaptive parameters which are initially seeded randomly between 0 and 1.

2) ZCS run with the parameters fixed at the suggested values.

3) ZCS run with fixed parameters at the average rate of the self-adaptive ZCS, i.e, 0.5.

The graph illustrates that with adaptive parameters the system is able to perform as well as the system with the suggested values. Fixing the parameter values at 0.5 results in disruptive performance. This is not entirely surprising as a mutation rate of 0.5 is high. If this experiment is carried out in the Woods 1 environment this disruptive effect is not detected (result not shown). This result indicates that the system is sensitive to parameter settings and that the environment is complex enough to demand specific settings of the parameters.

Fig. 2b shows the average values of the parameters in the rule base, i.e. when ZCS is run with the parameters initially seeded randomly between 0 and 1. The mutation rate falls off from its initial value (as in [Bull & Hurst 2000]), while the other parameters move little from their initial values. This last point is returned to.

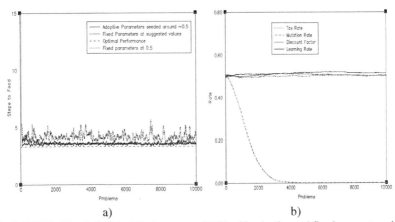

a)   b)

Fig. 2. ZCSj in Woods 14-06. a) Performance of ZCS with adaptive and fixed parameters. b) Parameter adaptation of ZCS with parameters seeded ~0.5

5   Non-stationary Wood 14-06 Environment

5.1   The Tasks

It has been noted that the use of self-adaptive mutation can be particularly useful within non-stationary/changing environments [Bäck 1998]. We have examined the behaviour of our fully self-adaptive classifier in a non-stationary version of the Woods 14-06 environment. This is achieved by moving the position of the food source from one end of the "passage" to the other. This forces a complete change in the rule-base as three new niches are created and the remaining niches have to change their optimal rule to obtain maximum reward. This environmental change is carried out halfway through the ZCS run, at problem 2500.

5.2   ZCS Performance

Figure 3 shows the results from experiments in the Woods 14-06 environment.

In Fig. 3a the results from two experiments are presented, ZCS is run with parameters fixed at the suggested values for the system and adaptive parameters. The adaptive parameters are initially seeded randomly between 0 and 1 as before. The graph indicates a significant benefit in performance using the adaptive parameters, over the fixed parameters at the suggested values.

Our previous work [Bull & Hurst 2000] [Bull et al 2000] has concentrated upon adapting the mutation rate in a learning classifier system and the advantage in doing so. Fig. 3b shows the performance of ZCS with all the parameters adapting and ZCS with only the mutation rate adapting with the other parameters fixed at the suggested values. It can be seen that the system with only the mutation rate adapting experiences a larger decline in performance than when all the other parameters adapt. However,

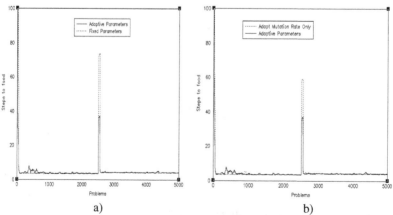

a)   b)

Fig. 3. ZCS in a changing Woods 14-06 environment.   a) Performance of ZCS with adaptive and fixed parameters. b) Performance of ZCS with adaptive parameters and adapting only the the mutation rate.

this performance is still better than when all the parameters are fixed at the suggested values.

The improvement in the performance when adapting all the parameters over just adapting the mutation rate could be due to the system either finding better values for the parameters initially or the dynamic response of the system in reaction to the change in the environment.

In Fig 4a the results from two experiments are shown:

1) ZCS run with fully adaptive parameters.

2) ZCS is run with parameters fixed at 0.5.

When the parameters are fixed at 0.5, we do not see a decline in performance at the point of change but overall the system is nosier and does not converge. This experiment further confirms that the system is indeed sensitive to parameter settings.

The result in Fig. 2b indicated that there is very little movement of the reinforcement learning parameters during the run from their initial seeding values, which on average were 0.5. To determine if 0.5 is the best setting for the reinforcement learning parameters further experiments were carried out.

In Fig. 4b the results from two experiments are shown:

1) ZCS run with adaptive mutation rate and reinforcement learning parameters fixed at the suggested values.

2) ZCS run with adaptive mutation rate and reinforcement learning parameters fixed at 0.5

Examination of the traces in Fig. 4b show that when the reinforcement learning parameters are fixed at 0.5 performance is better then fixing the reinforcement learning parameters at the suggested values, there is also a slight improvement over the fully adaptive reinforcement learning parameters (see Fig. 4a). In this environment 0.5 appears to be the best value for the reinforcement learning parameters. However, finding the parameters settings for machine learning algorithms can be a time consuming process, and the use of self-adaptive parameters may be an effective approach to side-step this problem.

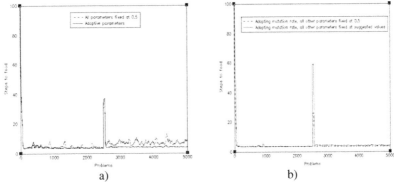

a)   b)

Fig. 4. ZCS in a changing Woods 14-06 environment. a) Performance of ZCS with adaptive parameters and parameters fixed at 0.5. b) Performance of ZCS with adaptive mutation rate all other parameters fixed at 0.5 and the suggested values.

6 Niche Analysis in Woods 14-06

Instead of considering the average parameter values for the entire rule-base the parameter values for each niche in the Woods 14-06 environment can be examined. In this way distortions caused by redundant rules in the rule-base can be removed. It also allows examination of the level of adaptation down the rule chain. At each step the parameter values of the rules which apply to the current niche are averaged. The niches are identified according to the scheme set out in Fig. 1. This analysis starts immediately after the change in the environment from Woods 14-06a to Woods 14-06b (see Fig. 1). It finishes after each niche has been updated 1500 times. Each niche is sampled every 50 updates. The results presented here are the average of ten runs. For clarity of presentation the results from only 3 of the 6 niches are shown.

Fig 5a. shows the analysis of the mutation rate in three niches after the change in environment from Woods 14-06a to Woods 14-06b. The Y axis shows the average mutation rate for the classifiers matching each niche, the X axis shows the number of times each niche is updated.

The mutation rate for all three niches initially increases after the change in environment. The size of this change varies according to how close the niche is to the reward. Niche 0 which is nearest the reward has the smallest change. While, Niche 5 which is the furthest niche from the reward has the largest increase in mutation rate. This pattern is repeated again in Fig. 5b. Instead of the mutation rate being extracted from the matching classifiers the learning rate is taken. The graph indicates that after starting off with fairly similar learning rates, the niches furthest from the reward move to a higher learning rate then the niches more proximal to the reward. This pattern was not clear for the discount factor or the tax rate (results not shown). The learning rate increase, in the niches more distant from the reward is not continous, but eventually forms a plateau (result not shown).

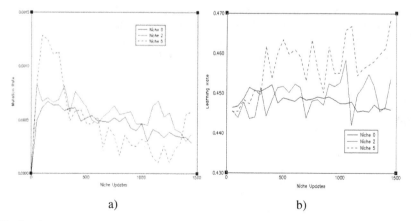

a)   b)

Fig. 5. Niche analysis of ZCS in Woods 14-06 after the change. a) Mutation rate analysis. b) Learning rate analysis.

Fig. 5 indicates that the adaptive parameters respond to changes in the environment, and that these adjustments are not uniform across the entire rulebase but are specific depending upon the local environment of each classifier.

7 Conclusions

There are two main justifications for using self-adaptive rather than fixed value parameters for controlling machine learning algorithms. First, suitable values for parameters are not usually known a priori, they are generally found by a process of trial and error. A self-adaptive approach will be able to bypass this step. Second, suitable values may depend upon the current environmental conditions which may change after changes in the environment.

Both of these advantages have been utilised in the experiments detailed in this paper. New suitable values for the reinforcement learning parameters in this environment have also been discovered (Fig. 4b), and the adaptive mutation rate and learning rate have displayed a dynamic response to changes in the environment (Fig. 5a).

ZCS is a robust and simple classifier system. The advantages of self-adaptation in these environments, while not dramatic appears promising. With more complex Classifier Systems and further challenging environments, these advantages may be more clearly realised. To determine if this is the case, we are implementing a fully adaptive CS to work in a robotic environment based at the Intelligent Autonomous Systems Laboratory, University of the West of England. Initial results from our XCS work indicates that adapting just the mutation rate shows similar behaviour to the ZCS implementation [Bull et al. 2000]. However, some difference may be expected with the other parameters, particularly in the non-stationary case because XCS generalizes over the problem space rather than solely identifying optima (after [Hartley 1999]).

Acknowledgements. The work has been supported by the University of the West of England and BT labs, Ipswich England. Many useful conversations were held with Dr. Chris Melhuish, IAS lab, University of the West of England. Conversations about "woods" environments with Andy Tomlinson, University of the West of England were also invaluable.

References

Angeline, P.J., Fogel, D.B., Fogel, L.J. (1996) A Comparison of Self-Adaptation Methods for Finite State Machines in a Dynamic Environment. In L.J. Fogel, P.J. Angeline, & T. Bäck (eds.) *Evolutionary Programming V*, MIT Press, pp. 441-449.

Bäck, T. (1992) Self-Adaptation in Genetic Algorithms. In F.J. Varela & P. Bourgine (eds.) *Toward a Practice of Autonomous Systems: Proceedings of the First European Conference on Artificial Life*, MIT Press, pp263-271.

Bäck, T. (1998) On the Behaviour of Evolutionary Algorithms in Dynamic Environments. In *Proceedings of the Fifth IEEE Conference on Evolutionary Computation*, IEEE Press, pp.446-451.

Bull, L. & Hurst, J. (2000) Self-Adaptive Mutation in ZCS Controllers. In S. Cagnoni, R. Poli, G. Smith, D. Corne, M. Oates, E. Hart, P-L. Lanzi, E. Willem, Y. Li, B. Paecther & T.C. Fogarty (eds) *Real-World Applications of Evolutionary Computing: Proceedings of the EvoNet Workshops - EvoRob 2000.* Springer, pp339-346.

Bull, L. Hurst, J. & Tomlinson, A. (2000) Self-Adaptive Mutation in Classifier System Controllers. In J-A. Meyer, A. Berthoz, D. Floreano, H. Roitblatt & S.W. Wilson (eds) *From Animals to Animats 6 - The Sixth International Conference on the Simulation of Adaptive Behaviour,* MIT Press.

Fogel, D.B. (1992) *Evolving Artificial Intelligence.* PhD dissertation, University of California.

Hartley, A.R. (1999) Accuracy-based Fitness Allows Similar Performance to Humans in Static and Dynamic Classification Environments. In W. Banzaff, J. Daida, A.E. Eiben, M.H. Garzon, V. Honavar, M. Jakiela & R.E. Smith (eds) *Proceedings of the Genetic and Evolutionary Computation Conference - Gecco'99*, Morgan Kauffman, pp. 266-273.

Holland, J.H. (1975) *Adaptation in Natural and Artificial Systems.* University of Michigan Press.

Holland, J.H., Holyoak, K.J., Nisbett, R.E. & Thagard, P.R. (1986) *Induction: Processes of Inference, Learning and Discovery.*

Hurst, J., Bull, L. *Using a self-adaptive learning rate in ZCS* (2000) to appear in University of West of England CSM Technical Reports 2000.

Koza, J.R. (1991) *Genetic Programming.* MIT Press.

Rechenberg, I. (1973) *Evolutionsstrategie; Optimierung technischer Systeme nach Prinzipen der biologischen Evolution.* Frommann-Holzboog Verlag.

Ross,S., Cliff,D. (1995) "Adding temporary memory to ZCS", *Adaptive Behavior,* 3(2):101-150, MIT Press

Watkins, C. (1989) *Learning from Delayed Rewards.* PhD dissertation, University of Cambridge.

Wilson, S.W. (1985) Knowledge Growth in an Artificial Animal. In J.J. Grefenstette (ed.) *Proceedings of the First International Conference on Genetic Algorithms and their Applications*, Lawrence Erlbaum Associates, pp 16-23.

Wilson, S.W. (1987) Classifier Systems and the Animat Problem. *Machine Learning* 2:199-228.

Wilson, S.W. (1994) ZCS: A Zeroth-level Classifier System. *Evolutionary Computation* 2(1):1-18.

Wilson, S.W. (1995) Classifier Fitness Based on Accuracy. *Evolutionary Computation* 3(2):149-177.

What Makes a Problem Hard for XCS?

Tim Kovacs and Manfred Kerber

School of Computer Science
The University of Birmingham
Birmingham B15 2TT England
{T.Kovacs,M.Kerber}@cs.bham.ac.uk
http://www.cs.bham.ac.uk/

Abstract. Despite two decades of work learning classifier systems researchers have had relatively little to say on the subject of what makes a problem difficult for a classifier system. Wilson's accuracy-based XCS, a promising and increasingly popular classifier system, is, we feel, the natural first choice of classifier system with which to address this issue. To make the task more tractable we limit our considerations to a restricted, but very important, class of problems. Most significantly, we consider only single step reinforcement learning problems and the use of the standard binary/ternary classifier systems language. In addition to distinguishing several dimensions of problem complexity for XCS, we consider their interactions, identify bounding cases of difficulty, and consider complexity metrics for XCS. Based on these results we suggest a simple template for ternary single step test suites to more comprehensively evaluate classifier systems.

1 Introduction

Two basic questions to ask about any learning system are: to what kinds of problems is it well suited? To what kinds of problems is it poorly suited? Despite two decades of work, Learning Classifier Systems (LCS) researchers have had relatively little to say on the subject. Although this may in part be due to the wide range of systems and problems the LCS paradigm encompasses, it is certainly a reflection of deficiency in LCS theory.

Delving into the subject more deeply, a host of other questions arise. What is it about a problem that makes it difficult or easy for a given system? In other words, what factors are involved in determining a problem's difficulty? How do these factors interact? What effects do the representation(s) used by the system have? What effects does the rule discovery system have? In short, we want to know about the dimensions of problem complexity for the system of interest. Clearly this is a difficult subject even for one particular learning system. At present we consider only Wilson's *XCS* [10] classifier system, although we hope much of the approach and some of the results will transfer to other LCS. To simplify matters, we restrict consideration to the standard ternary LCS language, to a binary action space and to single step reinforcement learning problems.

P.L. Lanzi, W. Stolzmann, and S.W. Wilson (Eds.): IWLCS 2000, LNAI 1996, pp. 80–99, 2001.
© Springer-Verlag Berlin Heidelberg 2001

One reason to ask questions like those above is, of course, to find out when we can hope to successfully apply a given system to a given problem. Another reason is to better understand how to evaluate a system. Since we can't test our systems on all possible problems, we must consider only a subset. How can we choose this subset? There are at least two conflicting criteria. First, the subset should maximise the coverage of the dimensions of difficulty in order to more fully represent the space of all possible problems. That is, it should include as many as possible of the features which make a problem difficult for the system in question. Otherwise the test set may not detect deficiencies in an algorithm which would become apparent on other problems. Second, we would like to minimise the number of tests which must be made in order to make testing more manageable. Optimising these two criteria requires a good understanding of the dimensions of problem complexity for the system in question.

We address questions of problem complexity by considering the space of all possible test functions (i.e. learning problems) given our various restrictions. Based on our insights into this space we suggest a simple ternary single step test suite for LCS, and provide some results for XCS on it. To begin with, however, we consider how to approach the study of problem complexity in XCS.

2   Methodological Considerations

In this section we briefly motivate our study, consider some representational issues, and outline our approach.

2.1   Why Study Single Step Tests?

Single step functions are those in which the LCS's actions have no influence on which inputs it receives in the future. This contrasts with *sequential* (also called *multi step*) functions, in which actions *do* influence future inputs.[1]

In previous work we have mainly studied single step functions and we continue that practice here for two reasons. First, some applications, e.g. data mining, are single step, so it is of interest to understand and to optimise LCS for single step problems. Second, single step functions avoid many complications of sequential ones. Even if we're interested only in sequential problems, it seems reasonable to first evaluate, understand, and possibly improve our systems in the simpler single step case. When we have a good understanding of the basic LCS mechanisms we can go on to look at issues which are specific to the sequential case. This seems easier than starting with the more complex case and having to face a host of additional problems at the outset. We would argue that present understanding of LCS is limited enough to justify this approach. (Clearly, however, useful work *is* being done with sequential tests, not all of it addressing problems exclusive to them.)

Of course we have to be careful when evaluating potential improvements to ensure that we're not overfitting; optimising performance in single step problems

---

[1] We'll refer to states and inputs interchangeably.

at the expense of sequential ones. If we are interested in sequential problems we need sequential tests in our test suite.

2.2   Representing and Manipulating Functions

In Reinforcement Learning (RL), feedback to the learner about the value of its actions consists only of numeric values, called *rewards*, and the goal of any reinforcement learner is to maximise (some function of) the rewards it receives. Rewards are defined a priori by the experimenter in the form of a *reward function*, which (for our purposes) maps input/action pairs to integers. The reward function is an essential component of any RL problem specification; changing the reward function changes the problem.

As an aside, XCS – like most other reinforcement learners, but unlike traditional LCS – learns an approximation of the entire reward function. That is, every input/action pair is represented. Traditional LCS, in contrast, are only concerned with representing the more rewarding parts of this space [10,6].

Specification of SL and RL Problems. Working with LCS, we often refer to test problems in terms of an input/output mapping. One example is the 6 multiplexer, which has often been used as an LCS test. Figure 1 shows the 3 multiplexer, a related but simpler function. This exhaustive listing of input/output cases is called a *truth table*.

The 3 multiplexer is defined on binary strings of length 3, and treats the string as being composed of an index segment (the first bit) and a data segment (the remaining two bits). The value of the function is the value of the indexed bit in the data segment, so, for example, the value of 000 is 0, the value of 001 is 0, the value of 101 is 1 and so on. Knowing the value of the string, we can do Supervised Learning (SL); that is, we know which action the LCS must respond with in order to be correct.

However, the input/output mapping of Fig. 1 alone is not a complete specification of an RL problem, since it does not specify rewards. In adapting a boolean function to an RL paradigm we need to extend it by defining a reward function. So the 3 multiplexer is not a complete RL problem – we need to extend it with a reward function, which we have done in Fig. 2. (Horizontal lines have been inserted between different inputs in this and other long figures simply as a visual aid.) Note that this figure refers to *actions* rather than the *output* of the function, because we are now dealing with a learning agent which acts (predicts the output of the function). Note also that we specify the reward for both the correct and incorrect action for each input, since we must specify a reward for each possible input/action pair. By "correct" we mean the action which receives the higher reward for that input.

In RL Rewards Determine Input/Output Mappings. We associated certain rewards with input/action pairs in Fig. 2 but clearly could have used other values. Other rewards will produce a 3 multiplexer problem as long as the correct

Input	Action	Reward
000	0	1000
000	1	0
001	0	1000
001	1	0
010	0	0
010	1	1000
011	0	0
011	1	1000
100	0	1000
100	1	0
101	0	0
101	1	1000
110	0	1000
110	1	0
111	0	0
111	1	1000

Input	Output
000	0
001	0
010	1
011	1
100	0
101	1
110	0
111	1

Fig. 1. The 3 multiplexer function.

Fig. 2. The 3 multiplexer, with one possible reward function.

action in each state is the output specified for that state in Fig. 1. If this is not the case, we no longer have a 3 multiplexer problem since it is the rewards which determine what input/output mapping will be learnt.

Even when rewards *are* consistent with the 3 multiplexer input/output mapping, 3 multiplexer RL problems differ when their reward functions differ. We'll see an example of this shortly.

Representing Generalisations. In the original and standard representation used with XCS [10], each rule has a single fixed-length l-bit condition which is a string from $\{0, 1, \#\}^l$, and single action which is a string from $\{0, 1\}^a$. In this work $a = 1$. A condition c matches a binary input string i if the characters in each position in c and i are the same, or if the character in c is a $\#$, so the $\#$ is the means by which conditions generalise over inputs. For example, the condition 00$\#$ matches two inputs: 000 and 001. Actions do not contain $\#$s and so, using this representation, XCS cannot generalise over actions.

The input/action/reward structure of the 3 multiplexer in Fig. 2 admits a number of accurate generalisations over inputs, and XCS seeks to find them. Figure 3 shows how XCS will learn to represent the problem defined in Fig. 2 using ternary classifier conditions to express generalisations over inputs. Using generalisation allows us (and XCS) to represent functions with fewer rules.

Notice that a table like Fig. 3 can be used in two ways, both as a specification of the function to be learned by XCS, and by XCS to representation its hypotheses about the function it is learning.

Input	Action	Reward
00#	0	1000
00#	1	0
01#	0	0
01#	1	1000
1#0	0	1000
1#0	1	0
1#1	0	0
1#1	1	1000

Input	Output
000	1
001	0
010	0
011	1
100	0
101	1
110	1
111	0

Fig. 3. The 3 multiplexer, with rewards and generalisations expressed with the ternary syntax.

Fig. 4. The even 3 parity function.

Input/Output Functions Constrain Generalisation. The amount of generalisation possible depends on the input/output mapping and the representation used. Consider the even 3 parity function, whose output is 1 when there are an even number of 1s in the input, and 0 otherwise (Fig. 4). While the 3 multiplexer admits considerable generalisation using the ternary LCS language, a parity function admits none whatsoever. That is, any condition which contains 1 or more #s is overgeneral.

Consequently, to represent the even 3 parity function (regardless of what reward function is associated with it) XCS must use the full set of rules with fully specific conditions (i.e., conditions which have no #s) of the appropriate length. Note that this set includes rules with identical conditions but different actions. The 3-bit version of the fully specific rule set (with different rewards) can be found in Figs. 2 and 5. Note that we can represent *any* 3-bit Boolean function with this same rule set by introducing an appropriate reward function.

Rewards Can Constrain Generalisation. Input/output mappings and representations constrain what generalisation is possible, and adding rewards to an input/output mapping can further constrain what generalisations XCS can make. For example, if we choose a reward function in which the rewards for each state are sufficiently[2] different, as in Fig. 5, XCS will be unable to generalise at all.[3] In this case XCS needs to use the set of all rules with fully specific conditions to represent the function. That is, XCS will need a rule for each row in the table in Fig. 5 (16 rules) rather than a rule for each row in Fig. 3 (8 rules).

Note that the altered reward function still returns a higher reward for the correct action in each state, and a lower reward for the incorrect action. For

---

[2] What constitutes *sufficiently* different rewards depends on XCS's tolerance for differences in rewards, which in turn depends on how XCS has been parameterised.

[3] This reward function was constructed by allocating a reward of 1000 for the correct action and 0 for the incorrect action in the first (topmost) state and incrementing the rewards for correct and incorrect actions by 100 for each subsequent state.

Input	Action	Reward
000	0	1000
000	1	0
001	0	1100
001	1	100
010	0	200
010	1	1200
011	0	300
011	1	1300
100	0	1400
100	1	400
101	0	500
101	1	1500
110	0	1600
110	1	600
111	0	700
111	1	1700

Fig. 5. The 3 multiplexer with rewards which may cause XCS to learn to represent it without generalisation.

example, for input 000, action 0 receives more reward than action 1, and so is to be preferred by a system whose goal is to maximise the rewards it receives. This reward function is consistent with the input/output mapping we call a 3 multiplexer function. If we changed the rewards so that action 0 received less reward than action 1 for input 000 then we would no longer be dealing with a 3 multiplexer function.

Although the reward function in Fig. 5 is consistent with the 3 multiplexer function, from XCS's point of view, however, the change in rewards means the problem is equivalent to the 3-bit parity problem, since with the new reward function XCS cannot generalise accurately over inputs at all. That is, even though the input/output mapping remains that of a multiplexer problem, XCS cannot generalise and must represent each input/action pair individually, as in a parity problem. Thus the representational complexity of this particular 3 multiplexer problem is equivalent to that of a parity problem (again, assuming XCS is parameterised such that it cannot generalise). This demonstrates that referring to input/output functions (e.g. multiplexer and parity functions) can be misleading when we are really referring to RL problems.

To summarise, the representational complexity of a single step RL problem depends not only on the input/output mapping but on the rewards associated with actions, the representation used, and XCS's parameterisation.

Optimal Rule Sets. Notice how we represented the 3 multiplexer in Fig. 3 using the language of classifier conditions to express generalisations over inputs. That is, each line in the table can be interpreted as a classifier, and the function can be represented by a set of classifiers. We could have used other sets of rules to represent the function, e.g., the set of fully specific rules used in Figs. 2 and 5. The set we used was chosen because it has certain properties. It is:

1. **Complete.** The rule set maps the entire input/action space.
2. **Accurate.** For our purposes this means each rule maps only to a single reward.
3. **Non-Overlapping.** No input/action pair is described by more than one rule.
4. **Minimal.** The rule set contains no more rules than are needed to satisfy the other three properties.

A set of rules with these 4 characteristics is called an *optimal population* or *optimal rule set*, denoted [O] and pronounced as the letter O [4]. We'll see in Sect. 3.2 that it is interesting to know the size of an optimal population, denoted $\|[O]\|$.

We find it convenient to represent test functions by their optimal populations because we can easily manipulate them to produce other optimal populations with their own corresponding functions. Working directly with the target representation makes it obvious what effects a transformation has.

Minimality and Default Hierarchies. XCS does not support *Default Hierarchies* (see, e.g., [1]) so we do not consider solutions involving them when calculating minimality. Also, default hierarchies inherently violate the constraint that solutions be composed of non-overlapping rules, so no solution containing a default hierarchy can be an [O].

More Compact Representations. We can represent functions more compactly if we assume we have binary rewards, that is, a reward function in which all correct actions receive the same reward r_1, and all incorrect actions receive another reward r_2, where, again, correct actions are simply those which return more reward, i.e. $r_1 > r_2$. This allows us to omit the reward column and the incorrect actions when specifying a test function: if we know the correct action for a state, we know what reward it will receive (r_1), and also what reward the other action in that state will receive (r_2). (Alternatively, we can omit the correct actions instead of the incorrect ones.) These conventions allow us to represent complete RL problems in the input/output form of Figs. 1 and 4.

If we go further and also omit the action column we cannot specify unique functions, but we can, using only conditions, specify classes of functions. The advantage of this approach is slight, being only that we can omit actions in our specification, and to obtain fully specified functions from this representation requires some computation. To do so, we systematically assign correct actions to the conditions in such a way as to avoid making it possible to replace conditions with more general ones. Effectively, we require that the functions obtained from the condition set all have the same number of rules in their minimal representation (i.e., the same $\|[O]\|$). (We ignore the capacity of non-binary reward functions to influence the minimal number of rules required, since we continue to assume

00
01
1#

Fig. 6. A set of conditions used to specify a class of functions.

Input	Action
00	0
01	1
1#	0

Input	Action
00	1
01	0
1#	0

Input	Action
00	0
01	1
1#	1

Input	Action
00	1
01	0
1#	1

Fig. 7. The four [O]s represented by the conditions in Fig. 6.

binary rewards.) Adding actions to conditions yields fully specified input/output functions, which in turn specify full input/action/reward mappings if we assume some binary reward function.

For example, we can assign 1s and 0s as correct actions to the conditions in Fig. 6 as we like, as long as we avoid assigning the same correct action to both 00 and 01, which would make it possible to replace them with 0# and yield an [O] with only 2 rules, which consequently lies outside the class denoted by Fig. 6 (because it contains 3 conditions). By assigning 1s and 0s to a set of conditions in different ways, and avoiding the possibility of replacing conditions with more general ones, we can obtain different functions, all of which have $|[O]| = 4$. The 4 [O]s which can be produced from the condition set in Fig. 6 are shown in Fig. 7.

This approach of specifying only conditions is used in Fig. 12. Note that we are using these more compact representations for the specification of test functions, but XCS is not using them to represent its hypotheses about the function it is learning.

2.3   Measuring Problem Difficulty

So far we've discussed problem difficulty without defining its meaning. Different measures are possible. The primary measure we'll use is %[O], the proportion of the optimal population present in the classifier system on a given time step, which is useful as a measure of the progress of genetic search. An alternative metric, more commonly used with XCS, is that used by Wilson in, e.g., [10], simply called 'performance'. This is defined as the proportion of the last 50 inputs to which the system has responded correctly. It measures the extent to which XCS has found a population of classifiers constituting *a solution* to the problem. %[O], in contrast, measures the extent to which XCS has found *the optimal solution*. The latter is naturally more difficult to find, and requires more trials (inputs to the system) to learn. Even after XCS has reached a point where it responds perfectly correctly to all its inputs it still needs more time to find the optimal solution.

We prefer the use of %[O] because it is more sensitive to the progress of genetic search. As demonstrated in [5], %[O] can reveal differences which do not show up using the other performance measure. %[O] also seems a natural choice of metric given the discussion in Sect. 3.2.

Another metric we'll use is the *mean* %[O] *regret* (or simply *regret*) which is defined as the mean difference between 100% [O] and the observed %[O] averaged over all trials and all runs. This corresponds to the mean distance between the top of a %[O] graph and the %[O] curve. Perfect performance would produce a %[O] regret of 0, while the worst possible performance would produce a regret of 1.

2.4   Population Sizing

We could consider the population size required to efficiently learn a function as another measure of its complexity. Different test functions – even those of the same string length – can have rather different population size requirements. Because of this, it is important to take population size into consideration in any comparison of different test functions. Otherwise, differences in performance may be due to the suitability of the population size used, rather than to some other feature of the problem. Different search mechanisms may have different population size requirements too, so population size should also be considered when comparing them.

Population sizing experiments on a range of 6-bit functions showed that in each case performance plateaued around a certain point. We chose to use a population size limit of 2000 rules for all experiments as all 6-bit functions should have plateaued by this point.

2.5   Experimental Procedure

The tests used in the following sections followed the standard experimental setup defined in [10] and subsequently used in many other studies of XCS. The essence of a trial is that XCS is presented with a randomly generated binary string of a fixed length as input, it responds with either a 0 or a 1, and receives a numerical reward as specified by the reward function.

Unless otherwise stated, the settings used were the standard ones for the 6 multiplexer from [10]. We used the specify operator from [7], GA subsumption deletion [11], a niche GA in the action sets [11], and the t3 deletion scheme from [5] which protects newly generated rules (with a delay of 25 for all tests). This configuration represents our current best guess at a good implementation of XCS for the problems considered here (apart from the ommission of action set subsumption, which would probably generally improve performance). No attempt was made to optimise parameters for individual problems. Finally, we used uniform crossover rather than the 1 point crossover used in previous work with XCS in order to avoid any bias due to the length or position of building blocks [1] for the solution.

3   Dimensions of Problem Difficulty

Now that we have outlined our approach, we can finally ask the question: what dimensions of single step problem difficulty are there for XCS?

Wilson briefly investigated complexity in [11] using a series of boolean multiplexer functions of string length 6, 11 and 20. The size of the optimal populations $|[O]|$ for these functions is 16, 32, and 64 respectively. By evaluating the number of inputs XCS needed to learn each function, Wilson worked out an expression relating $|[O]|$ and difficulty, and another relating string length and difficulty [11]. Not surprisingly, functions of greater string length and $|[O]|$ were more difficult. Our experience with multiplexer-based functions of various $|[O]|$ [2] and multiplexer and parity functions [4] indicates that larger $|[O]|$ is more difficult even when string length is constant. But, as we will soon see, string length and $|[O]|$ are not the only dimensions of problem complexity.

3.1   String Length

The lengths of the input and action strings determine the size of the space of rules XCS searches in, so it seems reasonable that difficulty would generally increase with string length. But if we consider the Kolmogorov complexity of binary strings we can see that it is quite possible for a long string to have low complexity while a much shorter string has high complexity. (See [9] for an introduction to Kolmogorov complexity.) For example, it seems intuitive that a string of 10,000 zeroes has low complexity, while a binary string of 100 randomly distributed ones and zeroes has higher complexity. Technically this assumes the use of an appropriate language to represent the strings, but intuitively the longer string has much greater regularity than the shorter one. If the strings were computer files the longer string could be compressed into a smaller file than the shorter string.

Just as some strings are much more regular than others, some functions are much more regular than others (assuming a given language in both cases). If our language can capture the regularities in a function we can represent it much more compactly. We'll see in Sect. 3.2 that how compactly we can represent a function correlates well with the difficulty XCS has in learning it, which means that string length does not have as great an effect on difficulty as we might think. That is, some functions of a given input length will be much easier than others, and will even be easier than some others of lesser input length.

3.2 $|[O]|$

It makes some intuitive sense that $|[O]|$ would be a major factor in problem complexity for XCS, because $|[O]|$ is determined by how much useful generalisation XCS can express, and XCS is largely concerned with finding generalisations. Unlike earlier LCS, XCS was designed to learn a complete mapping from state/action pairs to their values [10,6]. Further, it was designed with accurate generalisation over this mapping in mind, and accurate generalisation has been a focus of XCS research from the beginning (see [10,2,4,3,7,11,8]).

Since an optimal population for a function is – assuming the ternary language – a minimal representation of the function, $\|[O]\|$ is a measure of its complexity using this language. Thus we can think of $\|[O]\|$ as a representation-specific measure of Kolmogorov complexity.

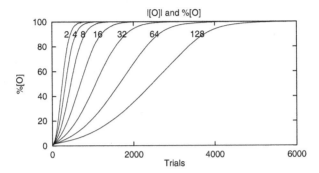

Fig. 8. %[O] for 6-bit functions with $\|[O]\|$ equal to 2, 4, 8, 16, 32, 64 and 128. Curves are averages of 1000 runs.

Figure 8 shows the difficulty of a series of 6-bit functions of increasing $\|[O]\|$ (the series is defined in Sect. 5). Difficulty increases with $\|[O]\|$, but the rate of increase of difficulty slows as $\|[O]\|$ rises. That is, changes in $\|[O]\|$ make less difference to difficulty at higher values.

Why exactly does difficulty increase with $\|[O]\|$? One factor seems to be that as $\|[O]\|$ increases, the rules in the population become, on the whole, more specific. More specific rules may be more difficult for XCS to find because XCS updates rules and affords them opportunities to reproduce only when they match an input. This has two consequences. First, more specific rules match fewer inputs and so are updated less frequently, and reproduce less frequently. The reproductive trial allocation scheme used in XCS (see [10]) balances out the difference between general and specific rules to some extent, but specific rules still reproduce less than more general ones. Now consider that a specific rule is likely to have been generated by the reproduction of another specific rule. This means that specific rules are generated less frequently because they reproduce less frequently.

The second reason more specific rules may be more difficult to find is that rules start with low fitness and only gain fitness as they are updated. It takes a number of updates for a rule to reach its full fitness, and more specific rules will take longer because they are updated less frequently. Because it takes such rules longer to reach their full fitness, they reproduce less than do more general rules.

A third reason is that genetic search in XCS seems to move mainly from specific to more general rules. Rules which are too general are unfit, whereas rules which are too specific are fit (although not as fit as rules which are as general as possible without being too general). So rules which are too general do not reproduce, while rules which are too specific do. If we think of a fitness landscape, more general rules have larger basins of attraction, while more specific rules have smaller ones. It should take longer for the GA to create a rule which falls in the basin of a specific rule – the GA seems inefficient at finding these rules. Lanzi noticed this problem and added a "specify" operator to XCS which detects the situation when all rules matching an input are overgeneral and creates a more specific version of a randomly chosen matching rule [7].

A final reason may be that as $\|[O]\|$ increases, the proportion of inaccurate to accurate rules increases in the space of all possible rules. To see this, consider the extreme case of the constant function, in which all rules are accurate. The 3-bit version of this function is shown as an [O] in Fig. 9. Its [O] has only 1 rule for each action, so it has the smallest possible $\|[O]\|$ of any function. Any other function will have some inaccurate rules and a greater $\|[O]\|$.

As the proportion of accurate rules decreases, the proportion of reproductive events which generate inaccurate rules should rise. If XCS does indeed search mainly from accurate to more general accurate rules, the generation of new inaccurate rules would contribute little to the search process. This would mean that reproductive events which generate inaccurate rules contribute little to search, so search would be slower on functions with more inaccurate rules, i.e. those of greater $\|[O]\|$.

Input	Action	Reward
###	0	1000
###	1	0

Fig. 9. The 3-bit constant function, with one possible reward function.

3.3 The Reward Function

As we saw in Sect. 2.2, the reward function can constrain what generalisations are possible. Apart from this, however, we expected the form of the reward function to have little effect on problem difficulty, because in XCS fitness is based on the accuracy with which a rule predicts rewards, and not on the magnitude of the reward prediction. However, results show the range of rewards – that is, the difference between the highest and lowest reward – has a potentially strong effect on problem difficulty.

To study the effect of reward range we used 4-bit parity functions in which the rewards for most of the function were binary and held constant, but the rewards for one state (1111) were varied (see Fig. 10). The population size limit was 500 and other settings were as defined in Sect. 2.5 and used for the 6-bit tests shown in Fig. 8.

Input	Action	Reward
0000	0	100
0000	1	0
0001	0	0
0001	1	100
0010	0	0
0010	1	100
$\vdots$	$\vdots$	$\vdots$
0110	0	100
0110	1	0
1111	0	x
1111	1	y

Fig. 10. The 4-bit parity function, with rewards.

As the range in rewards increases, problem difficulty initially decreases, but then increases (see Fig. 11). To explain the means by which the reward range has its effects we must refer to the XCS update rules [10], in particular the prediction error update:

$$\varepsilon_j \leftarrow \varepsilon_j + \beta(\frac{|R - p_j|}{R_{max} - R_{min}} - \varepsilon_j)$$

and the rule accuracy update:

$$\kappa_j = \begin{cases} 1 & \text{if } \varepsilon_j \leq \varepsilon_o \\ 0.1e^{(\ln \alpha)(\varepsilon_j - \varepsilon_o)/\varepsilon_o} & \text{otherwise} \end{cases}$$

where ε_j is the prediction error of rule j, $0 < \beta \leq 1$ is the learning rate, R is the reward, p_j is the prediction of rule j, R_{max} and R_{min} are the highest and lowest rewards possible in any state, κ_j is the accuracy of rule j, ε_o is a constant controlling the tolerance for prediction error and $0 < \alpha < 1$ is a constant controlling the rate of decline in accuracy when the threshold ε_o is exceeded (see [10]).[4]

We can see that in the prediction error update the error between prediction and reward $|R - p_j|$ is normalised to fall between 0 and 1 by dividing it by the range in rewards $R_{max} - R_{min}$. This means the error of a rule is inversely proportional to reward range; the larger the range the smaller the error.

---

[4] Wilson has since changed the accuracy update to:

$$\kappa_j = \begin{cases} 1 & \text{if } \varepsilon_j < \varepsilon_o \\ \alpha(\varepsilon_j/\varepsilon_o)^{-v} & \text{otherwise} \end{cases}$$

where $0 < v$ is another constant controlling the rate of decline in accuracy when ε_o is exceeded.

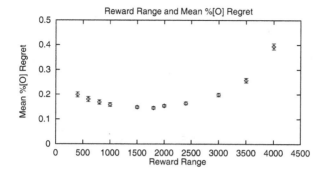

Fig. 11. Mean %[O] regret with 95% confidence intervals vs. reward range on the 4-bit parity problem (Fig. 10). Curves are averages of 400 runs.

The accuracy update says something like: the larger the error the lower the accuracy. Since fitness is based on accuracy, larger errors mean lower fitness. Putting all this together, larger reward ranges mean the fitness calculation is less sensitive to prediction error – it takes a larger error to produce the same effect. This means that, with larger reward ranges, XCS will *often* have more difficulty distinguishing accurate from inaccurate rules. We attribute the increase in difficulty as the reward range grows to this effect.

However, with larger reward ranges XCS will not *always* have more difficulty distinguishing accurate from inaccurate rules. In the extreme case a rule may be updated towards both R_{max} and R_{min}, and will have a large error. The errors of other rules will, in comparison, be small. This may allow XCS to more easily distinguish the overgenerality of some rules, and may account for the initial decrease of problem difficulty as reward range increases. We hypothesise that as reward range increases further this effect is then swamped by the more significant effect (that XCS becomes less sensitive to prediction error) and problem difficulty increases.

In order to avoid confounding effects of rewards, in this investigation we use only binary reward functions with the same reward range unless otherwise noted.

3.4 Mean Hamming Distance

The hamming distance between two strings is defined as the number of characters which must be changed to transform one into the other. The mean hamming distance (MHD) of an [O] is the mean distance between each pair of condition/action strings in the population, including comparison of a given string with itself.

To study the effect of MHD on difficulty we used the 4 functions represented in Fig. 12. This figure shows 4 sets of conditions, each of which can be transformed into a fully specified [O] by assigning alternating 0s and 1s as the correct action for each condition, commencing with 0 as the correct action for the topmost condition and working downwards. Correct actions received a reward of 100 while incorrect actions received a reward of 0.

The 4 [O]s represented in Fig. 12 each have $|[O]| = 8$ and string length 6, but each has a different mean hamming distance. Figure 13 shows that difficulty increases with MHD on this set of functions.

	H1	H2		H3		H4	
	000 ###	00#	0##	00#	0##	000	###
	001 ###	00#	1##	00#	1##	001	###
	010 ###	01#	0##	01#	0##	01#	0##
	011 ###	01#	1##	01#	1##	01#	1##
	100 ###	10#	#0#	10#	#0#	10#	#0#
	101 ###	10#	#1#	10#	#1#	10#	#1#
	110 ###	11#	#0#	11#	##0	11#	##0
	111 ###	11#	#1#	11#	##1	11#	##1
MHD	2	2.75		2.9375		3.125	

Fig. 12. From left to right: [O]s with increasing mean hamming distance, but constant $|[O]|$ and string length.

We hypothesise that this effect is partly due to the greater ease of transforming more similar strings into each other by crossover and mutation. In [O]s with shorter mean hamming distances it is easier to move from one accurate general rule to another.

An additional factor may be involved. In Sect. 3.2 we hypothesised that inaccurate rules contributed little to genetic search. If this is the case, mutation of an accurate rule into an inaccurate rule is a waste of effort, and slows the rate of genetic search. Rules which are more similar to other accurate rules are more likely to mutate into them, and less likely to mutate into inaccurate rules. Even if the accurate rule already exists, there may be more benefit in creating another copy of it than in creating an inaccurate rule. Optimal populations with smaller hamming distances between their rules are less likely to waste their efforts by producing inaccurate rules.

4   The Space of Single Step Functions

In the preceding sections we've identified several dimensions of single step problem complexity for XCS. In this section we consider some characteristics of the space of single step functions and how these dimensions structure it.

The space of single step functions grows rapidly with string length – there are 2^{2^l} possible binary functions for a binary string of length l. We know that some of these functions are more difficult for XCS than others. One dimension which affects difficulty is $|[O]|$ – results from Sect. 3.2 show that difficulty increases

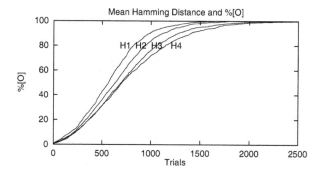

Fig. 13. %[O] for [O]s with different mean hamming distances. Difficulty increases with MHD. Curves are averages of 100 runs.

with $|[O]|$. We can use $|[O]|$ to structure the space of l-bit functions: at one extreme, with $|[O]|$ maximised for a given l, we have a parity function. In this case $[O]$ consists of $2^l \cdot 2$ fully specific rules. (There are 2^l inputs to match, and each maps to 2 actions.) At the other extreme, with $|[O]|$ minimised, we have a constant function. In this case $[O]$ consists of 2 rules with fully generalised conditions (since the fully generalised condition maps to 2 actions).

Although the parity and constant function bound $|[O]|$ for a given string length, they are atypical: of the 2^{2^l} functions for a given l there are only 2 parity and 2 constant functions. The vast majority of functions have $|[O]|$ somewhere between the two.

If $|[O]|$ was the only dimension relevant to difficulty we would be justified in stating that the difficulty of a function $d([O_1])$ is greater than another $d([O_2])$ if its $|[O]|$ is greater. That is, if $|[O_1]| > |[O_2]|$ then $d([O_1]) > d([O_2])$. This would mean that, for l-bit functions, parity was the hardest and the constant function the easiest. This would give us bounding cases on complexity for l-bit functions and a unique ordering among them (by $|[O]|$). Further, it would give us only $2^l \cdot 2$ *complexity classes* (sets of functions of equivalent difficulty) in a much larger space of 2^{2^l} functions. That is, if we wanted to test XCS on all different levels of difficulty for l-bit functions, we would only have to test $2^l \cdot 2$ rather than 2^{2^l} functions.

However, we know that $|[O]|$ is not the only dimension of problem difficulty. Let's consider the others we've identified. Mean hamming distance, for a given string length l, covaries with $|[O]|$: the constant and parity functions – the bounding cases for $|[O]|$ of a given l – have fixed mean hamming distances. MHD is only variable away from these extremes, so we need only consider its effect away from them. For example, we need not worry about whether MHD can make one parity function more difficulty than another, since they must have the same MHD. This suggests that, unless MHD has a very strong effect – and our studies suggest it does not – then complexity for l-bit functions is indeed bounded by the constant and parity functions. This issue deserves further study.

Unlike MHD, the reward range is independent of $||O||$: we can use any rewards we like with any function. This suggests that in comparing the complexity of functions, we should hold reward range constant, unless reward range is itself the object of comparison, in which case we should hold all other dimensions constant. This was the approach taken in Sect. 3.3.

The above suggests that, for a given string length and reward range, $||O||$ may be a reasonable metric for problem difficulty, and that the idea of dividing the space of functions into 2^l complexity classes defined by $||O||$ is also reasonable.

It is unfortunate that we have been unable to devise a more theoretically satisfying model of complexity than the "$||O||$ + noise" model proposed above. However, it is perhaps not surprising given the complexity of XCS: the classifier update rules, genetic algorithm, generalisation mechanism, deletion scheme, triggered operators and other mechanisms all affect the system's performance. While no simple precise model of all the above has been found, we are pleased that a single dimension, $||O||$, provides a simple and seemingly reasonable metric for problem difficulty. A somewhat more precise metric could perhaps be devised by combining $||O||$ and MHD, but we will not consider this here.

What other dimensions of single step problem difficulty exist for XCS, and what their significance is, remains to be seen. Because of this, it also remains to be seen whether $||O||$ is sufficient as a complexity metric.

5   A Ternary Single Step Test Suite

In Sect. 3.2 we noted that generalisation is an important subject for XCS, and that $||O||$ is a measure of the degree to which generalisation is possible using the ternary language. We also saw that $||O||$ has a major effect on problem difficulty. In Sect. 4 we saw how $||O||$ can be used to structure the space of functions of a given string length, and how using $||O||$ as a complexity metric divides the space of functions into a set of complexity classes. There are many fewer complexity classes than functions, which means we have to test XCS on only a small fraction of the function space to evaluate it at all levels of difficulty. However, there seems little need to go into such detail, particularly since higher values of $||O||$ make increasingly fine distinctions about difficulty.

Based on these observations, we propose a single step test suite which ranges over the dimension of $||O||$, and – to the extent that $||O||$ captures problem difficulty – ranges over problem difficulty. The suite is generated for l-bit strings as follows:

1 The first function in the series is the parity function for strings of length l. This function allows no useful generalisation.
2 Obtain the next function by making one of the l bits in the string irrelevant to the string's value. In effect we have a parity function for a string of $l - 1$ bits computed from a string of l bits. This function allows XCS to generalise over the irrelevant bit.

3 Repeat step 2 to cumulatively make more bits irrelevant and to obtain more functions until we reach the constant function, in which all bits are irrelevant.

This algorithm yields a set of $l + 1$ functions for l-bit strings. Recall that the number of functions grows hyperexponentially with the input string, and that the number of complexity classes defined by $|[O]|$ grows exponentially with it. Using this test suite, however, the number of tests we have to make grows only linearly with the the input string. In other words, it scales well to longer string lengths in terms of the effort required to perform the tests.

Note that this test suite is specific to the ternary LCS language, and not to XCS. That is, it may be used with any LCS, or indeed any system employing the ternary LCS language.

A disadvantage of the test suite is that it considers $|[O]|$ as the only dimension of problem difficulty. We would argue that the reward range can be considered separately to $|[O]|$ – we can use any reward range with the test suite. We would also argue that the bounds on $|[O]|$ provide bounds on MHD, since there is no variation in MHD at the bounds of $|[O]|$. There is the possibility that other, as yet unknown, dimensions of single step problem difficulty exist for XCS. Note, however, that the algorithm for generating the test suite does not specify how to select bits to ignore. By selecting bits in different orders we end up with different versions of the test suite. To cater for the possibility of unknown dimensions of problem complexity we could iterate the suite generation algorithm many times to produce many suites and average the results obtained from using them to test XCS.

The 6-bit tests shown in Fig. 8 were generated using this algorithm, with the leftmost relevant bit becoming irrelevant on each iteration of step 2.

6 Summary

We began with some methodological considerations, arguing that our approach of studying single step tasks is reasonable even if we're really interested in sequential ones. We then distinguished between the input/output functions we often speak of and the RL problems XCS is really applied to. Next we presented a way of representing RL problems which is particularly well suited to systems which use the ternary LCS language. Then we saw, for the first time in the literature, how population size affects performance in XCS and took measures to take its effect into account.

We've also taken some steps towards answering the questions posed at the start of the paper. We've examined a number of dimensions of problem complexity, some of them (reward range and MHD) previously unknown. We've illustrated how a significant dimension, $|[O]|$, structures the space of functions and defines complexity classes within it. Based on this we've presented a single step test suite template that's simple to describe and implement, and which scales to any length input string. We hope this test suite will prove useful, both by improving the way we evaluate LCS, that is, through its use, and by spurring the search for a better suite, and the knowledge needed to construct one.

The work begun here can be extended in many ways. To begin with, the search for additional dimensions of complexity for XCS seems important, as does evaluation of the many hypotheses introduced to account for the effects observed in Sect. 3. To what extent our approach is appropriate for other LCS remains to be seen, as does their sensitivity to the complexity dimensions we've examined with XCS.

Finally, we've provided a great deal of additional empirical evidence to support the suggestion in [4] that XCS reliably evolves [O]s for boolean functions. We suspect that XCS can reliably learn *any* function from the class studied here, given enough resources.

Acknowledgements. We'd like to thank the two anonymous reviewers for their helpful comments and Stewart Wilson for his support and inspiration over several years.

References

1. Goldberg, D. E. *Genetic Algorithms in Search, Optimization, and Machine Learning*. Addison-Wesley, 1989.
2. Kovacs, T. Evolving Optimal Populations with XCS Classifier Systems. MSc Thesis, University of Birmingham. Also Technical Report CSR-96-17 and CSRP-96-17, School of Computer Science, University of Birmingham, Birmingham, U.K., 1996.
3. Kovacs, T. Steady State Deletion Techniques in a Classifier System. Unpublished PhD report, 1997.
4. Kovacs, T. XCS Classifier System Reliably Evolves Accurate, Complete, and Minimal Representations for Boolean Functions. In Roy, Chawdhry, and Pant, editors, *Soft Computing in Engineering Design and Manufacturing*, pages 59–68. Springer–Verlag, 1997.
5. Kovacs, T. Deletion schemes for classifier systems. In W. Banzhaf, J. Daida, A. E. Eiben, M. H. Garzon, V. Honavar, M. Jakiela, and R. E. Smith, editors, *GECCO-99: Proceedings of the Genetic and Evolutionary Computation Conference*, pages 329–336. Morgan Kaufmann, 1999.
6. Kovacs, T. Strength or Accuracy? Fitness Calculation in Learning Classifier Systems. In P. L. Lanzi, W. Stolzmann, and S. W. Wilson, editors, *Learning Classifier Systems: An Introduction to Contemporary Research*, pages 143–160. Springer–Verlag, 2000.
7. Lanzi, P. L. A Study of the Generalization Capabilities of XCS. In Thomas Bäck, editor, *Proceedings Seventh International Conference on Genetic Algorithms (ICGA-7)*, pages 418–425. Morgan Kaufmann, 1997.
8. Lanzi, P. L. Generalization in Wilson's XCS. In A. E. Eiben, T. Bäck, M. Shoenauer, and H.-P. Schwefel, editors, *Proceedings of the Fifth International Conference on Parallel Problem Solving From Nature*, number 1498 in LNCS. Springer–Verlag, 1998.
9. Li, M. and Vitányi, P. *An Introduction to Kolmogorov Complexity and Its Applications*. 2nd edition. Springer–Verlag, 1997.
10. Wilson, S. W. Classifier fitness based on accuracy. *Evolutionary Computation*, 3(2):149–175, 1995.

11. Wilson, S. W. Generalization in the XCS classifier system. In J. Koza et al., editors, *Genetic Programming 1998: Proceedings of the Third Annual Conference*, pages 665–674. Morgan Kaufmann, 1998.

Part II

Applications

Applying a Learning Classifier System to Mining Explanatory and Predictive Models from a Large Clinical Database

John H. Holmes

Center for Clinical Epidemiology and Biostatistics
University of Pennsylvania School of Medicine
Philadelphia, PA 19104 USA
jholme@scceb.med.upenn.edu

Abstract. A stimulus-response LCS, called EpiCS, based upon the BOOLE and NEWBOOLE paradigms, was developed to work in single-step environments in which the goal is to generalize clinical decision rules from medical data by means of building explanatory and predictive models. This paper addresses the scalability of EpiCS to a large database, the Fatal Accident Reporting System (FARS), which is a large prospective database supported by the National Highway Traffic Safety Administration (NHTSA) of Transportation. This investigation used 1998 FARS data, the most recent complete year's data available at this time. The performance of EpiCS in building explanatory and predictive models compared very favorably with a decision tree inducer and logistic regression applied to these tasks.

1   Introduction

A central goal of clinical research is the discovery and refinement of concepts, or *rules*, that exist in medical databases. As it usually takes more than a single rule to form a complete concept in medicine, rules are often bundled together in a single *model*. These models serve one of two purposes: they can identify exposures and other factors that may *explain* a clinical outcome, usually disease or death, or they can *predict* an outcome, in terms of risk, given the presence of exposures and other factors found to be important. Traditionally, explanatory models are developed after difficult and painstaking work involving univariate and bivariate statistical procedures. A typical explanatory model would involve one or more IF..THEN rules, where the conditions express whether or not a set of exposures has occurred, and the consequent is a single clinical outcome. Predictive models require even more effort, as they require sophisticated multivariate techniques such as logistic regression. Both model building tasks are often hampered by preconceived mental models held by researchers that bias the investigation, especially during exploratory analysis. In addition, model building is a daunting exercise, requiring substantial time and effort. One way to address these issues is to incorporate *data mining* into the research endeavor as a first step in the model building process.

P.L. Lanzi, W. Stolzmann, and S.W. Wilson (Eds.): IWLCS 2000, LNAI 1996, pp. 103-113, 2001.

There has been increasing interest in applying evolutionary computation methods as data mining tools to knowledge discovery in databases (KDD). A number of KDD applications using genetic algorithms and genetic programming have been reported in the literature [3,10,12]. However, relatively few researchers have reported using Learning Classifier Systems (LCS) in this area [6,8,14,17]; even fewer have reported on their use on large-scale data mining problems. This paper reports on applying a LCS to mine a real-world clinical database of considerable size and complexity for explanatory and predictive models.

2   Methods

2.1   EpiCS: A Learning Classifier System for Epidemiologic Surveillance

A stimulus-response LCS, EpiCS [5] was developed from the NEWBOOLE model [2] to meet the demands posed by epidemiologic data. The distinctive features of EpiCS include algorithms for controlling under- and over-generalization of data, a methodology for determining risk as a measure of classification [6], and the ability to use differential negative reinforcement of false positive and false negative errors in classification during training. Real-number encoding was implemented in EpiCS for this investigation, using the approach suggested by Wilson [16].

2.2   Description of Data

The source of data for this investigation was the Fatal Accident Reporting System (FARS), which is a large prospective database supported by the National Highway Traffic Safety Administration (NHTSA) of the United States Department of Transportation. FARS documents all fatal automobile crashes occurring in the United States and Puerto Rico. These crashes are characterized in a large number of crash-, vehicle-, and person-specific variables that can be mined to determine their association with the outcome (fatality/no fatality). Data have been collected for FARS since 1975, and are available as ASCII files on the NHTSA Web site (www.nhtsa.gov). This investigation used 1998 data, the most recent complete year's data available.

FARS data comprises three files, each representing an accident, the vehicles involved in the accident, or the persons associated with each vehicle. Only the person-specific file was used, to allow for the investigation of associations of person-specific features with fatality. A total of 20 features were selected from the file; these are displayed in Table 1. In the 1998 FARS data, there were a total of 100,978 records, each representing a single person involved, but not necessarily killed, in a fatal crash. Of these, 41,471 (41.4%) represented fatalities.

Table 1. List of features in the FARS 1998 data used for this investigation

Feature	Values
Roadway function	Major urban, Major rural, Minor urban, Minor rural
Manner of collision	Rear-end, head-on, sideswipe, no collision
School bus related	No, Yes
Body type	Automobile, Utility vehicle, Minivan, Van, Pickup truck, Light truck, School bus, Bus, Truck, Motor home, Motorcycle, All-terrain vehicle, Farm/Construction vehicle, Other type, Unknown
Vehicle rollover	No, Yes
Emergency use vehicle	No, Yes
Fire occurrence	No, Yes
Age	Continuous
Sex	Male, Female, Unknown
Person type	Driver, Passenger, Pedestrian, Bicyclist, Unknown
Seating position	Non-motorist, Front, Second row, Third row, Fourth row, Other, Exterior of vehicle, Unknown
Non-motorist location	Occupant, Intersection, Non-intersection, Unknown
Ejected from vehicle	No, Totally, Partially, Unknown
Drinking	No, Yes, Unknown
Injury severity	No injury, Injury, Unknown
Work-related	No, Yes
Restraint	None, Seat belt, Child safety seat, Helmet, Other
Alcohol results	Negative, Within legal limit, Outside legal limit, Not administered, Unknown
Drug involvement	No, Yes, Unknown
Fatality (outcome)	No, Yes

2.3 Experimental Procedure

Procedures for creating and evaluating the explanatory and predictive models from FARS data were developed separately for EpiCS and the two comparison methods, decision tree induction using See5 [13] and logistic regression.

Preparation of Data

The original coding scheme for each feature, as used in FARS, was preserved. Codes representing unknown or not-applicable values were also used in their native form, rather than converted to missing values. This was done because in data mining, it is useful to understand the distribution of these types of codes, rather than forcing them into a single category representing missing values.

The database was separated into training and testing sets of equal size (50,489 records) with equal distribution of each of the two classes between them, but preserving the class distribution of the main database. The composition of the training and testing sets is shown in Table 2. Records were selected from the database randomly without replacement to ensure that all records were used and that the training and testing sets were mutually exclusive.

Table 2. Distribution of records in the training and testing sets

	Training Set	Testing Set	Total
Fatalities	20736	20735	41471
Non-fatalities	29753	29754	59507
Total	50489	50489	100978

The unequal distribution of the two classes in the FARS data is typical of clinical data in general. To ensure that EpiCS was exposed to all cases in the training and testing sets, a prevalence-based bootstrapping procedure [9] was employed. Prevalence-based bootstrapping is a type of frequency-based boosting [1,4,15] that ensures the even sampling of clinical data for training and testing the LCS.

See5 and logistic regression, like any classification system, are affected by classification pressure when operating in environments with unequal class prevalence. In order to ensure comparability with the procedures applied to EpiCS, the prevalence-based bootstrap procedure described in [9] was used to create 20 training-testing set pairs from the main dataset. These sets differed from those created for the EpiCS trials, in that they comprised equal numbers of positive and negative cases. In practice however, they were similar, in that the prevalence-based bootstrap procedure creates "virtual" training and testing sets of equal class distribution at run-time.

EpiCS

EpiCS was trained using the training data described above, over 20 trials, each consisting of 30,000 iterations. This was done to ensure that full convergence had been reached prior to stopping each trial, and that any inter-trial variance could be assessed. At each 100th iteration, the Area Under the Receiver Operating Characteristic Curve (AUC), corrected for the number of unclassifiable cases, was obtained using training set data. The AUC is a classification accuracy metric that is preferable to "percent correct" or "error rate" in data where the class distributions are unequal [7,11]. The training period lasted a total of 10,000 iterations, each defined as exposure of EpiCS to a single randomly selected training case.

After training, the classifier population was examined qualitatively for emergence of explanatory models, which were subsequently validated by a panel of clinical experts. The trained system was then exposed to the testing cases in the FARS database and its classification accuracy was determined by two methods. First, the classifications were tallied and compared with known classifications for each testing case, and the AUC was calculated, analogously to the procedure used during training. Second, EpiCS's risk assessment module was used to determine the risk of outcome for each case. For comparison with the RAM-derived model, a stepwise logistic model was created from the training set data and then applied to the testing data to determine its accuracy.

Logistic Regression

In logistic regression, the risk of developing an outcome is expressed as a function of a set of predictor (or independent) variables. The dependent variable in the logistic model is the natural logarithm of the odds of disease:

$$\ln\left[\frac{Px}{1-Px}\right] = \alpha + b_1X_1 + ... + bnXn \tag{1}$$

where P_x is the probability of disease for a specified covariate x, $\ln\left[\dfrac{Px}{1-Px}\right]$ is the log odds of developing the outcome (or logit), accounting for all exposure variables in the model (rather than a single exposure variable), a is the intercept, and b_i is the coefficient for the independent variable X_i.

Rewriting Eq. (1) produces a method for representing the estimated probability of developing the outcome of interest:

$$P\hat{y} = \frac{1}{1 + e^{-(\alpha + \beta_1 x_1 + ... + \beta_n x_n)}} \tag{2}$$

where $\hat{y}$ is the estimated probability of developing an outcome, given the presence of risk factors $x_1 ... x_n$. The formula in Eq. (2) is used to derive clinical decision rules.

One important implication of the logistic model is that one can calculate an *odds ratio* (OR) for an independent variable, adjusted for the effects of the other independent variables in the model. The OR indicates the degree of association of an independent variable with the outcome. ORs less than 1.0 indicate a "protective effect" in that exposure to the variable of interest is associated with decreased risk of outcome. ORs exceeding 1.0 indicate a positive association of the independent variable with the outcome.

The risk estimates from either adjusted ORs or from the entire logistic model, are used to create clinical prediction rules. These rules can be used to determine the classification of a patient by outcome status, given the patient's values for the variables that have been included in the model. For example, a single adjusted OR could be calculated for a person's odds of fatality when she is involved in an automobile crash and not restrained by seat belt. As described above, this OR would be adjusted by the other variables in the model, so it would automatically take into account such other factors as age, sex, alcohol use, etc. However, a more expansive rule can be created using Eq. (2); this rule provides an *overall* estimate of risk for the person, based on all variables in the model simultaneously and not just an estimate for a single exposure variable. Both approaches to prediction of risk are germane to this investigation.

Twenty separate stepwise logistic models were created from the training set data described above, using all 19 features as independent variables and the outcome, fatality, as the dependent variable. A permissive p-value (0.95) was used to ensure that all variables entered the model. Fixed models were then run, using the variables that were found to be significant ($p < 0.07$) on the respective stepwise models. The beta coefficients from each fixed model were used to create a clinical prediction rule, using the formula shown in Eq. (2). These rules were then applied to all cases in the respective testing set to determine the risk of outcome for each case. Dichotomous indicators of risk (Fatality/No fatality) were created at each decile of these risk estimates. The classification accuracy of each of models was assessed by calculating the AUC; these results were averaged and compared to those obtained from EpiCS.

Decision Tree Induction
See5 was used to derive pruned decision tree models from each of the 20 training sets, described above. In order to ensure comparability with EpiCS, See5's boosting and cross-validation procedures were not used; rather the prevalence-based bootstrap procedure, emulated through the separate datasets, was employed to optimize these models. From each of the models, See5 created a parsimonious rule set that was then used to classify the cases in each of the respective testing sets. The classification accuracy of these rule sets was determined by calculating the AUC. The results for the 20 models were averaged and compared with those obtained from EpiCS.

3   Results

3.1 Training

The performance of EpiCS during training is demonstrated in Fig. 1.

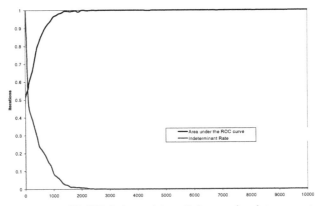

Fig. 1. Performance of EpiCS during training. Points on the plot represent areas under the receiver-operating characteristic curve obtained at each 100th iteration, corrected for training cases that could not be classified

As can readily be seen, EpiCS reached convergence quickly on FARS training data, within 2,000 iterations, attaining an AUC of 0.97, SD (1 standard deviation)=0.02. All training cases were classifiable after 2,200 iterations (Indeterminant Rate=0.0, SD=0.0. The time required for convergence was an average of 3.5 minutes (SD=0.01).

3.2 Emergence of Explanatory Models

The macrostate population after training demonstrated the emergence of generalized explanatory models. These models were judged to be useful by a panel of experts in automotive safety and injury epidemiology, and were found to be more informative and useful qualitatively than the pruned rule sets obtained from comparison runs with See5. These models included rules that were of little surprise, such as Rule 1, shown in Fig. 1. Other rules were not expected, yet suggested new, previously unconsidered hypotheses. One such rule was Rule 2, shown below; in this type of situation, one would expect that the lower speed limits imposed on urban roads would protect against fatal accidents. However, the panel responded with the hypothesis that increased traffic and possible increased drug or alcohol involvement might explain this rule. Subsequent investigation proved all three to contribute to the model, which would have not been built using traditional statistical methods. Some sample rules derived by EpiCS are shown in Fig. 2. These rules represent the most prevalent in the macrostate population at the end of training. In addition, the prevalence of these rules remained constant throughout each of the 20 EpiCS trials.

1.	IF		ROLLOVER=Yes or
			EJECTED=Yes or
			FIRE=Yes
	THEN		FATALITY=Yes
2.	IF		URBAN HIGHWAY=Yes
	THEN		FATALITY=Yes
3.	IF		COLLISION<>MOTOR VEHICLE or
			ALCOHOL=No or
			DRUGS=No
	THEN		FATALITY=No

Fig. 2. Rules extracted using EpiCS

The rules extracted from the model derived by logistic regression are shown below. No other rules were found across all 20 logistic regression runs; that is, only ROLLOVER, FIRE, and WORK-RELATED were found to be statistically significant in the logistic models.

The odds ratios for the features shown above were statistically significant, as shown below in Table 1. Of the odds ratios for the 19 candidate features, no others were found to be statistically significant.

Table 1. Odds ratios for signifcant features used in the logistic model derived from FARS data. Odds ratios >1 represent a poistive association between the feature and the outcome (fatality). Odds ratios <1 represent a protective effect

	Odds ratio	Confidence interval (95%)	
		Lower	Upper
ROLLOVER	1.8	1.3	2.6
FIRE	5.8	1.3	26.3
WORK-RELATED	0.5	0.4	0.5

```
    1.    IF          ROLLOVER=Yes or
                      FIRE=Yes
          THEN        FATALITY=Yes


    2.    IF          WORK-RELATED=Yes
          THEN        FATALITY=No
```

Fig. 3. Rules extracted using logistic regression

Sample rules derived by See5 are shown below:

```
    1.    IF          ROLLOVER=Yes
          THEN        FATALITY=Yes


    2.    IF          FIRE=Yes
          THEN        FATALITY=Yes


    3.    IF          DRUGS=No
          THEN        FATALITY=No
```

Fig. 4. Rules extracted using See5

The rules induced by See5 were extremely parsimonious, and often conflicting. For example, WORK-RELATED was associated with fatality and non-fatality alike. In addition, no rules induced by See5 contained more than one conjunct.

3.3 Classification Performance: Application of the Models to Prediction

Table 3 shows that the classification performance of EpiCS on testing data was excellent (AUC=0.98, IR=0.02). Comparison with See5 (AUC=0.97) showed EpiCS to be slightly better, but not significantly so (p>0.05). The risk models built by EpiCS performed significantly better than those derived by logistic regression (AUC from EpiCS=0.97; from logistic regression, 0.89; p<0.01). The terms in the logistic model were compared with those in the EpiCS models, and the former excluded many "interesting" terms that were included by the EpiCS models; this parsimony may have dampened the prediction performance of the logistic model.

Table 2. Comparison of EpiCS, See5, and logistic regression on classification performance. Areas under the receiver operating characteristic curve averaged over the 20 bootstrapped trials, one standard deviation shown in parentheses

	EpiCS	See5	Logistic regression
Area under the ROC curve	0.98 (0.01)	0.97 (0.01)	0.89 (0.01)

4   Discussion

This investigation focused on the application of EpiCS, a stimulus-response LCS, to a complicated problem in data mining: the discovery of explanatory and predictive models in a large epidemiologic surveillance database. Heretofore, most reports of the use of LCS in data mining have used relatively small databases that are standards in the machine learning repositories. However, the application of a LCS to mining the FARS database represents a significant departure from these efforts. Even with a relatively small number of features, the large number of records in FARS, and the subsequent possibility for a high-dimensional problem space, provides a substantial testbed for any data mining approach, let alone the LCS.

While not necessarily generalizable to other LCS paradigms such as XCS, EpiCS's performance on both learning new concepts from FARS and applying them to novel data was excellent. Given the size of the database, it was surprising that EpiCS so quickly reached convergence during training (within 2,500 iterations). One possible answer for this can be found in the parsimony of the rules that evolved during training for all three methods. These rules comprise the *explanatory models*. The FARS data appeared to partition well on relatively few features; that is, only several features contributed to the outcome. Examining the macrostate population evolved by EpiCS, the size of the decision trees and the subsequent rule sets induced by See5, and the number of candidate terms entered into the stepwise logistic model bears this out.

These results are shown in Figs. 2, 3, and 4. The rules evolved by EpiCS were found by an expert clinical panel to be more informative than the rules that comprised the See5 or logistic models. This was due to the coverage provided by Rule 1 (Fig. 2), in which rollover, occupant ejection, or fire were all associated with fatality. The rules induced by logistic regression never included occupant ejection as a possible predictor of fatality, and this is clinically counterintuitive. Additional sparseness was seen in the See5 models, where no disjunctions were found in the rulesets. Although rollover and fire were associated with fatality in these models, they were so only in the context of two separate rules, which makes their use potentially more cumbersome in applying them in a global clinical prediction rule.

Applying the macrostate classifiers to the task of *prediction*, or classifying unseen cases from the testing set, one can see that they performed very well, with nearly maximal AUCs. So too did the rules induced by See5, with no significant difference detected between the predictive accuracy of these rules compared with those of EpiCS. The predictive accuracy of the logistic regression models was significantly worse than that of the EpiCS or See5 models. This is an important finding, as logistic regression is considered the standard method for creating clinical prediction rules from population-based data.

5   Conclusions

This investigation demonstrated the ability of EpiCS, a stimulus-response LCS, to discover explanatory and predictive models in a large, real-world database used in epidemiologic surveillance. Additional research is needed into such issues as model interpretation and data visualization using the macrostate classifier population and applicability to other, even larger and more complex databases. However, this investigation indicates that the LCS is a promising paradigm from which to build practical data mining tools, and points to the feasibility of using other LCS approaches, particularly XCS, for knowledge discovery in databases.

References

1. Abe, N. and Mamitsuka, H.: Query learning strategies using boosting and bagging. In: Shavlik, J. (ed.): Machine Learning. Proceedings of the Fifteenth International Conference (ICML'98). San Francisco, Morgan Kaufmann Publishers (1998) 1-9.
2. Bonelli, P., Parodi, A., Sen, S., and Wilson, S.: NEWBOOLE: A fast GBML system, in: Porter, B. and Mooney, R. (eds.), Machine Learning: Proceedings of the Seventh International Conference. Morgan Kaufmann, San Mateo, CA (1990) 153-159.
3. Catral, R., Oppacher, F. and Duego, D.: Rule acquisition with a genetic algorithm. In Banzhaf, W., Daida, J., Eiben, A.E., et al (eds.): Proceedings of the Genetic and Evolutionary Computation Conference GECCO 99. Morgan Kaufmann, San Francisco (1999), 778.
4. Harries, M.: Boosting a strong learner: evidence against the minimum margin. In: Bratko, I. and Dzeroski, S. (eds.): Machine Learning. Proceedings of the Sixteenth International Conference (ICML '99). Morgan Kaufmann Publishers, San Francisco (1999) 171-180.
5. Holmes, J.H.: A genetics-based machine learning approach to knowledge discovery in clinical data, Journal of the American Medical Informatics Association Suppl (1996) 883.
6. Holmes, J.H.: Discovery of Disease Risk with a Learning Classifier System, in: Baeck, T. (ed.): Proceedings of the Seventh International Conference on Genetic Algorithms (SanFrancisco, Morgan Kaufmann (1997) 426-433.
7. Holmes J.H.: Quantitative methods for evaluating learning classifier system performance In forced two-choice decision tasks. In: Wu, A. (ed.) Proceedings of the Second International Workshop on Learning Classifier Systems (IWLCS99). Morgan Kaufmann, SanFrancisco (1999) 250-257.
8. Holmes JH, Durbin DR, Winston FK: The Learning Classifier System: An evolutionary computation approach to knowledge discovery in epidemiologic surveillance. Artificial Intelligence in Medicine 19(1): 53-74 (2000).
9. Holmes JH, Durbin DR, Winston FK: A new bootstrapping method to improve classification performance in learning classifier systems. Schoenauer M, Deb K, Rudolph G, et al (eds.): Parallel Problem Solving from Nature – PPSN VI, Proceedings of The Sixth International Conference: 745-754, 2000.
10. Marmelstein, R.E. and Lamont, G.: Pattern classification using a hybrid genetic program-decision tree approach. In: Koza J.R., Banzhaf W., Chellapilla K., et al (eds.): Genetic Programming 1998: Proceedings of the Third Annual Conference, Morgan Kaufmann, San Francisco (1998) 223-231.
11. McNeil, BJ; Hanley, JA. Statistical approaches to the analysis of receiver operating characteristic (ROC) curves. Medical Decision Making. 1984; 4:137-150.

12. Ngan, P.S., Wong, M.L., Leung, K.S., and Cheng, J.C.Y.: Using grammar-based genetic programming for data mining of medical knowledge. In: Koza J.R., Banzhaf W., Chellapilla K., et al (eds.): Genetic Programming 1998: Proceedings of the Third Annual Conference, Morgan Kaufmann, San Francisco (1998) 254-259.

13. Quinlan, J.R.: See5: Release 1.13, 2000.

14. Saxon, S. and Barry, A. XCS and the Monk's Problem. In Banzhaf, W., Daida, J., Eiben, A.E., et al (eds.): Proceedings of the Genetic and Evolutionary Computation Conference GECCO 99. Morgan Kaufmann, San Francisco (1999), 809.

15. Schapire, R.E.: Theoretical views of boosting. In: Computational Learning Theory, 4th European Conference, EuroCOLT'99. Springer-Verlag, Berlin (1999) 1-10.

16. Wilson, S.W., " Get real! XCS with continuous-valued inputs" In Booker, L., Forrest, S., Mitchell, M., and Riolo, R. (eds.): Festschrift in Honor of John H. Holland, May 15-18, 1999 (pp. 111-121),. Center for the Study of Complex Systems, The University of Michigan, Ann Arbor, MI.

17. Wilson, S.W.: Mining oblique data with XCS. To appear in Lanzi, P. L., Stolzmann, W., and S. W. Wilson (Eds.), Advances in Learning Classifier Systems. Third International Workshop (IWLCS-2000), Lecture Notes in Artificial Intelligence (LNAI-1996). Berlin: Springer-Verlag (2001).

Strength and Money: An LCS Approach to Increasing Returns

Sonia Schulenburg and Peter Ross

School of Computing
Napier University
219 Colinton Road
Edinburgh EH14 1DJ
s.schulenburg@napier.ac.uk, peter@dcs.napier.ac.uk

Abstract. This paper reports on a number of experiments where three different groups of artificial agents learn, forecast and trade their holdings in a real stock market scenario given exogenously in the form of easily-obtained stock statistics such as various price moving averages, first difference in prices, volume ratios, etc. These artificial agent-types trade while learning during – in most cases – a ten year period. They normally start at the beginning of the year 1990 with a fixed initial wealth to trade over two assets (a bond and a stock) and end in the second half of the year 2000. The adaptive agents are represented as Learning Classifier Systems (LCSs), that is, as sets of bit-encoded rules. Each condition bit expresses the truth or falsehood of a certain real market condition. The actual conditions used differ between agents. The forecasting performance is then compared against the performance of the *buy-and-hold* strategy, a *trend-following* strategy and finally against the *bank* investment over the same period of time at a fixed compound interest rate. To make the experiments as real as possible, agents pay commissions on every trade. The results so far suggest that this is an excellent approach to make trading decisions in the stock market.

1 Introduction

Many techniques have been used to model financial time series data such as stock prices, including linear and nonlinear statistical methods and more inscrutable methods such as neural nets. The hope is that if the time series can be predicted fairly well, the predictions can be used to make profitable buy/sell/hold decisions. Time series modelling may work well for physical systems, such as blood flow in veins, because the underlying physical laws do not change with time even though their effects (such as the rhythmic expansion and contraction of blood vessels) may do so. However, time series modelling in the financial world often seems to fail to track any of the causes of the data, and the causes themselves change over time. All that happens is that the model ceases to fit the real data well, and then it has become time to re-train or re-fit.

So what can we do? Continual re-training may not be the answer; in the case of (e.g.) neural networks it may be expensive, and certainly performance cannot

P.L. Lanzi, W. Stolzmann, and S.W. Wilson (Eds.): IWLCS 2000, LNAI 1996, pp. 114–137, 2001.

always improve, so there is a potential problem about when to switch from the old model to a new one. Another drawback of such models is that they do not tend to identify or explain anything about the relevant phenomena that is being modelled; this is not their main goal. As a result, there is no added knowledge or hypothesis about the underlying causes of the changes in the environment being modelled.

Our approach here is different. Because financial markets are complex systems where the players are human traders, we try to address these issues by focusing on the agent rather than on the data. The idea is to model traders' decision-making processes as they decide repeatedly whether to buy, sell or hold a particular stock. Modelling individual traders may not be ideal – individuals are extremely complex, their actions are affected by their private knowledge, their emotional make-up, even their breakfast!. Why then, not model the behaviour of whole groups of traders instead? We hypothesise that the aggregate behaviour of a group will be simpler to model than that of individuals and that it may still produce very good results.

What do we mean by modelling the behaviour of a *group of traders*? In this work it is a group of traders who use a certain set of information when making decisions. To make a simple start, we choose small and reasonable-looking sets, consisting of some binary indicators about how today's prices and volumes relate to various moving averages and historical extremes. The behaviour of the group is expressed as a set of rules that relate to a single stock, such as: if A and B and not C and D then buy 45%of what cash-in-hand allows; if not A and B and not C then sell 15%of current holdings; etc.

Initially the agent's rules are randomly generated, although with an inbuilt bias towards generality. Thereafter they are periodically modified by simulated evolution (see [3] for an introduction), so that rules which perform better than average are more likely to produce descendants, but the forces of recombination and mutation also work to produce new and steadily better rules.

2   The Model

In this paper we describe an artificial stock market model consisting of agents of different types each represented by a Michigan-style strength-based Learning Classifier System (LCS). Each agent learns and adapts to a market environment that is partially understood and where the domain characteristics can change rapidly over time. In the work reported here, the market environment consists of genuine daily price information about some genuine stock, typically over a ten-year period. The agents make investment decisions of whether to buy, sell or hold different proportions of two assets: a risky stock and a risk-free bond (essentially, an immediate-access bank account paying a reasonable but fixed rate of compound interest). Having different views about the market, each type of agent creates, develops and explores a vast pool of expectational models based on the recommendations of those strategies that perform best over time. There are three different types of agents in the model described in this paper.

Rather than describe the mechanics of a Michigan-style LCS, the interested reader is referred to [4] for a recent introduction and overview.

2.1   Evolution of Rules

It is important to emphasize that *trader types* are evolved rather than models of individual traders. The assumption is that the aggregate behaviour of a set of traders, each of whom is (say) basing buy/sell/hold decisions on certain sorts of data such as information about various moving averages and recent highs and lows, will be simpler to describe than the complex behaviour of only one trader. Any one trader might include in his decision-making factors such as personal knowledge of the people controlling the company, private knowledge of the local economy, etc. However, within a group who use the same basic methodology, the effects of such extra factors may tend to balance out so that the group's behaviour may at least be approximated in terms of only a modest set of easily available indicators.

For example, a *trader type* may pay attention to such factors as whether today's price is more than 20%higher than the 5-day-moving average, whether today's volume is larger than yesterday's and so on. At present, a *trader type* is characterised by the particular set of such factors f_i – each of them binary, a simple yes/no – that it pays attention to. Its behaviour is expressed in terms of rules whose conditions are a combination of terms such as $f_1 = $ yes, $f_2 = $ no, $f_3 = $ don't care (the *don't care* are wildcards, they match either yes or no). Rule actions can be to do nothing (hold), or to buy more stock using a certain proportion of current cash invested in the risk-free bond, or to sell a certain proportion of holdings in the stock and invest that in the risk-free bond.

In experiments, a *trader type* starts with a certain capital and gradually learns how to trade a certain stock, keeping cash not invested in that stock in a risk-free fixed-interest bond, essentially a high-interest immediate-access bank account paying 8%annual interest compounded daily. Every trade involves paying a commission too, normally set to 0.1%of the value of the transaction. The initial rules are created at random, except that there is a high proportion of wildcards involved. Rules that, with hindsight, contributed in some way to good trading decisions get rewarded and receive more attention whenever rules compete to make the next decision. Every so often a Genetic Algorithm (GA) is run in order to evolve the rules further; rules with a good track record are favoured in this process.

2.2   Previous Work

First, in order to explore the degree of reliability that artificially intelligent agents can have when applied to real life economic problems, we conducted an initial evaluation of whether an LCS is able to represent competent traders in a **real market scenario** in which daily stock prices, volume of transactions, dividends and information about other simple investment strategies are given to the agents **exogenously**, so permitting us to focus on the dynamics and evolution of the behaviour of these evolving traders without having to be concerned about how their actions affect the market.

See [6,7] for further details. In particular, these papers give details of the variables used in the rule conditions for each of three types of trader, and of the learning classifier system used. We do not repeat such details in this paper.

The results in those earlier papers, using the very well performing stock Merck and Co. over a period of ten years showed that the artificial agents, by displaying different and rich behaviours evolved over time, were indeed able to discover and refine novel and successful sets of market strategies that could outperform baseline strategies such as (i) *buy-and-hold*: simply put all available cash into the stock at the start and then keep it there, and (ii) *bank*: merely keep all money in the bank at a good rate of interest, never buying the stock. Note that the *buy-and-hold* strategy can be a very good one if the stock performs well over the years, and *bank* strategy can be very good if the stock performs poorly over the years.

Arguably, Merck and Co. is not a representative example of a stock (no stock would be), nor is it an unequivocally impressive illustration of our approach. Figure 1 shows how it performed over the years; in that figure, the lowest of the jagged lines shows how the value (in US dollars) of the *buy-and-hold* strategy grew over the years – the horizontal axis represents trading days. Apart from a fall over a period of about one and a half years in the middle, the stock's value grew fairly steadily, and at a very healthy rate in the most recent years. It was therefore fairly easy to make money from it. As the figure also shows, the best examples of the three *trader types* each managed to outperform the *buy-and-hold* strategy by a healthy margin. Although the fluctuations in their wealth were similar to the fluctuations in the stock's value (as shown by the wealth of the *buy-and-hold* strategy), they were able to do better by transferring money from the stock to the bank during downturns and transferring it back in upswings, as a close examination of the sequence of decisions revealed. The *bank* strategy of course did poorly; its wealth is shown by the lowest, smoothly rising line in Fig. 1.

Those results left open an number of important questions:

- how would our approach perform when applied to a stock that tended to drop in price over the years? Would it still be able to make money by buying in early in any upswing, even though those might be rare? How would that compare with the *bank* strategy?
- how would our approach perform when applied to a more temperamental stock, for which neither the *buy-and-hold* nor the *bank* strategy would be particularly effective?
- the rules are evolved by running a genetic algorithm every so often, to produce new rules by selection, recombination and mutation and then replace 20%of existing rules by crowding. Clearly, it matters how often the GA is invoked. If the GA is run too rarely, progress towards good rules will be slow; if it is run too often, there won't be time for rules to demonstrate their proper value. For example, a certain rule might apply only on rare occasions

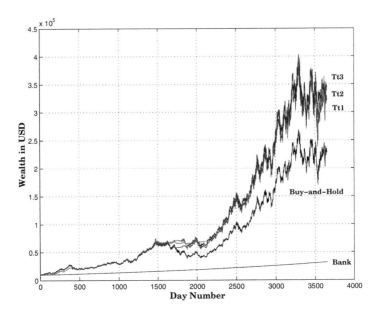

Fig. 1. Merck and Co. Stock. Wealth (in US dollars) of *Bank* Investment, *Buy-and-Hold* Strategy and *Trader-Types* 1,2 and 3 over a period of 11 years

but be crucial when it does. That rule only gets the chance to earn its keep when that rare situation arises. If the GA runs before that time, the potentially valuable rule will be an obvious candidate for replacement because it has not yet done anything, or perhaps anything particularly useful. This is an ongoing topic of research into LCSs which raises two fundamental issues: first, how can an LCS be made to behave fairly towards rarely-applicable yet valuable rules; and second, are such rules genuinely irreplaceable? Consider a car-driving rule system. A rule which says "if about to hit a wall, slam on the brakes" is very useful but (hopefully) applies very rarely; but is it needed at all, or is it possible to produce a rule system that ensures that such a situation will never even arise?

– not all runs produce any *trader types* that perform well. How much effort does it take to produce a good agent through repeated runs, and is this stock-dependent?

This paper addresses these questions.

3   Results

In order to test if our approach works, that is, whether the best of the sets of rules evolved perform more profitably than other common strategies, we typically use ten years of historical data. The simulated traders apportion their money between holdings in a reliable high-interest bond (8% a compound) and holdings of the stock in question, and they are obliged to pay a realistic commission on every trade (0.1% of transaction value). The best of them seriously outperform strategies such as keeping money in the high-interest bond, or buying then holding at the start of a prolonged general growth. The models are cheap to evolve, taking only minutes on a reasonable PC; not all models are great performers, but the cost of finding good performing models is still low.

Results with the stocks we use in this paper are consistent with our previous results, and not only do good percentages of the agents keep outperforming the *bank* investment and the *buy-and-hold* strategies, but also outperform a new *trend-following* strategy we have recently implemented. This strategy buys into a stock when the price starts to show an upward trend, and sells the stock when there is potential evidence that the price will continue to fall.

The *trend-following* strategy is simple and yet will outperform both the *buy-and-hold* strategy and the *bank* strategy if the stock price does not show a clear long-term trend upwards or downwards. It assumes that there will be an uptrend if is sees that the price of the stock today is higher than yesterday, and therefore buys the total number of shares that its available cash allows, minus the commission. If today's price is lower than yesterday's it assumes a continuation of that downward trend and sells all shares in possession. In both cases no other transaction is made until there is a reversal in trend. It pays commission in the same way the adaptive agents do. Note that when this strategy sells its stock and puts its money in the bank, the commission it pays on the transaction is higher than three days of interest earned on the bank deposit. On any given day, its holdings are either all shares valued at the current price, or all cash in the bank and earning interest. The frequency of transactions varies from stock to stock with this strategy, and as we will see in the next section, its performance is quite unpredictable and unreliable; it can be the best or the worst, depending on the stock.

Is it worth also using a fixed random strategy for comparison purposes? We believe not. The agents each start with a random strategy, and those random strategies do not survive long; they are replaced by better ones because of the learning process.

It is important to recall that the results of the following sections represent the performance of the best traders of a number of runs. This is an on-line learning model where the agents start trading in a real environment at day one with initially completely random strategies. Every new run is independent of previous ones and starts with a set of random strategies, with each agent initially having 10,000 dollars or pounds depending on whether the stock in question is a US or UK one. The random number seed is changed for each run; running the model with the same seed value would give exactly the same results. As described in [7], with probability 0.5 any bit-position in an initial rule's condition will be a #, so that the initial rule-set is reasonably general; 0s and 1s each occur with probability 0.25. However, random strategies are not uniformly bad. For a given run, the initial strategies that one agent gets can be genuinely better than what another agent gets.

Another novel property of this model is that in all results reported in this paper, the agents never see the stock price on any given day of the simulation more than once. The agent is trained according to how successful it will be (from day one) and later in the simulation, according to how successful it has been. Agents are not allowed to borrow money if they run out of it. The process is very different from other time series analysis models such as neural networks, where the data may be presented to the net for training literally thousands of times as part of the process of trying to minimise an error measure. Typically in a neural net system, when training is complete performance is then tested on unseen data. Such systems are usually very slow, need retraining at uncertain intervals and can be unsatisfactory because they offer no convenient explanation of why a given buy/sell/hold decision was made.

In the studies presented in this paper there is no separate testing phase that uses separate data. All the data are unseen, and the learning process is a continual one. The test of success is whether an agent continues to trade profitably, especially when compared with plausible non-evolutionary strategies. Remember, too, that the GA which is responsible for improving the rules runs in most cases reported in this paper only every 50-200 trading days. We do not want to try to examine whether it is possible for an artificial stock-market agent to be trained to learn good trading behaviour through repeated encounters with historical data. We are interested in exploring whether such agents can survive in the most human-like way we have found so far: where opportunities are given only once!.

In [7] we have already shown results where we trained for 9 years and tested for one further year during which the GA was turned off. In that particular example (Merck &Co.), the testing phase did produce better results than the *buy-and-hold* and the *bank* investments. But we believe that it is unrealistic to do such tests; in practice, traders do not use a fixed set of rules over an indefinitely long period but change them as market conditions alter.

As an example of this point, consider Luca Beltrametti's learning to forecast experiment [2] on the foreign exchange market with a LCS. In this experiment, the authors evaluated the performance of their adaptive agent against other decision rules which followed the prescription of various economic theories on exchange rate behaviour and the performance of forecasts given by Vector Auto Regression model (VAR) estimations of the exchange-rate's determinants. Although the out-of-sample forecasting ability of the adaptive agent under performed while in-sample forecasting outperformed the rival VAR model, it really doesn't matter. It is important to stress that the authors' purpose was to use the other methods as control devices to test the adaptive agent's goodness of fit by means of a formal statistical tool, i.e. whether the agent could learn to forecast the exchange rate under the conditions they specified in the experiment, not to compare if the adaptive agent was better or worse than the other models.

Our position is that the adaptive learning should never be frozen in non-stable environments such as real stock markets. Brian Arthur [1] in the Santa Fe Institute artificial stock market has also tested this, by injecting into his populations of strategies some that had been very good in the past. He observed that such transplanted strategies behaved badly in their new market environment; clearly they had been adapted to specific past conditions. As market behaviour remains unstable and never settles down, learning and forecasting should be continual activities. And because market conditions are ever-changing, our results do not show continuous improvements in performance throughout all time. They genuinely adapt.

3.1   Data

Although one single stock can capture some features of real markets, we feel that more investigation is needed across different stocks to analyse agent behaviour under a full range of market phenomena of interest such as abrupt changes in trading volume, bubbles, crashes, market psychology and moods. For this reason we present results of simulations of a selection of stocks representative of two potentially different market environments (the UK and the US), five of which trade in the London Stock Exchange and three in the New York Stock Exchange.

Table 1 describes general characteristics of the stocks analysed such as the company name, the industry sector they belong to and their index membership. Table 2 is a continuation that refers to their symbol and the actual dates used in the experiments we describe in this section. The length of the series is not the same in all stocks due to the fact that availability of both, prices and volumes is needed for the agents to process. There are two stocks with shorter series: Lloyds TSB Group (series of length 1,659) and WPP Group (length 1,752), the others are longer than 2,500 trading days. Unfortunately, Lloyds' price series after December 29th, 1995 was unavailable, as well as WPP's volume series up to June 30th, 1993. Note that one calendar year (365 days) corresponds roughly to only 253 financial or trading days.

Table 1. Profile of Stocks Analysed

COMPANY NAME	SECTOR	INDEX MEMBERSHIP
BP Amoco Plc.	Oil and Gas	FTSE 100
GKN Plc.	Automobiles	FTSE 100
Hanson Plc.	Construction	FTSE Mid 250
Lloyds TSB Group Plc.	Banking	FTSE 100
WPP Group Plc.	Media	FTSE 100
Microsoft Corp.	Tech., Software	Nasdaq 100, S&P 500, Dow Ind.
Cabletron Systems, Inc.	Tech., Comp. Networks	S&P 500
Forest Oil, Corp.	Oil and Gas	N/A

As we will see later in this section, these stocks include good performers that have generally grown over the period and other that have pretty steadily fallen. From now on, we will address them by their symbol as shown on table 2, and their properties and trends by day numbers rather than the actual dates when they occurred.

Table 2. Dates of Stocks Analysed Corresponding to Table 1

SYMBOL	FROM	TO	NO. OF DAYS
BP.L	06/19/89	06/07/00	2,780
GKN.L	06/19/89	06/07/00	2,780
HNS.L	06/19/89	06/07/00	2,780
LLOY.L	06/19/89	12/27/95	1,659
WPP.L	07/01/93	06/07/00	1,752
NASDAQNM: MSFT	13/03/86	25/08/00	3,654
NYSE: CS	31/05/89	28/04/00	2,757
NYSE: FST	26/03/90	13/03/00	2,513

3.2   Interest and Commission

To make the model as real as possible, we have introduced an annual fixed interest rate of 8% to all cash invested in the bank. This means that all the available cash the agents have is invested in the bank (with instant access) at this rate and it is compounded daily, meaning that at the end of each day the agents get their interest payment. Although it might seem a bit high in the year 2000, a decade ago interest rates were higher than at present times. We thought about making the interest variable rather than leaving it fixed for such a long period of time, but again, we faced limitations obtaining the data we needed. We would need, for example, quarterly or monthly interest rates for the whole past decade for the different countries these stocks trade in.

The commission we decided to charge is 0.1% of the total amount to trade. Commission costs are much lower than they used to be. Although it might seem low at first sight, we have found that this is a realistic figure. To make the point clear we will go through two examples. First if, let us say, on March 31st 2000 a trader decided to spend 75% of its cash available of MSFT shares (a bad decision, the price dropped from $06.25 to $0.875 in one day!), having only $6,000 of available cash, the commission charged at 0.1% would be $7.00. Nowadays most executions on the Internet charge less than $5.00 per transaction. These low fees normally include all types of orders – Market, Limit, and Stop – up to 5,000 shares traded online with no hidden costs. Total wealth and amount to trade vary from agent to agent. As a second example, imagine another agent has $,000,000 worth of MSFT shares and decides to sell 64% of them, then the commision it pays is ₤40, which is extremely high! We believe the commissions might average out, but another possibility is to charge a flat $5.00 (or £15.00 for UK stocks) per trade, no matter what size.

In the future we intend to experiment with models that use flat commissions and a lower bank interest rate. We do not expect dramatic differences with the results. Another factor is that we use the readily available **daily closing prices** rather than the actual bid and ask price (again these data was not obtainable), but the spread might be advantageous for our traders. For this reason we also intend to increase the commission to 2%a figure which should include more than the bid/ask difference (normally 1/16) plus commission. Note that using closing prices is less than ideal, since nobody can actually trade at those prices.

3.3   Description of the Layout of Results

Look at Fig. 2, which describes experiments with BP Amoco stock. The left-hand table shows the final wealth of various strategies: the *bank*, *buy-and-hold* and *trend-following* strategy; in this case the *trend-following* strategy is the most successful of these three, accumulating £74,943. The next table shows the wealth of the best-performing Tt1, Tt2 and Tt3 agents, for various values of how often the GA is run (every 50 days; every 75 days; ...; every 200 days). For each of these learning rates, 1001 runs were performed and the figure in the Tt1 column gives the final wealth of the most successful Tt1 agent in those 1001 runs. For example, when the GA is run every 50 trading days, the most successful Tt1 agent made £69,294, the most successful Tt2 agent made £80,122 and the most successful Tt3 agent made £65,843.

The graph associated with the table shows the growth in wealth of *bank*, *buy-and-hold*, and the best instance of each of the three *trader types* Tt1, Tt2 and Tt3 – taken from the best results with the GAs shown on the left-hand table. Due to space limitations daily wealth of the *trend-following* strategy is not graphed, but as explained before, the final wealth of this strategy is shown on the left-hand table.

The horizontal axis shows trading days, the vertical axis shows wealth – in pounds for UK stocks and in dollars for US stocks. All start with an initial 10,000 pounds or dollars. The smoothly rising line represents the wealth of the *bank* strategy. The lowest of the jagged lines is the wealth of the *buy-and-hold* strategy, and therefore reflects the stock price over time.

Over the last ten years the stock markets have generally shown an upward trend, so it makes sense to use the *buy-and-hold* strategy as a common baseline for assessment in judging how easy it is to produce a *trader type* that is at least reasonably effective at making money. The right-hand table shows the percentage of those 1001 runs in which each *trader type* was able to outperform the *buy-and-hold* strategy. For example, when the GA is run every 100 days, 32%f Tt1 strategies, 19%f Tt2 strategies and 18%f Tt3 strategies were able to beat *buy-and-hold* in terms of final wealth. These figures give at least some crude idea of how many times one might expect to have to run the LCS in order to arrive at an acceptable strategy by taking the best-performing *trader type*. And as the graph suggests, in general the *buy-and-hold* strategy is outclassed consistently from very early on; it is not the case that the *buy-and-hold* strategy leads for most of the time but fades near the end.

The graph conveys other interesting information too. For example, observe in this case that the price of BP Amoco stock showed a downward trend from around day 300 to around day 800. The *trader types* all managed to spot that it was best to keep their money in the bank during this period!

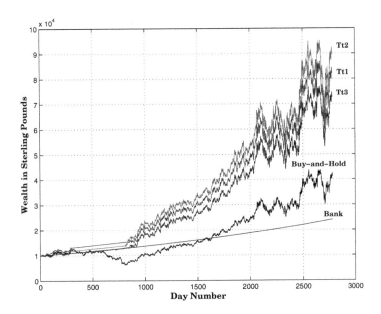

	GA	Tt1	Tt2	Tt3	Tt1	Tt2	Tt3
Bank	50	69,294	80,122	65,843	26%	18%	12%
24,107	75	80,166	79,876	68,464	32%	19%	18%
Buy-and-Hold	100	80,830	85,062	65,776	32%	19%	18%
41,248	125	81,964	83,640	64,689	32%	19%	17%
Trend-Following	150	75,942	86,959	66,430	32%	21%	20%
74,943	175	80,381	74,431	72,531	32%	20%	22%
	200	71,160	89,697	69,553	26%	21%	19%

Fig. 2. UK: BP Amoco Stock. See text for explanation

3.4   Some General Issues

It is noticeable that Tt2 sometimes outperforms the others by a large margin, for example in Fig. 2. Why is that? To understand, it is important to know what information the different *trader types* base their decisions on.

Trader type 1 uses price information: is today's price higher than yesterday's?, is it a new high?, is it a new low?, is it higher, by some small fixed percentage, than moving averages taken over periods ranging from 5 to 30 days? *Trader type* 2 pays attention to whether today's price is higher than yesterday's, and also some volume indicators such as whether today's volume is a new high or new low, or higher than yesterday's, or higher than the 20-day moving average. *Trader type* 3 pays attention to whether today's price and volume is higher than yesterday's, and also to how it compares to the bank and *buy-and-hold* strategies. It also knows what action it took yesterday, so it is crudely reflective.

Trader type 2 often benefits from knowing more about volume information than the others. Volume, when used in conjunction with other data, is a useful determinant in identifying whether a continuation of or a reversal in the prevailing trend is likely. Volume at low levels reflects uncertainty regarding the future direction of the market in question. If the volume is relatively high while the market is going up and remains relatively low during corrections, the inference is that the market is in a strong upward trend which should continue. In the other case, when the volume is high while the market is going down and relatively light during upward retracements, then the market is weak with a continuing downward trend more likely.

This does not necessarily mean that Tt2 is the best possible model for a *trader type*, of course. The whole question of what is a "good trader" is a complex one. In financial markets a good trader is not necessarily the person who makes the "right decision" most of the times. It could be someone who only makes three good decisions in a year, probably obtaining larger profits than another one who "got it right" most of the times, but with a smaller profit average. So as long as they keep earning a profit, they might stay in the market. But what about the others? Many others who report losses are also in the market. They are all survivors. Thus the market is composed of all sorts of traders (experienced and unexperienced, mathematical and gamblers, etc) each competing and hoping to get the most out of their investment at the expense of others. Some not only rely on their own tactics but might also copy what others, that they consider good ones, are doing. They imitate and possibly learn something by trial and error experimentation. In this pool of traders, some simply leave the system when they choose to do so, others are forced out (traders are kicked out of the market usually by punishment, negative criticisms, etc). Some can have a very short lifespan in the market place, others a long or even indefinite one. Our approach favours the "fund manager" model in which the aim is to learn to make a steady stream of reasonably good decisions, rather than (say) a single major killing followed by exit.

4   UK Stocks

4.1   Case 1: BP Amoco

This has been partly discussed in Sect. 3.3. Note again in Fig. 2 that Tt1 and Tt2 beat even the *trend-following* strategy, for most choices of GA-interval. It is also easy to find strategies that beat *buy-and-hold*, even though the stock has trended upward for most of the time. As mentioned earlier, the best strategies responded clearly and appropriately to the significant period when there was a pronounced slump in price.

4.2   Case 2: GKN

In the graph in Fig. 3, the *buy-and-hold* strategy is the lowest of the jagged lines. As the tables show, the *trend-following* strategy is hugely better than either *buy-and-hold* or *bank* strategies, because of the early gentle decline of prices and because the price fluctuated a lot towards the end of the period.

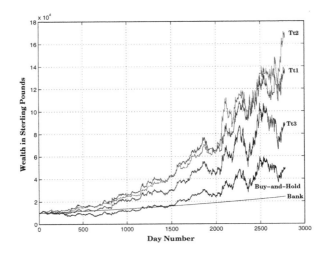

	GA	Tt1	Tt2	Tt3	Tt1	Tt2	Tt3
Bank	50	114,956	100,835	84,856	36%	26%	18%
24,107	75	91,232	106,680	81,436	38%	29%	19%
Buy-and-Hold	100	106,360	116,577	74,670	40%	28%	18%
49,072	125	108,628	105,056	83,179	35%	31%	18%
Trend-Following	150	98,655	112,793	88,491	32%	31%	19%
202,612	175	134,737	106,896	73,800	30%	29%	17%
	200	92,933	165,859	76,321	26%	30%	15%

Fig. 3. UK: GKN Stock. See text for explanation

The best *trader types* managed to avoid the early decline, and all managed to do very much better than *buy-and-hold* but not as well as *trend-following*. It was reasonably easy to generate strategies that beat *buy-and-hold* by a healthy margin.

In highly volatile stocks such as GKN, the *trend-following* strategy performs much better than the other methods because there are a large number of well-defined trends during the period analysed, specially from day 2,000 onwards. Figure 4 shows – in addition to the information plotted in Fig. 3 – the wealth of the *trend-following* strategy and it focuses only in the last part of the series, i.e. days 2,000 to 2,780. The arrow at around day 2,550 indicates a 100-day drop of the *trend-following*'s wealth: this strategy can have huge losses (far bigger than the losses of trader-types 1 &3 and   *buy-and-hold*) due to the highly risky operations of buying and selling so frequently. From the start of the arrow until the last day of the series, only Tt1 and Tt2 managed to make a profit.

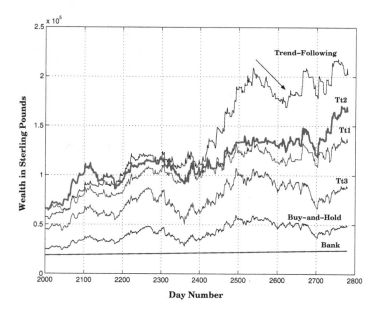

Fig. 4. UK: GKN Stock. Wealth (in Sterling Pounds) of *Bank* Investment, *Buy-and-Hold*, *Trend-Following* Strategy and *Trader-Types* 1,2 and 3 from day 2,000

During unstable periods such as this one, the traders usually manage to reduce their losses by keeping more money in the bank, by holding a small number of shares or by selling early in the downward trend. Figure 5 shows the shares owned by *buy-and-hold* (constant number of shares throughout), *trend-following* strategy (the lighter with more shares) and Tt2, which is the trader that can have a similar behaviour under highly volatile environments. To make the graph clear, it only covers the last 230 days of the series, i.e. from day 2,500 onwards. In this graph we show that Tt2's frequency of transactions is smaller than the *trend-following* strategy's and that it usually holds a smaller number of shares, thus minimising its losses when bad times arise.

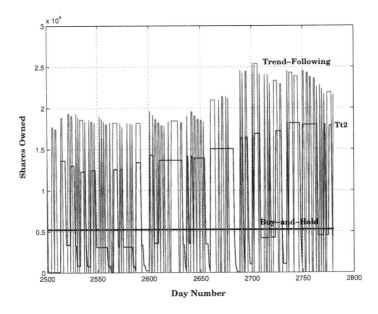

Fig. 5. UK: GKN Stock. Shares Owned by *Buy-and-Hold, Trend-Following* Strategy and *Trader-Type* 2 from day 2,500

4.3   Case 3: HNS

Figure 6 is interesting. Again, the *buy-and-hold* strategy is the poorly-performing one, the stock fluctuated a lot early on and then went into a pronounced decline before rallying and then fluctuating again. Tt3 did worse than the *bank* strategy for a while, but eventually learned to exploit the upswings to come out well. During the early decline, all the *trader types* rode out the slump by keeping money in the bank although Tt2 managed to creep ahead by successfully exploiting some of the upturns at that time. Overall the *trend-following* strategy did only slightly better than the *bank* strategy, and all the best *trader types* beat them both by a large margin. It was easy to generate strategies that beat both the *bank* and the *trend-following* strategies.

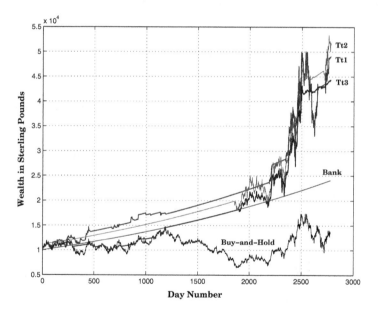

	GA	Tt1	Tt2	Tt3	Tt1	Tt2	Tt3
Bank	50	49,031	51,428	44,311	43%	79%	52%
24,107	75	38,321	48,026	35,044	43%	76%	54%
Buy-and-Hold	100	39,623	40,354	34,298	44%	77%	53%
13,437	125	33,996	39,046	32,981	47%	75%	51%
Trend-Following	150	33,194	41,593	30,185	49%	73%	51%
25,873	175	33,179	37,360	31,176	46%	75%	50%
	200	30,278	35,278	27,772	48%	72%	51%

Fig. 6. UK: HNS Stock. See text for explanation

4.4   Case 4: LLOY

Lloyds stock performed well over the six and a half year period, with a fairly steady upward trend punctuated by minor falls. In the graph in Fig. 7, there is only one long decline in prices from around day 1,200 to day 1,500. As a result, *buy-and-hold* soundly beat its non-evolved rivals, growing the initial £10,000 to £37,321. However, the best traders all did even better, with Tt2 being the best performer. It was, however, quite hard to generate *trader types* that beat *buy-and-hold*; only 4-8%of runs did so. A possible explanation for this is that Lloyd's prices change direction too often and too quickly (i.e. trends do not last more than a day or two), making it for the traders really expensive to respond to these changes by trading, so they tend to ignore small price movements and follow more or less what *buy-and-hold* suggests after day 400 approximately.

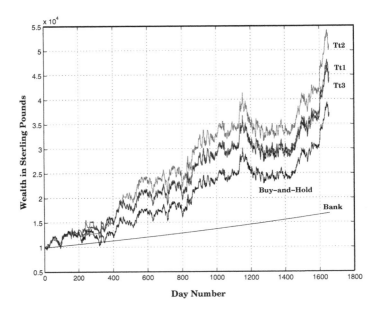

	GA	Tt1	Tt2	Tt3	Tt1	Tt2	Tt3
Bank	50	45,300	49,817	44,404	4%	5%	6%
16,906	75	41,453	44,724	43,961	4%	4%	8%
Buy-and-Hold	100	42,245	51,316	40,353	4%	5%	5%
37,321	125	40,651	45,664	43,082	4%	5%	6%
Trend-Following	150	40,407	43,170	44,375	4%	6%	7%
22,082	175	42,798	50,390	44,233	5%	4%	7%
	200	45,611	45,011	41,091	5%	6%	7%

Fig. 7. UK: LLOY Stock. See text for explanation

4.5   Case 5: WPP

As it can be seen in Fig. 8, this stock performed very well over the period, with a modest slump during a short interval around day 1,300. As with the previous cases, the buy-and-old strategy is the lowest jagged line. The best trader types learned to gradually pull ahead of *buy-and-hold*, but only Tt2 was able to do much better than the *trend-following* strategy. Tt2 was also the easiest type when it came to generating strategies that beat *buy-and-hold*.

Up to day 1,300 there was not much to be learned about this stock except that it is very stable. It steadily increases its value at a higher rate than the bank, so that all *trader types* prefer this option over the bank's investment over this period, but after it finishes, the price moves more often and we can see a quick response from the traders: it then becomes more profitable to trade the stock during the ups and downs. As a result they outperform *buy-and-hold*.

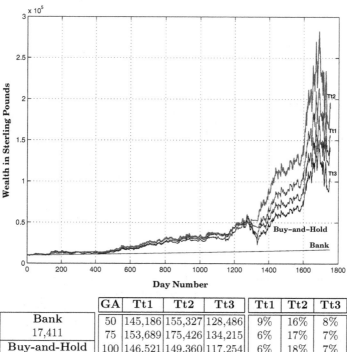

	GA	**Tt1**	**Tt2**	**Tt3**	**Tt1**	**Tt2**	**Tt3**
Bank	50	145,186	155,327	128,486	9%	16%	8%
17,411	75	153,689	175,426	134,215	6%	17%	7%
Buy-and-Hold	100	146,521	149,360	117,254	6%	18%	7%
100,465	125	130,382	146,653	127,413	7%	18%	8%
Trend-Following	150	143,507	188,925	134,263	5%	20%	7%
140,829	175	130,432	164,280	136,399	5%	20%	9%
	200	144,962	151,375	121,086	4%	20%	9%

Fig. 8. UK: WPP Stock. See text for explanation

5   US Stocks

5.1   Case 6: MSFT

Figure 9 corresponds to Microsoft's stock. This performed exceptionally well, so that the *buy-and-hold* strategy was excellent, far outperforming the *trend-following* strategy, which performs very poorly in this stock. As we can see from the table in the centre just below the graph, the best runs all happened with GA-period of 75.

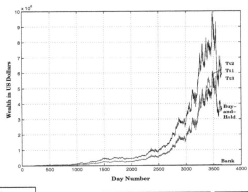

Bank	GA	Tt1	Tt2	Tt3	Tt1	Tt2	Tt3
31,791	75	6,229,070	6,285,237	5,878.406	4%	2%	8%
Buy-and-Hold	100	5,548,541	5,647,181	5,508,190	3%	2%	8%
3,629,278	125	5,509,811	5,878,918	5,171,595	3%	2%	6%
Trend-Following	150	4,733,077	7,615,733	4,598,360	3%	2%	7%
331,860							

Fig. 9. USA: Microsoft Stock. See text for explanation

As it is hard to recognise what is happening from this graph in such a large period, in Fig. 10 we zoomed the last 654 days of the series and added the *trend-following*'s wealth as well. All traders outperformed by far the *bank* investment, the *buy-and-hold* and the *trend-following* strategy. It is interesting to note how exactly they managed to do so: Tt1 was more or less holding a number of shares until around day 3,500; see Fig. 11, when on day 3,484, it abruptly sold all its 50,297 shares. This trader's profit from the last days comes from keeping its money in the bank (that is why its wealth steadily increases bank-like from this day on), it ends owning no shares at all.

Tt2's earned profit after the drop in prices comes from an interesting mix of buy/sell behaviour. It did not adopt any particular fashion, instead as you can see from Fig. 11, its shares oscillate somewhat during this unstable period, while before that time, it was steadily holding around 50,000 shares (all it could

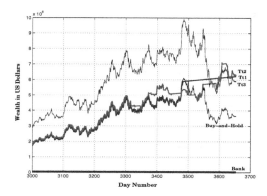

Fig. 10. USA: Microsoft Stock. Wealth of Bank, Buy_and_Hold, Trend_Strategy and Traders Tt1, Tt2 and Tt3 from day 3,000

afford). At the end it owns 88,994 shares. Note that with such transactions it earned almost 40,000 shares!

Tt3 almost precisely followed the *buy-and-hold* strategy until the end, when thanks to the generalised drop in technology stocks, lost about 40% of its wealth, still keeping at the end all its wealth in 83,234 shares.

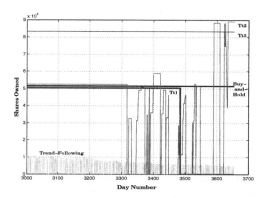

Fig. 11. USA: Microsoft Stock. Shares Owned by Buy_and_Hold, Trend_Strategy and Traders Tt1, Tt2 and Tt3 from day 3,000

5.2   Case 7: CS

Figure 12 shows Cabletron Systems, a very volatile stock that performed somewhat similar to GKN, where the *trend-following* strategy was unbeatable. However, Tt2 came close to equalling the trend strategy. The table below the figure
shows it was quite easy to generate strategies that beat the *buy-and-hold* strategy; in particular, Tt2 found it the easiest, as it beat it almost half of the time.

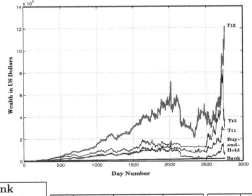

Bank							
23,933	**GA**	**Tt1**	**Tt2**	**Tt3**	**Tt1**	**Tt2**	**Tt3**
Buy-and-Hold	75	189,432	306,233	365,622	30%	45%	25%
69,772	100	175,472	1'175,583	194,739	30%	45%	26%
Trend-Following	125	199,400	399,772	260,258	28%	47%	23%
1,312,833							

Fig. 12. USA: Cabletron Systems Stock. See text for explanation

5.3   Case 8: FST

Figure 13 shows Forest Oil which, like many oil companies in the last decade, lost
value reasonably steadily. The *bank* strategy therefore beat *buy-and-hold* easily,
but all three *trader types* beat the *bank* spectacularly and Tt1 and Tt3 did very
well to exploit the brief upswing around day 2,250.

Trend-following strategy was the worst performer of all. As we have observed
in the previous cases, it seems that this strategy is particularly good for highly
volatile stocks. This stock shows the opposite. Low volatility and lower prices
persist throughout. So how can the agents make a profit under these conditions?
They have clearly learned to trade more during periods of high movement, keeping their money in the bank only when price constantly drops and shows no
signs of improvement. It was extremely easy to beat the *buy-and-hold* strategy.
In fact, in all cases it has been beaten by far margins.

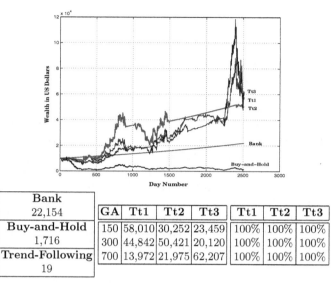

Bank							
22,154	**GA**	**Tt1**	**Tt2**	**Tt3**	**Tt1**	**Tt2**	**Tt3**
Buy-and-Hold	150	58,010	30,252	23,459	100%	100%	100%
1,716	300	44,842	50,421	20,120	100%	100%	100%
Trend-Following	700	13,972	21,975	62,207	100%	100%	100%
19							

Fig. 13. USA: Forest Oil Stock. See text for explanation

6   Conclusions and Future Work

We have found that it certainly seems more defensible to try to model the behaviour of a group of traders than to model the behaviour of a single trader, or to
try to predict the future of the time series that represents a stock's price, whether
by local linear methods, by neural net methods or by other nonlinear techniques.
Time series prediction methods generally model outcomes rather than causes,
and their predictions can be invalidated if the underlying causes change. Modelling genuinely different *trader types* is at least an attempt to model certain of
the causes of prices.

So what purpose could this serve? Such models could be used to actually
trade, or to assist human traders by making suggestions, or even as training
aids against which novice traders could compete. We plan to do further research
and development on the idea, both to gather more evidence to support it and to
explore ideas such as creating a portfolio management system involving a greater
number of *trader types*, each group being good at dealing in one stock, together
with an arbitrator system to apportion resources dynamically between them.

Before continuing to develop this section, we would like to stress some interesting properties one can learn and investigate further from a model of this
type:

- In order for the artificial agent to survive, it must adapt to market dynamics
  which are not affected directly or indirectly by the agent's actions, but rather
  by real traders and people's expectations in the stock market. In this sense

the adaptive agent can be viewed as trying to **mimic real behaviours** of which our understanding at present times is very limited. The causes of such complex behaviours are unknown to us and any attempts towards increasing our knowledge in this area are greatly valued.

- Also at the agent level, we showed in this paper that it is possible to develop strategies for trading successfully with highly summarised and easy to process market information. It might be possible to transfer experience across different stocks in search for some universal strategies as well as testing specific rules that apply to a stock across a finite length of time

- We are currently working on issues concerning the learning procedure and rule complexity. It appears that according to the agent's profitability, it might be better to have a good mix of rules, including specific ones and of higher complexity (with very few wild-card symbols). More analysis needs to be done regarding default hierarchy formation and whether we wish to obtain it at all times during the simulation. In order to control hierarchy formation in our model, we have implemented in the reinforcement procedure a reward scheme according to specificity

- The model allows us to learn about three important aspects: (i) market data, what items of information are more important than others or whether they are important at all; (ii) the evolutionary process of adaptive agents of these types; and finally (iii) about the environmental reward, whether the reward function is affecting profitability in a positive way or not. A better understanding of these aspects can guide us in the design of better trader models. For example, there is considerable scope both for experimenting with the mixture of rule conditions and for seeing whether some form of hill-climbing might manage to improve the rules even further.

- Technical trading is a valid outcome in this model, but it appears to be more relevant at some times than at others. The technical type of trader does not always outperform other non-technical traders. There is the possibility of creating a "super trader" which gets its investment signals from whichever trader is performing better than the rest. In this way the super trader actions can be guided by traders who are active and are performing really well. When the performance of the best trader starts to decrease, the super trader can adapt its actions by doing what a new best performer is doing.

Finally, it is important to stress that our approach is not capable of evolving agents that can spot the right moment to invest heavily in order to make a quick "killing" and then exit. Our agents have a trading opportunity only once per day, rather than trading in some event-driven way. The approach as shown in this paper is therefore more suited to tasks such as portfolio management than the pursuit of quick profits. The use of intra-daily data could be alternative method for short-time investments. However, it is important to mention that in no cases did the agents lost all their initial wealth in any of the runs presented in this paper. The great majority of cases show a clear return, much higher than the *bank's* investment.

References

1. W. Brian Arthur. On lerning and adaptation in the economy. Working paper 92-07-038, Santa Fe Institute, 1992.
2. Luca Beltrametti, Riccardo Fiorentini, Luigi Marengo, and Roberto Tamborini. A learning-to-forecast experiment on the foreign exchange market with a classifier system. *Journal of Economic Dynamics and Control*, 21(8-9):1543–1575, 1997.
3. David E. Goldberg. *Genetic Algorithms in Search, Optimization and Machine Learning.* Addison-Wesley, Reading, MA., 1989.
4. John H. Holland, Lashon B. Booker, Marco Colombetti, Marco Dorigo, David E. Goldberg, Stephanie Forrest, Rick L. Riolo, Robert E. Smith, Pier Luca Lanzi, Wolfgang Stolzmann, and Stewart W. Wilson. What is a Learning Classifier System? In Lanzi et al. [5], pages 3–32.
5. Pier Luca Lanzi, Wolfgang Stolzmann, and Stewart W. Wilson, editors. *Learning Classifier Systems: From Foundations to Applications*, volume 1813 of *LNAI*. Springer-Verlag, Berlin, 2000.
6. Sonia Schulenburg and Peter Ross. An evolutionary approach to modelling the behaviours of financial traders. In *Genetic and Evolutionary Computation Conference Late Braking Papers*, pages 245–253, Orlando, Florida, 1999.
7. Sonia Schulenburg and Peter Ross. An Adaptive Agent Based Economic Model. In Lanzi et al. [5], pages 265–284.

Using Classifier Systems as Adaptive Expert Systems for Control

Olivier Sigaud[1] and Pierre Gérard[1,2]

[1] Dassault Aviation, DGT/DPR/ESA
78, Quai Marcel Dassault, 92552 St-Cloud Cedex
[2] AnimatLab-LIP6, 8, rue du capitaine Scott, 75015 PARIS
`olivier.sigaud@dassault-aviation.fr`, `pierre.gerard@lip6.fr`

Abstract. In complex simulations involving several interacting agents, the behavior of the overall program is difficult to predict and control. As a consequence, the designers have to adopt a trial-and-error strategy. In this paper we want to show that helping experts to design simulation automata as classifier systems (CSs) by hand and using a semi-automated improvement functionality can be a very efficient engineering approach. Through the example of a simple multiagent simulation, we show how simulation automata can be implemented into the CS formalism. Then we explain how the obtained CS can be improved either by hand or thanks to adaptive algorithms. We first show how giving indications on the non-Markov character of the problems faced by the classifiers can help the experts to improve the controllers and we explain why adding modularity in the CS formalism is important. Then we show how the adaptive algorithms inherent to Learning Classifier Systems (LCSs)[1] can be used in such a context, we discuss our methodology and we present an experimental study of the efficiency of this approach. Finally, we point to difficulties raised by our perspective, we present directions for future research and conclude.

1 Introduction

In the domain of military operations, the simulations of fights between several aircrafts, whether at a tactical or a strategic scale, are becoming increasingly complex. The behaviors are more and more intertwined, there are more and more relationships between the actors in the air battle field, and the combinatorial of possible situations makes the evolution more and more difficult to foresee. In these domains, industrial and military studies make an intensive use of simulations. The core of these simulations are *simulation automata*[2], *i.e.* the parts of the programs which explicitly control the behavior of the agents. In

---

[1] In order to make clear that we sometimes use the Classifier Systems formalism without applying learning algorithms, we will distinguish Classifier Systems (CS) as a formalism and Learning Classifier Systems (LCS) throughout this paper.

[2] We call them automata whether these programs are explicitly implemented as finite state machines or not.

P.L. Lanzi, W. Stolzmann, and S.W. Wilson (Eds.): IWLCS 2000, LNAI 1996, pp. 138–157, 2001.

such a context, designing an automaton for a single agent in a simulator so that it manifests an appropriate behavior in any situation is becoming increasingly complex, too. As a consequence, the designers of automata which control the aircrafts tend to adopt a trial-and-error strategy and spend more and more time on this activity.

As a researcher in the industry of defense, our mission consists in helping these experts to automate this trial-and-error process by providing to them with the best of what adaptive techniques can do. Our challenge is to put into the hands of the experts a tool favoring the emergence of better solutions and minimizing the amount of work necessary to reconsider their design. Thus, in contrast with most researchers in adaptive behavior who tackle small scale problems or even toy-problems from scratch, we have to tackle very large scale problems where previously hand-crafted solutions exist.

There are many techniques and formalisms into which adaptive simulation automata can be designed. In our context, two key requirements for these techniques are that, as a starting point, the expert knowledge can be easily expressed in the formalism and that the result of the adaptation process is easily understandable by the experts. This is not the case, for instance, with recurrent neural networks [Beer and Gallagher, 1991], despite their efficiency. We have chosen the CS formalism because it meets these requirements and combines the adaptive power of both genetic algorithms [Goldberg, 1989] and reinforcement learning [Sutton and Barto, 1998].

In this paper we want to show that helping experts to design simulation automata as CSs by hand and using a semi-automated improvement functionality can be a very efficient engineering approach. We will present and discuss our methodology through an example. Since confidentiality concerns prevents us from publishing on the domain of military simulations, we have chosen to implement a simpler multiagent simulation for illustration purposes.

The rest of the paper is organized as follows.

In Sect. 2, we present our illustrative simulation, and we show how we build a new simulation automaton. In Sect. 3, we show how one can rephrase an existing simulation automaton written as a classical program into the CS formalism. Then we give in Sect. 4 some methodological hints on how to improve these simulation automata by hand. In particular, we explain how giving indications on the non-Markov character of the problems faced by the classifiers can help the experts to improve the controllers. In Sect. 4.4, we introduce the need for modularity and present how we can split a CS into modules.

In Sect. 5, we turn towards the use of adaptive algorithms to improve these automata. We breifly present the LCS framework in general and the particular algorithm which we have developed. In Sect. 6, we show through an empirical study how efficient these adaptive algorithms can be to improve the performance of the automata. We discuss the benefits of our methodology in Sect. 7.

In Sect. 8, at last, we present the problems which arise when adaptation results in the necessity of a global reorganization rather than in minor changes and discuss some areas which need further improvements. Finally, we conclude in Sect. 9.

2   An Illustrative Experiment

In order to present in details some methodological aspects of our work, we will first present a simulator developed for illustration purposes.

We are inspired by the Robot Sheepdog Project from [Vaughan et al., 1998], involving a robot driving a flock of ducks towards a target position. The algorithm controlling the robot was first tested in simulation and then implemented on a real robot driving a real flock of ducks. As a testbed, we will use a simulated extension of the task to the case where several agents share the goal mentioned above. Since it is neither oversimplified nor too complex, we believe that this experiment is a good case-study to meet and tackle the difficulties arising when one tries to combine adaptive capabilities and multiagent coordination schemes, which corresponds to our industrial problem.

2.1   Description of the Problem

Our simulated environment is shown in Fig. 1. It includes a circular arena, a flock of ducks and some *sheepdog agents* who must drive the flock towards a target area. We tested all controllers in simulations involving three sheepdog agents and six ducks. The ducks and the sheepdog agents have the same maximum velocity. The goal is achieved as soon as all the ducks are inside the target area.

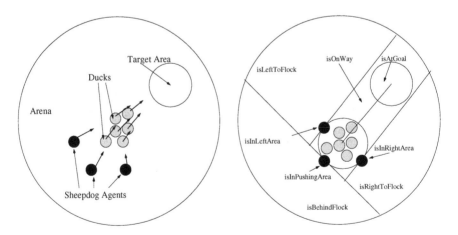

Fig. 1. The arena, ducks and sheepdogs   **Fig. 2.** Description of the situation

The behavior of the ducks results from a combination of three tendencies. They tend:

- to keep away from the walls of the arena[3];

- to join their mates when they see them, *i.e.* when they are within their visual range;

- to flee from the sheepdog agents which are within their visual range.

Once the behavior of the ducks is implemented, we must design the controllers of the sheepdog agents so that they drive the flock towards the target area. A first step of this design process consists in finding which features of the simulated environment are relevant to achieve the goal of the sheepdog agents. This is what we present in the next section.

2.2 Description of the Pre-conceived Strategy

When one programs the sheepdog agents as simply being attracted by the center of the flock, it appears that, when a sheepdog agent is close to the flock and follows it, the flock tends to scatter because each duck goes away from the sheepdog along a radial straight line.

In order to solve this scattering problem, the strategy we adopted was to design the behavior of the agents so that at least one agent should push the flock towards the target area from behind, while at least one other agent should follow the flock on its left hand side and another one on its right hand side so that the flock would not scatter while being pushed.

As a result of this design, the description of the situation given to the agents consists in a set of tests on their position, as shown in Fig. 2. This gives us a first set of conditions:

- isAtGoal
- isOnWay
- isLeftToFlock
- isRightToFlock
- isInLeftArea
- isInRightArea
- isBehindFlock
- isInPushingArea

The important point is that we defined pushing and guiding areas relative to current position of the flock in order to implement the pushing and guiding behaviors.

In order to coordinate the actions of the agents, we also added the following tests on the situation of other agents:

- nobodyBehindFlock
- nobodyPushing
- nobodyInLeftArea
- nobodyInRightArea
- nobodyLeftToFlock
- nobodyRightToFlock
- nobodyOnWay
- isFlockFormed

All the behaviors of the sheepdog agents consist in going towards a certain point. In general, when the flock is formed, the sheepdog agents react to the center of the flock. But, when the flock is scattered, they can also react to the duck which is closest to them or the one which is the further from the center of

---

[3] Therefore, if they are left on their own, they tend to go to the center of the arena.

the flock. The name of each behavior can be interpreted straight-forwardly. In the case of the "*driveXtoY*" behaviors, it consists in going behind X with respect to Y so as to push X towards Y. The overall behavior set is the following:

- doNothing
- goToFlockCenter
- goBehindFlock
- goToLeftArea
- goToRightOfFlock
- driveOutmostDuckToFlock
- driveClosestDuckToGoal
- goToOutmostDuck

- goToGoalCenter
- followFlockToGoal
- goToPushingPoint
- goToRightArea
- goToLeftOfFlock
- driveClosestDuckToFlock
- goToClosestDuck
- goAwayFromFlock

The controllers of our sheepdog agents involve 16 conditions and 16 basic behaviors. Designing the controller involving these sensori-motor capabilities consists in finding a good mapping between the conditions and the behaviors.

3   Rephrasing an Existing Program in the CS Formalism

As mentioned above, we want to use a formalism into which we can put some expert control knowledge. But we also want to use adaptive techniques. In this context, the CS formalism [Holland, 1975] appears as a natural candidate.

Since the work of [Wilson, 1994], a classical CS can be seen as composed of a population of rules, or *classifiers*, containing observations, consisting in a set of conditions, and actions:

$$[Condition] \rightarrow [Action](Strength)$$

The different parts of the classifier are strings of symbols in $\{0, 1, \#\}$, where $\#$, the "*don't care symbol*", means "either 0 or 1". This formalism can be extended from boolean numbers to integers without difficulty. The $[Condition]$ parts of the classifier are compared with an *input message* assigning its truth value to each condition at a given time step of the simulation. If the input message matches the $[Condition]$ part of one particular classifier, it can fire the corresponding action.

The complex simulation automata implemented by experts in conventional programs can be formalized very straight-forwardly into the CS formalism. A programmer who designs a simulation automaton must provide with two things:
- methods instantiating *conditions* in which the behaviors can be fired;
- methods (or functions, in the case of functional programming) implementing *basic behaviors* of the automaton or combinations of basic behaviors into more complex ones, and computing *parameters* to these behaviors (for instance, the relative position of the location where one agent must go).

In all the industrial simulators which we have examined, the conditions are expressed in terms of parameters describing the situation of the agent, either intrinsic to their own state or relative to relevant objects in the simulation.

It is easy to rephrase such a sequence of tests into a set of classifiers. The output of each *condition method* makes an entry in the input message, and one different action message must be mapped to each possible behavior, taking into account the fact that a method implementing a parameterized behavior makes as many behaviors as there are possible values for the parameters. This is what we have described in Sect. 2.2 in the case of our ducks experiments.

Adding new conditions and parameters generally consists in considering new relevant objects, which may eventually be virtual (for instance, a position behind another object). As it will be emphasized later, this process of adding new conditions cannot be reduced to merely considering a logical combination of other available conditions.

Then the programmer must design a higher level function or method combining the conditions, the behaviors and their parameters. This function can take the form of a long sequence of successive tests stating under which conditions which behavior can be fired. Building the automaton in the CS formalism merely consists in designing as many classifiers as necessary to tell under which conditions each behavior should be fired. The CS in charge of controlling our sheepdog agents is shown on Table 1.

4   Improving the CS Automaton by Hand

4.1   Reasons for Not Using Fully Automatized Learning Algorithms

Since CSs are well known to be a kind of adaptive tool, why should we not apply their learning algorithms as such to the classifiers written by experts ? There are three main reasons.

The reinforcement signal may not be available. To apply learning algorithms to CSs, one must provide to the automaton with some reinforcement signals. In particular application domains, some reinforcement signals may be obvious: if our agents are aircrafts, every behavior which leads to their destruction must be avoided, so it must be punished. Depending on the purpose of the simulation, there may also be a goal, and agents could be rewarded when they reach it.

But, though a simulation driven only by these efficiency criteria could reveal interesting solutions, it is also necessary to take into account the necessity to design realistic behaviors with respect to behaviors found in real-world situations. For instance, if we want to test the potentialities of one aircraft against standard opponents, it is important that the simulated opponents act in a way as similar as possible to what a real opponent would do.

Eliciting what makes a behavior realistic is well known to be very hard. This is generally achieved through programming a first version of the automaton, observing the resulting behavior, then adding constraints and re-iterating until satisfaction. In this process, the control of the expert is necessary to check whether a proposed behavior matches the realism requirements or not. Hence this cannot be completely automated.

Table 1. A hand-crafted controller

isBehindFlock	isInPushingArea	isLeftToFlock	isRightToFlock	isInLeftArea	isInRightArea	isOnWay	nobodyBehindFlock	nobodyPushing	nobodyLeftToFlock	nobodyRightToFlock	nobodyOnWay	isFlockFormed	Action
#	1	#	#	#	#	#	#	#	#	#	1	1	goToGoalCenter
#	1	#	#	#	#	#	#	#	#	#	1	1	goToFlockCenter
1	#	#	#	#	#	#	#	1	#	#	#	#	goToPushingPoint
#	#	1	#	#	#	#	1	#	#	#	#	#	goBehindFlock
#	#	1	#	#	#	#	1	#	#	#	#	#	goBehindFlock
#	#	#	1	#	#	#	1	#	#	#	#	#	goBehindFlock
#	#	#	1	#	#	#	1	#	#	#	#	#	goBehindFlock
#	#	1	#	1	#	#	0	0	#	#	1	1	followFlockToGoal
#	#	1	#	1	#	#	0	0	#	#	1	1	followFlockToGoal
#	#	1	#	0	#	#	#	#	#	#	1	1	goToLeftPushingPoint
#	#	1	#	0	#	#	#	#	#	#	1	1	goToRightPushingPoint
#	#	#	#	#	#	1	#	#	#	1	#	#	goToRightPushingPoint
#	#	#	#	#	#	1	0	#	0	#	#	#	goToRightPushingPoint
#	#	#	#	#	#	1	#	#	1	#	#	#	goToLeftofFlock
#	#	#	#	#	#	1	0	#	0	#	#	#	goToLeftofFlock
#	#	#	#	#	#	1	#	#	1	#	#	#	goToLeftPushingPoint
#	#	#	#	#	#	1	0	#	#	0	#	#	goToLeftPushingPoint
#	#	#	#	#	#	1	#	#	1	#	#	#	goToRightofFlock
#	#	#	#	#	#	1	0	#	#	0	#	#	goToRightofFlock
#	#	#	#	#	#	#	#	#	#	#	#	0	driveClosestDuckToFlock
#	#	#	#	#	#	#	#	#	#	#	#	0	goToOutmostDuck
#	#	#	#	#	#	#	#	#	#	#	#	0	goToClosestDuck
#	#	#	#	#	#	#	#	#	#	#	#	0	driveOutmostDuckToFlock
#	#	#	#	#	#	#	#	#	#	#	#	0	goAwayFromFlock

The evolved CSs need validation. One strong reason for not using a fully-automated LCS in operational context is that the experts want to keep control of what the system is doing. It may be important that they can formally approve or reject the solution built by the system. Particularly, in the military domain, people are very reluctant to let the system take unforeseen decisions (and we won't blame them for that, will we?).

There are two complementary strategies to tackle this concern. The first one consists in giving to the experts a control on the evolution of the classifiers. The second one consists in applying adaptive algorithms off-line and validating the obtained controllers before using them in operational situations.

Experts learn from improving the system. Another strong argument for letting the experts monitor the adaptation of their classifiers is that they may also learn a lot from the evolution of the classifiers and of the behavior of the simulation. The LCS may propose new solutions where the automaton needs improvement, and thus reveals weaknesses or misconceptions. This is perhaps the main justification for using adaptive programs in that context nowadays. The more the experts are involved in the adaptation process, the more they learn about the dynamics of the system.

Furthermore, observing the external behavior of the system can reveal some solutions which are both unforeseen by the expert and more efficient than the one they have designed. We describe such a case in an experimental framework in [Sigaud and Gérard, 2000]. In these favorable cases of emergence, it is important that the experts have a perfect knowledge of the underlying automaton, so that they can interpret what is happening.

4.2   Adjusting the CS Automaton

As explained in Sect. 3, once rephrased into the CS formalism, the classifiers controlling the behavior of the automaton take the form of a module whose inputs are conditions on the environment and whose outputs are the basic behaviors of the automaton. This module contains a list of classifiers which appears as a table. Most of the time, only a few conditions are relevant for firing one particular basic behavior, so there are many more don't care symbols ("#") than 0s and 1s in the table.

In Table 1, we present the controller that we designed in order to implement the solution of our flock control simulator described in Sect. 2.2. It can be seen that we only use 13 of the 16 available inputs.

There are two ways of improving a simulation automaton. The first one is to optimize the set of classifiers. As we will present in Sect. 5, this is what fully automated LCS are good at. Indeed, once the CS description is settled, the only thing learning algorithms may do is to optimize the mapping between conditions and actions with respect to the fitness criteria. But the way experts improve their automata cannot be reduced to this optimizing process. From our experience, it is clear that the key difficulty for adjusting efficient simulation automata consists more in finding good inputs and basic behaviors than in optimizing the mapping between them.

Thus it seems necessary to help the experts to find where new conditions and actions should be added before trying to optimize the mapping between them. We address this point in the next section.

4.3   Non-Markov Indicators

In the *Markov Decision Process* (MDP) framework, an agent moves from *state* to *state* thanks to *actions*, and the distribution of probability of reaching the next state only depends on the state of the agent and on its action. When this condition, called the *Markov hypothesis*, is not verified, there is a *hidden state*, the agent must solve a *non-Markov* problem.

Trying to tackle non-Markov problems is hard. The algorithms which are intended to solve the hidden state planning problem from the formal framework – see [Kaelbing et al., 1998] for a very clear presentation – face a problem of combinatorial explosion and are restricted to solving very small-size *non-Markov* problems.

Alternatively, some people who work in reinforcement learning – for instance, [Whitehead and Lin, 1995,McCallum, 1996,Donnart, 1998,Lanzi, 1998] – try to adapt their algorithms to the non-Markov case, since it is well-known that the proof of convergence underlying the reinforcement learning algorithms are restricted to the Markov case [Lanzi, 2000].

In the case of multiagent simulations, designing the input and output of the agents so that the problem they solve is Markov is very hard, since agents cannot have a perfect knowledge of every relevant feature of all other agents and of the behavior of these agents. Hence we are doomed to solving non-Markov problems.

Some researchers [McCallum, 1993,Witkowski, 1997,Dorigo, 1994] have proposed algorithms which pick the relevant inputs from a set given beforehand. In these approaches, adding a new input strongly relies on the non-Markov character of the problem: if the system receives different rewards for the same action in what it considers as the same situation, this means that in fact the situation is not the same, then the problem is non-Markov and one input must be added in order to distinguish better. Thus, checking whether a problem is Markov might be a key factor in the improvement process.

If the problem solved by an agent is non-Markov, then there must be at least one module of the agent which solves a non-Markov problem. In such a module, there must be at least one classifier facing a hidden state. The fewer hidden states there are in the problem which an agent must solve, the easier it is to find a good policy, and the more efficient the agent will be. Furthermore, improving it with a learning algorithm will be easier.

This has lead us to the intuition that giving to the experts indications that some elements in their solution are facing a non-Markov problem would be very informative to them. And it is!

Classifiers facing a hidden state can be identified by recording, for each classifier and each state into which it has been fired, a list of all the subsequent states. If there are several subsequent states for the same initial state, the problem is non-Markov. We can define the *non-Markov rate* NMR of the classifiers as the number of subsequent states divided by the number of initial states into which it has been fired.

$$NMR = \frac{|non\text{-}Markov\ cases|}{|cases\ when\ fired|}$$

Modifying by hand the classifiers which have the highest non-Markov rate has proven to result in very efficient improvements of the automata. As long as the classifier contains some "#" in its [*Condition*] part, it can be further specialized. Interestingly, adding inputs to classifiers is what most fully automated LCS do when they rely on specialization mechanisms, but they do so by picking a new condition in a set of inputs already available. But when the [*Condition*] part is completely specialized, the only possible improvement consists in adding new inputs to the global automaton. The easiest solution, here, rather than trying to learn to solve the non-Markov problem as such, is that the expert adds new inputs when necessary.

4.4   Modular Classifier Systems

From Table 1, it can be seen that the representation using a basic controller could be more compact: there are a lot of "#", which means that each expert classifier uses very few of the available inputs. As a result, the controller is difficult to design, since any change in the input set involves reconsidering all the lines in the table. As it will appear in Sect. 6, the controller could also be more efficient.

Furthermore, the adaptive algorithms of the LCS are slow to converge on such a representation, since the search space is very large. Here we have only used 13 inputs, but simulation automata designed for industrial purpose can be huge. In the case of simulations of military operations, some automata designed by experts to control a single agent involve around 200 inputs.

Representing such automata as tables with 200 columns would make them unreadable for experts. Hence, it seems necessary to split the automata into smaller modules, building *modular classifier systems* (MCS).

One good way of splitting a CS devoted to fulfilling a behavior into modules is to identify several lower level behaviors whose conjunction acheives the global behavior. The lower level behaviors can in turn be split into even lower level behaviors, or they can be represented directly as CSs. This gives rise to a hier-archical decomposition of the global behavior. Then, if they act on independent actuators, some of the basic level behaviors could be run independently. If this is not the case, one must find a way to synchronize them.

Among many architectures which may result from these considerations, we chose to develop a simple one where a high level CS, or *decision CS*, is de-voted to monitoring the execution of several basic behavior CSs, choosing one among them at each time step. The decision CS shares their inputs with the behavior CSs, but it also needs an information on previous decisions. Its out-put tells which basic behavior must be fired at a given time step. Interestingly, our architecture is very similar to those of [Wiering and Schmidhüber, 1997] and [Sun and Sessions, 2000], how both presented learning algorithms devoted to applying adaptive algorithms to them.

4.5   Modularity in Our Experimental Set-Up

The notion of role appears naturally in the strategy we presented in Sect. 2.2. In our solution, at least one agent must push the flock from behind (playing a PUSHER role) and at least one agent must guide the flock on its left hand side and another one on its right hand side (playing LEFTGUIDE and RIGHTGUIDE roles respectively). Therefore, we tried to modify the controller presented in Table 1 so as to make an explicit use of roles. Our new architecture contains two kinds of components:

• The *role CS* is a CS stating under which conditions on the situation a agent changes its role into another role. If no observation matches, the role remains the same. The roles are initialized so that each agent chooses between FUTUREPUSHER, FUTURELEFTGUIDE and FUTURERIGHTGUIDE randomly, but in such a way that each role is assigned to at least one agent. Our *role CS* is shown in Table 2.

• The *behavior CSs* are CSs which fire actions of the agent according to conditions on the situation. There is one CS for each role. Hence, there is only one *behavior CS* active at a time, the one which corresponds to the role played by the agent.

In that particular case, each lower level module is seen as devoted to achieve one particular basic behavior, and the higher level module is seen as deciding which basic behavior should be fired according to the role of the agent. The role itself depends on the situation of the agent.

Table 2. The role table (F. stands for Future)

isInPushingArea	isInLeftArea	isInRightArea	isFlockFormed	Former Role	New Role
1	#	#	1	F.Pusher	Pusher
#	1	#	1	F.LeftGuide	LeftGuide
#	#	1	1	F.RightGuide	RightGuide
1	#	#	0	F.Pusher	F.Pusher
#	1	#	0	F.LeftGuide	F.LeftGuide
#	#	1	0	F.RightGuide	F.RightGuide
1	#	#	0	Pusher	F.Pusher
#	1	#	0	LeftGuide	F.LeftGuide
#	#	1	0	RightGuide	F.RightGuide
0	#	#	#	Pusher	F.Pusher
#	0	#	#	LeftGuide	F.LeftGuide
#	#	0	#	RightGuide	F.RightGuide

We have six behaviors, each one corresponding to the fulfillment of one particular role, *i.e.* FUTUREPUSHERBEHAVIOR, PUSHERBEHAVIOR, FUTURELEFT-GUIDEBEHAVIOR, LEFTGUIDEBEHAVIOR, FUTURERIGHTGUIDEBEHAVIOR and RIGHTGUIDEBEHAVIOR.

As an example, the initial PUSHERBEHAVIOR CS is shown in Table 3. The complete set of behavior tables can be found in [Sigaud and Gérard, 2000].

Table 3. The PUSHERBEHAVIOR table

isInPushingArea	isFlockFormed	isBehindFlock	Action
0	1	#	goToPushingPoint
1	1	#	goAwayFromFlock
#	0	0	goBehindFlock
#	0	1	driveClosestDuckToFlock

5   Applying Adaptive Algorithms

Up to that point, we have shown how to rephrase an expertise into the CS formalism. This formalism is convenient for improving the automata since adjusting by hand the global behavior of one automaton merely consists in changing some values into others in the classifiers. Using CSs in such a way that the knowledge of an expert is coded into a set of classifiers would make the reader feel that we have re-invented a sort of expert system devoted to control. But a CS is more than an expert system. Since adaptive algorithms can sometimes be applied to it, our framework is rather what we call an *Adaptive Expert System*.

5.1   Learning Classifier Systems

Up to that point, we have presented CSs as a formalism to code an hand-crafted automaton. Rather than being done by hand, the adjustment process can be more or less automated, using LCS algorithms. The first LCSs were designed by [Holland, 1975]. In these initial versions, the strength of classifiers was modified by the *Bucket Brigade* algorithm according to the estimated reward received by the agent for firing the classifier. The population of classifiers was evolved thanks to a *genetic algorithm* (GA) – see [Goldberg, 1989] – using the strength of the classifiers as a fitness measure. When several classifiers could be fired in the same state, the strength was also used to select the one which would be fired.

A major improvement of the LCS framework was acheived by [Wilson, 1995] in designing XCS, replacing a *strength-based* LCS by an *accuracy-based* one.

Recently, a new way of using the LCS framework has received a growing interest [Stolzmann, 1998]. Based on ideas of [Riolo, 1990], it consists in adding in the classifiers an [*Effect*] part which allows the system to use the classifiers for anticipating rather than merely reacting to the environment. It uses direct experience in order to build new classifiers, instead of relying on a GA. The classifiers of such LCSs contain the following components:

$$[Condition][Action] \rightarrow [Effect] \ (quality \ parameters)$$

The learning process of such LCSs can be decomposed into two complementary processes:

• *latent learning* consists in building a reliable model of the dynamics of the environment, by ensuring that the [*Effect*] part of all classifiers are correct. This new part stores information about state transitions and allows lookahead planning. The latent learning process can take place at each time step without any reward, hence it is very efficient. In particular, as [Witkowski, 1997] has shown, the quality of anticipation of every classifier which can be fired at a time can be updated according to the subsequent input message, even if the classifier has not actually been fired;

• *reinforcement learning* consists in improving a policy using the experience of the system, so that it becomes able to choose the optimal action in every state. This process takes advantage of latent learning to converge faster.

These new approaches can be seen as replacing the blind search performed by the GA by an heuristic search which takes advantage of the previous experience to improve the classifiers. As a result, they are less general since, for instance, they are devoted to tackling multi-steps problems whereas GA-based LCS can also tackle single-step problems, but they are also much more efficient in what they are designed for.

5.2   Our Algorithm

Our algorithm, YACS, is an instance of heuristic search LCS based on anticipation. Its classifiers contain the following components:

$$[Condition][Action] \rightarrow [Effect] \ R$$

where R estimates the immediate reward received by the system when the classifier is fired.

The latent learning process creates and deletes classifiers. The creation process can be split in two main parts:

• the effect covering mechanism adjusts the effect parts by comparing successive observations and correcting mistakes;

• the condition specialization process identifies the most general of relevant conditions.

A classifier which sometimes anticipates well and sometimes not is such that its [*Condition*] part matches several distinct states. It is too general and must be replaced by new classifiers with more specialized [*Condition*] parts.

These mechanisms allow the system to converge towards a set of accurate classifiers anticipating correctly. We use this information about the state transitions in order to improve the reinforcement learning process.

The first part of this process consists in estimating the immediate reward resulting from the firing of each classifier. At each time step, we use the received reward to update an estimation of the immediate reward (R) of every classifier involving the last action and the last state, even if it has not actually been fired. The state transition informations and the immediate reward estimations allow to use a Dynamic Programming algorithm [Bellman, 1957] to compute a policy. A more detailed description of this algorithm can be found in [Gérard and Sigaud, 2000], in this volume.

6   Empirical Study

In order to check whether our role-based controller was more efficient than the basic one, and whether it could be improved by our learning algorithm, we conducted the following experimental study.

We first ran 2000 experiments to get a statistically significant view of the results obtained with these controllers. Although the hand-crafted role-based controllers appeared more efficient than the ones without roles with three sheepdogs, we did want to check whether it would be more or less robust with respect to the size of the agents population, since the role-based controllers are designed for a group of three sheepdogs.

Therefore, we decided to test the robustness of both control policies when the number of sheepdog agents was increased from three to twenty.

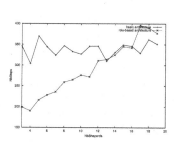

Fig. 3. Robustness of basic and role-based controllers to an increasing number of sheepdogs

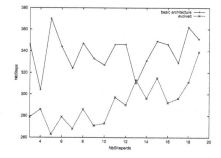

Fig. 4. Robustness of basic and evolved controllers to an increasing number of sheepdogs

The results are shown on Fig. 3. Each point in the curves represents an average performance over 100 trials, and each set of 100 trials starts with the same 100 random initial positions. We must also mention that the goal is never reached in less than 95 time steps, which is the minimum time for the sheepdog agents to surround the flock and drive it to the target area from a lucky initial situation.

If a trial lasts more the 4000 time steps, it is stopped and counted as a failure. Failures are not taken into account in the computation of the average, since their duration is arbitrary. But, since there are very few failures, their impact on the results is not very significant. More precisely, the worst case was four failures over the 100 trials that give one point on the figures. It appears that the role-based controller failed ten times on the $18 \times 100 = 1800$ trials, while the basic and learned basic controllers only failed respectively five times and two times over the 1800 trials. The failures happen more often with more than twelve sheepdogs in the role-based case, which supports our diagnosis of a lack of robustness of this solution.

It can be seen in Fig. 3 that the role-based architecture performs much better with three sheepdogs than the basic one, but that the basic architecture is more robust to an increasing number of sheepdogs. The complete presentation of this robustness study and further results are given in [Sigaud and Gérard, 2000].

It can also be seen in Fig. 4 that the controller obtained form applying adaptive algorithms to the basic architecture during two trials performs better than the hand-crafted one, and is still robust.

Hence, it must be highlighted that applying adaptive algorithms to our hand-crafted controllers results in a significant improvement of the performance. From an engineering perspective, it means that the expert who has to design a controller can write a first draft of this controller before applying adaptive algorithms to optimize it. Hence he spends much less time in this design, which is very appealing in an industrial context. This finding shows that the CS formalism is adapted for coding controllers both because the knowledge of the expert can be easily represented in it and because applying optimization algorithms is straight-forward in the formalism.

7   Discussion

7.1   Controlling the Adaptation

If we want experts to control the adaptation of classifiers, our tool should highlight all the modifications of the initial classifiers and let them approve or reject the changes. Another way to tackle the validation concern could be to let the expert constrain the exploration of the state space. Actually, what we do is a combination of the two.

The YACS system presented in [Gérard and Sigaud, 2000] is a combination of different functionalities used to improve the classifiers. One of them, the anticipation learning mechanism, improves the $[Effect]$ part, another one specializes the [*Condition*] part, and one is devoted to combining conditions with new actions. Each of these functionalities can be switched on or off, depending on the use we want to make of the LCS. Typically, in a fully automated experiment, all the switches are set on. In the case where we use expert classifiers as a starting point, we set some of them off in order to insure that the classifiers only get adjusted thanks to specialization. This guarantees that the system only explores the domain of the state space the expert want it to explore. This is an indirect way to constrain the adaptation process. But in our view, this does not eliminate the necessity of a validation of the resulting classifiers by the expert.

7.2   Benefits of Our Methodology

Letting the experts elicit their knowledge to set the initial CS is beneficial with respect to using a LCS from scratch with a random CS. It is well known that, when we use a LCS from scratch, the initial exploration phase before the system starts to converge can be very long even for simple problems. Using the expert knowledge that way allows us to cut through that phase which may be prohibitively long for our real-world applications.

Furthermore, introducing roles in our architecture brings several benefits.

● It is easier to design a *behavior CS* devoted to fulfill one particular role, since a particular role corresponds to a specialized part of the global behavior. Hence, each *behavior CS* is much smaller than the CS presented in Sect. 4.2.

● It is easier to design an internal reinforcement signal policy when we use roles. Generally, fulfilling a role corresponds to reaching a particular situation which can be detected by the agent, and/or to insure that some validity conditions hold. Then the agents can be rewarded or punished if the first condition holds or the second one is broken. In our flock control simulation, for example, playing a FUTURELEFTGUIDE role involves reaching the *leftArea* while playing a LEFTGUIDE role involves keeping the flock formed. Hence, an agent in charge of the left side of the flock can be rewarded when it reaches the *leftArea*, becoming a LEFTGUIDE, and punished if the flock is scattered, coming back to FUTURELEFTGUIDE. We think that this is a good way of introducing intermediate reinforcement signals, in a more natural framework than in [Matarić, 1994], for instance.

8   Future Work

8.1   Global Reorganizations

We have shown that an expert must have a pre-conception of the way by which his agents will solve the problem at hand in order to define their inputs and behavior sets. This is only once he has implemented the agents and observed their behavior that he will be able to refine his initial conception, making changes in the behavior modules.

But it sometimes happens that observing the behavior of the system during the adaptation process reveals a completely different strategy to solve the problem. In these cases, implementing the new solution may require new inputs, new behaviors and new mappings between the two.

These cases where a global reorganization seems necessary give a strong argument for adopting a modular approach, since some modules may remain unchanged despite the new perspective. But the design of a fully-automated LCS which would be able to tackle such global reorganizations is a very challenging research goal. Therefore these cases also give a strong argument for adopting a semi-automated approach, since the eye of the expert is necessary to identify when such global redescriptions are necessary.

8.2   Improving the Tool

In order to get more convenient, our tool should include a graphical interface, devoted both to the design of adaptive automata and to their improvement.

In order to help to improve adaptive automata, the interface must highlight the classifiers which need to be improved according to the non-Markov indicators. It must also let the users validate or reject new classifiers.

We have presented a way to use CSs as a particular case of expert systems. Rather than expressing the knowledge of the expert directly into the CS formalism, which makes it hard to read, we should also use a higher level input/output language to translate strings of 0, 1 and # into readable assertions like "if $(param_1 > 50.0)$ and $(condition2$ holds) and $(...)$ then $actThisWay$". For instance, the SAMUEL system [Grefenstette et al., 1990] uses such a language for interface concerns.

8.3   Solving Non-Markov Problems

More interestingly for the scientific community, we also want to automate more processes. We have shown that we can indicate to the users the classifiers which have a high non-Markov rate. If a correlation can be found between the variability in subsequent situations and an input which does not appear in the condition part of the classifier, then adding this input to the classifier might solve the missing information problem. We have to go into further investigation in this area before presenting results, but solving non-Markov problems is the next stage in the agenda of YACS.

8.4   Structural Modularity

Structural modularity is not the kind of temporal modularity presented in Sect. 4.4. High level conditions can be a logical combination of lower level conditions. In such cases, the computation of the truth value of these conditions can be rephrased into a small CS whose conditions are the lower level ones and the action is the assertion of the truth value of the higher level one. These modules are connected one to another so that the output of one module makes an entry in the input message of another module. This can be a good way to break the complexity of the conditions of the automata.

It is interesting to use this form of modularity when one lower level module can be re-used by several higher level modules. Our attempt to use this form of modularity in our flock driving experiment was not successful, but the need for structural modularity is not obvious in such a problem, since the automaton is not very complicated. In our industrial applications, on the contrary, there should be a lot of reusable modules.

Combining learning algorithms with structural modularity raises interesting questions. When a higher level module is reinforced, how should it share its reinforcement with lower level modules which give its inputs?

Though we did not tackle this question yet, the learning algorithm presented in [Gérard and Sigaud, 2000] already measures how relevant is a particular input to a particular classifier. We will use this information to design a structural reinforcement sharing algorithm.

9   Conclusion

In this paper, we have presented an application of CSs to a moderately complicated multiagent problem. We have drawn some lessons out of this experiments on how could CSs be used in real world domains.

The main message of that paper is that using the CS formalism can be a very efficient way to implement or rephrase simulation automata written by experts. It provides with both a clear and concise representation of the "intelligence" of the system, which can be easily handled through a graphical interface, and a convenient way to adapt this intelligence through a trial-and-error process, either by hand, automatically, or even through a mixture of the two.

The second message is that pointing out classifiers dealing with the non-Markov property of the problem is very helpful and gives an efficient indication of what must be improved in the design of the automaton. This is not a surprise since this is at the core of the algorithms of XCS [Wilson, 1995], but we proposed a new methodology to involve the experts in the improvement process when it is necessary.

Acknowledgements. The author wants to thank the reviewers of an early version of this paper and all the IWLCS2000 workshop attendees for valuable comments on this work.

References

[Beer and Gallagher, 1991] Beer, R. D. and Gallagher, J. C. (1991). Evolving dynamic neural networks for adaptive behavior. *Adaptive behavior*, 1(1):91–122.

[Bellman, 1957] Bellman, R. E. (1957). *Dynamic Programming*. Princeton University Press, Princeton, NJ.

[Donnart, 1998] Donnart, J.-Y. (1998). *Architecture cognitive et propriétés adaptatives d'un animat motivationnellement autonome.* PhD thesis, Université Pierre et Marie Curie, Paris, France.

[Dorigo, 1994] Dorigo, M. (1994). Genetic and non-genetic operators in ALECSYS. *Evolutionary Computation*, 1(2):151–164.

[Gérard and Sigaud, 2000] Gérard, P. and Sigaud, O. (to appear, 2000). Yacs: Combining dynamic programming with generalization in classifier systems. In Stolzmann, W., Lanzi, P.-L., and Wilson, S. W., (Eds.), *LNCS: Proceedings of the Third International Workshop on Learning Classifier Systems.* Springer-Verlag.

[Goldberg, 1989] Goldberg, D. E. (1989). *Genetic Algorithms in Search, Optimization, and Machine Learning.* Addison Wesley.

[Grefenstette et al., 1990] Grefenstette, J. J., Ramsey, C. L., and Schultz, A. C. (1990). Learning sequential decision rules using simulation models and competition. *Machine Learning*, 5(4):355–381.

[Holland, 1975] Holland, J. H. (1975). *Adaptation in Natural and Artificial Systems.* The University of Michigan Press.

[Kaelbling et al., 1998] Kaelbling, L. P., Littman, M. L., and Cassandra, A. R. (1998). Planning and acting in partially observable stochastic domains. *Artificial Intelligence*, 101.

[Lanzi, 1998] Lanzi, P. L. (1998). Adding memory to XCS. In *Proceedings of the IEEE Conference on Evolutionary Computation (ICEC98).* IEEE Press.

[Lanzi, 2000] Lanzi, P. L. (2000). Adaptive agents with reinforcement and internal memory. In Meyer, J.-A., Wilson, S. W., Berthoz, A., Roitblat, H., and Floreano, D., (Eds.), *From Animals to Animats 6: Proceedings of the Sixth International Conference on Simulation of Adaptive Behavior*, pages 333–342, Paris. MIT Press.

[Matarić, 1994] Matarić, M. J. (1994). Rewards functions for accelerated learning. In Cohen, W. W. and Hirsch, H., (Eds.), *Proceedings of the Eleventh International Conference on Machine Learning*, San Francisco, CA. Morgan Kaufmann Publishers.

[McCallum, 1993] McCallum, R. A. (1993). Overcoming incomplete perception with utile distinction memory. In *Proceedings of the Tenth International Conference on Machine Learning*, pages 190–196, Amherst, MA. Morgan Kaufmann.

[McCallum, 1996] McCallum, R. A. (1996). Learning to use selective attention and short-term memory. In Maes, P., Mataric, M., Meyer, J.-A., Pollack, J., and Wilson, S. W., (Eds.), *From Animals to Animats 4: Proceedings of the Fourth International Conference on Simulation of Adaptive Behavior*, pages 315–324, Cambridge, MA. MIT Press.

[Riolo, 1990] Riolo, R. L. (1990). Lookahead planning and latent learning in a classifier system. In *From Animals to Animats: Proceedings of the First International Conference on Simulation of Adaptive Behavior*, pages 316–326, Cambridge, MA. MIT Press.

[Sigaud and Gérard, 2000] Sigaud, O. and Gérard, P. (to appear, 2000). Being reactive by exchanging roles: an empirical study. In Hannebauer, M., Wendler, J., and Pagello, E., (Eds.), *LNCS : Balancing reactivity and Social Deliberation in Multiagent Systems.* Springer-Verlag.

[Stolzmann, 1998] Stolzmann, W. (1998). Anticipatory classifier systems. In Koza, J. R., Banzhaf, W., Chellapilla, K., Deb, K., Dorigo, M., Fogel, D. B., Garzon, M. H., Golberg, D. E., Iba, H., and Riolo, R., (Eds.), *Genetic Programming.* Morgan Kaufmann Publishers, Inc., San Francisco, CA.

[Sun and Sessions, 2000] Sun, R. and Sessions, C. (2000). Multi-agent reinforcement learning with bidding for segmenting action sequences. In Meyer, J.-A., Wilson, S. W., Berthoz, A., Roitblat, H., and Floreano, D., (Eds.), *From Animals to Animats 6: Proceedings of the Sixth International Conference on Simulation of Adaptive Behavior*, pages 317–324, Paris. MIT Press.

[Sutton and Barto, 1998] Sutton, R. S. and Barto, A. G. (1998). *Reinforcement Learning, an introduction*. MIT Press, Cambridge, MA.

[Vaughan et al., 1998] Vaughan, R., Stumpter, N., Frost, A., and Cameron, S. (1998). Robot sheepdog project achieves automatic flock control. In Pfeifer, R., Blumberg, B., Meyer, J.-A., and Wilson, S. W., (Eds.), *From Animals to Animats 5: roceedings of the Fifth International Conference on Simulation of Adaptive Behavior*, pages 489–493, Cambridge, MA. MIT Press.

[Whitehead and Lin, 1995] Whitehead, S. D. and Lin, L.-J. (1995). Reinforcement learning of non-Markov decision processes. *Artificial Intelligence*, 73(1-2):271–306.

[Wiering and Schmidhüber, 1997] Wiering, M. and Schmidhüber, J. (1997). HQ-learning. *Adaptive Behavior*, 6(2):219–246.

[Wilson, 1994] Wilson, S. W. (1994). ZCS, a zeroth level classifier system. *Evolutionary Computation*, 2(1):1–18.

[Wilson, 1995] Wilson, S. W. (1995). Classifier fitness based on accuracy. *Evolutionary Computation*, 3(2):149–175.

[Witkowski, 1997] Witkowski, C. M. (1997). *Schemes for Learning and behaviour: A New Expectancy Model*. PhD thesis, Department of Computer Science, University of London, England.

Mining Oblique Data with XCS

Stewart W. Wilson

The University of Illinois, Urbana-Champaign IL 61801, USA
Prediction Dynamics, Concord MA 01742, USA
wilson@prediction-dynamics.com

Abstract. The classifier system XCS was investigated for data mining applications where the dataset discrimination surface (DS) is generally oblique to the attribute axes. Despite the classifiers' hyper-rectangular predicates, XCS reached 100% performance on synthetic problems with diagonal DS's and, in a train/test experiment, competitive performance on the Wisconsin Breast Cancer dataset. Final classifiers in an extended WBC learning run were interpretable to suggest dependencies on one or a few attributes. For data mining of numeric datasets with partially oblique discrimination surfaces, XCS shows promise from both performance and pattern discovery viewpoints.

1 Introduction

Data mining has been described as "the process of discovering patterns in data" [17]. The discovered patterns are often represented by rules that, given a data instance, can be used to predict an outcome or consequence of interest. Similarly, XCS [13], a learning classifier system, evolves rules (classifiers) through which the system gradually improves its ability to obtain environmental reward. In effect, XCS *mines its environment* for patterns that, expressed in classifiers, allow it to make increasingly remunerative decisions. XCS is potentially applicable to data mining problems because in many environments it evolves accurate, maximally general rules in which the patterns are easily seen.

Some of the relevant XCS work has involved learning Boolean functions [13, 5,14]. From a data-mining point of view, a Boolean function is a very strongly patterned dataset containing all two-valued attribute strings of a given length. The ability to learn Boolean functions indicates XCS's ability to find highly non-linear patterns among attributes. Saxon and Barry [9] tested XCS on The Monk's Problems [11], a widely used non-Boolean test set for comparing learning algorithms. The domain has six attributes taking up to four nominal values (e.g., the head_shape attribute takes values round, square, and octagon). The Monk's 1 problem is a relatively simple concept,

(head_shape = body_shape) or (jacket_color = red).

The second problem is a more complicated concept not simply described by a disjunction of conjunctions of attribute-value pairs. Monk's 3 is again a simple concept but contains noise in the form of approximately 5% misclassified examples in the training set. Comparing the results with published results for other

P.L. Lanzi, W. Stolzmann, and S.W. Wilson (Eds.): IWLCS 2000, LNAI 1996, pp. 158–174, 2001.
© Springer-Verlag Berlin Heidelberg 2001

systems led Saxon and Barry to conclude that on The Monk's Problems XCS "performed at least as well as traditional Machine Learning techniques", and that XCS was "also able to produce and maintain an easily identifiable accurately general set of classifiers representing the concepts within the data sets". Wilson [15] showed that XCS could learn a problem in which there was a Boolean relation among real-valued attributes, showing that XCS could be adapted to take continuous inputs.

Promising as these results are, in all the problems addressed the concept or function sought is essentially "logical". I.e., it can be expressed by a combination of and, or, and not applied to attribute values, simple recodings of them, or, in the case of [15], ranges of the values. XCS appears well suited to "logical" data-mining problems, including realistically large ones (as suggested by preliminary complexity results in [14]). However, in many data-mining problems the function sought is *not* expressible logically. This is because the problem's discrimination surface (DS) is *oblique* – neither parallel nor perpendicular to – the attribute axes. Datasets with oblique DS's form a large class and their instances typically have numeric attributes.

XCS is good at logical problems because the classifier conditions define hyper-rectangles, which can evolve to fit the shape of a logical DS exactly. However, if the DS is oblique, hyper-rectangles can only approximate the shape. Many classifiers may be required, and the shape may be difficult to see in the classifiers. One approach to oblique problems is to modify the syntax of classifier conditions so that oblique DS's can be approximated. The most general method is to use *S-classifiers* [7,12], where the conditions are Lisp S-expression predicates and can be based on arithmetic function primitives. Our aim in this paper, however, is to apply basic XCS (modified for numeric inputs) to oblique data, using the well-known Wisconsin Breast Cancer dataset [2] as test bed. The WBC dataset offers an opportunity to test XCS's performance and the interpretability of its evolved rules on a realistic, oblique, data-mining problem.

The next section gives a brief introduction to XCS. Section 3 presents modifications needed for the WBC problem. We warm up on some synthetic data in Sect. 4. Section 5 presents results on the WBC dataset, including a stratified cross-validation (train/test) experiment, and an experiment that reveals patterns. Sections 6 and 7 contain discussion and conclusion.

2   XCS in Brief

The following, drawn from [15], is an abbreviated description of XCS. (For more detail, see [13], [5], and [14]; [3] gives an algorithmic description.) XCS is designed for both single- and multiple-step tasks, but the discussion here applies only to XCS for independent single-step tasks in which an input is presented, the system makes a decision, and the environment provides some reward.

Structurally, each classifier C_j in XCS's population [P] has a *condition*, an *action*, and a set of associated parameters. The condition is a string from $\{0,1,\#\}$; the action is an integer. The three principal parameters are: (1) *payoff prediction*

p_j, which estimates the payoff the system will receive if C_j matches and its action is chosen by the system; (2) *prediction error* ϵ_j, which estimates the error in p_j with respect to actual payoffs received; and (3) *fitness* F_j, computed as later explained. It is convenient to divide the description of a single operating cycle or time-step into the traditional performance, update (reinforcement), and discovery components.

2.1   Performance

Upon presentation of an input – a binary string – XCS forms a *match set* [M] of classifiers in [P] whose conditions are satisfied by the input. The condition is satisfied if and only if each of its non-# positions is the same as the corresponding bit of the input string.

[If no classifiers match, the input is "covered" by creating matching classifiers with each of the possible actions, and placing them in [M]. Each new classifier's condition is a copy of the input except that #'s ("don't cares") are inserted with probability $P_\#$ per position. Parameters are given initial values. If [P] has reached its allowable maximum N, deletion of classifiers occurs to make room for the new ones (deletion is generally not necessary; initial populations are empty and covering normally occurs only at the very beginning of a run)].

Then, for each action a_k represented in [M], the system computes a fitness-weighted average P_k of the predictions p_j of each classifier in [M] having that action: $P_k = \sum_j F_j p_j / \sum_j F_j$. P_k is termed the *system prediction* for action a_k.

Next, XCS chooses an action from those represented in [M] and sends it to the environment. According to the *action-selection* regime in force, the action may be picked randomly or otherwise probabilistically based on the P_k, or it may be picked deterministically – i.e., the action with the highest P_k is chosen. Finally, an *action set* [A] is formed consisting of the subset of [M] having the chosen action.

2.2   Update

In this component, the parameters of the classifiers in [A] are re-estimated according to the *reward* R returned by the environment as a consequence of the system's taking action a_k. First, the predictions are updated: $p_j \leftarrow p_j + \beta(R - p_j)$. Next, the errors: $\epsilon_j \leftarrow \epsilon_j + \beta(|R - p_j|)$. Third, for each C_j, an *accuracy* κ_j is computed: $\kappa_j = 0.1(\epsilon_j/\epsilon_0)^{-n}$, for $\epsilon_j > \epsilon_0$, else 1.0. Then, from the κ_j, each classifier's *relative accuracy* κ'_j is computed: $\kappa'_j = \kappa_j / \sum_j \kappa_j$. Finally the fitnesses F_j are updated according to: $F_j \leftarrow F_j + \beta(\kappa'_j - F_j)$.

2.3   Discovery

On some time-steps, XCS executes a *genetic algorithm* (GA) within [A]. Two classifiers are chosen probabilistically based on their fitnesses and copied. The copies are crossed (two-point crossover) with probability χ, and then mutated with probability μ per allele. The resulting offspring are inserted into [P]; if the population size is already at its maximum value, N, two classifiers are deleted. The probability of deletion of a classifier is determined by Kovacs's method [6] and is designed to preferentially remove low-fitness classifiers that have participated in a threshold number of action sets – that is, have had sufficient time for their parameters to be accurately estimated.

Whether or not to execute the GA on a given time-step is determined as follows. The system keeps a count of the number of time-steps since the beginning of a run. Every time a GA occurs, the classifiers in that [A] are "time-stamped" with the current count. Whenever an [A] is formed, the time-stamp values of its members are averaged and subtracted from the current count; if the difference exceeds a threshold θ_{GA}, a GA takes place.

A *macroclassifier* technique is used to speed processing and provide a more perspicuous view of population contents. Whenever a new classifier is generated by the GA (or covering), [P] is scanned to see if there already exists a classifier with the same condition and action. If so, the *numerosity* parameter of the existing classifier is incremented by one, and the new classifier is discarded. If not, the new classifier is inserted into [P]. The resulting population consists entirely of structurally unique classifiers, each with numerosity ≥ 1. If a classifier is chosen for deletion, its numerosity is decremented by 1, unless the result would be 0, in which case the classifier is removed from [P]. All operations in a population of macroclassifiers are carried out as though the population consisted of conventional classifiers; that is, the numerosity is taken into account. In a macroclassifier population, the sum of numerosities equals N, the traditional population size. [P]'s actual size in macroclassifiers, M, is of interest as a measure of the population's space complexity.

2.4   Overall Picture

XCS's overall objective is to maximize the rate of reward it obtains from the environment. If the environment (or trainer, teacher, etc.) gives high reward for actions (decisions) that it regards as "correct" or "best", then XCS's achieving a high reward rate will be equivalent to learning or solving the problem presented by the environment. This is the framework of *reinforcement learning* [10]. Data mining problems can be cast in terms of reinforcement learning if rewards given the system correlate with the correctness of its decisions.

XCS is designed to evolve classifiers that accurately predict environmental reward in all the situations (inputs) the system might encounter. Having these it can choose the actions that maximize reward. XCS evolves accurate classifiers by a process of trial and error in which, given an input and a match set, a particular action is tried, the reward (if any) is received, and the associated classifiers are updated as previously described. Classifiers that predict accurately tend to be reproduced, while inaccurate classifiers are eventually deleted.

XCS not only evolves accurate classifiers, it evolves ones that are accurate and *maximally general*. That is, if several *different* input situations result in the same reward when a particular action is made by the system, then XCS will tend to evolve a *single* (macro)classifier having that action that matches all of those situations. As a result, the system achieves compactness of representation, and the evolved classifiers display the structure of the environment or problem in a way that is often readily interpretable by users. This important tendency of XCS occurs because if there are two equally accurate classifiers but one matches a subset of the states matched by the other, the more general classifier will win out since it occurs in more action sets and will have more reproductive opportunities [13,5,14,16].

2.5   Subsumption Deletion

The generalization mechanism just mentioned, while powerful, may sometimes not go as far as one would wish. Winning classifiers will be those that match more inputs – environmental *states* – than equally accurate rivals. Usually, a classifier whose condition is formally more general (has more #'s) will match more states. However, in certain environments (termed *sparse*), not all states may actually be present, with the result that some formally more general classifiers, while still perfectly accurate, cannot "drive out" their rivals. The resulting population will be larger than is strictly necessary to solve the problem, and its knowledge will not be as perspicuous. To deal with sparseness and evolve classifiers that are as formally general as possible without sacrificing accuracy, an optional procedure called "subsumption deletion" was introduced [14,16,3].

Two forms of subsumption deletion are used. In *GA subsumption*, a new offspring is examined to see if its condition is logically subsumed by the condition of either of its parents. If so, and if the subsuming parent is both highly accurate and sufficiently experienced (its parameters have been updated a threshold number of times), the offspring is not added to the population but the parent's numerosity is incremented. *Action-set subsumption* is different from and independent of GA subsumption. Each action set is searched for the most general classifier that is both accurate and sufficiently experienced. Then all other classifiers in the set are tested against the general one to see if it subsumes them. Any that are subsumed are deleted from the population.

3   XCSI: XCS Modified for Integer Inputs

The attributes of WBC dataset instances are integer-valued, from 1 to 10 inclusive. To handle this format, XCS was modified in its input interface, the mutation operator, covering, and subsumption. For convenience, we call the modified system "XCSI". The changes are analogous to those made for real-valued inputs in XCSR [15]. The classifier condition is changed from a string from $\{0,1,\#\}$ to a concatenation of "interval predicates", $int_i = (l_i, u_i)$, where l_i ("lower") and u_i ("upper") are integers. A classifier matches an input x with attributes x_i if and only if $l_i \leq x_i \leq u_i$ for all x_i. A consequence of using interval predicates is that the number of numerical values or alleles in the condition is twice the number of components in x.

Crossover (two-point) operates in direct analogy to crossover in XCS. A crossover point can occur between any two alleles, i.e., within an interval predicate or between predicates, and also at the ends of the condition (the action is not involved in crossover). Mutation, however, is different. Preliminary experiments were done, and the best method appears to be to mutate an allele by adding an amount $\pm rand(m_0)$, where m_0 is a fixed integer, $rand$ picks an integer uniform randomly from $(0, m_0]$, and the sign is chosen uniform randomly. If a new value of l_i is less than the minimum possible input value, in this case 1, the new value is set to 1. If the new value is greater than u_i, it is set equal to u_i. A corresponding rule holds for mutations of u_i.

The condition of a "covering" classifier has components $l_0, u_0, ..., l_n, u_n$, where each $l_i = x_i - rand_1(r_0)$, but limited to the minimum possible input value, and each $u_i = x_i + rand_1(r_0)$, limited to the maximum possible input value; $rand_1$ picks a random integer from $[0, r_0]$, with r_0 a fixed integer.

Subsumption of one classifier by another occurs if every interval predicate in the first classifier's condition subsumes the corresponding predicate in the second classifier's condition. An interval predicate subsumes another one if its l_i is less than or equal to that of the other and its u_i is greater than or equal to that of the other. For purposes of action-set subsumption, a classifier is more general than another if its *generality* is greater. Generality is defined as the sum of the widths $u_i - l_i + 1$ of the interval predicates, all divided by the maximum possible value of this sum.

4   Experiments on Synthetic Oblique Data

To get a feel for its behavior, we began by applying XCSI to some synthetic oblique data. In the first experiment the problem had just two dimensions, in order to give a clear picture of the resulting classifiers, In the other experiment, the problem had the same dimensionality as the WBC dataset – nine. In both cases the DS (discrimination surface) was diagonal to all the axes, i.e., maximally oblique.

4.1   Experiment 1 – Two Dimensions

A dataset, "Random-Data2", was constructed as follows. Random vectors (x_1, x_2) were created, with each x_i a random integer from $(1, 10)$. The correct outcome o for each vector was chosen according to

$$o = \text{ if } x_1 + x_2 \geq 11 \text{ then } 1 \text{ else } 0.$$

Each vector and its outcome constituted an instance of Random-Data2. The dataset had 683 such instances (comparable to the size of the WBC dataset), and the attribute range from 1 through 10 corresponded to the WBC's attribute range. Note that the DS for this problem is indeed diagonal to the x_1 and x_2 axes.

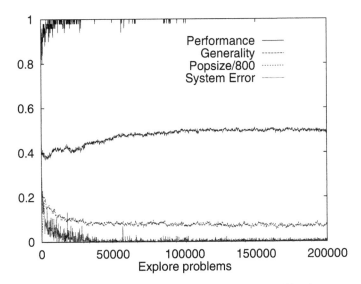

Fig. 1. Performance (fraction correct), generality, population size (/800), and system error vs. number of explore problems in Experiment 1

In the experiment, XCSI operated in a *pure explore* mode in which on each time-step the system was given a randomly selected instance from Random-Data2, it carried out the performance, update, and discovery procedures as explained in Sects. 2 and 3, but its action selection rule was to choose its output action (its decision as to the correct outcome) randomly. If the action was correct, XCSI received a reward of 1000; if incorrect, 0. Both forms of subsumption deletion were enabled.

To determine whether the system was actually learning something, the explore steps alternated with *test* steps in which XCSI deliberately chose as its decision the action with the maximum system prediction. During test steps the update, discovery, and subsumption components were disabled.

The following parameters of XCSI were the same for all experiments in this paper: $\beta = 0.2$, $\epsilon_0 = 1$, $n = 5$, $\theta_{GA} = 48$, $\chi = 0.8$, $\mu = 0.04$, and $m_0 = 2$. Also the same were the experience threshold for deletion and for GA subsumption, $\theta_{del} = 50$ (*experience* is the number of times a classifier has been in an updated action set) and a separate experience threshold for action-set subsumption, $\theta_{as} = 1000$. The space of parameter settings is obviously large, and a number of experiments preceded those reported here. Principally, it was found that ϵ_0 should be quite small (to push toward high accuracy) and θ_{as} should be quite large (to ensure that a classifier's accuracy is reliable before allowing it to delete another classifier in action-set subsumption). Parameters for this experiment that were not the same through all experiments were $N = 800$ and $r_0 = 4$.

Figure 1 shows results for a typical run of XCSI on Random-Data2. The quantities are all moving averages over the past 50 problems (instances seen);

CONDITION	ACT	PRED	ERR	FITN	NUM	GEN	EXPER
0. |......0000|...0000000|	1	1000.	.000	282.	15	.55	29435
1. |000000....|0000......|	0	1000.	.000	359.	26	.50	22546
2. |0000......|000000....|	0	1000.	.000	153.	13	.50	22780
3. |00000.....|00000.....|	0	1000.	.000	358.	19	.50	23150
4. |0000000...|000.......|	0	1000.	.000	295.	19	.50	18197
5. |....000000|.....00000|	1	1000.	.000	150.	12	.55	29394
6. |000000000.|0.........|	0	1000.	.000	435.	28	.50	7924
7. |......000|..00000000|	1	1000.	.000	250.	23	.55	26022
8. |00000000..|00........|	0	1000.	.000	236.	16	.50	12647
9. |........00|.000000000|	1	1000.	.000	229.	29	.55	17336
10. |.........0|0000000000|	1	1000.	.000	429.	22	.55	9401
11. |..00000000|.......000|	1	1000.	.000	213.	10	.55	19615
12. |0.........|......000.|	0	1000.	.000	515.	29	.20	1658
13. |00........|00000000..|	0	1000.	.000	501.	24	.50	12346
25. |0000000...|0000......|	0	991.	.032	0.	1	.55	46
26. |0000......|0000000...|	0	990.	.037	0.	1	.55	41
27. |000000....|00000.....|	0	966.	.081	5.	3	.55	80
28. |00........|000000000.|	0	930.	.135	0.	1	.55	51
29. |000.......|00000000..|	0	800.	.161	0.	2	.55	39
30. |...0000000|...0000000|	1	754.	.308	3.	1	.70	16
47. |00000.....|00000.....|	1	0.	.000	202.	15	.50	21652
48. |........00|.000000000|	0	0.	.000	232.	20	.55	17411
49. |.........0|0000000000|	0	0.	.000	284.	23	.55	10208
50. |....000000|.....00000|	0	0.	.000	407.	32	.55	27947
51. |..00000000|.......000|	0	0.	.000	345.	8	.55	21179
52. |000.......|0000000...|	1	0.	.000	251.	27	.50	18306
53. |0000000...|000.......|	1	0.	.000	188.	20	.50	16057
54. |.....00000|....0000000|	0	0.	.000	234.	20	.55	25685
55. |0.........|......000.|	1	0.	.000	556.	28	.20	1735

Fig. 2. Some classifiers from Experiment 1. Condition predicates shown graphically (see text). Also shown: ACTion, PREDiction, ERRor, FITNess, NUMerosity, GENerality, and EXPERience of each classifier

values are plotted every 100 problems. Individual plots appear in the top-to-bottom order shown in the legend.

Approximately 100,000 explore problems (instances) were required for the system to reach 100% performance. However, 98% performance (one error in 50 problems) was reached quickly, so most of the time was needed to get the last few instances – usually just one or two – right. "Generality" is a fitness-weighted average of classifier generality. It climbs slowly and seems to level off at around 0.5. "Popsize/800" is the number of macroclassifiers divided by N, the total numerosity. It falls quickly to approximately 0.08. The actual number of classifiers at the end was 63. Finally, "System Error" is the difference (divided by 1000) between the system prediction for the chosen action and the actual reward received. It falls quickly to a very small value.

Figure 2 depicts 29 representative classifiers from the 63 in the final population of Experiment 1, ordered by descending prediction. A graphic notation is used to represent the conditions. In each interval predicate (shown between "\|"s), the range of input values accepted is indicated by a sequence of 0's. Thus the first classifier accepts (matches) input vectors for which $7 \leq x_1 \leq 10$ and $4 \leq x_2 \leq 10$.

Notice that the first classifier is always correct in its prediction: all accepted inputs satisfy $x_1 + x_2 \geq 11$, the classifier advocates action 1, and the reward received is indeed 1000. Furthermore, the classifier is maximally general: neither of its predicates can be expanded without causing an error. For the second classifier, all accepted inputs satisfy $x_1 + x_2 < 11$, it advocates action 0, and it is completely accurate predicting a reward of 1000. It, too, is maximally general. In fact all classifiers in the first group are accurate (error 0.000) and maximally general except no. 12 which is merely accurate.

The second group represents the 13 classifiers that were not accurate. Note that this is reflected in their very small fitnesses (all fitness values are shown multiplied by 1000). Because system predictions are a fitness-weighted sum (Sect. 2.1), low-fitness classifiers have minimal effect on the system, and are soon deleted. They represent GA offspring that turned out not to be accurate.

The classifier conditions in the first and third groups can be thought of as "boxes" – hyper-rectangles in 2-d – fitting into the space on either side of the line defined by the dataset's DS. The fit is awkward: apart from nos. 12 and 55, each box is as big as it can be without causing an error, but they overlap in such a way that none subsumes any other and all survive. In effect, the boxes are trying to approximate the diagonally divided input space but can't do it elegantly because they are rectangular. Despite this frustration, the system did its job: of the 63 classifiers in the set, all with substantial fitness (and thus able to affect the system prediction) were accurate, and all of these except nos. 12 and 55 were maximally general.

Still, this experiment's input space had only two dimensions. Despite the system's high performance and relatively small population (space complexity) in this case, what can be expected for more realistic data mining problems such as the WBC with its nine dimensions? Will XCSI's "boxes" approximation be adequate, and what insight will it give into the problem's structure? As a first step in answering these questions, we tested XCSI on a nine-dimensional problem with a "diagonal" DS.

4.2   Experiment 2 – Nine Dimensions

A second random dataset, "Random-Data9", was constructed like Random-Data2, except that there were nine dimensions and the expression determining the outcomes was

$$o = \text{ if } x_1 + \ldots + x_9 \geq 50 \text{ then } 1 \text{ else } 0.$$

The dataset contained 683 examples, 361 of which had outcome 1.

Experiment 2 was conducted like Experiment 1 except that $N = 3200$ and $r_0 = 6$. Larger values for these parameters are generally needed as the input space becomes larger. In general, they are chosen empirically such that the total number of classifiers does not exceed approximately $0.75N$ and any initial covering ceases quickly.

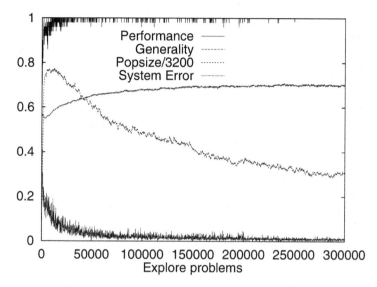

Fig. 3. Performance (fraction correct), generality, population size (/3200), and system error vs. number of explore problems in Experiment 2

Results are presented in Fig. 3, showing a typical run. In comparison with Experiment 1, performance took somewhat longer to reach 100%, system error fell more slowly, and the maximum and final population sizes were substantially larger. On the other hand, the input space is exponentially larger – 10^9 vs. 10^2 – whereas the results differ by a factor of 10 or less. Why the 9-d problem is not harder is not clear at present. It may have to do with the input space being only sparsely occupied by dataset instances, in comparison with the much fuller coverage in the 2-d case. Sparse coverage makes the DS irregular and thus less strictly diagonal; this may aid the classifiers in approximating it.

The 974 classifiers of the final population were examined, but examples are not shown here. As in Experiment 1, roughly 80% of the classifiers were accurate, with the remaining inaccurate ones having very low fitness. Because of the dimensionality and sparseness of the dataset, and unlike Experiment 1, it was not readily possible to judge if the accurate classifiers were maximally general. The accurate classifiers showed no clear pattern in their predicates, as would be expected from the obliqueness of the formula for creating the dataset, together with the sparseness. Nevertheless, as seen in Fig. 3, the dataset was learned. It appears that XCSI can deal with nine-dimensional oblique data, at least from the point of view of performance.

5   Experiments on the WBC Dataset

We used the "original" Wisconsin Breast Cancer Database which was donated to the UCI Repository by Prof. Olvi Mangasarian and contains 699 cases (instances) collected over time by Dr. William H. Wolberg. For concreteness, the nine attributes of each instance are: Clump Thickness, Uniformity of Cell Size, Uniformity of Cell Shape, Marginal Adhesion, Single Epithelial Cell Size, Bare Nuclei, Bland Chromatin, Normal Nucleoli, and Mitoses. Each attribute has a value between 1 and 10 inclusive. Sixteen instances contain an attribute whose value is unknown. The outcome distribution is 458 Benign (65.5%), 241 Malignant (34.5%). The following is a small sample of the raw data.

```
1070935,3,1,1,1,1,1,2,1,1,2
1071760,2,1,1,1,2,1,3,1,1,2
1072179,10,7,7,3,8,5,7,4,3,4
1074610,2,1,1,2,2,1,3,1,1,2
1075123,3,1,2,1,2,1,2,1,1,2
1079304,2,1,1,1,2,1,2,1,1,2
1080185,10,10,10,8,6,1,8,9,1,4
1081791,6,2,1,1,1,1,7,1,1,2
1084584,5,4,4,9,2,10,5,6,1,4
1091262,2,5,3,3,6,7,7,5,1,4
1096800,6,6,6,9,6,?,7,8,1,2
```

The first number is a label, the next nine are the attribute values, and the last is the outcome, 2 for Benign and 4 for Malignant. Clearly, Malignant is associated with larger attribute values. But the precise borderline (DS) is not obvious, nor is it clear whether certain attributes are more important than others. The obliqueness of the data is reflected in the fact that a summation of attribute values or "weight of evidence" appears broadly to be decisive. On an earlier (smaller) version of the data, Wolberg and Mangasarian [18] used a statistical method with multiple hyperplanes to obtain accuracies as high as 95.9%. The UCI Repository states "highest reported accuracy" on the current dataset to be 94%.

XCSI will first be applied to the WBC dataset in a "train/test" experiment using a well-known procedure for evaluating learning algorithms for data mining. After that, we will present an experiment in which XCSI extracted some of the patterns contained in the data.

5.1   Experiment 3 – WBC Train/Test

A practical learning algorithm for data mining must of course be able to categorize instances correctly that it hasn't seen before. In the experiments of Sect. 4, XCSI learned a dataset perfectly, but was not tested on further examples. In this experiment, we applied XCSI to the WBC data in a stratified tenfold cross-validation procedure in which the system learned on part of the data and was tested on the remainder.

According to Witten and Frank [17], "Tenfold cross-validation is the standard way of measuring the error rate of a learning scheme on a particular dataset; for reliable results, ten times tenfold cross-validation." We followed the procedure as they explain it, adding stratification, but left the 10 times repeat for later work.

Briefly, the procedure is as follows. The dataset is divided into 10 parts called "folds". The system is then tested on each fold, after being trained on the balance of the dataset. Then the results on the 10 test folds are averaged giving the final score. The folds are made as equal in size as possible, given the size of the actual dataset. "Stratification" means that in each fold the possible outcomes have approximately the same prevalences as in the whole dataset.

The folds were created from the dataset by random selection without replacement. To get stratification in a fold, it was actually made up of two parts, one containing instances randomly selected without replacement from the remaining 0-outcomes in the dataset, the other from the remaining 1-outcomes. Then the two fold parts were shuffled randomly together. The actual numbers of outcomes selected for each fold were given by a predetermined pair of numbers. For eight of the ten folds, the pair was (46, 24) for 0-outcomes and 1-outcomes, respectively. For the last two folds, the pairs were (45, 24) and (45, 25), thus accounting for all the instances as evenly as possible. (The WBC outcome notation of 2 and 4 was replaced by 0 and 1.)

Parameters for the experiment were the same as previously described, except $N = 6400$ and $r_0 = 4$. If an attribute value was missing, it was assumed to match. Calling each fold an "Out" set and the corresponding balance of the dataset an "In" set, XCSI learned on each of In sets for 50,000 explore problems, then was tested on the associated Out set. Each learning run reached 100% performance by 40,000 problems, with no mistakes after that, except for three runs that reached 100% at approximately 49,500, 49,000, and 40,100 problems. Testing consisted of a simple sweep through the Out set with XCSI in test mode. The test results are shown in Table 1.

With a mean performance of about 95.5%, XCSI appears on this problem to be in the same league as the best of other approaches. Of course, the present experiments are exploratory, and further testing is called for on the WBC data – using different fold sets – and on other oblique data problems.

5.2   Experiment 4 – Discovering Patterns

As XCSI grinds through thousands of data instances, its generalization and subsumption mechanisms evolve increasingly general, accurate classifiers. On Boolean functions or The Monk's Problems the result is a small set of classifiers in which the problem structure is evident. On oblique data, however, the discrimination surface must be approximated by hyper-rectangles defined by the classifier conditions. To the extent the data are truly oblique, the evolved classifiers may reveal little about the DS. In Experiment 1, for instance, no individual classifier in Fig. 2 offers any hint as to the shape of the DS, even though each one having high fitness is accurate and maximally general. On the other hand, if

Table 1. Results of stratified tenfold cross-validation test on WBC dataset. Each line has results for one fold. Last line is mean of fold scores

Correct	Incorrect	Not Matched	Fraction Correct
68	2	0	0.9714
69	1	0	0.9857
65	5	0	0.9286
66	4	0	0.9429
65	3	2	0.9286
64	3	3	0.9143
70	0	0	1.0000
69	1	0	0.9857
65	3	1	0.9420
67	2	1	0.9571
		MEAN ⇒	0.9556

the data while largely oblique contains some "logical" structure – i.e., structure that hyper-rectangles can more directly approximate – we should be able to see it in the evolved classifiers.

An oblique dataset like WBC can be tested for logical structure by continuing the evolution far past the point of 100% performance. Evolutionary search does not stop if the GA is running and further generalization of existing classifiers is possible. We can tell that the search continues as long as population generality is rising and population size is falling. In Experiment 4 we carried a learning run on the entire WBC dataset out to 2,000,000 time-steps (instances seen) and examined the resulting classifiers. Graphs of the experiment are shown in Fig. 4. Notice that 100% performance is reached by roughly 50,000 problems, but generality and population size are still changing at 2,000,000 problems.

Figure 5 shows the 27 most experienced classifiers in the final population (their experiences ranged from 50,810 to 414,215). These are rules that make no mistakes in predicting the payoff for any WBC dataset instance that they match. Because of their large experiences, it is quite safe to assume that they are generalized up to the point where expanding any of the interval predicates, even slightly, would cause an error. In short they are never contradicted by the dataset, and they are maximally general.

High experience means a classifier matches a large fraction of the dataset. The classifiers in Fig. 5 should offer some insight about the dataset's structure and by extension, the domain from which the data were drawn. For example, No. 3 appears to say, "Regardless of the values of the remaining attributes, if attribute 1 is 7 or above and attribute 2 is 5 or above, the case is malignant." In medical terms, this would be, "If clump thickness is 7 or above and uniformity of cell size is 5 or above, malignancy is indicated."

The statement is an hypothesis derived from the data, certainly not a proven fact. In fuller terms, it would be: "To the extent the dataset accurately samples the universe of breast cancer cases, it is hypothesized that no case fitting the

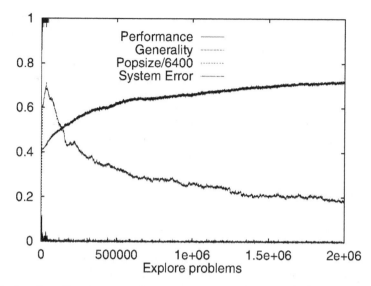

Fig. 4. Performance (fraction correct), generality, population size (/6400), and system error vs. number of explore problems in Experiment 4

```
 0. |0000000...|0000000000|00000 00000|0 0........|00........|000000 0000|0000000000|00000000 00|000000000 0|  0 1000
 1. |0000000000|0.........|0000000000|000000 000|00 00000 000|0 000.....|0000000000 0|0000000000|0000000000|  1    0
 2. |00000000..|0000000000|0000000000|0 000000000|0000000 0000|0000......|00........|00 0000000|0000000000 0|  0 1000
 3. |.....0000|....000000|0000000000|0000000000|00 00000000|0000000000|0000000 000|0000000000|00 00000000|  1 1000
 4. |......0000|....000000|000000000|000000 000|0000000000|0000000000|0000000000|0000000000|0000 000000|  0    0
 5. |0000000000|000000 000|......0000|.000000000|00 00000000|0000000000|0000000000|..000000000|0000000000|  0    0
 6. |0000000000|....00000|0000000000|00000 000|0000000000|0 000000 00|0000000000|0000000000|.0 00 000000|  0    0
 7. |0000000000|0000000000|0000. ....|000000 0000|00 00000 0000|0 000 .....|000.......|0.........|0000000000|  1    0
 8. |0000000000|....000000|00000 00000|00000 0000|0000000000|0 00000 000|0 0000 00000|00 0|000000000|.000 00000 0|  1 1000
 9. |.......00|0000000000|000000000|0 00000000|00000000|000000 0000|0000000000|0000000000|00 00 00 00000|  1 1000
10. |.......00|0000000000|0000000000|00000000|00 00000000|000000 0000|00 00000 000|0000000000|0000000000|  0    0
11. |0000000000|0000000000|......00|0000000000|0000000000|0 00000 0000|0000000000 0|0000000000|0000 000000|  1 1000
12. |0000000000|0000000000|0000......|000000 0000|00 000000000|0 0.......|00000000000|00........|0000000000|  0 1000
13. |0000000000|0000000000|0000000000|00000000000|000000 0000|0 000000 00|0000000 00 0|........0|00 00000000|  1 1000
14. |0000000000|0000000000|0000000000|0 000000000|0000000000|000000000000|0000000000|.......0|000000000 0|  0    0
15. |.....0000|0000000000|0000000000|00000000000|0000000000|.......0 00|0000000 000|000 000000000|000000000 0|  1 1000
16. |.....0000|0000000 0000|00000000000|0000000000|00000 000|......00|00000000 00|000000000 00|00 000000000|  0    0
17. |0000000000|000000 0000|..00000000|.....0 000|00 00000 000|000000 00000|0000 00000000|0000000...|00 00000000|  0    0
18. |0000000000|0000000000|0000. .....|0 000000000|000000 00000|.......0|00000000 0|0.........|0000000000 0|  1    0
19. |0000000000|0000000000|0000000000|0000000000|00 00000000|......0000|....000000|000 000...|0000000000 0|  0    0
20. |0000000...|0000000000|000000000|00........|00........|0000000000|0000000 00|0000000000 00|00 00 0000 0|  1    0
21. |0000000000|0000000000|00000 00000|0000000000|00 00000000|.....00000|....000 00|000 0000...|0000 00000 0|  1 1000
22. |00000.....|0000000000|.....00000|0 00000 0000|0000000000|00 000000 00|0000000 0000|00000000000|0000000000|  0    0
23. |00000.....|0000000000|.....00000|00000000000|00 0000 0000|0 000000000|0000000 00|0000000000|0000000000|  1 1000
24. |.....00000|000000 0000|00000 00000|00.......|0000000000|...00 00 0000|00 000 0000|0000000000|00 0000000|  1 1000
25. |00000000..|000000 0000|0000000000|0 000000000|0000000000|0000.....|00........|000 00000|00 00000000 0|  1    0
26. |0000000000|0000000000|0000000000|0000000000|00 000000|0000000000|.......000|000000 0000|00 00 000000|  1 1000
```

Fig. 5. The most experienced classifiers from the final population of Experiment 4

ranges of No. 3 will not be malignant. Furthermore, there are cases that fit No. 3 except for clump thickness less than 7 or uniformity of cell size less than 5 that are benign." Thus the classifier makes an hypothesis about cases that fit its condition, and a weaker hypothese about cases that nearly fit its condition.

Figure 5 includes some classifiers in which a single attribute is decisive. For example No. 9 says, "If clump thickness is 9 or above, then malignant." No. 26 says, "If bland chromatin is 8 or greater, then malignant." Some are very close to depending on a single attribute. No. 11 says, "If uniformity of cell shape is 8 or above and marginal adhesion is not 1, then malignant. Similarly for Nos. 6 and 8. Furthermore, rules dependent on just two attributes can be identified, for instance Nos. 1 (which indicates benign), 5, and 15. In all of these we have omitted the associated weaker hypothesis.

6   Discussion

XCSI's good performance on both the synthetic oblique problems and the WBC dataset suggests that the apparent mismatch between the obliqueness of the discrimination surface and XCSI's hyper-rectangular predicates is not a fundamental limitation. The boxy predicates might have been expected to lead to *overfitting*, i.e., excessively detailed learning of the training data causing poor performance on new instances. But test performance on the WBC data was at a competitive level, suggesting that overfitting was not in fact a problem. Still, it is not clear why this pleasant outcome should have occurred. Perhaps there is something about the "boxes" approximation that actually tends to prevent overfitting.

The emergence of some pattern information in the WBC data suggests that the set is not totally oblique, but instead contains regions where there is a strong dependence on one or a few attributes. XCSI seems to zero in on such patterns. Hopefully, the patterns will make sense to clinicians or practitioners, aiding confidence in the system's predictions, and providing suggestive domain hypotheses.

Beyond the patterns shown in Fig. 5, the final population contained of course a great many others having a more intricate structure. Some of these classifiers are concerned with the region close to the DS, where discrimination is complex. The patterns of Fig. 5, though they cover huge subspaces, may not in fact apply in "close cases" near the DS. There, however, the match set will often indicate the degree of uncertainty of the decision, because it will contain high fitness classifiers that vote strongly each way. A measure of match set agreement could assist practitioners in the close cases. Holmes [4] used this sort of technique for evaluating risk of disease.

Next steps for research on XCS and oblique data should include further fold tests on WBC and tests on additional representative datasets. Classifier patterns such as those seen in Fig. 5 should be shown to domain practitioners for plausibility. Analysis is needed of the boxes approximation, including the result that the learning complexity of XCSI on oblique data is apparently far below exponential. The conditions of the classifiers of evolved populations contain a great deal of information about the structure of the dataset, but only a fraction of it is directly interpretable as in Sect. 5.2. It would be desirable to find algorithms for extracting all the classifiers' implications as rules of thumb and in other representations.

7 Conclusion

XCS, suitably modified for numeric inputs, appears to have considerable potential for mining oblique datasets. On tests so far, performance was high, and simple as well as more complex patterns describing the structure of the data emerged. Further investigation on a wide range of problems may show that systems based on XCS are a very good choice for high performance combined with clear pattern discovery.

Acknowledgment. The author acknowledges helpful conversations with John H. Holmes and Pier Luca Lanzi, and support from the Automated Learning Group at the National Center for Supercomputer Applications in Urbana-Champaign.

References

1. Wolfgang Banzhaf, Jason Daida, Agoston E. Eiben, Max H. Garzon, Vasant Honavar, Mark Jakiela, and Robert E. Smith, editors. *Proceedings of the Genetic and Evolutionary Computation Conference (GECCO-99)*. Morgan Kaufmann: San Francisco, CA, 1999.
2. C.L. Blake and C.J. Merz. UCI repository of machine learning databases, 1998. http://www.ics.uci.edu/~mlearn/MLRepository.html.
3. Martin V. Butz and Stewart W. Wilson. An algorithmic description of XCS. This volume.
4. John H. Holmes. Discovering Risk of Disease with a Learning Classifier System. In Thomas Bäck, editor, *Proceedings of the 7th International Conference on Genetic Algorithms (ICGA97)*. Morgan Kaufmann: San Francisco CA, 1997.
5. Tim Kovacs. XCS classifier system reliably evolves accurate, complete, and minimal representations for boolean functions. In Roy, Chawdhry, and Pant, editors, *Soft Computing in Engineering Design and Manufacturing*, pages 59–68. Springer-Verlag, London, 1997.
6. Tim Kovacs. Deletion schemes for classifier systems. In Banzhaf et al. [1], pages 329–336.
7. Pier Luca Lanzi. Extending the representation of classifier conditions. Part II: From messy coding to S-expressions. In Banzhaf et al. [1], pages 345–352.
8. Pier Luca Lanzi, Wolfgang Stolzmann, and Stewart W. Wilson, editors. *Learning Classifier Systems: From Foundations to Applications*, volume 1813 of *LNAI*. Springer-Verlag, Berlin, 2000.
9. Shaun Saxon and Alwyn Barry. XCS and The Monk's Problems. In Lanzi et al. [8], pages 223–242.

10. Richard S. Sutton and Andrew G. Barto. *Reinforcement Learning: An Introduction.* The MIT Press/Bradford Books, Cambridge, MA, 1998.

11. Sebastian B. Thrun et al. The monk's problems: A performance comparison of different learning algorithms. Technical Report CMU-CS-91-197, Carnegie Mellon University, Pittsburgh, PA, 1991.

12. Stewart W. Wilson. ZCS: A zeroth level classifier system. *Evolutionary Computation,* 2(1):1–18, 1994.

13. Stewart W. Wilson. Classifier fitness based on accuracy. *Evolutionary Computation,* 3(2):149–175, 1995.

14. Stewart W. Wilson. Generalization in the XCS classifier system. In John R. Koza, Wolfgang Banzhaf, Kumar Chellapilla, Kalyanmoy Deb, Marco Dorigo, David B. Fogel, Max H. Garzon, David E. Goldberg, Hitoshi Iba, and Rick Riolo, editors, *Genetic Programming 1998: Proceedings of the Third Annual Conference,* pages 665–674. Morgan Kaufmann: San Francisco, CA, 1998.

15. Stewart W. Wilson. Get Real! XCS with Continuous-Valued Inputs. In Lanzi et al. [8], pages 209–220.

16. Stewart W. Wilson. State of XCS Classifier System Research. In Lanzi et al. [8], pages 63–82.

17. Ian H. Witten and Eibe Frank. *Data Mining: Practical Machine Learning Tools and Techniques with Java Implementations.* Morgan Kaufmann, San Francisco, CA, 2000.

18. W. H. Wolberg and O. L. Mangasarian. Multisurface method of pattern separation for medical diagnosis applied to breast cytology. *Proceedings of the National Academy of Sciences,* 87:9193–9196, 1990.

Part III

Advanced Architectures

A Study on the Evolution of Learning Classifier Systems

Tiago Sepúlveda and Mário Rui Gomes

IST, Instituto Superior Técnico
INESC, Instituto de Engenharia de Sistemas e Computadores
R. Alves Redol, 9, 6°, 1000 Lisboa, Portugal.
{tiago.sepulveda,mrg}@inesc.pt

Abstract. In this paper we propose an evolutionary approach to aggregate and control multiple Learning Classifier Systems (LCS) within a tree architecture. Our approach relies on two main principles. First, to base the tree control flow on a metaphor of a classifier attribute - strength, taking it as an expression of the classifier system excitement at a given time step. The tree control mechanism takes the excitement level of standard classifier systems to feed higher-level coordinator classifier systems, which will become responsible for choosing the appropriate host agent behavior. The second principle consists in relying on evolution to be the judge of the suitability of LCS aggregation. We believe that a "running time" aggregation mechanism will be useless if it is not provided a method to assess the suitability of the resulting structure. In the approach we propose, this role is played by simulated evolution of synthetic LCS based agents. The test-bed of our claims was *Saavana*, an Artificial Life environment modeled after a natural ecosystem where synthetic LCS based antelopes were subjected to simulated evolution. The preliminary results showed us that this approach improves the progressive adaptation of agent populations to the environment they are facing and looks promising regarding the emergence of high-level agents capable of dealing with multi-goal tasks.

1 Introduction

Learning Classifier Systems (LCS) [1] are a very promising methodology for the simulation and modeling of artificial agent adaptive behavior. The power of this methodology relies on the level of independence between LCS design and specific application details. The system designer does not need to implement internal world models. Instead, to set the system, the designer needs only to provide its performance landscape.

1.1 Learning Classifier Systems

A LCS is a type of parallel production rule system where rules – *classifiers*, relate the information that the system acquires (encoded in the condition part of the classifier) to system behavior (resulting from the action part of the classifier), trying, this way, to establish a bond between world events and the system actions. Classifiers constitute

P.L. Lanzi, W. Stolzmann, and S.W. Wilson (Eds.): IWLCS 2000, LNAI 1996, pp. 177-191, 2001.

self-formulated world hypotheses that need to be validated (and improved) as the LCS accumulates experience.

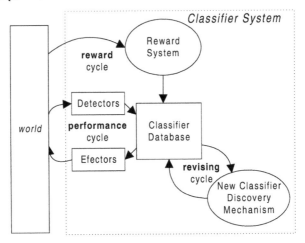

Fig. 1. Functional levels of an LCS

An LCS (Fig. 1) can be described by a functional structure composed of 3 levels:

- **Performance Level**. According the match between world state and classifiers conditions, the actions of selected classifiers determine the system behavior. The performance cycle can be divided in the following phases:
  1. Detection: environmental data is sensed (through detectors), converted into system messages.
  2. Matching: the system messages are compared with the conditions of the system classifiers (classifier database).
  3. Classifier competition: The classifiers that were successfully matched in the previous step compete to take control of the system effectors. Competition is based on classifier strength.
  4. Action: The commands that selected classifiers (classifiers that won the competition) issue trigger the corresponding effectors actions.
- **Reward Level**. The impact of LCS actions on the environment is evaluated. The evaluation result is assigned to the respective classifiers, adding the evaluation result to the classifier strength.
- **Revising Level**. From time to time, the most successful classifiers are chosen to be the basis of a new generation of classifiers. The new classifiers replace the classifiers who present the worst performance, tuning the current world model.

This architecture defines two levels of learning (reward and revising). At the reward level, world hypotheses (expressed in LCS classifiers) are rated individually. At the revising level, new ones are generated.

1.2 The Problem

LCS have proven to be very successful finding solutions to problems where it is easy to provide a fitness landscape. However, when the tasks that LCS must cope with are non-trivial, corresponding to environments where the fitness landscapes are hard to define, LCS are not adequate. One class of such environments corresponds to environments involving multiple goals. The inadequacy of LCS to deal with multiple goals is closely related with the need of providing the system a single reward value that must take into account the impact of the system actions on the pursue of all goals; often, a very challenging task.

We believe, however, that LCS scope can be extended to this class of environments as long as it can be provided a way to couple specific LCS, in the sense that each individual LCS handles a particular system goal, within a common control structure. Examples of this "divide-and-conquer" approach can be found both in Nature and in other scientific areas, like, for instance, the case of Brooks' subsumption architecture [2]. Our research goal is, then, to build a framework where LCS based performance units can learn simple behaviors and afterwards to provide a mechanism to aggregate them in order to construct higher-level control structures (that we will call agents) capable of exhibiting richer behavior.

From the discussion of the research problem it is notorious our concern avoiding to introduce environment specific details in the design of our approach. This goal suits our approach to an evolutionary framework, since the assessment of the aggregation suitability of basic performance units can be a product of a simulated evolution process

2   Related Work

The major influence in the development of our work was the research line followed by Colombetti and Dorigo, during the mid 90's. These two researchers were the first to envision the role of LCS like basic units of higher-level agent control architectures [3]. Taking advantage of the development of a transputer platform supporting the distributed execution of multiple LCS – ALECSYS [4], they proved that LCS hierarchical architectures could accomplish multi-goal tasks. Beside the experimental work performed with LCS controlled robots, they defined the notions of basic and coordination modules and defended the use of a bottom-up approach to join those building blocks in a tree like fashion.

In 1993, Dorigo and Schnepf [5] pointed out that like Nature provided evolution to enhance the performance of living organisms, AI should provide mechanisms that could induce the self-adaptation of an artificial system, arguing that "adaptation takes place only in the mind of the designer of such an autonomous system". Following this line of thought, they proposed the extension of the tree architecture of 1992 to a general LCS graph structure, configuring an approach to ethological behavior models, like the one from Tinbergen [6]. Unfortunately, the experimental work that was reported in the paper did not exploit thoroughly the role that simulated evolution could play in the construction of instances of the presented model. Hierarchical LCS structures are again referenced in 1996 [7], but in this paper the authors did not present significant progresses regarding past research.

As the tasks being dealt by artificial systems rose in complexity, evolution and adaptation became important research issues because they could become precious tools to handle it. Following this trend, several researchers began to investigate the implication of evolution in the LCS learning process. Lattaud, in particular, returned to light the issue of multifaceted LCS based agents [8]. He induced the emergence of new behaviors of Non Homogeneous Classifier Systems agents adding or changing classes of agent-environment relationships as the agents evolved. Although arising important representational issues and showing promising results, the architecture depended excessively on the environment, do not looking clear how to extend it to other types of applications.

3 Our Framework

In this section we will describe the framework corresponding to the approach we took. The principles behind our approach are:

- Adoption of the tree architecture of Colombetti and Dorigo.
- Enable the aggregation of different trees in "running time".
- Evolution like the judge of the aggregation suitability of LCS trees.

These principles narrow the application of our approach to environments where it can be established a process of simulated evolution – Artificial Life (AL) environments. This limitation poses also requirements regarding the architecture of the LCS host agents.

3.1 The Environment: *Saavana*

Saavana is the AL system embedding our agents. *Saavana* was modeled after a simplified natural ecosystem. Like *woods* [9], *Saavana* topology is defined by a 2D toroidal[1] grid.

Each grid cell constitutes a synthetic agent available location. In these locations, the agents collect the cell available resource. Each type of resource is characterized by a energy value. There are a couple of distinguishable types of resources: poison and grass. A grass cell is characterized by a high positive energy value. A poison cell exhibits a negative energy level. All other cells are neutral regarding energy.

For monitoring purposes it was found useful to have a three-dimensional graphical visualization of the environment. For this sake, it was used a graphical interface called *3D Saavana*. A snapshot of *3D Saavana* is presented in Fig. 2.

---

[1] When an agent steps into a grid boundary, it reappears on the opposite side.

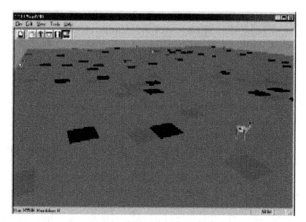

Fig. 2. A *3D Saavana* snapshot

3.2 Agent Architecture

Saavana is the stage. The actors – our virtual agents, are artificial antelopes whose "life" is regulated by a biological model, and, whose behavior is dictated by a control model. The interaction between these models is the engine powering the evolution of antelope population towards a progressive adaptation to the environment.

3.2.1 Biological Model

Health is the only attribute included in the antelope biological model and, thus, it is linked with all aspects of antelope behavior (moving, breeding and dying).

Motion is the antelopes basic behavior. Antelopes are able to move from cell to cell. The collection of the resources is automatic, i.e., an antelope collects the resource available in the location it is standing without having to issue a directive specifically for that purpose.

Antelope reproduction is asexual. It is triggered when the value of an antelope health reaches a pre-defined reproduction threshold. The reproduction procedure follows:

1. Another antelope is created at the same location.
2. Half of the parent's health is transferred to its offspring.
3. The parent control model is copied into its offspring.
4. Application of mutation to the offspring control model.

An antelope can die either of exhaustion (health level decreased below a minimum threshold) or of old age.

This simple model is sufficient for natural selection[2] to occur. Natural selection assures a way to differentiate the antelopes regarding their success, pushing the popu-

---

[2] Differential reproductive success.

lation of synthetic antelopes to improve their ability to increase health. This can be done either by augmenting the efficiency of collecting resources or either by making the agents to avoid standing on poison cells.

3.2.2 Control Model

The antelope control model is the structure responsible for reasoning and, therefore, for defining the actions that the antelopes perform. The control model architecture is a LCS tree. Like in Colombetti and Dorigo's system, we also specify two types of tree nodes: basic and coordinator nodes.

A basic node corresponds to a LCS that is an interface with the environment, while a coordinator node (or LCS) is responsible for supervising the execution of its coordinated nodes. It is important to make this distinction because, due to its different functions, these types of LCS have different implementations: basic nodes have detectors and effectors suited to interact with external environment, while coordinators have detectors and effectors suited to supervise the activity of other classifier systems.

In order to simplify the explanation of the mechanisms underlying the antelopes control model, we will describe it in 3 steps:

- First, the system fundamental units: the *basic agents*.
- Afterwards, we extend the control model to accommodate *aggregate agents*.
- Finally, we describe the *aggregation mechanism* enabling the aggregation of any two (or more) agents.

Basic Agent

Basic agents possess a plain control model. Although it can be considered like a LCS tree, the control model of a basic antelope is composed by a single basic LCS.

In *Saavana*, a basic LCS searches for poison and grass cells in the antelope neighborhood and then determines what is the cell to which the antelope should move (Fig. 3). A 3-bit action encodes the motion direction.

The only characteristic that is worthwhile to mention about the control model of a basic *Saavana* agent is the inclusion of a bit mask, called *vision mask*, in the LCS detector.

Each agent can acquire the information about its 8 neighboring cells. If a LCS agent is meant to deal with all available information, the LCS should work with 16 bit classifiers: 8 bits for each cell grass flag plus 8 bits for each cell poison flag). The action of the vision mask is to limit the acquired knowledge to the mask positive bits. This "implementional" artifact was introduced to provide more flexibility in the design of the basic agent control model, enabling, thus, the generation of agents dealing with distinct features of the environment.

This way we found a way to simulate an environment where co-exist agents handling several types of information; one of the characteristics of the research problem we are addressing.

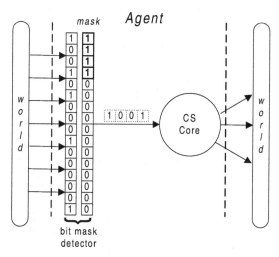

Fig. 3. Control model of a basic *Saavana* agent

Aggregate Agent
Assume two basic agents: *A*, dealing with E and NE cells, and *B*, dealing with S and SW cells (Fig. 4).

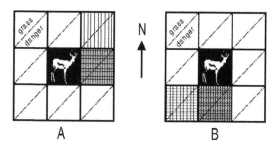

Fig. 4. Visibility of *A* and *B* agents

The goal we are pursuing is to find a way to join basic agents, like *A* and *B*, in order to build a new aggregate agent that could take advantage of the knowledge that both have acquired over time (Fig. 5).

To use *A* and *B* using a simple tree hierarchical model it is required the existence of a mechanism to decide whenever to use the knowledge of agent *A* or the knowledge of agent *B*.

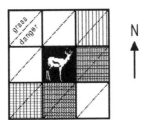

Fig. 5. An agent resulting from the aggregation of *A* and *B* agents

We began to look for variables that might be suited to play this role, i.e., to assess the usefulness of the solutions provided by both agents. Dorigo and Colombetti used two methods to pass information about the solutions proposed by LCS along the tree. One relied on delivering the bit strings corresponding to the actions the LCS proposes to other nodes. The other relied on delivering pre-defined LCS excitation bits. Both methods were very dependent on the environment and required the intervention of the system designer. Instead, we looked in the LCS framework for a variable "translating" the importance of the solutions proposed by LCS. Metaphorically, we see that matched classifiers can be mirrored as structures that get excited proportionally the strength they exhibit. Following this line of thought, we found that the strength of a classifier was the good candidate to be the variable weighted in order to decide which of the lower levels LCS is going to control the agent.

Functionally, the control model of an aggregate agent will step through 4 distinct phases. In order to illustrate them we will take the aggregate agent of figure 5, so that the basic LCS corresponding to the control models of agents A and B are now the branches of the control tree of the aggregate agent of fig. 5 (Fig.6).

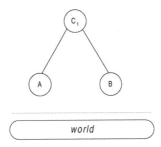

Fig. 6. Control tree of the agent resulting from the aggregation of *A* and *B* agents. The circle A represents the basic LCS from agent A. The circle B represents the basic LCS from agent B. The circle C_1 represents the coordinator LCS

Since the basic LCS of both A and B agents handle the poison and grass data regarding two neighboring cells, both will have classifiers with 4-bit conditions and 3-bit actions. The referred phases are:

1. Execution of the performance cycle of the lower level LCS, leaving the action phase (the execution of the selected actions) on hold (Fig. 7a).

2. The strength of the classifiers that were selected on lower level LCS is encoded in bit strings and sent to the respective coordinators. Control climbs the several levels of the structure until the top node (Fig. 7b).
3. At the top level, a coordination classifier is selected determining the node that becomes active. The procedure is repeated throughout the control model structure, defining the path followed in the tree (Fig. 7c).
4. Finally, at the bottom level, the selected basic unit completes its performance cycle issuing a behavior directive that will cause the antelope to move (Fig. 7d).

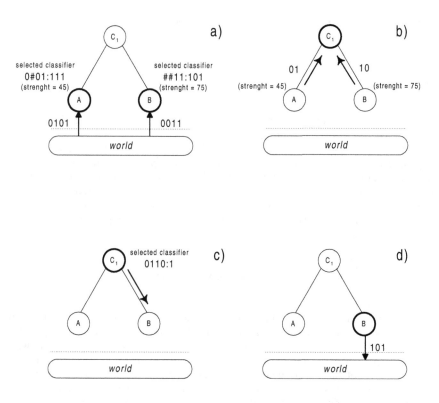

Fig. 7. Control flow in the LCS tree of the agent resulting from the aggregation of basic agent A and basic agent B

Aggregation
When two or more LCS agents aggregate, a new agent is created, whose control tree have a coordinator LCS as its root and the source agent trees as its branches (Fig. 8). The source agents are removed form the environment, thus reducing the population size.

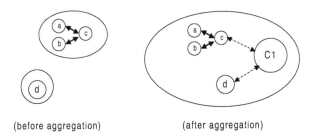

(before aggregation)   (after aggregation)

Fig. 8. Aggregation of generic LCS based agents

4   Results

The experiments performed so far are just the first steps to gather data in order to perform the analysis of our approach.

With the exception of agent features, the conditions of the several sets of experiments performed remained the same. In all experiments, the population of antelopes sharing the same features was initialized with 8 individuals. The dimension of the grid was 40x40. The number of both grass and poison cell introduced initially in the environment was 100. Grass cells were renewed every 25 cycles. Poison cells were not renewed because they are not removed from the grid when they are consumed by an antelope.

4.1   No Evolution: More Information, Better Performance

With this first set of experiments we wanted to verify the assumption that the aggregation of individuals dealing with different sets of environment information could, in fact, produce a lineage of agents exhibiting a better performance.

The initial antelope population was divided into two groups of basic agents with non-overlapping 4-bit vision masks. The strategies[3] of the basic LCS constituting the control model of the agents belonging to both groups were hand-designed. In the simulation, it was allowed the occurrence of a single aggregation event. The agents being aggregated must belong to different groups. A strategy for the coordinator of the resulting aggregate agent was also pre-defined. A null mutation rate prevented the agents to evolve and change the characteristics that were defined *a priori*.

The evolution of the number of elements in both basic agent groups and aggregate population are shown in Fig. 9. The graph presented corresponds to results obtained in a system typical run.

---

[3]   A LCS strategy is the set of classifiers constituting the LCS classifier database in a particular time step.

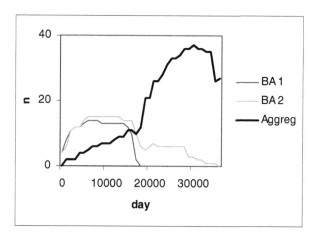

Fig. 9. Number of individuals *versus* time (BA1 - Basic Agents of group 1, BA2 - Basic Agents of group 2 and Aggreg. – Aggregate agents)

Under such a static environment the population originated by the single aggregated entity rapidly dominates both groups of basic antelopes leading them to extinction, demonstrating that an agent able to use the knowledge acquired by simpler agents gets a significant competitive advantage.

4.2 Coordinator Evolution

The goal of this set of experiments was to monitor the evolution of aggregate agents performance if the strategy of the coordinator LCS was allowed to evolve, instead of being pre-defined.

The conditions of the former set of experiments changed in the following points:

- The number of aggregation events allowed between elements of distinct groups was not limited. The occurrence of an aggregation event depended on a system parameter we called aggregation rate.
- The coordinator strategy of aggregated agents is created randomly.
- Learning and mutation (acting when the aggregate agents breed) are the mechanisms responsible for the adaptation of the coordinator strategy.

The graphic depicted in Fig. 10 presents the evolution of the number of individuals within the studied populations on a typical run of this set of experiments.

The results show that a population of aggregate agents can evolve in order to dominate the environment and produce results similar to the previous set of experiments. As we might expect, the extinction of the basic groups took longer when the aggregate agents were subjected to evolution, since the coordination strategy that is provided to the aggregate agent immediately after the aggregation event is worst, since it is random, that the coordinator strategy provided to the aggregate agents in the former case.

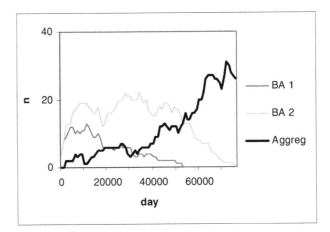

Fig. 10. Number of individuals *versus* time (BA1 - Basic Agents of group 1, BA2 - Basic Agents of group 2 and Aggreg. – Aggregate agents)

From the set of experiments performed, we estimate that are necessary an average of about 10 aggregation events to find an agent presenting a sufficiently good random coordinator strategy to establish a new antelope lineage. In one of the best examples, a successful aggregation, in the sense we just described, occurred after 7 aggregation events. In this case, the aggregated agent had an initially randomized coordination strategy that guaranteed an offspring of 3 sons during its lifetime. In this example, it took about 50000 cycles and 8 generations to extinct the basic populations.

4.3 Full Evolution: Pangeia

The next step in our experimental path implied to leave several types of basic agents to evolve and aggregate freely. This step presented, however, several problems concerned with the co-evolution of agents within the same environment. All individuals have a similar biological model, meaning that all individuals fight over the same resources. From the outcome of a few preliminary experiments we performed, the evolution of a random population of antelopes, where random means that both the vision mask and the LCS strategy of the basic agents were initialized stochastically, ended up with the dominance of a single type of basic agent. Therefore, it seemed impossible to maintain a heterogeneous population of synthetic, a condition that is essential in order to apply successfully our approach.

We thought in several solutions to overcome this problem like diversifying the biological model of our agents, introducing an extra resource or imposing a share on the number of individuals in sub-populations. However, these solutions raised other problems on their own.

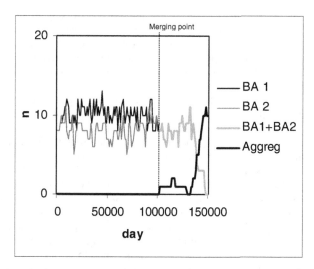

Fig. 11. Number of individuals *versus* time (BA1 - Basic Agents in environment 1, BA2 - Basic Agents in environment 2, BA1+BA2 – Basic Agents in the merged environment and Aggreg. – Aggregate agents in the merged environment)

The solution we finally adopted was based on a model of speciation by geographic separation [10]. This model predicts the development of species with different characteristics, if a group of similar individuals is subjected to evolution in environments that are apart.

In order to simulate this model, we ran two parallel instances of our environment, not allowing any aggregation, letting each *Saavana* instance to *saturate*, where by saturation we mean the emergence of a dominant group of agents with similar features. Then, we merged half of the populations in a single instance and allowed the individuals to aggregate and evolve. We called this experimental framework the *Pangeia model*.

The results from experiments ran with the Pangeia model show that, if basic agents have sufficient time to evolve, we still can obtain a lineage of aggregate agents performing better than the agents belonging to basic agent populations. In the particular experiment that the graphic of figure 11 refers to, the populations of basic agents that dominated the environments of the two initial *Saavana* instances possessed 4-bit vision masks that overlapped in two bits, meaning that the capabilities of the aggregated agent were therefore enhanced only with 2 bits of non-redundant information. Even with such a handicap the aggregated agents lead the basic agents to extinction demonstrating the efficiency of the evolutionary approach we propose.

5   Future Work

Since the issues focused in this paper are the subjects of ongoing research, we have much work planned for the next months.

First, we want to continue to analyze our approach, assessing its real range. The analysis procedure will follow with experiments where we will use the Pangeia framework to allow the populations to step trough several *separation-saturation-aggregation-saturation* cycles, possibly, with more than two *Saavana* instances running simultaneously, and then, examine what are the characteristics that become dominant in the final populations.

From the analysis of the results of our experiments, we hope to improve the current evolutionary model, since the results of evolving the top node of the LCS tree relying only on the mutation of classifiers and classifier strengths are poor.

We intend to compare the efficiency of our approach with the learning efficiency of a single complete (having full information) LCS. The goal is to see, if even in an environment where it is easy to find a good measure of performance, the convergence of aggregate agents does not outdo the convergence speed of the full 16 bit LCS.

From the observation of the characteristics of *Saavana*, we can see that the task dealt by the agents is not really a multi-goal task and that the problem could easily be solved with a unique LCS. As we have stated, in the development of our approach we simulated an environment with multiple goals bounding the capability of our basic agents to acquire information with a vision mask. Therefore, one of our goals, on a longer term, is to test our approach on environments where the agents ability to survive depends on their success in dealing with uncorrelated goals.

Other aspect deserving a careful analysis is the evaluation of the validity of this approach if it is applied to LCS with different classifier utility definitions, like for instance Wilson's XCS.

Finally, we would like to take advantage of the structure of our architecture in order to improve its efficiency; the tree structure is very appropriate to use genetic programming techniques, see how Iba [11] used them to provide genetic operators to tree structured classifiers. The goal of applying these techniques can be to optimize the topology of the tree, deleting, for instance, redundant coordinators.

6 Conclusions

Although the presentation of our approach has been interlaced with the description of the development environment, we believe that the approach we propose is generic. The approach consists in the application of a methodology enabling the evolution and control of multiple LCS based agents. The methodology relies on a hierarchical LCS tree structure and a correspondent mechanism enabling the aggregation of the control trees of individual agents.

From the results gathered so far, our evolutionary approach seems promising. If validated, we can anticipate several advantages in using this approach:

- Several units can be aggregated at the same time.
- The mechanism can be applied to all scales.
- Preserves acquired knowledge.
- Is generic, there is no dependence on the application domain.
- Is a simple solution, does not requiring any increase in the complexity of the agent architecture

This approach still lacks a good evolutionary model to evolve the top node of the control LCS tree. The operators used so far do not take full advantage of the LCS learning potential. The usefulness of this approach to solve multi-goal tasks needs to be assessed in further detail.

Acknowledgments. This work is sponsored by FCT's PRAXIS XXI program (BD/9375).

References

1. Holland, J., *Adaptation in Natural and Artificial Systems*, MIT Press, 1992.
2. Brooks, R. A., "A Robust Layered Control System For A Mobile Robot", *IEEE Journal of Robotics and Automation*, Vol. RA-2, n° 1, 1986.
3. Colombetti, M. and Dorigo, M., "Learning to Control an Autonomous Robot by Distributed Genetic Algorithms", *Proceedings of From Animals to Animats, Second International Conference on Simulation of Adaptable Behavior (SAB92)*, pp. 305-312, MIT Press, 1992.
4. Dorigo, M. and Sirtori, E., "ALECSYS: A Parallel Laboratory for Learning Clasiifir Systems", *Proceedings of the 4th International Conference on Genetic Algorithms*, USA, 1991.
5. Dorigo, M. and Schnepf, U., "Genetics-based Machine Learning and Behavior Based Robotics: a New Synthesis", *IEEE Transactions on Systems, Man and Cybernetics*, 23, 1, 1993.
6. Tinbergen, N., *The study of instinct*, Oxford University Press, 1978.
7. Colombetti, M., Dorigo, M. and Borghi, G., "Robot Shaping: The Hamster Experience", *Proceedings of ISRAM'96, Sixth International Symposium on Robotics and Manufacturing*, M. Jamshidi et al. (Eds.), May 28-30, 1996, Montpellier, France.
8. Lattaud, C., "Non-Homogeneous Classifier Systems in a Macro-Evolution Process", Proceedings of 2nd International Workshop on Learning Classifier Systems, USA, 1999.
9. Wilson, S. W., "ZCS: A Zeroth Level Classifier System", *Evolutionary Computation*, Vol. 2, 1, pp. 1-18, 1994.
10. Dawkins, R., *O Relojoeiro Cego*, Universo da Ciência. Edições 70, 1986, Portugal.
11. Iba, H., de Garis, H., and Higuchi, T., "Evolutionary learning of predatory behaviors based on structured classifiers", *From Animals to Animats 2: Proceedings of the Second International Conference on Simulation of Adaptive Behaviour*, Meyer, J. A., Roitblat, H. L. and Wilson, S. W. (editors), MIT Press, 1993.

Learning Classifier Systems Meet Multiagent Environments

Keiki Takadama[1], Takao Terano[2], and Katsunori Shimohara[3]

[1] ATR International, 2-2-2 Hikaridai, Seika-cho, Soraku-gun, Kyoto 619-0288 Japan
Tel: +81-774-95-1007, Fax: +81-774-95-2647
[2] Univ. of Tsukuba, 3-29-1, Otsuka, Bunkyo-ku, Tokyo 112-0012 Japan
Tel: +81-3-3942-6855, Fax: +81-3-3942-6829
[3] ATR International, 2-2-2 Hikaridai, Seika-cho, Soraku-gun, Kyoto 619-0288 Japan
Tel: +81-774-95-1070, Fax: +81-774-95-2647
{keiki,katsu}isd.atr.co.jp, terano@gssm.otsuka.tsukuba.ac.jp

Abstract. An Organizational-learning oriented Classifier System(OCS) is an extension of Learning Classifier Systems (LCSs) to multiagent environments, introducing the concepts of organizational learning (OL) in organization and management science. Unlike conventional research on LCSs which mainly focuses on single agent environments, OCS has an architecture for addressing multiagent environments. Through intensive experiments on a complex scalable domain, the following implications have been revealed: (1) OCS finds good solutions at small computational costs in comparison with conventional LCSs, namely the Michigan and Pittsburgh approaches; (2) the learning mechanisms at the organizational level contribute to improving the performance in multiagent environments; (3) an estimation of environmental situations and utilization of records of past situations/actions must be implemented at the organizational level to cope with non-Markov properties in multiagent environments.

Keywords: learning classifier system, multiagent system, non-Markov environment, organizational learning

1   Introduction

Currently, *non-Markov* environments are studied on in the context of Learning Classifier Systems (LCSs) [Goldberg 89], and the capability of LCSs in such environments is investigated in the framework of *reinforcement learning* [Sutton 98]. In particular, these researches mostly address the POMDP (partially observable Markov decision process) environments where an agent cannot distinguish different situations due to a lack of global environmental information. This non-Markov property is related to a location in single agent environments. As a major approach towards such environments, estimation of environmental situations, which is a model-based approach, showed its effectiveness in the POMDP environments [Chirsman 92,MacCallum 93], while utilization of records of past

P.L. Lanzi, W. Stolzmann, and S.W. Wilson (Eds.): IWLCS 2000, LNAI 1996, pp. 192–210, 2001.
© Springer-Verlag Berlin Heidelberg 2001

situations/actions contributed to coping with such environments by adding temporary memory [Cliff 95,Lanzi 98,Lanzi 99].

However, the property in the POMDP environments is one of non-Markov properties and another property are still embedded in multiagent environments [Weiss 99]. Another property is peculiar in multiagent environments and is related to a change of an agent's internal state. Specifically, this property makes it difficult for an agent to recognize an environmental change caused by the change of another agent's internal state, due to a lack of the other agents' information. From this characteristic, the effective actions of the agent vary due to such kinds of changes even if the agent stays in the same location. Here, defining this environment as the NOMDP (non observable Markov decision process) environment, the non-Markov properties in multiagent environments include both properties in the POMDP and NOMDP environments. Thus, addressing multiagent environments is more complex than addressing single agent environments.

Due to these difficulties, there is no standard and promising method to address the above non-Markov properties in multiagent environments. Therefore, as one of the methods, this paper explores elements needed in LCSs to cope with multiagent environments using our Organizational-learning oriented Classifier System (OCS) [Takadama 99] which is an extension of LCS to multiagent environments. Concretely, we investigate such elements by analyzing results that compare the performance of OCS in multiagent environments with those of the conventional LCSs, namely the *Michigan* [Holland 78] and *Pittsburgh* [Smith 83] approaches.

This paper is organized as follows. Section 2 starts by describing organizational learning (OL) which is introduced in our LCS. Section 3 explains the architecture of OCS. A multiagent example is given in Sect. 4. Sections 5 shows simulations of a comparison between OCS and conventional LCSs. Section 6 discusses elements for coping with multiagent environments. Finally, our conclusions are made in Sect. 7.

2   Organizational Learning

2.1   Four Loop Learning in Organizational Learning

Organizational learning (OL) [Argyris 78,Cohen 95] has been studied in the context of organization and management science and is roughly characterized as organizational activities that improve organizational performance which cannot be achieved at an individual level. In particular, OL consists of the following four kinds of learning [Kim 93,Argyris 78].

- **Individual single-loop learning** improves the performance within an individual norm.
- **Individual double-loop learning** improves the performance through the change of an individual norm itself.
- **Organizational single-loop learning** improves the performance within an organizational norm.

- **Organizational double-loop learning** improves the performance through the change of an organizational norm itself.

2.2   Reinterpretation of Four Loop Learning

The categorization in the previous section stipulates that (1) there are individual and organizational levels in learning, and (2) each learning can be classified as a single or a double type. However, the term *norm*[1] in the above learning has not been defined clearly from a computational viewpoint. This allows us to implement such learning in many ways from a computational viewpoint, and this way of implementation may lead to different results. Since such ambiguity is not appropriate to discuss focused issues consistently, this paper starts by assuming the norms as follows.

- **Individual norm** is implemented by individual knowledge.
- **Organizational norm** is implemented by organizational knowledge.

Next, these two types of knowledge are assumed as follows.

- **Individual knowledge** is implemented by a rule set.
- **Organizational knowledge** is implemented by a set of individual knowledge (rule set).

These assumptions may seem to define only parts of organizational learning, but they come from the consideration that individual (or organizational) norms are kinds of behavior established in an individual (or an organization) and these behaviors are derived from individual (or organizational) knowledge. By clarifying such norms through the above assumptions, we can potentially find new results which cannot be derived from the conventional definitions. Based on this claim, this paper defines *computational organizational learning* as "learning that includes four kinds of computationally interpreted loop learning".

3   Organizational-Learning Oriented Classifier System

An Organizational-learning oriented Classifier System (OCS) [Takadama 99] has GBML (Genetics–Based Machine Learning) architecture and includes multiple Learning Classifier Systems (LCSs) extended to introduce the concepts of organizational learning.

3.1   Agents

In OCS, agents are implemented by their own LCSs, which are extended to introduce four kinds of learning mechanisms in OL. In order to solve problems that cannot be solved at an individual level, agents cooperate with other agents

---

[1] For instance, a routine and a weltanschauung are examples of an individual norm and an organizational norm, respectively.

by specializing their own roles. This indicates that OCS is based on problem solving through role specialization. Since these roles are implemented by *rule sets* in agents' own LCSs, the *aim* of the agents is defined as acquiring appropriate *rule sets* through interaction with other agents. Specifically, the learning mechanisms make these rule sets appropriate by varying *if-then* rules and the strength[2] values of these rules.

3.2   Architecture

As shown in Fig. 1, OCS is composed of many agents, and each agent has the same architecture which includes the following components.

< Problem Solver >
  – **Detector** and **Effector** translate a part of an environment state into an internal state of an agent and derive actions based on this internal state [Russell 95], respectively.

< Memory >
  – **Organizational knowledge memory** stores a set comprising each agent's rule set as organizational knowledge. In OCS, this knowledge is shared by all agents and represents knowledge on role specializations.

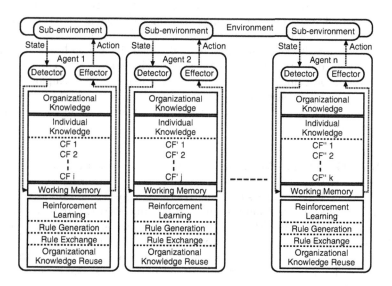

Fig. 1. OCS architecture

---

[2] The term strength in this paper is defined as the worth or weight of rules.

- **Individual knowledge memory** stores a rule set (a set of classifiers (CFs)) as individual knowledge. In OCS, agents independently store different CFs that are composed of *if-then* rules with a strength factor. In particular, a fixed number (FIRST_CF) of rules in each agent is generated at random in advance, and the strength values of all rules are set to the same initial value. In this case, one primitive action is included in the *then* part.
- **Working memory** stores the recognition results of sub-environmental states and also stores the internal states of actions of fired rules.

< **Mechanisms** >

- **Reinforcement learning mechanism, rule generation mechanism, rule exchange mechanism,** and **organizational knowledge reuse mechanism** are computationally interpreted from the four kinds of learning in OL (Details are described later). These mechanisms are not improved by specific or elaborate techniques but by simple and ordinary ones.

3.3   Learning in OCS

(1) Reinforcement Learning Mechanism. In OCS, the reinforcement learning (RL) mechanism enables agents to acquire their own appropriate actions that are required to solve given problems. In particular, RL supports the learning of the appropriate order of fired rules by changing the strength values of the rules. Since this mechanism improves problem solving efficiency at an individual level not by creating/deleting rules but by utilizing them while changing the order of the fired rules, it works as a kind of "individual single-loop learning," which is interpreted to improve performance within individual rules in computational organizational learning. To implement this mechanism, OCS employs a *profit sharing* method [Grefenstette 88] that reinforces the sequence of all rules when agents obtain some rewards.[3] The concrete mechanism of RL in OCS follows as shown in Fig. 4–1.

(2) Rule Generation Mechanism. The rule generation mechanism in OCS creates new rules when none of the stored rules match the current environmental state. This mechanism adapts to the current environment, and works as shown in Fig. 4–2. Concretely, the condition (if) part of a rule is created to reflect the current situation, the action (then) part is determined at random, and the strength value of the rule is set to the initial value. When the number of rules is MAX_CF (maximum number of rules), in particular, the rule with the lowest strength is removed and a new rule is generated. Since this mechanism improves the problem solving range at an individual level by creating/deleting rules, it works as a kind of "individual double-loop learning," which is interpreted to improve performance through the change of individual rules themselves in computational organizational learning.

---

[3] The detailed credit assignment in OCS was proposed in [Takadama 98].

In addition to the above basic mechanism, the strength value of the fired rule (*e.g.*, the No. i rule) temporarily decreases as $ST(i) = ST(i) - FN(i)$, where $ST(i)$ indicates the strength of the No. i rule and $FN(i)$ indicates the fired number of the No. i rule. In particular, $FN(i)$ is counted when the No. i rule is fired and is reset to 0 when the situation changes. With this mechanism, the strength value of fired rules decreases as long as the situation does not change as in deadlocked situations where the same rules are selected repeatedly. Then, these rules become candidates that capable of being replaced by new rules, while the strength value of these rules is recovered when the situation changes.

(3) Rule Exchange Mechanism. In OCS, agents exchange rules with other agents at particular time intervals (GA_STEP)[4] in order to solve given problems that cannot be solved at an individual level as shown in Fig. 4–3. Since this mechanism improves the problem solving efficiency at the organizational level not by creating/deleting a set comprising each agent's rule set but by utilizing it among the agents, this mechanism works as a kind of "organizational single-loop learning," which is interpreted to improve performance within a set comprising each agent's individual rules in computational organizational learning.

In this mechanism, a particular number ((the number of rules) × GENERATION _GAP[5]) of rules with low strength values is replaced by rules with high strength values between two arbitrary agents. For example, when agents X and Y are selected as shown in Fig. 2, the CFs in each agent are sorted by order of their strength values (upper CFs have high strength values). After this sorting, $CF_{j-2} \sim CF_j$ and $CF'_{k-2} \sim CF'_k$ in this case are replaced by $CF'_1 \sim CF'_3$ and $CF_1 \sim CF_3$, respectively. However, rules that have higher strength values than a particular value (BORDER_ST) are not replaced to avoid unnecessary rule exchanges. The strength values of replaced rules are reset to their initial values, because effective rules in some agents are not always effective for other agents in multiagent environments.

(4) Organizational Knowledge Reuse Mechanism. Finally, agents in OCS store a set comprising each agent's rule set (individual knowledge) as knowledge on the role specialization when they most effectively solve given problems.[6] After storing this knowledge, agents reuse it for future problem solving, instead of using the initial individual knowledge generated at random. This mechanism enables agents to use the best knowledge acquired previously. We call the organizational knowledge as knowledge on role specialization, because organizational knowledge is a set comprising each agent's rule set and each rule set works as one of the roles to solve given problems at the organizational level. The concrete mechanism of organizational knowledge reuse in OCS follows as shown in

---

[4] This step is defined in Sect. 4.2.
[5] The ratio of removed rules.
[6] Since the efficiency depends upon the problem, it is generally difficult to define the efficiency. However, as one of the methods, agents can be made to solve a given problem most effectively by measuring a "good solution" or a "small cost".

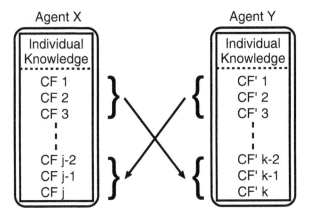

Fig. 2. Rule exchange

Fig. 4–4. Considering the situation in which n agents address a given problem, organizational knowledge (*i.e.*, a set comprising each agent's rule set) can be represented by {RS (1), RS (2), $\cdots$, RS (n)} as shown in Fig. 3, where RS(x) is the rule set for the x-th agent. Since this mechanism improves the problem solving range at an organizational level by creating/deleting organizational knowledge, it works as a kind of "organizational double-loop learning," which is interpreted to improve performance through the change of a set comprising each agent's individual rules itself in computational organizational learning.

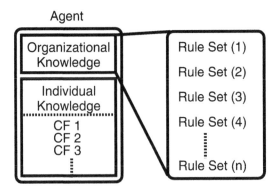

Fig. 3. Organizational knowledge reuse

procedure reinforcement learning
  begin
    if solution is converged **then**
      for all agents **do**
        fired rules are reinforced;
  end

Figure 4–1

procedure rule generation
  begin
    for all agents **do**
      if no matched rules **then**
        begin
          if number of rules = MAX_CF **then**
            the rule with the lowest strength value is deleted;
            a new rule is created;
            a strength value of the new rule is set to an initial one;
        end
  end

Figure 4–2

procedure rule exchange
  begin
    if mod (step, GA_STEP)=0 **then**
      for all pairs of agents **do**
        for (number of rules)×GENERATION_GAP rules **do**
          if the lowest strength value of rule ≤ BORDER_ST **then**
            begin
              a rule with a low strength value is replaced by
                a rule with a high strength value between two agents;
              a strength value of the replaced rule is reset to its
                initial value;
            end
  end

Figure 4–3

procedure organizational knowledge reuse
  begin
    if iteration=0 **then**
      stored organizational knowledge is utilized;
    else if solution is the best **then**
      begin
        if organizational knowledge is stored **then**
          stored organizational knowledge is deleted;
        current organizational knowledge is stored;
      end
  end

Figure 4–4

Fig. 4. Algorithms of four learning mechanisms

Furthermore, other characteristics of organizational knowledge are summarized as follows:

- Each agent at the current stage of OCS does not store the entire individual rule sets of all of the other agents independently, but shares the rule sets of all agents with other agents.
- Organizational knowledge is different from ordinary effective knowledge in a single LCS, because the former knowledge represents role specialization and is used in the unit of *multiple agents*, while the latter knowledge is utilized in the unit of *one agent*. Note that organizational knowledge is composed of a lot of redundant rules, but each agent does not reuse this knowledge by itself. Each agent reuses a part of the organizational knowledge, which means the knowledge that the same or other agent acquired in previous problem solving.
- Agents cannot use both individual and organizational knowledge at the same time, because the former knowledge is modified by each agent *during* problem solving while the latter knowledge is stored or reused by all agent *after* or *before* problem solving.

3.4   Relationships among the Four Learning Mechanisms

The total algorithm of OCS follows the procedure shown in Fig. 5. Briefly, organizational knowledge is reused if it is stored before agents solve a problem, and then, both the rule generation and rule exchange mechanisms are executed until the solution converge. After the convergence of the solution, both the reinforcement learning and organizational knowledge reuse mechanisms are executed, and agents continue to address the same problem until the iteration arrives at the maximum number of iterations, which is set by a human designer.

3.5   Comparison between Conventional LCSs and OCS

In the context of LCS, conventional LCSs can be roughly divided into two types: the Michigan [Holland 78] and Pittsburgh [Smith 83] approaches. As shown in Table 1, the former approach includes many rules in a population, and these rules are evaluated by credit assignment. The latter approach, on the other hand, includes many rule sets in a population, and these rule sets are evaluated through elitist preserving selection [DeJong 75].[7] Compared to these two conventional LCSs, OCS includes many rule sets in a population, but the rules in the rule sets are evaluated by credit assignment. Although other differences between conventional LCSs and OCS can be found in both genetic operations (crossover, mutation, inversion) and a concept of OL as shown in Table 1, the decisive difference is that (1) OCS has a multiagent learning architecture which

---

[7] Although several methods for an elitist preserving selection are proposed, the method in this paper just means to remove rule sets with a bad evaluation by introducing GA operated rule sets with a good evaluation.

Table 1. Comparison of characteristics between conventional LCSs and OCS

	Michigan	Pittsburgh	OCS
Population	rule	rule set	rule set
Evaluation	rule	rule set	rule
	credit assignment	elitist preserving selection	credit assignment
Crossover	between rules	between rule sets	between rule sets
Mutation	rule	rule	—
Inversion	—	rule set	—
Concept of OL	a part *	a part *	whole
Problem solving	single agent type	single agent type	multiagent type
	a LCS solves a problem	LCSs solve their own problems	LCSs solve a problem together

* Detail analysis is discussed in Sect. 6.

```
procedure OCS
  begin
    iteration=0;
    organizational knowledge reuse;
    while iteration < max iteration do
      begin
        step=0;
        while solution does not converge do
          begin
            rule generation;
            rule exchange;
            step=step+1;
          end
        iteration=iteration+1;
        reinforcement learning;
        organizational knowledge reuse;
      end
  end
```

Fig. 5. Algorithm of OCS

solves given problems through the cooperation of multiple agents, and (2) OCS addresses the role specialization in multiple agents. Both issues are difficult to achieve in the framework of conventional approaches.

4   Pentomino Tiling Problem

4.1   Problem Description

A pentomino is a figure that combines five squares as shown in Fig. 6 (a), and its tiling problem is to appropriately place the pentominos while minimizing the

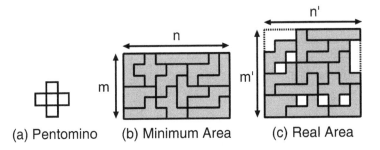

Fig. 6. Pentominos

area that encloses all of the pentominos without any overlap. We select this domain because (1) this problem can be considered as a multiagent problem when one pentomino is assumed to be one agent; (2) it is easy to generate POMDP and NOMDP environments by preparing rules which include local environmental information without other agents information; (3) the minimum solution is known as shown in Fig. 6 (b); and (4) this problem can be directly applied to engineering domains such as printed circuit boards (PCBs) design problems (in this case, each part corresponds to each pentomino [Takadama 99]).

4.2   Pentomino Design and Problem Setting

In the task, each pentomino is designed as an agent in OCS and learns to acquire an appropriate sequence of actions that minimizes the area enclosing all of the pentominos without any overlap. In detail, the pentominos have 17 primitive actions including stay, move, and rotate, and the pentominos get a turn in order, to execute such actions. In a concrete problem setting, all of the pentominos are initially placed at random without considering any overlap, and thus most of the pentominos actually overlap with others. After this initial placement, the pentominos start to perform some primitive actions to reduce such overlap while minimizing the area that encloses all of them. When the size of this area converges without any overlap, all of the pentominos evaluate their own sequences of actions according to the size of the area. Then, the pentominos restart from the initial placement to acquire more appropriate sequences of actions to find a smaller area. In this cycle, one *step* is counted when all of the pentominos perform one primitive action, and one *iteration* is counted when the size of the area converges without overlap. Note that the size of the area enclosing all of the pentominos at each iteration always converges, because its value finally gets into a local minimum when all of the pentominos can no longer find new locations of smaller area than in the current situation without breaking the non-overlap situation.

4.3   Index of Evaluation

The following two indexes are employed as evaluation criteria in the task, and the *performance* in this paper is defined as a criterion which considers the two indexes.

$$Solution = (Real\ area)/(Minimum\ area) \tag{1}$$

$$Computational\ cost = \sum_{i=1}^{n} step(i) \tag{2}$$

The first index (*solution*) evaluates the area enclosing all pentominos and shows how the current area, like that shown in Fig. 6 (c), is small compared with the minimum area in Fig. 6 (b). The next index (*computational cost*) calculates the accumulated steps. Especially in the latter equation, "*step* (*i*)" and "*n*" indicate the steps counted until the size of the area converges in *i* iterations, and the maximum number of iterations, respectively.

Note that real computational cost must include all content shown in Table 2. For example, when $cost1(i)$, $cost2(i)$, and $cost3(i)$ in OCS are respectively assumed as the cost of every step, the cost of every GA_STEP, and the cost of every iteration, the three costs in an *i* iteration are calculated as follows.

$$cost1(i) = n_a s(i) \cdot (n_r l c + k_a c)$$
$$cost2(i) = n_a \frac{s(i)}{GA\_STEP} \cdot (n_r g l c)$$
$$cost3(i) = n_a(s(i) \cdot c + n_r l c)$$

In the above equations, n_a, $s(i)$, n_r, l, c, k_a, and g indicate the number of agents, the number of steps in an *i* iteration, the number of rules, the length of a rule, the cost for one value (or bit) match, the coefficient that adjusts the cost for

Table 2. Real computational cost

	Michigan	Pittsburgh	OCS
Every step	n_a agents[*] perform one action	pn_a agents[*] perform one action	n_a agents[*] perform one action
Every GA_STEP[†]	crossover + mutation	—	crossover
Every iteration	credit assignment	crossover + mutation + inversion	credit assignment + organizational knowledge

[*] n_a indicates the number of agents in an organization.
   p indicates the number of LCSs that solve the same problem at the same iteration.
[†] GA_STEP in Pittsburgh approach can be considered as one iteration.

an action ($k_a \gg 1$: In general, the cost of performing an action is much larger than c), and the generation gap ($0 < g < 1$), respectively. In particular, the first and second terms in $cost1$ indicate the cost of rule matching and the cost of performing an action, respectively. In $cost3$, the first and second terms indicate the cost of a credit assignment and the cost of storing organizational knowledge, respectively. These equations derive a relationship $cost1(i) \gg \{cost2(i), cost3(i)\}$ that is also satisfied in both the Michigan and Pittsburgh approaches. Thus, the computational cost in an i iteration can be calculated as follows.

$$Computational\ cost(i) = Cost1(i) + Cost2(i) + Cost3(i)$$
$$\approx Cost1(i)$$
$$= C \cdot s(i)$$

In this equation, C indicates a constant number represented by $n_a(n_r lc + k_a c)$. From this equation, this paper employs the Eq. (2) as the computational cost. Note that the computational cost of the Pittsburgh approach must be calculated as $p \cdot s(i)$ instead of $s(i)$, because the p number of LCSs solve the same problem at the same iteration.

4.4   Rule Set Design

The classifiers (CFs) in the rule sets of the pentominos are designed as follows for the pentomino tiling problem. These rules are use both for individual and organizational knowledge.

- **The condition part**
    - A previously performed primitive action (the 17 types described in the previous section);
    - A flag distinguishing whether a pentomino overlaps with others or not (1 or 0);
    - A flag distinguishing whether a pentomino is totally adjoined to other surrounding pentominos or not (1 or 0); and
    - A flag distinguishing whether a pentomino removes an overlapping area within a certain time or not (1 or 0). This condition only requires two types of memory for both the one past situation and the count of not removing an overlapping area.
- **The action part:** primitive action (17 types).
- **The strength part:** Strength value.

According to this rule design, an example of 2 1 0 # 6 : 0.5 in CF indicates that *if* a previous action is the 2nd action and there is an overlap and the pentomino is not totally adjoined, *then* employ the 6th action, with a 0.5 strength value. In this rule, the # mark indicates "don't care."

5   Simulation

5.1   Experiment Design

To explore elements that cope with non-Markov properties in multiagent environments, we conduct a simulation to compare the following three cases in the pentomino tiling problem with 24 pentominos.

- Michigan Approach [Holland 78]
- Pittsburgh Approach [Smith 83]
- OCS

We select the Michigan and Pittsburgh approaches as our targets to compare with OCS, because both approaches are standard in the context of LCS literature and have different aspects from those of OCS.

5.2   Experimental Setup

For the pentomino tiling problem, organizational knowledge and valuables in OCS are designed as follows.

- **Organizational knowledge** in this simulation is a set comprising each pentominos rule set acquired by 12 pentominos in the prior simulations and is reused as the initial rule sets of 24 pentominos. Note that this knowledge is not randomly generated but is acquired by 12 pentominos. Concretely, 24 pentominos utilize the rule sets as follows, where $RS_{24}(x)$ indicates the rule set of the x-th pentomino whose total number is 24.

$$RS_{24}(x) \leftarrow RS_{12}(mod((x-1), 12) + 1), \ x = 1, \cdots, 24$$

  Through this reuse, the role specialization of 12 pentominos is transfered to that of 24 pentominos as a double role specialization.
- **Parameters** in the Michigan approach, the Pittsburgh approach and OCS are shown in Table 3. Note that the tendency of the results does not change drastically with the parameter setting.

5.3   Experimental Results

Figure 7 shows results of both *solution* and *computational cost* in the Michigan approach, the Pittsburgh approach, and OCS. In this experiment, all results are averaged from five situations with different random seeds. The steps needed to acquire the organizational knowledge are added to the results in OCS, and the *computational cost* in the Pittsburgh approach is adjusted by multiplying p, which is the number of LCSs. The reason for the multiplication is because the same problem is solved by each LCS at the same iteration in the Pittsburgh approach. From this figure, we find the following characteristics.

- The computational cost in the Michigan approach is small, but the solution itself is not good.

Table 3. Parameters in Michigan, Pittsburgh, and OCS

	Michigan	Pittsburgh	OCS
Population size	1 LCS	24 LCSs	
FIRST_CF	30		
MAX_CF	50		
GA_STEP	20 steps	1 iteration	20 steps
Crossover	1 point crossover		rule exchange
GENERATION_GAP	0.1		
BORDER_ST	—		−50
Mutation	1 bit change		—
Mutation rate	0.05		—
Inversion rate	—	0.05	—
Credit assignment	profit sharing	—	profit sharing

* FIRST_CF, MAX_CF, GA_STEP, GENERATION_GAP, and BORDER_ST indicate the number of initial rules of each pentomino, the maximum number of rules of each pentomino, the interval steps in GA operations, the ratio of removed rules, and the lowest strength of the rule not for removal, respectively

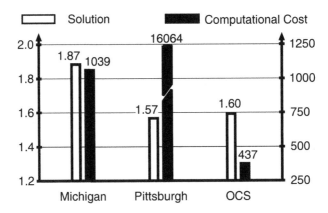

Fig. 7. Solution and computational cost: comparison of Michigan, Pittsburgh and OCS

- The solution in the Pittsburgh approach is quite good, but requires a huge computational cost.
- In comparison with the above results, the solution of OCS is almost the same as that of the Pittsburgh approach, and has the smallest computational cost.

6   Discussion

(1) Analysis from the Viewpoint of OL

As shown in Fig. 7, OCS finds better solutions at smaller computational costs than the Michigan and Pittsburgh approaches. This section investigates why we obtained this result from the viewpoint of OL. We employ the concept of OL as a method for measuring a capability of LCSs towards multiagent environments, because our previous research found that the integration of the four learning mechanisms in OL contributes to finding good solutions at small computational costs in multiagent environments [Takadama 99].

An analysis from the viewpoint of OL tells us that some of the learning mechanisms in OL are missing both in the Michigan and Pittsburgh approaches whereas OCS includes all four of them. Concretely, the Michigan approach includes individual single-loop learning (reinforcement learning) and individual double-loop learning (crossover and mutation),[8] but the other two mechanisms are missing. The Pittsburgh approach, on the other hand, includes individual single- and double-loop learning (inversion and mutation) and organizational single-loop learning (crossover), but lacks organizational double-loop learning. In particular, the lack of the rule exchange mechanism for organizational single-loop learning in the Michigan approach prevents the solution from improving. This is because pentominos in the Michigan approach are limited to independently acquire their own appropriate rules that contribute to finding good solutions. This means that the explored results of other pentominos is required to overcome the limitation of the search range of one pentomino. Furthermore, the lack of the organizational knowledge reuse mechanism for organizational double-loop learning in both the Michigan and Pittsburgh approaches requires large computational costs. This is because pentominos in both the Michigan and Pittsburgh approaches do not originally have an architecture for utilizing pre-learned rules at an organizational level, which contribute to reducing the computational costs.

From this analysis, the learning mechanisms at the *organizational level* are required to overcome limitations in the performance of conventional LCSs in *multiagent environments*. This indicates that such learning mechanisms can be one of the elements to cope with multiagent environments. Here, what we should point to notice is that the organizational level learning mechanisms can maintain their effectiveness owing to the individual level learning mechanisms. For example, the profit sharing as credit assignment procedures of RL in OCS is generally useful only in stationary (*e.g.* single agent) environments, but the rule exchange mechanism and organizational knowledge reuse mechanism in OCS contribute to coping with non-stationary (*e.g.* multiagent) environments by utilizing locally optimized rules acquired by the profit sharing. It is important to utilize locally optimized rules rather than optimize rules in multiagent environments.

---

[8] The crossover and mutation in the Michigan approach contribute to creating new rules but do not work at an organizational level.

(2) Analysis of Non-Markov Properties

The previous analysis suggests that both organizational single- and double-loop learning are required to improve the performance in multiagent environments. However, this implication is derived only from the viewpoint of OL, and we have not yet understood the relationship between the concept of OL and non-Markov properties. Therefore, this section investigates this relationship to explore elements for coping with multiagent environments.

First, organizational single-loop learning has the capability of estimation of environmental situations at the organizational level. This is because the behavior selection after others' rule acquisition through a rule exchange as organizational single-loop learning can be roughly approximated as behavior selection based on estimation of environmental situation. This means behavior selection based on other agents' internal model (*i.e.*, rule sets in OCS) partly acquired by exchanging rules among agents. Second, organizational double-loop learning, on the other hand, has the capability of utilization of records of past situations/actions at the organizational level. This is because rule sets of all pentominos acquired through organizational double-loop learning can be roughly considered as a condensation of the records on the past situations/actions.

From these facts, both the estimation of environmental situations and the utilization of records of past situations/actions at the *organizational level* have the great potentials to cope with *multiagent environments*. Specifically, an integration of both methods at the *organizational level* has a capability of handling the NOMDP environments, while both methods at the *individual level* cope with the POMDP environments. This indicates that it is quite important to consider such methods at the organizational level to improve the performance in multiagent environments. Furthermore, the NOMDP environments might be effectively addressed by combining methods for the POMDP environments. Moreover, we must not forget that the performance at the organizational level can be improved just by introducing methods at the organizational level, even though they are simple and not elaborated one. In OCS, the rule exchange mechanism and organizational knowledge reuse mechanisms contribute to improving the performance in multiagent environments, even though they are implemented quite simply.

7   Conclusion

This paper focused on non-Markov properties in LCSs and discussed difficulties of addressing the properties in multiagent environments. Towards such difficulties, this paper explored elements for coping with non-Markov properties in multiagent environments by comparing the performance of OCS with those of the conventional LCSs. Although this exploration does not cover entire non-Markov properties in multiagent environments, intensive simulations of the pentomino tiling problem have revealed the following potential implications: (1) OCS finds good solutions at small computational costs in comparison with conventional LCSs, namely the Michigan and Pittsburgh approaches; (2) the learning mechanisms at the organizational level, which means the organizational single- and double-loop learning mechanisms in OL, contribute to improving the performance in multiagent environments; (3) an estimation of environmental situations and utilization of records of past situations/actions must be implemented at the organizational level to cope with non-Markov properties in multiagent environments.

Future research will include the following: (a) a theoretical analysis of the implications found in this paper; (b) a comparison of the performance of OCS with those of ZCS [Wilson 94], XCS [Wilson 95], and plain GA in multiagent environments; (c) other elements required in LCSs to cope with non-Markov properties in multiagent environments; and (d) categorization of non-Markov properties in multiagent environments.

References

[Argyris 78] C. Argyris and D. A. Schön: *Organizational Learning*, Addison-Wesley, 1978.

[Chirsman 92] L. Chirsman: "Reinforcement Learning with Perceptual Aliasing: The Perceptual Distinctions Approach", *The 10th National Conference on Artificial Intelligence (AAAI '92)*, pp. 183–188, 1992.

[Cliff 95] D. Cliff and S. Ross: "Adding Temporary Memory to ZCS", *Adaptive Behavior*, Vol. 3, No. 2, pp. 101–150, 1995.

[Cohen 95] M. D. Cohen and L. S. Sproull: *Organizational Learning*, SAGE Publications, 1995.

[DeJong 75] K. Dejong: *An analysis of the behavior of a class of genetic adaptive system*, Ph.D. Thesis, University of Michigan, 1975.

[Goldberg 89] D. E. Goldberg: *Genetic Algorithms in Search, Optimization, and Machine Learning*, Addison-Wesley, 1989.

[Grefenstette 88] J. J. Grefenstette: "Credit Assignment in Rule Discovery Systems Based on Genetic Algorithms," *Machine Learning*, Vol. 3. pp. 225–245, 1988.

[Holland 78] J. H. Holland and J. Reitman: "Cognitive Systems Based on Adaptive Algorithms," in D. A. Waterman and F. Hayes-Roth (Eds.), *Pattern Directed Inference System*, Academic Press, 1978.

[Kim 93] D. Kim: "The Link between individual and organizational learning," *Sloan Management Review*, Fall, pp. 37–50, 1993.

[Lanzi 98] P. L. Lanzi: "Adding Memory to XCS", *IEEE International Conference on Evolutionary Computation (ICEC '98)*, pp. 609–614, 1998.

[Lanzi 99] P. L. Lanzi and S. W. Wilson: "Optimal Classifier System Performance in Non-Markov Environments", *technical report N.99.36, Dipartimento di Elettronica e Informazione*, 1999.

[MacCallum 93] R. A. MacCallum: "Overcoming Incomplete Perception with Utile Distinction Memory", *The 10th International Conference on Machine Learning (ICML '93)*, pp. 190–196, 1993.

[Russell 95] S. J. Russell and P. Norving: *Artificial Intelligence: A Modern Approach*, Prentice-Hall International, 1995.

[Smith 83] S. F. Smith: "Flexible learning of problem solving heuristics through adaptive search," *1983 International Joint Conference on Artificial Intelligence (IJCAI '83)*, pp. 422–425, 1983.

[Sutton 98] R. S. Sutton, A. G. Bart: *Reinforcement Learning – An Introduction –*, The MIT Press, 1998.

[Takadama 98] K. Takadama, S. Nakasuka, and T. Terano: "Multiagent Reinforcement Learning with Organizational-Learning Oriented Classifier System," *IEEE 1998 International Conference On Evolutionary Computation (ICEC '98)*, pp. 63–68, 1998.

[Takadama 99] K. Takadama, T. Terano, K. Shimohara, K. Hori, and S. Nakasuka: "Making Organizational Learning Operational: Implications from Learning Classifier System", *Computational and Mathematical Organization Theory (CMOT)*, Kluwer Academic Publishers, Vol. 5, No. 3, pp. 229–252, 1999.

[Weiss 99] G. Weiss: *Multiagent Systems – Modern Approach to Distributed Artificial Intelligence*, The MIT Press, 1999.

[Wilson 94] S. W. Wilson: "ZCS: A Zeroth Level Classifier System", *Evolutionary Computation*, Vol. 2, No. 1, pp. 1–18, 1994.

[Wilson 95] S. W. Wilson: "Classifier Fitness Based on Accuracy", *Evolutionary Computation*, Vol. 3, No. 2, pp. 149–175, 1995.

Part IV

The Bibliography

A Bigger Learning Classifier Systems Bibliography

Tim Kovacs[1] and Pier Luca Lanzi[2]

[1] School of Computer Science
The University of Birmingham
Birmingham B15 2TT England
T.Kovacs@cs.bham.ac.uk
http://www.cs.bham.ac.uk/
[2] Dipartimento di Elettronica e Informazione
Politecnico di Milano
Piazza Leonardo da Vinci 32
I-20133 Milano – Italia
pierluca.lanzi@polimi.it
http://www.elet.polimi.it/people/lanzi/

Abstract. With over 600 entries, this is by far the most comprehensive bibliography of the machine learning systems introduced by John Holland.

1 Introduction

In 1999 the authors compiled a Learning Classifier Systems (LCS) bibliography [343] of 467 entries, the largest of its kind. Since then the bibliography has grown to 610 entries, largely thanks to many small contributions by numerous individuals. Further contributions (and corrections) are solicited and can be sent by email to the first author.

Learning classifier systems have a long and rich history. We hope this bibliography will both illustrate this point and prove a useful resource for researchers. Although the first classifier system, CS-1, was reported in 1978 [293], the development of LCS was foreshadowed by some of Holland's earlier work [277,278, 279] dating back as far as 1971. In the early 80's much progress was in the form of PhD theses [512,49,238,461,213] (but see also [588,589]), following which LCS papers began to appear steadily in conferences. Later landmarks include the publication of books by Holland in 1986 [291] and Goldberg in 1989 [241], and the first, second and third International Workshops on LCS (IWLCS), in 1992, 1999 and 2000 respectively.

As the bibliography shows, LCS papers appear in a wide range of conferences and journals. The following table shows the distribution of entries by type as of November 7, 2000. (The conference papers category includes 1-page poster papers.)

P.L. Lanzi, W. Stolzmann, and S.W. Wilson (Eds.): IWLCS 2000, LNAI 1996, pp. 213–249, 2001.
© Springer-Verlag Berlin Heidelberg 2001

Category	Number
Books	15
Book chapters	28
Journal papers	86
Conference proceedings	30
Conference papers	353
Technical reports	40
PhD theses	25
Masters theses	15
Unpublished papers	12
Miscellaneous entries	5

Acknowledgements. We are grateful to Alwyn Barry for the contribution of his large LCS bibliography to ours, and to the many other individuals who have contributed.

References

1. Emergent Computation. Proceedings of the Ninth Annual International Conference of the Center for Nonlinear Studies on Self-organizing, Collective, and Cooperative Phenomena in Natural and Artificial Computing Networks. A special issue of Physica D. Stephanie Forrest (Ed.), 1990.
2. *Collected Abstracts for the First International Workshop on Learning Classifier System (IWLCS92)*, 1992. October 6–8, NASA Johnson Space Center, Houston, Texas.
3. *Proceedings of the 2000 Congress on Evolutionary Computation (CEC00)*. IEEE Press, 2000.
4. Proceedings of the International Workshop on Learning Classifier Systems (IWLCS-2000), in the Joint Workshops of SAB 2000 and PPSN 2000, 2000. Pier Luca Lanzi, Wolfgang Stolzmann and Stewart W. Wilson (workshop organisers).
5. Jose L. Aguilar and Mariela Cerrada. Reliability-Centered Maintenance Methodology-Based Fuzzy Classifier System Design for Fault Tolerance. In Koza et al. [345], page 621. One page paper.
6. Manu Ahluwalia and Larry Bull. A Genetic Programming-based Classifier System. In Banzhaf et al. [18], pages 11–18.
7. Rudolf F. Albrecht, Nigel C. Steele, and Colin R. Reeves, editors. *Proceedings of the International Conference on Artificial Neural Nets and Genetic Algorithms.* Spring-Verlag, 1993.
8. Peter J. Angeline, Zbyszek Michalewicz, Marc Schoenauer, Xin Yao, and Ali Zalzala, editors. *Proceedings of the 1999 Congress on Evolutionary Computation CEC99*, Washington (DC), 1999. IEEE Press.
9. W. Brian Arthur, John H. Holland, Blake LeBaron, Richard Palmer, and Paul Talyer. Asset Pricing Under Endogenous Expectations in an Artificial Stock Market. Technical report, Santa Fe Institute, 1996. This is the original version of LeBaron1999a.
10. Thomas Bäck, editor. *Proceedings of the 7th International Conference on Genetic Algorithms (ICGA97)*. Morgan Kaufmann: San Francisco CA, 1997.

11. Thomas Bäck, David B. Fogel, and Zbigniew Michalewicz, editors. *Handbook of Evolutionary Computation.* Institute of Physics Publishing and Oxford University Press, 1997. http://www.iop.org/Books/Catalogue/.

12. Thomas Bäck, Ulrich Hammel, and Hans-Paul Schwefel. Evolutionary computation: Comments on the history and current state. *IEEE Transactions on Evolutionary Computation,* 1(1):3–17, 1997.

13. Jalal Baghdadchi. A Classifier Based Learning Model for Intelligent Agents. In Whitely et al. [586], page 870. One page poster paper.

14. Anthony J. Bagnall. A Multi-Adaptive Agent Model of Generator Bidding in the UK Market in Electricity. In Whitely et al. [586], pages 605–612.

15. Anthony J. Bagnall and G. D. Smith. An Adaptive Agent Model for Generator Company Bidding in the UK Power Pool. In *Proceedings of Artificial Evolution,* page ??, 1999.

16. Anthony J. Bagnall and G. D. Smith. Using an Adaptive Agent to Bid in a Simplified Model of the UK Market in Electricity. In Banzhaf et al. [18], page 774. One page poster paper.

17. N. R. Ball. Towards the Development of Cognitive Maps in Classifier Systems. In Albrecht et al. [7], pages 712–718.

18. Wolfgang Banzhaf, Jason Daida, Agoston E. Eiben, Max H. Garzon, Vasant Honavar, Mark Jakiela, and Robert E. Smith, editors. *Proceedings of the Genetic and Evolutionary Computation Conference (GECCO-99).* Morgan Kaufmann: San Francisco, CA, 1999.

19. Alwyn Barry. The Emergence of High Level Structure in Classifier Systems - A Proposal. *Irish Journal of Psychology,* 14(3):480–498, 1993.

20. Alwyn Barry. Hierarchy Formulation Within Classifiers System – A Review. In Goodman et al. [246], pages 195–211.

21. Alwyn Barry. Aliasing in XCS and the Consecutive State Problem: 1 – Effects. In Banzhaf et al. [18], pages 19–26.

22. Alwyn Barry. Aliasing in XCS and the Consecutive State Problem: 2 – Solutions. In Banzhaf et al. [18], pages 27–34.

23. Alwyn Barry. Specifying Action Persistence within XCS. In Whitely et al. [586], pages 50–57.

24. Alwyn Barry. *XCS Performance and Population Structure within Multiple-Step Environments.* PhD thesis, Queens University Belfast, 2000.

25. Richard J. Bauer. *Genetic Algorithms and Investment Strategies.* Wiley Finance Editions. John Wiley & Sons, 1994.

26. Eric Baum and Igor Durdanovic. An Evolutionary Post Production System. In *Proceedings of the International Workshop on Learning Classifier Systems (IWLCS-2000), in the Joint Workshops of SAB 2000 and PPSN 2000* [4]. Extended abstract.

27. Richard K. Belew and Stephanie Forrest. Learning and Programming in Classifier Systems. *Machine Learning,* 3:193–223, 1988.

28. Richard K. Belew and Michael Gherrity. Back Propagation for the Classifier System. In Schaffer [463], pages 275–281.

29. Hugues Bersini and Francisco J. Varela. Hints for Adaptive Problem Solving Gleaned From Immune Networks. In Schwefel and Männer [470], pages 343–354.

30. Janine Beunings, Ludwig Bölkow, Bernd Heydemann, Biruta Kresling, Claus-Peter Lieckfeld, Claus Mattheck, Werner Nachtigall, Josef Reichholf, Bertram J. Schmidt, Veronika Straaß, and Reinhard Witt. *Bionik: Natur als Vorbild.* WWF Dokumentationen. PRO FUTURA Verlag, München, 1993.

31. J. Biondi. Robustness and evolution in an adaptive system application on classification task. In Albrecht et al. [7], pages 463–470.

32. Andrea Bonarini. ELF: Learning Incomplete Fuzzy Rule Sets for an Autonomous Robot. In Hans-Jürgen Zimmermann, editor, *First European Congress on Fuzzy and Intelligent Technologies – EUFIT'93*, volume 1, pages 69–75, Aachen, D, September 1993. Verlag der Augustinus Buchhandlung.

33. Andrea Bonarini. Evolutionary Learning of General Fuzzy Rules with Biased Evaluation Functions: Competition and Cooperation. *Proc. 1st IEEE Conf. on Evolutionary Computation*, pages 51–56, 1994.

34. Andrea Bonarini. Learning Behaviors Represented as Fuzzy Logic Controllers. In Hans Jürgen Zimmermann, editor, *Second European Congress on Intelligent Techniques and Soft Computing - EUFIT'94*, volume 2, pages 710–715, Aachen, D, 1994. Verlag der Augustinus Buchhandlung.

35. Andrea Bonarini. Extending Q-learning to Fuzzy Classifier Systems. In Marco Gori and Giovanni Soda, editors, *Proceedings of the Italian Association for Artificial Intelligence on Topics in Artificial Intelligence*, volume 992 of *LNAI*, pages 25–36, Berlin, 1995. Springer.

36. Andrea Bonarini. Delayed Reinforcement, Fuzzy Q-Learning and Fuzzy Logic Controllers. In Herrera and Verdegay [274], pages 447–466.

37. Andrea Bonarini. Delayed Reinforcement, Fuzzy Q-Learning and Fuzzy Logic Controllers. In F. Herrera and J. L. Verdegay, editors, *Genetic Algorithms and Soft Computing, (Studies in Fuzziness, 8)*, pages 447–466, Berlin, D, 1996. Physica-Verlag.

38. Andrea Bonarini. Evolutionary Learning of Fuzzy rules: competition and cooperation. In W. Pedrycz, editor, *Fuzzy Modelling: Paradigms and Practice*, pages 265–284. Norwell, MA: Kluwer Academic Press, 1996.
ftp://ftp.elet.polimi.it/pub/Andrea.Bonarini/ELF/ELF-Pedrycz.ps.gz.

39. Andrea Bonarini. Anytime learning and adaptation of fuzzy logic behaviors. *Adaptive Behavior*, 5(3–4):281–315, 1997.

40. Andrea Bonarini. Reinforcement Distribution to Fuzzy Classifiers. In *Proceedings of the IEEE World Congress on Computational Intelligence (WCCI) – Evolutionary Computation*, pages 51–56. IEEE Computer Press, 1998.

41. Andrea Bonarini. Comparing reinforcement learning algorithms applied to crisp and fuzzy learning classifier systems. In Banzhaf et al. [18], pages 52–59.

42. Andrea Bonarini. An Introduction to Learning Fuzzy Classifier Systems. In Lanzi et al. [364], pages 83–104.

43. Andrea Bonarini and Filippo Basso. Learning to compose fuzzy behaviors for autonomous agents. *Int. Journal of Approximate Reasoning*, 17(4):409–432, 1997.

44. Andrea Bonarini, Claudio Bonacina, and Matteo Matteucci. Fuzzy and crisp representation of real-valued input for learning classifier systems. In Wu [623], pages 228–235.

45. Andrea Bonarini, Claudio Bonacina, and Matteo Matteucci. Fuzzy and Crisp Representations of Real-valued Input for Learning Classifier Systems. In Lanzi et al. [364], pages 107–124.

46. Andrea Bonarini, Marco Dorigo, V. Maniezzo, and D. Sorrenti. AutonoMouse: An Experiment in Grounded Behaviors. In *Proceedings of GAA91 – Second Italian Workshop on Machine Learning, Bari, Italy*, 1991.

47. Pierre Bonelli and Alexandre Parodi. An Efficient Classifier System and its Experimental Comparison with two Representative learning methods on three medical domains. In Booker and Belew [59], pages 288–295.

48. Pierre Bonelli, Alexandre Parodi, Sandip Sen, and Stewart W. Wilson. NEW-BOOLE: A Fast GBML System. In *International Conference on Machine Learning*, pages 153–159, San Mateo, California, 1990. Morgan Kaufmann.

49. Lashon B. Booker. *Intelligent Behavior as an Adaptation to the Task Environment*. PhD thesis, The University of Michigan, 1982.

50. Lashon B. Booker. Improving the performance of genetic algorithms in classifier systems. In Grefenstette [250], pages 80–92.

51. Lashon B. Booker. Classifier Systems that Learn Internal World Models. *Machine Learning*, 3:161–192, 1988.

52. Lashon B. Booker. Triggered rule discovery in classifier systems. In Schaffer [463], pages 265–274.

53. Lashon B. Booker. Instinct as an Inductive Bias for Learning Behavioral Sequences. In Meyer and Wilson [385], pages 230–237.

54. Lashon B. Booker. Representing Attribute-Based Concepts in a Classifier System. In Rawlins [422], pages 115–127.

55. Lashon B. Booker. Viewing Classifier Systems as an Integrated Architecture. In *Collected Abstracts for the First International Workshop on Learning Classifier System (IWLCS-92)* [2]. October 6–8, NASA Johnson Space Center, Houston, Texas.

56. Lashon B. Booker. Do We Really Need to Estimate Rule Utilities in Classifier Systems? In Wu [623], pages 236–241.

57. Lashon B. Booker. Classifier systems, endogenous fitness, and delayed reward: A preliminary investigation. In *Proceedings of the International Workshop on Learning Classifier Systems (IWLCS-2000), in the Joint Workshops of SAB 2000 and PPSN 2000* [4]. Extended abstract.

58. Lashon B. Booker. Do We Really Need to Estimate Rule Utilities in Classifier Systems? In Lanzi et al. [364], pages 125–142.

59. Lashon B. Booker and Richard K. Belew, editors. *Proceedings of the 4th International Conference on Genetic Algorithms (ICGA91)*. Morgan Kaufmann: San Francisco CA, July 1991.

60. Lashon B. Booker, David E. Goldberg, and John H. Holland. Classifier Systems and Genetic Algorithms. *Artificial Intelligence*, 40:235–282, 1989.

61. Lashon B. Booker, Rick L. Riolo, and John H. Holland. Learning and Representation in Classifier Systems. In Vassant Honavar and Leonard Uhr, editors, *Artificial Intelligence and Neural Networks*, pages 581–613. Academic Press, 1994.

62. H. Brown Cribbs III and Robert E. Smith. Classifier System Renaissance: New Analogies, New Directions. In Koza et al. [347], pages 547–552.

63. Will Browne. *The Development of an Industrial Learning Classifier System for Application to a Steel Hot Strip Mill*. PhD thesis, University of Wales, Cardiff, 1999.

64. Will Browne, Karen Holford, and Carolynne Moore. An Industry Based Development of the Learning Classifier System Technique. Submitted to: 4th International Conference on Adaptive Computing in Design and Manufacturing (ACDM 2000).

65. Will Browne, Karen Holford, Carolynne Moore, and John Bullock. The implementation of a learning classifier system for parameter identification by signal processing of data from steel strip downcoilers. In A. T. Augousti, editor, *Software in Measurement. IEE Computer and Control Division*, 1996.

66. Will Browne, Karen Holford, Carolynne Moore, and John Bullock. A Practical Application of a Learning Classifier System for Downcoiler Decision Support in a Steel Hot Strip Mill. *Ironmaking and Steelmaking*, 25(1):33–41, 1997. Engineering Doctorate Seminar '97. Swansea, Wales, Sept. 2nd, 1997.

67. Will Browne, Karen Holford, Carolynne Moore, and John Bullock. A Practical Application of a Learning Classifier System in a Steel Hot Strip Mill. In Smith et al. [491], pages 611–614.

68. Will Browne, Karen Holford, Carolynne Moore, and John Bullock. An Industrial Learning Classifier System: The Importance of Pre-Processing Real Data and Choice of Alphabet. *To appear in: Engineering Applications of Artificial Intelligence*, 1999.

69. Larry Bull. *Artificial Symbiology: evolution in cooperative multi-agent environments*. PhD thesis, University of the West of England, 1995.

70. Larry Bull. On ZCS in Multi-agent Environments. *Lecture Notes in Computer Science*, 1498:471–480, 1998.

71. Larry Bull. On Evolving Social Systems. *Computational and Mathematical Organization Theory*, 5(3):281–298, 1999.

72. Larry Bull. On using ZCS in a Simulated Continuous Double-Auction Market. In Banzhaf et al. [18], pages 83–90.

73. Larry Bull. Simple markov models of the genetic algorithm in classifier systems: Accuracy-based fitness. In *Proceedings of the International Workshop on Learning Classifier Systems (IWLCS-2000), in the Joint Workshops of SAB 2000 and PPSN 2000* [4]. Extended abstract.

74. Larry Bull. Simple markov models of the genetic algorithm in classifier systems: Multi-step tasks. In *Proceedings of the International Workshop on Learning Classifier Systems (IWLCS-2000), in the Joint Workshops of SAB 2000 and PPSN 2000* [4]. Extended abstract.

75. Larry Bull and Terence C. Fogarty. Coevolving Communicating Classifier Systems for Tracking. In Albrecht et al. [7], pages 522–527.

76. Larry Bull and Terence C. Fogarty. Evolving Cooperative Communicating Classifier Systems. In A. V. Sebald and L. J. Fogel, editors, *Proceedings of the Third Annual Conference on Evolutionary Programming*, pages 308–315, 1994.

77. Larry Bull and Terence C. Fogarty. Parallel Evolution of Communicating Classifier Systems. In *Proceedings of the 1994 IEEE Conference on Evolutionary Computing*, pages 680–685. IEEE, 1994.

78. Larry Bull and Terence C. Fogarty. Evolutionary Computing in Cooperative Multi-Agent Systems. In Sandip Sen, editor, *Proceedings of the 1996 AAAI Symposium on Adaptation, Coevolution and Learning in Multi-Agent Systems*, pages 22–27. AAAI, 1996.

79. Larry Bull and Terence C. Fogarty. Evolutionary Computing in Multi-Agent Environments: Speciation and Symbiogenesis. In H-M. Voigt, W. Ebeling, I. Rechenberg, and H-P. Schwefel, editors, *Parallel Problem Solving from Nature – PPSN IV*, pages 12–21. Springer-Verlag, 1996.

80. Larry Bull, Terence C. Fogarty, S. Mikami, and J. G. Thomas. Adaptive Gait Acquisition using Multi-agent Learning for Wall Climbing Robots. In *Automation and Robotics in Construction XII*, pages 80–86, 1995.

81. Larry Bull, Terence C. Fogarty, and M. Snaith. Evolution in Multi-agent Systems: Evolving Communicating Classifier Systems for Gait in a Quadrupedal Robot. In Eshelman [186], pages 382–388.

82. Larry Bull and O. Holland. Internal and External Representations: A Comparison in Evolving the Ability to Count. In *Proceedings of the First Annual Society for the Study of Artificial Intelligence and Simulated Behaviour Robotics Workshop*, pages 11–14, 1994.

83. Larry Bull and Jacob Hurst. Self-Adaptive Mutation in ZCS Controllers. In *Proceedings of the EvoNet Workshops - EvoRob 2000*, pages 339–346. Springer, 2000.

84. Larry Bull, Jacob Hurst, and Andy Tomlinson. Mutation in Classifier System Controllers. In et al. [187], pages 460–467.

85. Martin Butz, David E. Goldberg, and Wolfgang Stolzmann. New challenges for an ACS: Hard problems and possible solutions. Technical Report 99019, University of Illinois at Urbana-Champaign, Urbana, IL, October 1999.

86. Martin Butz, David E. Goldberg, and Wolfgang Stolzmann. The anticipatory classifier system and genetic generalization. Technical Report 2000032, Illinois Genetic Algorithms Laboratory, 2000.

87. Martin Butz and Wolfgang Stolzmann. Action-Planning in Anticipatory Classifier Systems. In Wu [623], pages 242–249.

88. Martin V. Butz. An Implementation of the XCS classifier system in C. Technical Report 99021, The Illinois Genetic Algorithms Laboratory, 1999.

89. Martin V. Butz. XCSJava 1.0: An Implementation of the XCS classifier system in Java . Technical Report 2000027, Illinois Genetic Algorithms Laboratory, 2000.

90. Martin V. Butz, David E. Goldberg, and Wolfgang Stolzmann. Introducing a Genetic Generalization Pressure to the Anticipatory Classifier System – Part 1: Theoretical Approach. In Whitely et al. [586], pages 34–41. Also Technical Report 2000005 of the Illinois Genetic Algorithms Laboratory.

91. Martin V. Butz, David E. Goldberg, and Wolfgang Stolzmann. Introducing a Genetic Generalization Pressure to the Anticipatory Classifier System – Part 2: Performance Analysis. In Whitely et al. [586], pages 42–49. Also Technical Report 2000006 of the Illinois Genetic Algorithms Laboratory.

92. Martin V. Butz, David E. Goldberg, and Wolfgang Stolzmann. Investigating Generalization in the Anticipatory Classifier System. In *Proceedings of Parallel Problem Solving from Nature (PPSN VI)*, 2000. Also tech. report 2000014 of the Illinois Genetic Algorithms Laboratory.

93. Martin V. Butz, David E. Goldberg, and Wolfgang Stolzmann. Probability-enhanced predictions in the anticipatory classifier system. In *Proceedings of the International Workshop on Learning Classifier Systems (IWLCS-2000), in the Joint Workshops of SAB 2000 and PPSN 2000* [4]. Extended abstract.

94. Martin V. Butz and Stewart W. Wilson. An Algorithmic Description of XCS. Technical Report 2000017, Illinois Genetic Algorithms Laboratory, 2000.

95. Alessio Camilli. Classifier systems in massively parallel architectures. Master's thesis, University of Pisa, 1990. (In Italian).

96. Alessio Camilli and Roberto Di Meglio. Sistemi a classificatori su architetture a parallelismo massiccio. Technical report, Univ. Delgi Studi di Pisa, 1989.

97. Alessio Camilli, Roberto Di Meglio, F. Baiardi, M. Vanneschi, D. Montanari, and R. Serra. Classifier System Parallelization on MIMD Architectures. Technical Report 3/17, CNR, 1990.

98. Y. J. Cao, N. Ireson, L. Bull, and R. Miles. Distributed Learning Control of Traffic Signals. In *Proceedings of the EvoNet Workshops - EvoSCONDI 2000*, pages 117–126. Springer, 2000.

99. Y. J. Cao, N. Ireson, Larry Bull, and R. Miles. Design of a Traffic Junction Controller using a Classifier System and Fuzzy Logic. In *Proceedings of the Sixth International Conference on Computational Intelligence, Theory, and Applications*. Springer-Verlag, 1999.

100. A. Carbonaro, G. Casadei, and A. Palareti. Genetic Algorithms and Classifier Systems in Simulating a Cooperative Behavior. In Albrecht et al. [7], pages 479–483.

101. Brian Carse. Learning Anticipatory Behaviour Using a Delayed Action Classifier System. In Fogarty [203], pages 210–223.

102. Brian Carse and Terence C. Fogarty. A delayed-action classifier system for learning in temporal environments. In *Proceedings of the 1st IEEE Conference on Evolutionary Computation*, volume 2, pages 670–673, 1994.

103. Brian Carse and Terence C. Fogarty. A Fuzzy Classifier System Using the Pittsburgh Approach. In Davidor and Schwefel [136], pages 260–269.

104. Brian Carse, Terence C. Fogarty, and A. Munro. Distributed Adaptive Routing Control in Communications Networks using a Temporal Fuzzy Classifier System. In *Proceedings of the Fifth IEEE Conference on Fuzzy Systems*, pages 2203–2207. IEEE, 1996.

105. Brian Carse, Terence C. Fogarty, and A. Munro. Evolutionary Learning of Controllers using Temporal Fuzzy Classifier Systems. In I. C. Parmee, editor, *Proceedings of the Second Conference on Adaptive Computing in Engineering Design and Control*, pages 174–180, 1996.

106. Brian Carse, Terence C. Fogarty, and A. Munro. Evolving fuzzy rule based controllers using genetic algorithms. *International Journal for Fuzzy Sets and Systems*, 80:273–293, 1996.

107. Brian Carse, Terence C. Fogarty, and A. Munro. The Temporal Fuzzy Classifier System and its Application to Distributed Control in a Homogeneous Multi-Agent ecology. In Goodman et al. [246], pages 76–86.

108. Brian Carse, Terence C. Fogarty, and Alistair Munro. Evolving Temporal Fuzzy Rule-Bases for Distributed Routing Control in Telecommunication Networks. In Herrera and Verdegay [274], pages 467–488.

109. Brian Carse, Terence C. Fogarty, and Alistair Munro. Artificial evolution of fuzzy rule bases which represent time: A temporal fuzzy classifier system. *International Journal of Intelligent Systems*, 13(issue 10-11):905–927, 1998.

110. G. Casadei, A. Palareti, and G. Proli. Classifier System in Traffic Management. In Albrecht et al. [7], pages 620–627.

111. Keith Chalk and George D. Smith. Multi-Agent Classifier Systems and the Iterated Prisoner's Dilemma. In Smith et al. [491], pages 615–618.

112. Keith W. Chalk and George D. Smith. The Co-evolution of Classifier Systems in a Competitive Environment. Poster presented at AISB94. Authors were from the University of East Anglia, U.K.

113. Pawel Cichosz. Reinforcement learning algorithms based on the methods of temporal differences. Master's thesis, Institute of Computer Science, Warsaw University of Technology, 1994.

114. Pawel Cichosz. *Reinforcement Learning by Truncating Temporal Differences*. PhD thesis, Department of Electronics and Information Technology, Warsaw University of Technology, 1997.

115. Pawel Cichosz and Jan J. Mulawka. GBQL: A novel genetics-based reinforcement learning architecture. In *Proceedings of the Third European Congress on Intelligent Techniques and Soft Computing (EUFIT'95)*, 1995.

116. Pawel Cichosz and Jan J. Mulawka. Faster temporal credit assignment in learning classifier systems. In *Proceedings of the First Polish Conference on Evolutionary Algorithms (KAE-96)*, 1996.

117. Dave Cliff and Seth G. Bullock. Adding 'Foveal Vision' to Wilson's Animat. *Adaptive Behavior*, 2(1):47–70, 1993.

118. Dave Cliff, Philip Husbands, Jean-Arcady Meyer, and Stewart W. Wilson, editors. *From Animals to Animats 3. Proceedings of the Third International Conference on Simulation of Adaptive Behavior (SAB94)*. A Bradford Book. MIT Press, 1994.

119. Dave Cliff and Susi Ross. Adding Temporary Memory to ZCS. *Adaptive Behavior*, 3(2):101–150, 1994. Also technical report: ftp://ftp.cogs.susx.ac.uk/pub/reports/csrp/csrp347.ps.Z.

120. Dave Cliff and Susi Ross. Adding Temporary Memory to ZCS. Technical Report CSRP347, School of Cognitive and Computing Sciences, University of Sussex, 1995. ftp://ftp.cogs.susx.ac.uk/pub/reports/csrp/csrp347.ps.Z.

121. H. G. Cobb and John J. Grefenstette. Learning the persistence of actions in reactive control rules. In *Proceedings 8th International Machine Learning Workshop*, pages 293–297. Morgan Kaufmann, 1991.

122. Philippe Collard and Cathy Escazut. Relational Schemata: A Way to Improve the Expressiveness of Classifiers. In Eshelman [186], pages 397–404.

123. Marco Colombetti and Marco Dorigo. Learning to Control an Autonomous Robot by Distributed Genetic Algorithms. In Roitblat and Wilson [447], pages 305–312.

124. Marco Colombetti and Marco Dorigo. Robot Shaping: Developing Situated Agents through Learning. Technical Report TR-92-040, International Computer Science Institute, Berkeley, CA, 1993.

125. Marco Colombetti and Marco Dorigo. Training Agents to Perform Sequential Behavior. Technical Report TR-93-023, International Computer Science Institute, Berkeley, CA, September 1993.

126. Marco Colombetti and Marco Dorigo. Training agents to perform sequential behavior. *Adaptive Behavior*, 2(3):247–275, 1994. ftp://iridia.ulb.ac.be/pub/dorigo/journals/IJ.06-ADAP94.ps.gz.

127. Marco Colombetti and Marco Dorigo. Verso un'ingegneria del comportamento. *Rivista di Automatica, Elettronica e Informatica*, 83(10), 1996. In Italian.

128. Marco Colombetti and Marco Dorigo. Evolutionary Computation in Behavior Engineering. In *Evolutionary Computation: Theory and Applications*, chapter 2, pages 37–80. World Scientific Publishing Co.: Singapore, 1999. Also Tech. Report. TR/IRIDIA/1996-1, IRIDIA, Université Libre de Bruxelles.

129. Marco Colombetti, Marco Dorigo, and G. Borghi. Behavior Analysis and Training: A Methodology for Behavior Engineering. *IEEE Transactions on Systems, Man and Cybernetics*, 26(6):365–380, 1996.

130. Marco Colombetti, Marco Dorigo, and G. Borghi. Robot shaping: The HAMSTER Experiment. In M. Jamshidi et al., editor, *Proceedings of ISRAM'96, Sixth International Symposium on Robotics and Manufacturing, May 28–30, Montpellier, France*, 1996.

131. M. Compiani, D. Montanari, R. Serra, and P. Simonini. Asymptotic dynamics of classifier systems. In Schaffer [463], pages 298–303.

132. M. Compiani, D. Montanari, R. Serra, and P. Simonini. Learning and Bucket Brigade Dynamics in Classifier Systems. In *Special issue of Physica D (Vol. 42)* [1], pages 202–212.

133. M. Compiani, D. Montanari, R. Serra, and G. Valastro. Classifier systems and neural networks. In *Parallel Architectures and Neural Networks–First Italian Workshop*, pages 105–118. World Scientific, Teaneck, NJ, 1989.

134. Clare Bates Congdon. Classification of epidemiological data: A comparison of genetic algorithm and decision tree approaches. In *Proceedings of the 2000 Congress on Evolutionary Computation (CEC00)* [3], pages 442–449.

135. O. Cordón, F. Herrera, E. Herrera-Viedma, and M. Lozano. Genetic Algorithms and Fuzzy Logic in Control Processes. Technical Report DECSAI-95109, University of Granada, Granada, Spain, 1995.

136. Y. Davidor and H.-P. Schwefel, editors. *Parallel Problem Solving From Nature – PPSN III*, volume 866 of *Lecture Notes in Computer Science*, Berlin, 1994. Springer Verlag.

137. Lawrence Davis. Mapping Classifier Systems into Neural Networks. In *Proceedings of the Workshop on Neural Information Processing Systems 1*, pages 49–56, 1988.

138. Lawrence Davis, editor. *Genetic Algorithms and Simulated Annealing*, Research Notes in Artificial Intelligence. Pitman Publishing: London, 1989.

139. Lawrence Davis. Mapping Neural Networks into Classifier Systems. In Schaffer [463], pages 375–378.

140. Lawrence Davis. Covering and Memory in Classifier Systems. In *Collected Abstracts for the First International Workshop on Learning Classifier System (IWLCS-92)* [2]. October 6–8, NASA Johnson Space Center, Houston, Texas.

141. Lawrence Davis and David Orvosh. The Mating Pool: A Testbed for Experiments in the Evolution of Symbol Systems. In Eshelman [186], pages 405–??

142. Lawrence Davis, Stewart W. Wilson, and David Orvosh. Temporary Memory for Examples can Speed Learning in a Simple Adaptive System. In Roitblat and Wilson [447], pages 313–320.

143. Lawrence Davis and D. K. Young. Classifier Systems with Hamming Weights. In *Proceedings of the Fifth International Conference on Machine Learning*, pages 162–173. Morgan Kaufmann, 1988.

144. Bart de Boer. Classifier Systems: a useful approach to machine learning? Master's thesis, Leiden University, 1994.
ftp://ftp.wi.leidenuniv.nl/pub/CS/MScTheses/deboer.94.ps.gz.

145. Kenneth A. De Jong. Learning with Genetic Algorithms: An Overview. *Machine Learning*, 3:121–138, 1988.

146. Michael de la Maza. A SEAGUL Visits the Race Track. In Schaffer [463], pages 208–212.

147. Daniel Derrig and James Johannes. Deleting End-of-Sequence Classifiers. In John R. Koza, editor, *Late Breaking Papers at the Genetic Programming 1998 Conference*, University of Wisconsin, Madison, Wisconsin, USA, July 1998. Stanford University Bookstore.

148. Daniel Derrig and James D. Johannes. Hierarchical Exemplar Based Credit Allocation for Genetic Classifier Systems. In Koza et al. [345], pages 622–628.

149. L. Desjarlais and Stephanie Forrest. Linked learning in classifier systems: A control architecture for mobile robots. In *Collected Abstracts for the First International Workshop on Learning Classifier System (IWLCS-92)* [2]. October 6–8, NASA Johnson Space Center, Houston, Texas.

150. P. Devine, R. Paton, and M. Amos. Adaptation of Evolutionary Agents in Computational Ecologies. In *BCEC-97, Sweden*, 1997.

151. Jean-Yves Donnart. *Cognitive Architecture and Adaptive Properties of an Motivationally Autonomous Animat*. PhD thesis, Université Pierre et Marie Curie. Paris, France., 1998. Thesis is in French.

152. Jean-Yves Donnart and Jean-Arcady Meyer. A hierarchical classifier system implementing a motivationally autonomous animat. In Cliff et al. [118], pages 144–153.

153. Jean-Yves Donnart and Jean-Arcady Meyer. Hierarchical-map Building and Self-positioning with MonaLysa. *Adaptive Behavior*, 5(1):29–74, 1996.

154. Jean-Yves Donnart and Jean-Arcady Meyer. Learning Reactive and Planning Rules in a Motivationally Autonomous Animat. *IEEE Transactions on Systems, Man and Cybernetics - Part B: Cybernetics*, 26(3):381–395, 1996.

155. Jean-Yves Donnart and Jean-Arcady Meyer. Spatial Exploration, Map Learning, and Self-Positioning with MonaLysa. In Maes et al. [377], pages 204–213.

156. Marco Dorigo. Message-Based Bucket Brigade: An Algorithm for the Apportionment of Credit Problem. In Y. Kodratoff, editor, *Proceedings of European Working Session on Learning '91, Porto, Portugal*, number 482 in Lecture notes in Artificial Intelligence, pages 235–244. Springer-Verlag, 1991.

157. Marco Dorigo. New perspectives about default hierarchies formation in learning classifier systems. In E. Ardizzone, E. Gaglio, and S. Sorbello, editors, *Proceedings of the 2nd Congress of the Italian Association for Artificial Intelligence (AI*IA) on Trends in Artificial Intelligence*, volume 549 of *LNAI*, pages 218–227, Palermo, Italy, October 1991. Springer Verlag.

158. Marco Dorigo. Using Transputers to Increase Speed and Flexibility of Genetic-based Machine Learning Systems. *Microprocessing and Microprogramming*, 34:147–152, 1991.

159. Marco Dorigo. Alecsys and the AutonoMouse: Learning to Control a Real Robot by Distributed Classifier System. Technical Report 92-011, Politecnico di Milano, 1992.

160. Marco Dorigo. *Optimization, Learning and Natural Algorithms*. PhD thesis, Politecnico di Milano, Italy, 1992. (In Italian).

161. Marco Dorigo. Genetic and Non-Genetic Operators in ALECSYS. *Evolutionary Computation*, 1(2):151–164, 1993. Also Tech. Report TR-92-075 International Computer Science Institute.

162. Marco Dorigo. Gli Algoritmi Genetici, i Sistemi a Classificatori e il Problema dell'Animat. *Sistemi Intelligenti*, 3(93):401–434, 1993. In Italian.

163. Marco Dorigo. Alecsys and the AutonoMouse: Learning to Control a Real Robot by Distributed Classifier Systems. *Machine Learning*, 19:209–240, 1995.

164. Marco Dorigo. The Robot Shaping Approach to Behavior Engineering. Thèse d'Agrégation de l'Enseignement Supérieur, Faculté des Sciences Appliquées, Université Libre de Bruxelles, pp.176, 1995.

165. Marco Dorigo and Hugues Bersini. A Comparison of Q-Learning and Classifier Systems. In Cliff et al. [118], pages 248–255.

166. Marco Dorigo and Marco Colombetti. Robot shaping: Developing autonomous agents through learning. *Artificial Intelligence*, 2:321–370, 1994.
ftp://iridia.ulb.ac.be/pub/dorigo/journals/IJ.05-AIJ94.ps.gz.

167. Marco Dorigo and Marco Colombetti. The Role of the Trainer in Reinforcement Learning. In S. Mahadevan et al., editor, *Proceedings of MLC-COLT '94 Workshop on Robot Learning, July 10th, New Brunswick, NJ*, pages 37–45, 1994.

168. Marco Dorigo and Marco Colombetti. Précis of Robot Shaping: An Experiment in Behavior Engineering. *Special Issue on Complete Agent Learning in Complex Environments, Adaptive Behavior*, 5(3–4):391–405, 1997.

169. Marco Dorigo and Marco Colombetti. Reply to Dario Floreano's "Engineering Adaptive Behavior". *Special Issue on Complete Agent Learning in Complex Environments, Adaptive Behavior*, 5(3–4):417–420, 1997.

170. Marco Dorigo and Marco Colombetti. *Robot Shaping: An Experiment in Behavior Engineering*. MIT Press/Bradford Books, 1998.

171. Marco Dorigo and V. Maniezzo. Parallel Genetic Algorithms: Introduction and Overview of Current Research. In J. Stenders, editor, *Parallel Genetic Algorithms: Theory and Applications*, Amsterdam, 1992. IOS Press.

172. Marco Dorigo, V. Maniezzo, and D. Montanari. Classifier-based robot control systems. In *IFAC/IFIP/IMACS International Symposium on Artificial Intelligence in Real-Time Control*, pages 591–598, Delft, Netherlands, 1992.

173. Marco Dorigo, Mukesh J. Patel, and Marco Colombetti. The effect of Sensory Information on Reinforcement Learning by a Robot Arm. In M. Jamshidi et al., editor, *Proceedings of ISRAM'94, Fifth International Symposium on Robotics and Manufacturing, August 14–18, Maui, HI*, pages 83–88. ASME Press, 1994.

174. Marco Dorigo and U. Schnepf. Organisation of Robot Behaviour Through Genetic Learning Processes. In *Proceedings of ICAR'91 – Fifth IEEE International Conference on Advanced Robotics, Pisa, Italy*, pages 1456–1460. IEEE Press, 1991.

175. Marco Dorigo and U. Schnepf. Genetics-based Machine Learning and Behaviour Based Robotics: A New Synthesis. *IEEE Transactions on Systems, Man and Cybernetics*, 23(1):141–154, 1993.

176. Marco Dorigo and E. Sirtori. A Parallel Environment for Learning Systems. In *Proceedings of GAA91 – Second Italian Workshop on Machine Learning, Bari, Italy*, 1991.

177. Marco Dorigo and Enrico Sirtori. Alecsys: A Parallel Laboratory for Learning Classifier Systems. In Booker and Belew [59], pages 296–302.

178. Barry B. Druhan and Robert C. Mathews. THIYOS: A Classifier System Model of Implicit Knowledge in Artificial Grammars. In *Proc. Ann. Cog. Sci. Soc.*, 1989.

179. John H. Holmes Dennis R. Durbin and Flaura K. Winston. A New Bootstrapping Method to Improve Classification Performance in Learning Classifier Systems. In *Proceedings of Parallel Problem Solving from Nature (PPSN VI)*, 2000.

180. Daniel Eckert and Johann Mitlöhner. Modelling individual and endogenous learning in games: the relevance of classifier systems. In *Complex Modelling for Socio-Economic Systems, SASA, Vienna*, 1997.

181. Daniel Eckert, Johann Mitlöhner, and Makus Moschner. Evolutionary stability issues and adaptive learning in classifier systems. In *OR'97 Conference on Operations Research, Vienna*, 1997.

182. G. Enee and C. Escazut. Classifier systems evolving multi-agent system with distributed elitism. In Angeline et al. [8], pages 1740–1745.

183. Cathy Escazut and Philippe Collard. Learning Disjunctive Normal Forms in a Dual Classifier System. In Nada Lavrač and Stefan Wrobel, editors, *Proceedings of the 8th European Conference on Machine Learning*, volume 912 of *LNAI*, pages 271–274. Springer, 1995.

184. Cathy Escazut, Philippe Collard, and Jean-Louis Cavarero. Dynamic Management of the Specificity in Classifier Systems. In Albrecht et al. [7], pages 484–491.

185. Cathy Escazut and Terence C. Fogarty. Coevolving Classifier Systems to Control Traffic Signals. In John R. Koza, editor, *Late Breaking Papers at the 1997 Genetic Programming Conference*, Stanford University, CA, USA, July 1997. Stanford Bookstore.

186. Larry J. Eshelman, editor. *Proceedings of the 6th International Conference on Genetic Algorithms (ICGA95)*. Morgan Kaufmann Publishers: San Francisco CA, 1995.

187. J. A. Meyer et al., editor. *From Animals to Animats 6: Proceedings of the Sixth International Conference on Simulation of Adaptive Behavior*, 2000.

188. Andrew Fairley and Derek F. Yates. Improving Simple Classifier Systems to alleviate the problems of Duplication, Subsumption and Equivalence of Rules. In Albrecht et al. [7], pages 408–416.

189. Andrew Fairley and Derek F. Yates. Inductive Operators and Rule Repair in a Hybrid Genetic Learning System: Some Initial Results. In Fogarty [203], pages 166–179.

190. I. De Falco, A. Iazzetta, E. Tarantino, and A. Della Cioppa. An evolutionary system for automatic explicit rule extraction. In *Proceedings of the 2000 Congress on Evolutionary Computation (CEC00)* [3], pages 450–457.

191. J. Doyne Farmer. A Rosetta Stone for Connectionism. In *Special issue of Physica D (Vol. 42)* [1], pages 153–187.

192. J. Doyne Farmer, N. H. Packard, and A. S. Perelson. The Immune System, Adaptation & Learning. *Physica D*, 22:187–204, 1986.

193. Francine Federman. NEXTNOTE: A Learning Classifier System. In Annie S. Wu, editor, *Proceedings of the Genetic and Evolutionary Computation Conference Workshop Program*, pages 136–138, 2000.

194. Francine Federman and Susan Fife Dorchak. Information Theory and NEXTPITCH: A Learning Classifier System. In Bäck [10], pages 442–449.

195. Francine Federman and Susan Fife Dorchak. Representation of Music in a Learning Classifier System. In Rad and Skowron, editors, *Foundations of Intelligent Systems: Proceedings 10th International Symposium (ISMIS'97)*. Springer-Verlag: Heidelberg, 1997.

196. Francine Federman and Susan Fife Dorchak. A Study of Classifier Length and Population Size. In Koza et al. [345], pages 629–634.

197. Francine Federman, Gayle Sparkman, and Stephanie Watt. Representation of Music in a Learning Classifier System Utilizing Bach Chorales. In Banzhaf et al. [18], page 785. One page poster paper.

198. Rhonda Ficek. Genetic Algorithms. Technical Report NDSU-CS-TR-90-51, North Dakota State University. Computer Science and Operations Research, 1997.

199. M. V. Fidelis, H. S. Lopes, and A. A. Freitas. Discovering comprehensible classification rules with a genetic algorithm. In *Proceedings of the 2000 Congress on Evolutionary Computation (CEC00)* [3], pages 805–810.

200. Gary William Flake. *The Computational Beauty of Nature*. MIT Press, 1998. (Contains a chapter on ZCS).

201. Peter Fletcher. Simulating the use of 'fiat money' in a simple commodity economy. Master's thesis, Schools of Psychology and Computer Science, University of Birmingham, 1996.

202. Terence C. Fogarty. Co-evolving Co-operative Populations of Rules in Learning Control Systems. In *Evolutionary Computing, AISB Workshop Selected Papers* [203], pages 195–209.

203. Terence C. Fogarty, editor. *Evolutionary Computing, AISB Workshop Selected Papers*, number 865 in Lecture Notes in Computer Science. Springer-Verlag, 1994.

204. Terence C. Fogarty. Learning new rules and adapting old ones with the genetic algorithm. In G. Rzevski, editor, *Artificial Intelligence in Manufacturing*, pages 275–290. Springer-Verlag, 1994.

205. Terence C. Fogarty. Optimising Individual Control Rules and Multiple Communicating Rule-based Control Systems with Parallel Distributed Genetic Algorithms. *IEE Journal of Control Theory and Applications*, 142(3):211–215, 1995.

206. Terence C. Fogarty, Larry Bull, and Brian Carse. Evolving Multi-Agent Systems. In J. Periaux and G. Winter, editors, *Genetic Algorithms in Engineering and Computer Science*, pages 3–22. John Wiley & Sons, 1995.

207. Terence C. Fogarty, Brian Carse, and Larry Bull. Classifier Systems – recent research. *AISB Quarterly*, 89:48–54, 1994.

208. Terence C. Fogarty, Brian Carse, and Larry Bull. Classifier Systems: selectionist reinforcement learning, fuzzy rules and communication. Presented at the First International Workshop on Biologically Inspired Evolutionary Systems, Tokyo, 1995.

209. Terence C. Fogarty, Brian Carse, and A. Munro. Artificial evolution of fuzzy rule bases which represent time: A temporal fuzzy classifier system. *International Journal of Intelligent Systems*, 13(10–11):906–927, 1998.

210. Terence C. Fogarty, N. S. Ireson, and Larry Bull. Genetic-based Machine Learning – Applications in Industry and Commerce. In Vic Rayward-Smith, editor, *Applications of Modern Heuristic Methods*, pages 91–110. Alfred Waller Ltd, 1995.

211. David B. Fogel. *Evolutionary Computation. The Fossil Record. Selected Readings on the History of Evolutionary Computation*, chapter 16: Classifier Systems. IEEE Press, 1998. This is a reprint of (Holland and Reitman, 1978), with an added introduction by Fogel.

212. Stephanie Forrest. *A study of parallelism in the classifier system and its application to classification in KL-ONE semantic networks*. PhD thesis, University of Michigan, Ann Arbor, MI, 1985.

213. Stephanie Forrest. Implementing semantic network structures using the classifier system. In Grefenstette [250], pages 24–44.

214. Stephanie Forrest. The Classifier System: A Computational Model that Supports Machine Intelligence. In *International Conference on Parallel Processing*, pages 711–716, Los Alamitos, Ca., USA, August 1986. IEEE Computer Society Press.

215. Stephanie Forrest. *Parallelism and Programming in Classifier Systems*. Pittman, London, 1991.

216. Stephanie Forrest, editor. *Proceedings of the 5th International Conference on Genetic Algorithms (ICGA93)*. Morgan Kaufmann, 1993.

217. Stephanie Forrest and John H. Miller. Emergent behavior in classifier systems. In *Special issue of Physica D (Vol. 42)* [1], pages 213–217.

218. Stephanie Forrest, Robert E. Smith, and A. Perelson. Maintaining diversity with a genetic algorithm. In *Collected Abstracts for the First International Workshop on Learning Classifier System (IWLCS-92)* [2]. October 6–8, NASA Johnson Space Center, Houston, Texas.

219. Peter W. Frey and David J. Slate. Letter Recognition Using Holland-Style Adaptive Classifiers. *Machine Learning*, 6:161–182, 1991.

220. Leeann L. Fu. The XCS Classifier System and Q-learning. In John R. Koza, editor, *Late Breaking Papers at the Genetic Programming 1998 Conference*, University of Wisconsin, Madison, Wisconsin, USA, 1998. Stanford University Bookstore.

221. Leeann L. Fu. What I have come to understand about classifier systems, 1998. Unpublished document. Dept. of Electrical Engineering and Computer Science. University of Michigan.

222. Takeshi Furuhashi. A Proposal of Hierarchical Fuzzy Classifier Systems. In Forrest [216].

223. Takeshi Furuhashi, Ken Nakaoka, Koji Morikawa, and Yoshiki Uchikawa. Controlling Excessive Fuzziness in a Fuzzy Classifier System. In Forrest [216], pages 635–635.

224. Takeshi Furuhashi, Ken Nakaoka, and Yoshiki Uchikawa. A Study on Fuzzy Classifier System for Finding Control Knowledge of Multi-Input Systems. In Herrera and Verdegay [274], pages 489–502.

225. Santiago Garcia, Fermin Gonzalez, and Luciano Sanchez. Evolving Fuzzy Rule Based Classifiers with GAP: A Grammatical Approach. In Riccardo Poli, Peter Nordin, William B. Langdon, and Terence C. Fogarty, editors, *Genetic Programming, Proceedings of EuroGP'99*, volume 1598 of *LNCS*, pages 203–210, Goteborg, Sweden, May 1999. Springer-Verlag.

226. Chris Gathercole. A Classifier System Plays a Simple Board Game. Master's thesis, Department of AI, University of Edinburgh, U.K., 1993.

227. Pierre Gerard and Olivier Sigaud. Combining Anticipation and Dynamic Programming in Classifier Systems. In *Proceedings of the International Workshop on Learning Classifier Systems (IWLCS-2000), in the Joint Workshops of SAB 2000 and PPSN 2000* [4]. Extended abstract.

228. Andreas Geyer-Schulz. Fuzzy Classifier Systems. In Robert Lowen and Marc Roubens, editors, *Fuzzy Logic: State of the Art*, Series D: System Theory, Knowledge Engineering and Problem Solving, pages 345–354, Dordrecht, 1993. Kluwer Academic Publishers.

229. Andreas Geyer-Schulz. *Fuzzy Rule-Based Expert Systems and Genetic Machine Learning*. Physica Verlag, 1995.
    Book review at: http://www.apl.demon.co.uk/aplandj/fuzzy.htm.

230. Andreas Geyer-Schulz. Holland Classifier Systems. In *Proceedings of the International Conference on APL (APL'95)*, volume 25, pages 43–55, New York, NY, USA, June 1995. ACM Press.

231. Antonella Giani. A Study of Parallel Cooperative Classifier Systems. In John R. Koza, editor, *Late Breaking Papers at the Genetic Programming 1998 Conference*, University of Wisconsin, Madison, Wisconsin, USA, July 1998. Stanford University Bookstore.

232. Antonella Giani, Fabrizio Baiardi, and Antonina Starita. Q-Learning in Evolutionary Rule-Based Systems. In Davidor and Schwefel [136], pages 270–289.

233. Antonella Giani, A. Sticca, F. Baiardi, and A. Starita. Q-learning and Redundancy Reduction in Classifier Systems with Internal State. In Claire Nédellec and Céline Rouveirol, editors, *Proceedings of the 10th European Conference on Machine Learning (ECML-98)*, volume 1398 of *LNAI*, pages 364–369. Springer, 1998.

234. A. H. Gilbert, Frances Bell, and Christine L. Valenzuela. Adaptive Learning of Process Control and Profit Optimisation using a Classifier System. *Evolutionary Computation*, 3(2):177–198, 1995.

235. Attilio Giordana and Filippo Neri. Search-Intensive Concept Induction. *Evolutionary Computation*, 3:375–416, 1995.

236. Attilio Giordana and L. Saitta. REGAL: An integrated system for learning relations using genetic algorithms. In *Proc. 2nd International Workshop on Multistrategy Learning*, pages 234–249, 1993.

237. Attilio Giordana and L. Saitta. Learning disjunctive concepts by means of genetic algorithms. In *Proc. Int. Conf. on Machine Learning*, pages 96–104, 1994.

238. David E. Goldberg. *Computer-Aided Gas Pipeline Operation using Genetic Algorithms and Rule Learning*. PhD thesis, The University of Michigan, 1983.

239. David E. Goldberg. Dynamic System Control using Rule Learning and Genetic Algorithms. In *Proceedings of the 9th International Joint Conference on Artificial Intelligence (IJCAI-85)*, pages 588–592. Morgan Kaufmann, 1985.

240. David E. Goldberg. Genetic algorithms and rules learning in dynamic system control. In Grefenstette [250], pages 8–15.

241. David E. Goldberg. *Genetic Algorithms in Search, Optimization, and Machine Learning*. Addison-Wesley, Reading, Mass., 1989.

242. David E. Goldberg. Probability Matching, the Magnitude of Reinforcement, and Classifier System Bidding. *Machine Learning*, 5:407–425, 1990. (Also TCGA tech report 88002, U. of Alabama).

243. David E. Goldberg. Some Reflections on Learning Classifier Systems. Technical Report 2000009, Illinois Genetic Algorithms Laboratory, University of Illinois at Urbana-Champaign, 2000. This appeared as part of Holland2000a.

244. David E. Goldberg, Jeffrey Horn, and Kalyanmoy Deb.   What Makes a Problem Hard for a Classifier System?   In *Collected Abstracts for the First International Workshop on Learning Classifier System (IWLCS-92)* [2].   (Also tech. report 92007 Illinois Genetic Algorithms Laboratory, University of Illinois at Urbana-Champaign). Available from ENCORE (ftp://ftp.krl.caltech.edu/pub/EC/Welcome.html) in the section on Classifier Systems.

245. S. Y. Goldsmith. *Steady state analysis of a simple classifier system*. PhD thesis, University of New Mexico, Albuquerque, USA, 1989.

246. E. G. Goodman, V. L. Uskov, and W. F. Punch, editors. *Proceedings of the First International Conference on Evolutionary Algorithms and their Application EVCA '96*, Moscow, 1996. The Presidium of the Russian Academy of Sciences.

247. David Perry Greene and Stephen F. Smith. Competition-based induction of decision models from examples. *Machine Learning*, 13:229–257, 1993.

248. David Perry Greene and Stephen F. Smith. Using Coverage as a Model Building Constraint in Learning Classifier Systems. *Evolutionary Computation*, 2(1):67–91, 1994.

249. A. Greenyer. The use of a learning classifier system JXCS. In P. van der Putten and M. van Someren, editors, *CoIL Challenge 2000: The Insurance Company Case*. June 2000. Technical report 2000-09, Leiden Institute of Advanced Computer Science.

250. John J. Grefenstette, editor. *Proceedings of the 1st International Conference on Genetic Algorithms and their Applications (ICGA85)*. Lawrence Erlbaum Associates: Pittsburgh, PA, July 1985.

251. John J. Grefenstette. Multilevel Credit Assignment in a Genetic Learning System. In *Proceedings of the 2nd International Conference on Genetic Algorithms (ICGA87)* [252], pages 202–207.

252. John J. Grefenstette, editor. *Proceedings of the 2nd International Conference on Genetic Algorithms (ICGA87)*, Cambridge, MA, July 1987. Lawrence Erlbaum Associates.

253. John J. Grefenstette. Credit Assignment in Rule Discovery Systems Based on Genetic Algorithms. *Machine Learning*, 3:225–245, 1988.

254. John J. Grefenstette. A System for Learning Control Strategies with Genetic Algorithms. In Schaffer [463], pages 183–190.

255. John J. Grefenstette. Lamarckian Learning in Multi-Agent Environments. In Booker and Belew [59], pages 303–310. http://www.ib3.gmu.edu/gref/publications.html.

256. John J. Grefenstette.   Learning decision strategies with genetic algorithms. In *Proc. Intl. Workshop on Analogical and Inductive Inference*, volume 642 of *Lecture Notes in Artificial Intelligence*, pages 35–50. Springer-Verlag, 1992. http://www.ib3.gmu.edu/gref/.

257. John J. Grefenstette. The Evolution of Strategies for Multi-agent Environments. *Adaptive Behavior*, 1:65–89, 1992. http://www.ib3.gmu.edu/gref/.

258. John J. Grefenstette. Using a genetic algorithm to learn behaviors for autonomous vehicles. In *Proceedings American Institute of Aeronautics and Astronautics Guidance, Navigation and Control Conference*, pages 739–749. AIAA, 1992. http://www.ib3.gmu.edu/gref/.

259. John J. Grefenstette. Evolutionary Algorithms in Robotics. In M. Jamshedi and C. Nguyen, editors, *Robotics and Manufacturing: Recent Trends in Research, Education and Applications, v5. Proc. Fifth Intl. Symposium on Robotics and Manufacturing, ISRAM 94*, pages 65–72. ASME Press: New York, 1994. http://www.ib3.gmu.edu/gref/.

260. John J. Grefenstette and H. G. Cobb. User's guide for SAMUEL, Version 1.3. Technical Report NRL Memorandum Report 6820, Naval Research Laboratory, 1991.

261. John J. Grefenstette, C. L. Ramsey, and Alan C. Schultz. Learning Sequential Decision Rules using Simulation Models and Competition. *Machine Learning*, 5(4):355–381, 1990. http://www.ib3.gmu.edu/gref/publications.html.

262. John J. Grefenstette and Alan C. Schultz. An evolutionary approach to learning in robots. In *Machine Learning Workshop on Robot Learning*, New Brunswick, NJ, 1994. http://www.ib3.gmu.edu/gref/.

263. Hisashi Handa, Takashi Noda, Tadataka Konishi, Osamu Katai, and Mitsuru Baba. Coevolutionary fuzzy classifier system for autonomous mobile robots. In Takadama [531].

264. Adrian Hartley. Genetics Based Machine Learning as a Model of Perceptual Category Learning in Humans. Master's thesis, University of Birmingham, 1998. ftp://ftp.cs.bham.ac.uk/pub/authors/T.Kovacs/index.html.

265. Adrian Hartley. Accuracy-based fitness allows similar performance to humans in static and dynamic classification environments. In Banzhaf et al. [18], pages 266–273.

266. U. Hartmann. Efficient Parallel Learning in Classifier Systems. In Albrecht et al. [7], pages 515–521.

267. U. Hartmann. On the Complexity of Learning in Classifier Systems. In Davidor and Schwefel [136], pages 280–289. Republished in: ECAI 94. 11th European Conference on Artificial Intelligence. A Cohn (Ed.), pp.438–442, 1994. John Wiley and Sons.

268. Marianne Haslev. A Classifier System for the Production by Computer of Past Tense Verb-Forms. Presented at a Genetic Algorithms Workshop at the Rowland Institute, Cambridge MA, Nov 1986, 1986.

269. Mozart Hasse and Aurora R. Pozo. Using Phenotypic Sharing in a Classifier Tool. In Whitely et al. [586], page 392. One page poster paper.

270. Akira Hayashi and Nobuo Suematsu. Viewing Classifier Systems as Model Free Learning in POMDPs. In *Advances in Neural Information Processing Systems 11*, pages 989–995, 1999.

271. Luis Miramontes Hercog. Hand-eye coordination: An evolutionary approach. Master's thesis, Department of Artificial Intelligence. University of Edinburgh, 1998.

272. Luis Miramontes Hercog and Terence C. Fogarty. XCS-based inductive intelligent multi-agent system. In *Late Breaking Papers at the 2000 Genetic and Evolutionary Computation Conference (GECCO-2000)*, pages 125–132, 2000.

273. Luis Miramontes Hercog and Terence C. Fogarty. XCS-based Inductive Multi-Agent System. In *Proceedings of the International Workshop on Learning Classifier Systems (IWLCS-2000), in the Joint Workshops of SAB 2000 and PPSN 2000* [4]. Extended abstract.

274. F. Herrera and J. L. Verdegay, editors. *Genetic Algorithms and Soft Computing, (Studies in Fuzziness, 8)*. Physica-Verlag, Berlin, 1996.

275. E. Herrera-Viedma. Sistemas Clasificadores de Aprendizaje. Aproximaciones Difusas. Technical Report DECSAI-95132, Dept. of Computer Science and A.I., University of Granada, 1995.

276. M. R. Hilliard, G. E. Liepins, Mark Palmer, Michael Morrow, and Jon Richardson. A classifier based system for discovering scheduling heuristics. In Grefenstette [252], pages 231–235.

277. John H. Holland. Processing and processors for schemata. In E. L. Jacks, editor, *Associative information processing*, pages 127–146. New York: American Elsevier, 1971.

278. John H. Holland. *Adaptation in Natural and Artificial Systems*. University of Michigan Press, Ann Arbor, 1975. Republished by the MIT press, 1992.

279. John H. Holland. Adaptation. In R. Rosen and F. M. Snell, editors, *Progress in theoretical biology*. New York: Plenum, 1976.

280. John H. Holland. Adaptive algorithms for discovering and using general patterns in growing knowledge bases. *International Journal of Policy Analysis and Information Systems*, 4(3):245–268, 1980.

281. John H. Holland. Genetic Algorithms and Adaptation. Technical Report 34, University of Michigan. Department of Computer and Communication Sciences, Ann Arbor, 1981.

282. John H. Holland. Escaping brittleness. In *Proceedings Second International Workshop on Machine Learning*, pages 92–95, 1983.

283. John H. Holland. Properties of the bucket brigade. In Grefenstette [250], pages 1–7.

284. John H. Holland. A Mathematical Framework for Studying Learning in a Classifier System. In Doyne Farmer, Alan Lapedes, Norman Packard, and Burton Wendroff, editors, *Evolution, Games and Learning: Models for Adaptation in Machines and Nature*, pages 307–317, Amsterdam, 1986. North-Holland.

285. John H. Holland. A Mathematical Framework for Studying Learning in Classifier Systems. *Physica D*, 22:307–317, 1986.

286. John H. Holland. Escaping Brittleness: The possibilities of General-Purpose Learning Algorithms Applied to Parallel Rule-Based Systems. In Mitchell, Michalski, and Carbonell, editors, *Machine learning, an artificial intelligence approach. Volume II*, chapter 20, pages 593–623. Morgan Kaufmann, 1986.

287. John H. Holland. Genetic Algorithms and Classifier Systems: Foundations and Future Directions. In Grefenstette [252], pages 82–89.

288. John H. Holland. Concerning the Emergence of Tag-Mediated Lookahead in Classifier Systems. In *Special issue of Physica D (Vol. 42)* [1], pages 188–201.

289. John H. Holland, Lashon B. Booker, Marco Colombetti, Marco Dorigo, David E. Goldberg, Stephanie Forrest, Rick L. Riolo, Robert E. Smith, Pier Luca Lanzi, Wolfgang Stolzmann, and Stewart W. Wilson. What is a Learning Classifier System? In Lanzi et al. [364], pages 3–32.

290. John H. Holland and Arthur W. Burks. Adaptive Computing System Capable of Learning and Discovery. Patent 4697242 United States 29 Sept., 1987.

291. John H. Holland, Keith J. Holyoak, Richard E. Nisbett, and P. R. Thagard. *Induction: Processes of Inference, Learning, and Discovery*. MIT Press, Cambridge, 1986.

292. John H. Holland, Keith J. Holyoak, Richard E. Nisbett, and Paul R. Thagard. Classifier Systems, Q-Morphisms, and Induction. In Davis [138], pages 116–128.

293. John H. Holland and J. S. Reitman. Cognitive systems based on adaptive algorithms. In D. A. Waterman and F. Hayes-Roth, editors, *Pattern-directed inference systems*. New York: Academic Press, 1978. Reprinted in: Evolutionary Computation. The Fossil Record. David B. Fogel (Ed.) IEEE Press, 1998. ISBN: 0-7803-3481-7.

294. John H. Holmes. *Evolution-Assisted Discovery of Sentinel Features in Epidemiologic Surveillance*. PhD thesis, Drexel University, 1996. http://cceb.med.upenn.edu/holmes/disstxt.ps.gz.

295. John H. Holmes. A genetics-based machine learning approach to knowledge discovery in clinical data. *Journal of the American Medical Informatics Association Supplement*, 1996.

296. John H. Holmes. Discovering Risk of Disease with a Learning Classifier System. In Bäck [10]. http://cceb.med.upenn.edu/holmes/icga97.ps.gz.

297. John H. Holmes. Differential negative reinforcement improves classifier system learning rate in two-class problems with unequal base rates. In Koza et al. [345], pages 635–642. http://cceb.med.upenn.edu/holmes/gp98.ps.gz.

298. John H. Holmes. Evaluating Learning Classifier System Performance In Two-Choice Decision Tasks: An LCS Metric Toolkit. In Banzhaf et al. [18], page 789. One page poster paper.

299. John H. Holmes. Quantitative Methods for Evaluating Learning Classifier System Performance in Forced Two-Choice Decision Tasks. In Wu [623], pages 250–257.

300. John H. Holmes. Applying a Learning Classifier System to Mining Explanatory and Predictive Models from a Large Database. In *Proceedings of the International Workshop on Learning Classifier Systems (IWLCS-2000), in the Joint Workshops of SAB 2000 and PPSN 2000* [4]. Extended abstract.

301. John H. Holmes. Learning Classifier Systems Applied to Knowledge Discovery in Clinical Research Databases. In Lanzi et al. [364], pages 243–261.

302. John H. Holmes, Dennis R. Durbin, and Flaura K. Winston. The learning classifier system: an evolutionary computation approach to knowledge discovery in epidemiologic surveillance. *Artificial Intelligence In Medicine*, 19(1):53–74, 2000.

303. Keith J. Holyoak, K. Koh, and Richard E. Nisbett. A Theory of Conditioning: Inductive Learning within Rule-Based Default Hierarchies. *Psych. Review*, 96:315–340, 1990.

304. Jeffrey Horn. *The Nature of Niching: Genetic Algorithms and the Evolution of Optimal, Cooperative Populations*. PhD thesis, University of Illinois at Urbana-Champaign (UMI Dissertation Service No. 9812622, 1997.

305. Jeffrey Horn and David E. Goldberg. Natural Niching for Cooperative Learning in Classifier Systems. In Koza et al. [347], pages 553–564.

306. Jeffrey Horn and David E. Goldberg. A Timing Analysis of Convergence to Fitness Sharing Equilibrium. In *Parallel Problem Solving from Nature (PPSN)*, 1998.

307. Jeffrey Horn and David E. Goldberg. Towards a Control Map for Niching. In *Foundations of Genetic Algorithms (FOGA)*, pages 287–310, 1998.

308. Jeffrey Horn, David E. Goldberg, and Kalyanmoy Deb. Implicit Niching in a Learning Classifier System: Nature's Way. *Evolutionary Computation*, 2(1):37–66, 1994. Also IlliGAL Report No 94001, 1994.

309. Dijia Huang. A framework for the credit-apportionment process in rule-based systems. *IEEE Transactions on Systems, Man and Cybernetics*, 1989.

310. Dijia Huang. *Credit Apportionment in Rule-Based Systems: Problem Analysis and Algorithm Synthesis*. PhD thesis, University of Michigan, 1989.

311. Dijia Huang. The Context-Array Bucket-Brigade Algorithm: An Enhanced Approach to Credit-Apportionment in Classifier Systems. In Schaffer [463], pages 311–316.

312. Jacob Hurst and Larry Bull. A Self-Adaptive Classifier System. In *Proceedings of the International Workshop on Learning Classifier Systems (IWLCS-2000), in the Joint Workshops of SAB 2000 and PPSN 2000* [4]. Extended abstract.

313. Francesc Xavier Llorà i Fàbrega. Automatic Classification using genetic algorithms under a Pittsburgh approach. Master's thesis, Enginyeria La Salle - Ramon Llull University, 1998. http://www.salleurl.edu/~xevil/Work/index.html.

314. Francesc Xavier Llorà i Fàbrega and Josep Maria Garrell i Guiu. GENIFER: A Nearest Neighbour based Classifier System using GA. In Banzhaf et al. [18], page 797. One page poster paper appeared at GECCO. The full version is available at http://www.salleurl.edu/~xevil/Work/index.html.

315. Francesc Xavier Llorà i Fàbrega, Josep Maria Garrell i Guiu, and Ester Bernadó i Mansilla. A Classifier System based on Genetic Algorithm under the Pittsburgh approach for problems with real valued attributes. In Viceng Torra, editor, *Proceedings of Artificial Intelligence Catalan Workshop (CCIA98)*, volume 14–15, pages 85–93. ACIA Press, 1998. In Catalan http://www.salleurl.edu/~xevil/Work/index.html.

316. Josep Maria Garrell i Guiu, Elisabet Golobardes i Ribé, Ester Bernadó i Mansilla, and Francesc Xavier Llorà i Fàbrega. Automatic Classification of mammary biopsy images with machine learning techniques. In E. Alpaydin, editor, *Proceedings of Engineering of Intelligent Systems (EIS'98)*, volume 3, pages 411–418. ICSC Academic Press, 1998.
http://www.salleurl.edu/~xevil/Work/index.html.

317. Josep Maria Garrell i Guiu, Elisabet Golobardes i Ribé, Ester Bernadó i Mansilla, and Francesc Xavier Llorà i Fàbrega. Automatic Diagnosis with Genetic Algorithms and Case-Based Reasoning. *To appear in AIENG Journal*, 1999. (This is an expanded version of Guiu98a).

318. H. Iba, H. de Garis, and T. Higuchi. Evolutionary Learning of Predatory Behaviors Based on Structured Classifiers. In Roitblat and Wilson [447], pages 356–363.

319. H. Inoue, K. Takadama, M. Okada, K. Shimohara, , and O. Katai. Agent architecture based on self-reflection learning classifier system. In *The 5th International Symposium on Artificial Life and Robotics (AROB'2000)*, pages 454–457, 2000.

320. H. Inoue, K. Takadama, and K. Shimohara. Inference of user's internal states and its agent's architecture. In *The 20th System Engineering Meeting of SICE (The Society of Instrument and Control Engineers)*, pages 55–60, 2000.

321. N. Ireson, Y. J. Cao, L. Bull, and R. Miles. A Communication Architecture for Multi-Agent Learning Systems. In *Proceedings of the EvoNet Workshops - EvoTel 2000*, pages 255–266, 2000.

322. Hisao Ishibuchi and Tomoharu Nakashima. Linguistic Rule Extraction by Genetics-Based Machine Learning. In Whitely et al. [586], pages 195–202.

323. Yasushi Ishikawa and Takao Terano. Co-evolution of multiagents via organizational-learning classifier system and its application to marketing simulation. In *Proc. 4th Pacific-Asia Conf. on Information Systems (PACIS-2000)*, pages 1114–1127, 2000.

324. Kenneth A. De Jong and William M. Spears. Learning Concept Classification Rules using Genetic Algorithms. In *Proceedings of the Twelfth International Conference on Artificial Intelligence IJCAI-91*, volume 2, 1991.

325. K. Takadama, T. Terano, K. Shimohara, K. Hori and S. Nakasuka. Towards a multiagent design principle - analyzing an organizational-learning oriented classifier system. In V. Loia and S. Sessa, editors, *Soft Computing Agents: New Trends for Designing Autonomous Systems*, Series of Studies in Fuzziness and Soft Computing. Springer–Verlag, 2001.

326. Daisuke Katagami and Seiji Yamada. Real robot learning with human teaching. In Takadama [531].

327. Hiroharu Kawanaka, Tomohiro Yoshikawa, and Shinji Tsuruoka. A Study of Parallel GA Using DNA Coding Method for Acquisition of Fuzzy Control Rules. In *Late Breaking Papers at the 2000 Genetic and Evolutionary Computation Conference (GECCO-2000)*, pages 431–436, 2000.

328. Hiroaki Kitano, Stephen F. Smith, and Tetsuya Higuchi. GA-1: A Parallel Associative Memory Processor for Rule Learning with Genetic Algorithms. In Booker and Belew [59], pages 311–317.

329. Leslie Knight and Sandip Sen. PLEASE: A Prototype Learning System using Genetic Algorithms. In Eshelman [186], pages 429–??

330. Kostyantyn Korovkin and Robert Richards. Visual Auction: A Classifier System Pedagogical and Researcher Tool. In Scott Brave and Annie S. Wu, editors, *Late Breaking Papers at the 1999 Genetic and Evolutionary Computation Conference (GECCO-99)*, pages 159–163, 1999.

331. Tim Kovacs. Evolving Optimal Populations with XCS Classifier Systems. Master's thesis, School of Computer Science, University of Birmingham, Birmingham, U.K., 1996. Also tech. report CSR-96-17 and CSRP-96-17
ftp://ftp.cs.bham.ac.uk/pub/tech-reports/1996/CSRP-96-17.ps.gz.

332. Tim Kovacs. Steady State Deletion Techniques in a Classifier System. Unpublished document – partially subsumed by Kovacs1999a 'Deletion Schemes for Classifier Systems', 1997.

333. Tim Kovacs. XCS Classifier System Reliably Evolves Accurate, Complete, and Minimal Representations for Boolean Functions. In Roy, Chawdhry, and Pant, editors, *Soft Computing in Engineering Design and Manufacturing*, pages 59–68. Springer-Verlag, London, 1997.
ftp://ftp.cs.bham.ac.uk/pub/authors/T.Kovacs/index.html.

334. Tim Kovacs. XCS Classifier System Reliably Evolves Accurate, Complete, and Minimal Representations for Boolean Functions. Technical Report Version. Technical Report CSRP-97-19, School of Computer Science, University of Birmingham, Birmingham, U.K., 1997.
http://www.cs.bham.ac.uk/system/tech-reports/tr.html.

335. Tim Kovacs. Deletion schemes for classifier systems. In Banzhaf et al. [18], pages 329–336. Also technical report CSRP-99-08, School of Computer Science, University of Birmingham. http://www.cs.bham.ac.uk/~tyk.

336. Tim Kovacs. Strength or accuracy? A comparison of two approaches to fitness calculation in learning classifier systems. In Wu [623], pages 258–265.

337. Tim Kovacs. Strength or Accuracy? Fitness calculation in learning classifier systems. In Lanzi et al. [364], pages 143–160.

338. Tim Kovacs. Towards a theory of strong overgeneral classifiers. In Terence C. Fogarty, Worthy Martin, and William M. Spears, editors, *Proceedings of the Workshop on Foundations of Genetic Algorithms (FOGA2000)*, 2000. Also tech. report CSRP-00-20, School of Computer Science, University of Birmingham.

339. Tim Kovacs and Manfred Kerber. Some dimensions of problem complexity for XCS. In Annie S. Wu, editor, *Proceedings of the 2000 Genetic and Evolutionary Computation Conference Workshop Program*, pages 289–292, 2000.

340. Tim Kovacs and Manfred Kerber. What makes a problem hard for XCS? In *Proceedings of the International Workshop on Learning Classifier Systems (IWLCS-2000), in the Joint Workshops of SAB 2000 and PPSN 2000* [4]. Extended abstract.

341. Tim Kovacs and Manfred Kerber. What makes a problem hard for XCS? In Pier Luca Lanzi, Wolfgang Stolzmann, and Stewart W. Wilson, editors, *Advances in Learning Classifier Systems*, number 1996 in LNAI, page ?? Springer–Verlag, 2001.

342. Tim Kovacs and Pier Luca Lanzi. A Learning Classifier Systems Bibliography. Technical Report 99.52, Dipartimento di Elettronica e Informazione, Politecnico di Milano, 1999.

343. Tim Kovacs and Pier Luca Lanzi. A Learning Classifier Systems Bibliography. In Lanzi et al. [364], pages 321–347.

344. Yuhsuke Koyama. The emergence of the cooperative behaviors in a small group. In Takadama [531].

345. John R. Koza, Wolfgang Banzhaf, Kumar Chellapilla, Kalyanmoy Deb, Marco Dorigo, David B. Fogel, Max H. Garzon, David E. Goldberg, Hitoshi Iba, and Rick Riolo, editors. *Genetic Programming 1998: Proceedings of the Third Annual Conference*. Morgan Kaufmann: San Francisco, CA, 1998.

346. John R. Koza, Kalyanmoy Deb, Marco Dorigo, David B. Fogel, Max H. Garzon, Hitoshi Iba, and Rick Riolo, editors. *Genetic Programming 1997: Proceedings of the Second Annual Conference*. Morgan Kaufmann: San Francisco, CA, 1997.

347. John R. Koza, David E. Goldberg, David B. Fogel, and Rick L. Riolo, editors. *Genetic Programming 1996: Proceedings of the First Annual Conference*, Stanford University, CA, USA, 1996. MIT Press.

348. Pier Luca Lanzi. A Model of the Environment to Avoid Local Learning (An Analysis of the Generalization Mechanism of XCS). Technical Report 97.46, Politecnico di Milano. Department of Electronic Engineering and Information Sciences, 1997. http://ftp.elet.polimi.it/people/lanzi/report46.ps.gz.

349. Pier Luca Lanzi. A Study of the Generalization Capabilities of XCS. In Bäck [10], pages 418–425. http://ftp.elet.polimi.it/people/lanzi/icga97.ps.gz.

350. Pier Luca Lanzi. Solving Problems in Partially Observable Environments with Classifier Systems (Experiments on Adding Memory to XCS). Technical Report 97.45, Politecnico di Milano. Department of Electronic Engineering and Information Sciences, 1997.
http://ftp.elet.polimi.it/people/lanzi/report45.ps.gz.

351. Pier Luca Lanzi. Adding Memory to XCS. In *Proceedings of the IEEE Conference on Evolutionary Computation (ICEC98)*. IEEE Press, 1998.
http://ftp.elet.polimi.it/people/lanzi/icec98.ps.gz.

352. Pier Luca Lanzi. An analysis of the memory mechanism of XCSM. In Koza et al. [345], pages 643–651. http://ftp.elet.polimi.it/people/lanzi/gp98.ps.gz.

353. Pier Luca Lanzi. Generalization in Wilson's XCS. In A. E. Eiben, T. Bäck, M. Shoenauer, and H.-P Schwefel, editors, *Proceedings of the Fifth International Conference on Parallel Problem Solving From Nature – PPSN V*, number 1498 in LNCS. Springer Verlag, 1998.

354. Pier Luca Lanzi. *Reinforcement Learning by Learning Classifier Systems*. PhD thesis, Politecnico di Milano, 1998.

355. Pier Luca Lanzi. An Analysis of Generalization in the XCS Classifier System. *Evolutionary Computation*, 7(2):125–149, 1999.

356. Pier Luca Lanzi. Extending the Representation of Classifier Conditions Part I: From Binary to Messy Coding. In Banzhaf et al. [18], pages 337–344.

357. Pier Luca Lanzi. Extending the Representation of Classifier Conditions Part II: From Messy Coding to S-Expressions. In Banzhaf et al. [18], pages 345–352.

358. Pier Luca Lanzi. Adaptive Agents with Reinforcement Learning and Internal Memory. In *To appear in the Sixth International Conference on the Simulation of Adaptive Behavior (SAB2000)*, 2000.

359. Pier Luca Lanzi. Adaptive Agents with Reinforcement Learning and Internal Memory. In et al. [187], pages 333–342.

360. Pier Luca Lanzi. Learning Classifier Systems from a Reinforcement Learning Perspective. Technical Report 00-03, Dipartimento di Elettronica e Informazione, Politecnico di Milano, 2000.

361. Pier Luca Lanzi and Marco Colombetti. An Extension of XCS to Stochastic Environments. Technical Report 98.85, Dipartimento di Elettronica e Informazione - Politecnico di Milano, 1998.

362. Pier Luca Lanzi and Marco Colombetti. An Extension to the XCS Classifier System for Stochastic Environments. In Banzhaf et al. [18], pages 353–360.

363. Pier Luca Lanzi and Rick L. Riolo. A Roadmap to the Last Decade of Learning Classifier System Research (from 1989 to 1999). In Lanzi et al. [364], pages 33–62.

364. Pier Luca Lanzi, Wolfgang Stolzmann, and Stewart W. Wilson, editors. *Learning Classifier Systems. From Foundations to Applications*, volume 1813 of *LNAI*. Springer-Verlag, Berlin, 2000.

365. Pier Luca Lanzi and Stewart W. Wilson. Optimal classifier system performance in non-Markov environments. Technical Report 99.36, Dipartimento di Elettronica e Informazione - Politecnico di Milano, 1999. Also IlliGAL tech. report 99022, University of Illinois.

366. Pier Luca Lanzi and Stewart W. Wilson. Toward Optimal Performance in Classifier Systems. *Evolutionary Computation*, In press 2000.

367. Claude Lattaud. Non-Homogeneous Classifier Systems in a Macro-Evolution Process. In Wu [623], pages 266–271.

368. Claude Lattaud. Non-Homogeneous Classifier Systems in a Macro-Evolution Process. In Lanzi et al. [364], pages 161–174.

369. Blake Lebaron, W. Brian Arthur, and R. Palmer. The Time Series Properties of an Artificial Stock Market. *Journal of Economic Dynamics and Control*, 1999.

370. Martin Lettau and Harald Uhlig. Rules of Thumb and Dynamic Programming. Technical report, Department of Economics, Princeton University, 1994.

371. Martin Lettau and Harald Uhlig. Rules of thumb versus dynamic programming. *American Economic Review*, 89:148–174, 1999.

372. Gunar E. Liepins, M. R. Hillard, M. Palmer, and G. Rangarajan. Credit Assignment and Discovery in Classifier Systems. *International Journal of Intelligent Systems*, 6:55–69, 1991.

373. Gunar E. Liepins, Michael R. Hilliard, Mark Palmer, and Gita Rangarajan. Alternatives for Classifier System Credit Assignment. In *Proceedings of the Eleventh International Joint Conference on Artificial Intelligence (IJCAI-89)*, pages 756–761, 1989.

374. Gunar E. Liepins and Lori A. Wang. Classifier System Learning of Boolean Concepts. In Booker and Belew [59], pages 318–323.

375. Derek A. Linkens and H. Okola Nyongesah. Genetic Algorithms for fuzzy control - Part II: Off-line system development and application. Technical Report CTA/94/2387/1st MS, Department of Automatic Control and System Engineering, University of Sheffield, U.K., 1994.

376. Juliet Juan Liu and James Tin-Yau Kwok. An extended genetic rule induction algorithm. In *Proceedings of the 2000 Congress on Evolutionary Computation (CEC00)* [3], pages 458–463.

377. Pattie Maes, Maja J. Mataric, Jean-Arcady Meyer, Jordan Pollack, and Stewart W. Wilson, editors. *From Animals to Animats 4. Proceedings of the Fourth International Conference on Simulation of Adaptive Behavior (SAB96)*. A Bradford Book. MIT Press, 1996.

378. Chikara Maezawa and Masayasu Atsumi. Collaborative Learning Agents with Structural Classifier Systems. In Banzhaf et al. [18], page 777. One page poster paper.

379. Bernard Manderick. Selectionist Categorization. In Schwefel and Männer [470], pages 326–330.

380. Ester Bernadó I Mansilla and Josep Maria Garrell i Guiu. MOLeCS: A MultiObjective Learning Classifier System. In Whitely et al. [586], page 390. One page poster paper.

381. Ramon Marimon, Ellen McGrattan, and Thomas J. Sargent. Money as a Medium of Exchange in an Economy with Artificially Intelligent Agents. *Journal of Economic Dynamics and Control*, 14:329–373, 1990. Also Tech. Report 89-004, Santa Fe Institute, 1989.

382. Maja J Mataric. A comparative analysis of reinforcement learning methods. A.I. Memo No. 1322, Massachusetts Institute of Technology, 1991.

383. Alaster D. McAulay and Jae Chan Oh. Image Learning Classifier System Using Genetic Algorithms. In *Proceedings IEEE NAECON '89*, 1989.

384. Chris Melhuish and Terence C. Fogarty. Applying A Restricted Mating Policy To Determine State Space Niches Using Immediate and Delayed Reinforcement. In Fogarty [203], pages 224–237.

385. J. A. Meyer and S. W. Wilson, editors. *From Animals to Animats 1. Proceedings of the First International Conference on Simulation of Adaptive Behavior (SAB90)*. A Bradford Book. MIT Press, 1990.

386. Zbigniew Michalewicz. *Genetic Algorithms + Data Structures = Evolution Programs*. Springer-Verlag, 1996. Contains introductory chapter on LCS.

387. John H. Miller and Stephanie Forrest. The dynamical behavior of classifier systems. In Schaffer [463], pages 304–310.

388. M. Mitchell and S. Forrest. Genetic Algorithms and Artificial Life. Technical Report 93-11-072, Santa Fe Institute, 1993. Contains a 2 page review of work on LCS.

389. Johann Mitlöhner. Classifier systems and economic modelling. In *APL '96. Proceedings of the APL 96 conference on Designing the future*, volume 26 (4), pages 77–86, 1996.

390. Chilukuri K. Mohan. *Expert Systems: A Modern Overview*. Kluwer, 2000. Contains an introductory survey chapter on LCS.

391. D. Montanari. Classifier systems with a constant-profile bucket brigade. In *Collected Abstracts for the First International Workshop on Learning Classifier System (IWLCS-92)* [2]. October 6–8, NASA Johnson Space Center, Houston, Texas.

392. David E. Moriarty, Alan C. Schultz, and John J. Grefenstette. Evolutionary Algorithms for Reinforcement Learning. *Journal of Artificial Intelligence Research*, 11:199–229, 1999.
    http://www.ib3.gmu.edu/gref/papers/moriarty-jair99.html.

393. Rémi Munos and Jocelyn Patinel. Reinforcement learning with dynamic covering of state-action space: Partitioning Q-learning. In Cliff et al. [118], pages 354–363.

394. Jorge Muruzábal. Fuzzy and Probabilistic Reasoning in Simple Learning Classifier Systems. In *Proceedings of the 2nd IEEE International Conference on Evolutionary Computation*, volume 1, pages 262–266. IEEE Press, 1995.

395. Jorge Muruzábal. Mining the space of generality with uncertainty-concerned cooperative classifiers. In Banzhaf et al. [18], pages 449–457.

396. Jorge Muruzábal and A. Muñoz. Diffuse pattern learning with Fuzzy ARTMAP and PASS. In Davidor and Schwefel [136], pages 376–385.

397. Ichiro Nagasaka and Toshiharu Taura. 3D Geometric Representation for Shape Generation using Classifier System. In Koza et al. [346], pages 515–520.

398. Filippo Neri. *First Order Logic Concept Learning by means of a Distributed Genetic Algorithm*. PhD thesis, University of Milano, Italy, 1997.

399. Filippo Neri. Comparing local search with respect to genetic evolution to detect intrusions in computer networks. In *Proceedings of the 2000 Congress on Evolutionary Computation (CEC00)* [3], pages 238–243.

400. Filippo Neri and Attilio Giordana. A distributed genetic algorithm for concept learning. In Eshelman [186], pages 436–443.

401. Filippo Neri and L. Saitta. Exploring the power of genetic search in learning symbolic classifiers. *IEEE Trans. on Pattern Analysis and Machine Intelligence*, PAMI-18:1135–1142, 1996.

402. Volker Nissen and Jörg Biethahn. Determining a Good Inventory Policy with a Genetic Algorithm. In Jörg Biethahn and Volker Nissen, editors, *Evolutionary Algorithms in Management Applications*, pages 240–249. Springer Verlag, 1995.

403. M. O. Odetayo and D. R. McGregor. Genetic algorithm for inducing control rules for a dynamic system. In Schaffer [463], pages 177–182. It could be argued this is a GA as opposed to a classifier system approach.

404. Jae Chan Oh. Improved Classifier System Using Genetic Algorithms. Master's thesis, Wright State University, ??

405. Norihiko Ono and Adel T. Rahmani. Self-Organization of Communication in Distributed Learning Classifier Systems. In Albrecht et al. [7], pages 361–367.

406. G. Deon Oosthuizen. Machine Learning: A mathematical framework for neural network, symbolic and genetics-based learning. In Schaffer [463], pages 385–390.

407. F. Oppacher and D. Deugo. The Evolution of Hierarchical Representations. In *Proceedings of the 3rd European Conference on Artificial Life*. Springer-Verlag, 1995.

408. Alexandre Parodi and P. Bonelli. The Animat and the Physician. In Meyer and Wilson [385], pages 50–57.

409. Alexandre Parodi and Pierre Bonelli. A New Approach to Fuzzy Classifier Systems. In Forrest [216], pages 223–230.

410. Mukesh J. Patel, Marco Colombetti, and Marco Dorigo. Evolutionary Learning for Intelligent Automation: A Case Study. *Intelligent Automation and Soft Computing*, 1(1):29–42, 1995.

411. Mukesh J. Patel and Marco Dorigo. Adaptive Learning of a Robot Arm. In Fogarty [203], pages 180–194.

412. Mukesh J. Patel and U. Schnepf. Concept Formation as Emergent Phenomena. In Francisco J. Varela and P. Bourgine, editors, *Proceedings First European Conference on Artificial Life*, pages 11–20. MIT Press, 1992.

413. Ray C. Paton. Designing Adaptable Systems through the Study and Application of Biological Sources. In Vic Rayward-Smith, editor, *Applications of Modern Heuristic Methods*, pages 39–54. Alfred Waller Ltd, 1995.

414. Rolf Pfeifer, Bruce Blumberg, Jean-Arcady Meyer, and Stewart W. Wilson, editors. *From Animals to Animats 5. Proceedings of the Fifth International Conference on Simulation of Adaptive Behavior (SAB98)*. A Bradford Book. MIT Press, 1998.

415. Steven E. Phelan. *Using Artificial Adaptive Agents to Explore Strategic Landscapes*. PhD thesis, School of Business, Faculty of Law and Management, La Trobe University, Australia, 1997.

416. A. G. Pipe and Brian Carse. A Comparison between two Architectures for Searching and Learning in Maze Problems. In Fogarty [203], pages 238–249.

417. A. G. Pipe and Brian Carse. Autonomous Acquisition of Fuzzy Rules for Mobile Robot Control: First Results from two Evolutionary Computation Approaches. In Whitely et al. [586], pages 849–856.

418. R. Piroddi and R. Rusconi. A Parallel Classifier System to Solve Learning Problems. Master's thesis, Dipartimento di Elettronica e Informazione, Politecnico di Milano, Milano, Italy., 1992.

419. Mitchell A. Potter, Kenneth A. De Jong, and John J. Grefenstette. A Coevolutionary Approach to Learning Sequential Decision Rules. In Eshelman [186], pages 366–372.

420. C. L. Ramsey and John J. Grefenstette. Case-based initialization of genetic algorithms. In Forrest [216], pages 84–91. http://www.ib3.gmu.edu/gref/.

421. C. L. Ramsey and John J. Grefenstette. Case-based anytime learning. In D. W. Aha, editor, *Case-Based Reasoning: Papers from the 1994 Workshop*. 1994. Also Tech. Report WS-94-07 http://www.ib3.gmu.edu/gref/.

422. Gregory J. E. Rawlins, editor. *Proceedings of the First Workshop on Foundations of Genetic Algorithms (FOGA91)*. Morgan Kaufmann: San Mateo, 1991.

423. Robert A. Richards. *Zeroth-Order Shape Optimization Utilizing a Learning Classifier System*. PhD thesis, Stanford University, 1995. Online version available at: http://www-leland.stanford.edu/~buc/SPHINcsX/book.html.

424. Robert A. Richards. Classifier System Metrics: Graphical Depictions. In Koza et al. [345], pages 652–657.

425. Robert A. Richards and Sheri D. Sheppard. Classifier System Based Structural Component Shape Improvement Utilizing I-DEAS. In *Iccon User's Conference Proceeding*. Iccon, 1992.

426. Robert A. Richards and Sheri D. Sheppard. Learning Classifier Systems in Design Optimization. In *Design Theory and Methodology '92*. The American Society of Mechanical Engineers, 1992.

427. Robert A. Richards and Sheri D. Sheppard. Two-dimensional Component Shape Improvement via Classifier System. In *Artificial Intelligence in Design '92*. Kluwer Academic Publishers, 1992.

428. Robert A. Richards and Sheri D. Sheppard. A Learning Classifier System for Three-dimensional Shape Optimization. In H. M. Voigt, W. Ebeling, I. Rechenberg, and H. P. Schwefel, editors, *Parallel Problem Solving from Nature – PPSN IV*, volume 1141 of *LNCS*, pages 1032–1042. Springer-Verlag, 1996.

429. Robert A. Richards and Sheri D. Sheppard. Three-Dimensional Shape Optimization Utilizing a Learning Classifier System. In Koza et al. [347], pages 539–546.

430. Rick L. Riolo. Bucket Brigade Performance: I. Long Sequences of Classifiers. In Grefenstette [252], pages 184–195.

431. Rick L. Riolo. Bucket Brigade Performance: II. Default Hierarchies. In Grefenstette [252], pages 196–201.

432. Rick L. Riolo. CFS-C: A Package of Domain-Independent Subroutines for Implementing Classifier Systems in Arbitrary User-Defined Environments. Technical report, University of Michigan, 1988.

433. Rick L. Riolo. *Empirical Studies of Default Hierarchies and Sequences of Rules in Learning Classifier Systems*. PhD thesis, University of Michigan, 1988.

434. Rick L. Riolo. The Emergence of Coupled Sequences of Classifiers. In Schaffer [463], pages 256–264.

435. Rick L. Riolo. The Emergence of Default Hierarchies in Learning Classifier Systems. In Schaffer [463], pages 322–327.

436. Rick L. Riolo. Lookahead Planning and Latent Learning in a Classifier System. In Meyer and Wilson [385], pages 316–326.

437. Rick L. Riolo. Modelling Simple Human Category Learning with a Classifier System. In Booker and Belew [59], pages 324–333.

438. Rick L. Riolo. The discovery and use of forward models for adaptive classifier systems. In *Collected Abstracts for the First International Workshop on Learning Classifier System (IWLCS-92)* [2]. October 6–8, NASA Johnson Space Center, Houston, Texas.

439. Joaquin Rivera and Roberto Santana. Improving the Discovery Component of Classifier Systems by the Application of Estimation of Distribution Algorithms. In *Proceedings of Student Sessions ACAI'99: Machine Learning and Applications*, pages 43–44, Chania, Greece, July 1999.

440. A. Robert, F. Chantemargue, and M. Courant. Grounding Agents in EMud Artificial Worlds. In *Proceedings of the First International Conference on Virtual Worlds, Paris (France), July 1-3*, 1998.

441. Gary Roberts. A Rational Reconstruction of Wilson's Animat and Holland's CS-1. In Schaffer [463], pages 317–321.

442. Gary Roberts. Dynamic Planning for Classifier Systems. In Forrest [216], pages 231–237.

443. George G. Robertson. Parallel Implementation of Genetic Algorithms in a Classifier System. In Grefenstette [252], pages 140–147. Also Tech. Report TR-159 RL87-5 Thinking Machines Corporation.

444. George G. Robertson. Population Size in Classifier Systems. In *Proceedings of the Fifth International Conference on Machine Learning*, pages 142–152. Morgan Kaufmann, 1988.

445. George G. Robertson. Parallel Implementation of Genetic Algorithms in a Classifier System. In Davis [138], pages 129–140.

446. George G. Robertson and Rick L. Riolo. A Tale of Two Classifier Systems. *Machine Learning*, 3:139–159, 1988.

447. J. A. Meyer H. L. Roitblat and S. W. Wilson, editors. *From Animals to Animats 2. Proceedings of the Second International Conference on Simulation of Adaptive Behavior (SAB92)*. A Bradford Book. MIT Press, 1992.

448. S. Ross. Accurate Reaction or Reflective Action? Master's thesis, School of Cognitive and Computing Sciences, University of Sussex, 1994.

449. S. E. Rouwhorst and A. P. Engelbrecht. Searching the forest: Using decision trees as building blocks for evolutionary search in classification databases. In *Proceedings of the 2000 Congress on Evolutionary Computation (CEC00)* [3], pages 633–638.

450. A. Sanchis, J. M. Molina, P. Isasi, and J. Segovia. Knowledge acquisition including tags in a classifier system. In Angeline et al. [8], pages 137–144.

451. Adrian V. Sannier and Erik D. Goodman. Midgard: A Genetic Approach to Adaptive Load Balancing for Distributed Systems. In *Proc. Fifth Intern. Conf. Machine Learning*. Morgan Kaufmann, 1988.
452. Manuel Filipe Santos. *Learning Classifiers in Distributed Environments*. PhD thesis, Departamento de Sistemas de Informação, Universidade do Minho, Portugal, 2000.
453. Cédric Sanza, Christophe Destruel, and Yves Duthen. Agents autonomes pour l'interaction adaptative dans les mondes virtuels. In *5ème Journées de l'Association Francaise d'Informatique Graphique. Décembre 1997, Rennes, France*, 1997. In French.
454. Cédric Sanza, Christophe Destruel, and Yves Duthen. A learning method for adaptation and evolution in virtual environments. In *3rd International Conference on Computer Graphics and Artificial Intelligence, April 1998, Limoges, France*, 1998.
455. Cédric Sanza, Christophe Destruel, and Yves Duthen. Autonomous actors in an interactive real-time environment. In *ICVC'99 International Conference on Visual Computing Feb. 1999, Goa, India*, 1999.
456. Cédric Sanza, Christophe Destruel, and Yves Duthen. Learning in real-time environment based on classifiers system. In *7th International Conference in Central Europe on Computer Graphics, Visualization and Interactive Digital Media'99*, Plzen, Czech Republic, 1999.
457. Cédric Sanza, Cyril Panatier, Hervé Luga, and Yves Duthen. Adaptive Behavior for Cooperation: a Virtual Reality Application. In *8th IEEE International Workshop on Robot and Human Interaction September 1999, Pisa, Italy*, 1999.
458. Shaun Saxon and Alwyn Barry. XCS and the Monk's problem. In Wu [623], pages 272–281.
459. Shaun Saxon and Alwyn Barry. XCS and the Monk's Problems. In Lanzi et al. [364], pages 223–242.
460. Andreas Schachtner. A classifier system with integrated genetic operators. In H.-P. Schwefel and R. Männer, editors, *Parallel Problem Solving from Nature*, volume 496 of *Lecture Notes in Computer Science*, pages 331–337, Berlin, 1990. Springer.
461. J. David Schaffer. *Some experiments in machine learning using vector evaluated genetic algorithms*. PhD thesis, Vanderbilt University, Nashville, 1984.
462. J. David Schaffer. Learning Multiclass Pattern Discrimination. In Grefenstette [250], pages 74–79.
463. J. David Schaffer, editor. *Proceedings of the 3rd International Conference on Genetic Algorithms (ICGA89)*, George Mason University, June 1989. Morgan Kaufmann.
464. Sonia Schulenburg and Peter Ross. An Adaptive Agent Based Economic Model. In Lanzi et al. [364], pages 263–282.
465. Sonia Schulenburg and Peter Ross. Strength and Money: An LCS Approach to Increasing Returns. In *Proceedings of the International Workshop on Learning Classifier Systems (IWLCS-2000), in the Joint Workshops of SAB 2000 and PPSN 2000* [4]. Extended abstract.
466. Alan C. Schultz and John J. Grefenstette. Evolving Robot Behaviors. Poster at the Artificial Life Conference. http://www.ib3.gmu.edu/gref/.
467. Alan C. Schultz and John J. Grefenstette. Improving Tactical Plans with Genetic Algorithms. In *Proceedings of the Second International Conference on Tools for Artificial Intelligence*. IEEE, 1990.

468. Alan C. Schultz, Connie Logia Ramsey, and John J. Grefenstette. Simulation as-
     sisted learning by competition: Effects of noise differences between training model
     and target environment. In *Proceedings of Seventh International Conference on
     Machine Learning (ICML)*, pages 211–215. Morgan Kaufmann, 1990.

469. Dale Schuurmans and Jonathan Schaeffer. Representational Difficulties with Clas-
     sifier Systems. In Schaffer [463], pages 328–333.
     http://www.cs.ualberta.ca/~jonathan/Papers/Papers/classifier.ps.

470. Hans-Paul Schwefel and Reinhard Männer, editors. *Parallel Problem Solving from
     Nature: Proceedings of the First International Workshop. Dortmund, FRG, 1–3
     Oct 1990*, number 496 in Lecture Notes in Computer Science, Heidelberg, 1990.
     Springer.

471. Tod A. Sedbrook, Haviland Wright, and Richard Wright. Application of a Genetic
     Classifier for Patient Triage. In Booker and Belew [59], pages 334–338.

472. Sandip Sen. Classifier system learning of multiplexer function. Dept. of Electrical
     Engineering, University of Alabama, Tuscaloosa, Alabama. Class Project, 1988.

473. Sandip Sen. Sequential Boolean Function Learning by Classifier System. In *Proc.
     of 1st International Conference on Industrial and Engineering Applications of
     Artificial Intelligence and Expert Systems*, 1988.

474. Sandip Sen. Noise Sensitivity in a simple classifier system. In *Proc. 5th Conf. on
     Neural Networks & Parallel Distributed Processing*, 1992.

475. Sandip Sen. Improving classification accuracy through performance history. In
     Forrest [216], pages 652–652.

476. Sandip Sen. A Tale of two representations. In *Proc. 7th International Conference
     on Industrial and Engineering Applications of Artificial Intelligence and Expert
     Systems*, pages 245–254, 1994.

477. Sandip Sen. Modelling human categorization by a simple classifier system. WSC1:
     1st Online Workshop on Soft Computing. Aug 19-30, 1996.
     http://www.bioele.nuee.nagoya-u.ac.jp/wsc1/papers/p020.html, 1996.

478. Sandip Sen and Mahendra Sekaran. Multiagent Coordination with Learning Clas-
     sifier Systems. In Gerhard Weiß and Sandip Sen, editors, *Proceedings of the IJ-
     CAI Workshop on Adaption and Learning in Multi-Agent Systems*, volume 1042
     of *LNAI*, pages 218–233. Springer Verlag, 1996.

479. Tiago Sepulveda and Mario Rui Gomes. A Study on the Evolution of Learn-
     ing Classifier Systems. In *Proceedings of the International Workshop on Learn-
     ing Classifier Systems (IWLCS-2000), in the Joint Workshops of SAB 2000 and
     PPSN 2000* [4]. Extended abstract.

480. F. Seredynski, Pawel Cichosz, and G. P. Klebus. Learning classifier systems in
     multi-agent environments. In *Proceedings of the First IEE/IEEE International
     Conference on Genetic Algorithms in Engineering Systems: Innovations and Ap-
     plications (GALESIA'95)*, 1995.

481. F. Seredynski and C. Z. Janikow. Learning nash equilibria by coevolving dis-
     tributed classifier systems. In Angeline et al. [8], pages 1619–1626.

482. Sotaro Shimada and Yuichiro Anzai. Component-Based Adaptive Architecture
     with Classifier Systems. In Pfeifer et al. [414].

483. Sotaro Shimada and Yuichiro Anzai. Fast and Robust Convergence of Chained
     Classifiers by Generating Operons through Niche Formation. In Banzhaf et al.
     [18], page 810. One page poster paper.

484. Sotaro Shimada and Yuichiro Anzai. On Niche Formation and Corporation in
     Classifier System. In Takadama [531].

485. Takayuki Shiose and Tetsuo Sawaragi. Extended learning classifier systems by
     dual referencing mechanism. In Takadama [531].

486. Lingyan Shu and Jonathan Schaeffer. VCS: Variable Classifier System. In Schaffer [463], pages 334–339.
http://www.cs.ualberta.ca/~jonathan/Papers/Papers/vcs.ps.

487. Lingyan Shu and Jonathan Schaeffer. Improving the Performance of Genetic Algorithm Learning by Choosing a Good Initial Population. Technical Report TR-90-22, University of Alberta, CS DEPT, Edmonton, Alberta, Canada, 1990.

488. Lingyan Shu and Jonathan Schaeffer. HCS: Adding Hierarchies to Classifier Systems. In Booker and Belew [59], pages 339–345.

489. Olivier Sigaud. On the usefulness of a semi-automated Classifier System: the engineering perspective. In *Proceedings of the International Workshop on Learning Classifier Systems (IWLCS-2000), in the Joint Workshops of SAB 2000 and PPSN 2000* [4]. Extended abstract.

490. George D. Smith. Economic Applications of Genetic Algorithms. In Vic Rayward-Smith, editor, *Applications of Modern Heuristic Methods*, pages 71–90. Alfred Waller Ltd, 1995. Contains 2 pages on LCS.

491. George D. Smith, Nigel C. Steele, and Rudolf F. Albrecht, editors. *Artificial Neural Networks and Genetic Algorithms*. Springer, 1997.

492. R. E. Smith, B. A. Dike, B. Ravichandran, A. El-Fallah, and R. K. Mehra. The Fighter Aircraft LCS: A Case of Different LCS Goals and Techniques. In Lanzi et al. [364], pages 283–300.

493. Robert E. Smith. *Default Hierarchy Formation and Memory Exploitation in Learning Classifier Systems*. PhD thesis, University of Alabama, 1991.

494. Robert E. Smith. A Report on The First International Workshop on Learning Classifier Systems (IWLCS-92). NASA Johnson Space Center, Houston, Texas, Oct. 6-9.
ftp://lumpi.informatik.uni-dortmund.de/pub/LCS/papers/lcs92.ps.gz or from ENCORE, The Electronic Appendix to the Hitch-Hiker's Guide to Evolutionary Computation (ftp://ftp.krl.caltech.edu/pub/EC/Welcome.html) in the section on Classifier Systems, 1992.

495. Robert E. Smith. Is a classifier system a type of neural network? In *Collected Abstracts for the First International Workshop on Learning Classifier System (IWLCS-92)* [2]. October 6–8, NASA Johnson Space Center, Houston, Texas.

496. Robert E. Smith. Memory exploitation in learning classifier systems. In *Collected Abstracts for the First International Workshop on Learning Classifier System (IWLCS-92)* [2]. October 6–8, NASA Johnson Space Center, Houston, Texas.

497. Robert E. Smith. Genetic Learning in Rule-Based and Neural Systems. In *Proceedings of the Third International Workshop on Neural Networks and Fuzzy Logic*, volume 1, page 183. NASA. Johnson Space Center, January 1993.

498. Robert E. Smith. Memory Exploitation in Learning Classifier Systems. *Evolutionary Computation*, 2(3):199–220, 1994.

499. Robert E. Smith. Derivative Methods: Learning Classifier Systems. In Bäck et al. [11], pages B1.2:6–B1.5:11. http://www.iop.org/Books/Catalogue/.

500. Robert E. Smith and H. Brown Cribbs. Is a Learning Classifier System a Type of Neural Network? *Evolutionary Computation*, 2(1):19–36, 1994.

501. Robert E. Smith and Henry Brown Cribbs. What Can I do with a Learning Classifier System? In C. Karr and L. M. Freeman, editors, *Industrial Applications of Genetic Algorithms*, pages 299–320. CRC Press, 1998.

502. Robert E. Smith, B. A. Dike, R. K. Mehra, B. Ravichandran, and A. El-Fallah. Classifier Systems in Combat: Two-sided Learning of Maneuvers for Advanced Fighter Aircraft. In *Computer Methods in Applied Mechanics and Engineering*. Elsevier, 1999.

503. Robert E. Smith, B. A. Dike, B. Ravichandran, A. El-Fallah, and R. K. Mehra. The Fighter Aircraft LCS: A Case of Different LCS Goals and Techniques. In Wu [623], pages 282–289.

504. Robert E. Smith, Stephanie Forrest, and A. S. Perelson. Searching for diverse, cooperative subpopulations with Genetic Algorithms. *Evolutionary Computation*, 1(2):127–149, 1993.

505. Robert E. Smith, Stephanie Forrest, and Alan S. Perelson. Population Diversity in an Immune System Model: Implications for Genetic Search. Technical report, Unknown institution, 1992.

506. Robert E. Smith and David E. Goldberg. Reinforcement Learning with Classifier Systems: Adaptive Default Hierarchy Formation. Technical Report 90002, TCGA, University of Alabama, 1990.

507. Robert E. Smith and David E. Goldberg. Variable Default Hierarchy Separation in a Classifier System. In Rawlins [422], pages 148–170.

508. Robert E. Smith and David E. Goldberg. Reinforcement learning with classifier systems: adaptative default hierarchy formation. *Applied Artificial Intelligence*, 6, 1992.

509. Robert E. Smith and H. B. Cribbs III. Cooperative Versus Competitive System Elements in Coevolutionary Systems. In Maes et al. [377], pages 497–505.

510. Robert E. Smith and H. B. Cribbs III. Combined biological paradigms. *Robotics and Autonomous Systems*, 22(1):65–74, 1997.

511. Robert E. Smith and Manuel Valenzuela-Rendón. A Study of Rule Set Development in a Learning Classifier System. In Schaffer [463], pages 340–346.

512. S. F. Smith. *A Learning System Based on Genetic Adaptive Algorithms*. PhD thesis, University of Pittsburgh, 1980.

513. S. F. Smith. Flexible Learning of Problem Solving Heuristics through Adaptive Search. In *Proceedings Eight International Joint Conference on Artificial Intelligence*, pages 422–425, 1983.

514. S. F. Smith and D. P. Greene. Cooperative Diversity using Coverage as a Constraint. In *Collected Abstracts for the First International Workshop on Learning Classifier System (IWLCS-92)* [2]. October 6–8, NASA Johnson Space Center, Houston, Texas.

515. Piet Spiessens. PCS: A Classifier System that Builds a Predictive Internal World Model. In *PROC of the 9th European Conference on Artificial Intelligence, Stockholm, Sweden, Aug. 6–10*, pages 622–627, 1990.

516. Bryan G. Spohn and Philip H. Crowley. Complexity of Strategies and the Evolution of Cooperation. In Koza et al. [346], pages 521–528.

517. Wolfgang Stolzmann. Learning Classifier Systems using the Cognitive Mechanism of Anticipatory Behavioral Control, detailed version. In *Proceedings of the First European Workshop on Cognitive Modelling*, pages 82–89. Berlin: TU, 1996. http://www.psychologie.uni-wuerzburg.de/stolzmann/.

518. Wolfgang Stolzmann. *Antizipative Classifier Systeme*. PhD thesis, Fachbereich Mathematik/Informatik, University of Osnabrueck, 1997.

519. Wolfgang Stolzmann. Two Applications of Anticipatory Classifier Systems (ACSs). In *Proceedings of the 2nd European Conference on Cognitive Science*, pages 68–73. Manchester, U.K., 1997. http://www.psychologie.uni-wuerzburg.de/stolzmann/.

520. Wolfgang Stolzmann. Anticipatory classifier systems. In *Proceedings of the Third Annual Genetic Programming Conference*, pages 658–664, San Francisco, CA, 1998. Morgan Kaufmann. http://www.psychologie.uni-wuerzburg.de/stolzmann/gp-98.ps.gz.

521. Wolfgang Stolzmann. Untersuchungen zur adäquatheit des postulats einer antizipativen verhaltenssteuerung zur erklärung von verhalten mit ACSs. In W. Krause and U. Kotkamp, editors, *Intelligente Informationsverarbeitung*, pages 130–138. Deutscher Universitäts Verlag, 1998.

522. Wolfgang Stolzmann. Latent Learning in Khepera Robots with Anticipatory Classifier Systems. In Wu [623], pages 290–297.

523. Wolfgang Stolzmann. An Introduction to Anticipatory Classifier Systems. In Lanzi et al. [364], pages 175–194.

524. Wolfgang Stolzmann and Martin Butz. Latent Learning and Action-Planning in Robots with Anticipatory Classifier Systems. In Lanzi et al. [364], pages 301–317.

525. Wolfgang Stolzmann, Martin Butz, J. Hoffmann, and D. E. Goldberg. First cognitive capabilities in the anticipatory classifier system. In et al. [187], pages 287–296. Also Technical Report 2000008 of the Illinois Genetic Algorithms Laboratory.

526. K. Takadama, H. Inoue, M. Okada, K. Shimohara, , and O. Katai. Agent architecture based on interactive self-reflection classifier system. *International Journal of Artificial Life and Robotics (AROB)*, 2001.

527. K. Takadama, H. Inoue, and K. Shimohara. How to autonomously decide boundary between self and others? In *The Third Asia-Pacific Conference on Simulated Evolution And Learning (SEAL'2000)*, 2000.

528. K. Takadama, S. Nakasuka, and T. Terano. Multiagent reinforcement learning with organizational-learning oriented classifier system. In *The IEEE 1998 International Conference On Evolutionary Computation (ICEC'98)*, pages 63–68, 1998.

529. K. Takadama and T. Terano. Good solutions will emerge without a global objective function: Applying organizational-learning oriented classifier system to printed circuit board design. In *The IEEE 1997 International Conference On Systems, Man and Cybernetics (SMC'97)*, pages 3355–3360, 1997.

530. K. Takadama, T. Terano, and K. Shimohara. Designing multiple agents using learning classifier systems. In *The 4th Japan-Australia Joint Workshop on Intelligent and Evolutionary Systems (JA'2000)*, 2000.

531. Keiki Takadama, editor. *Exploring New Potentials in Learning Classifier Systems. A Session of the 4th Japan-Australia Joint Workshop on Intelligent and Evolutionary Systems*. Ashikaga Institute of Technology, 2000.

532. Keiki Takadama. Organizational-learning oriented classifier system. Technical Report TR-H-290, ATR, 2000. In Japanese.

533. Keiki Takadama, S. Nakasuka, and Takao Terano. On the credit assignment algorithm for organizational-learning oriented classifier system. In *The 1997 System/information joint Symposium of SICE (The Society of Instrument and Control Engineers)*, pages 41–46, 1997. In Japanese.

534. Keiki Takadama, S. Nakasuka, and Takao Terano. Organizational-learning oriented classifier system. In *The 11th Annual Conference of JSAI (Japanese Society for Artificial Intelligence)*, pages 201–204, 1997. In Japanese.

535. Keiki Takadama, S. Nakasuka, and Takao Terano. Organizational-learning oriented classifier system for intelligent multiagent systems. In *The 6th Multi Agent and Cooperative Computation (MACC '97) of JSSST (Japan Society for Software Science and Technology)*, page ???, 1997. In Japanese.

536. Keiki Takadama, S. Nakasuka, and Takao Terano. Analyzing the roles of problem solving and learning in organizational-learning oriented classifier system. In H. Y. Lee and H. Motoda, editors, *Lecture Notes in Artificial Intelligence*, volume 1531, pages 71–82. Springer–Verlag, 1998.

537. Keiki Takadama, Shinichi Nakasuka, and Kasunori Shimohara. Designing multiple agents using learning classifier systems - suggestions from three levels analyses. In Takadama [531].

538. Keiki Takadama, Takao Terano, and Katsunori Shimohara. Agent-based model toward organizational computing: From organizational learning to genetics-based machine learning. In *The IEEE 1999 International Conference On Systems, Man and Cybernetics (SMC'99)*, volume 2, pages 604–609, 1999.

539. Keiki Takadama, Takao Terano, and Katsunori Shimohara. Can multiagents learn in organization? – analyzing organizational learning-oriented classifier system. In *IJCAI'99 Workshop on Agents Learning about, from and other Agents*, 1999.

540. Keiki Takadama, Takao Terano, and Katsunori Shimohara. Learning Classifier Systems meet Multiagent Environments. In *Proceedings of the International Workshop on Learning Classifier Systems (IWLCS-2000), in the Joint Workshops of SAB 2000 and PPSN 2000* [4]. Extended abstract.

541. Keiki Takadama, Takao Terano, Katsunori Shimohara, H. Hori, and S. Nakasuka. Making Organizational Learning Operational: Implications from Learning Classifier System. *Computational and Mathematical Organization Theory (CMOT)*, 5(3):229–252, 1999.

542. Keiki Takadama, Takao Terano, Katsunori Shimohara, H. Hori, and S. Nakasuka. Toward emergent problem solving by distributed classifier systems based on organizational learning. *Transactions of SICE (the Society of Instrument and Control Engineers)*, 35(11):1486–1495, 1999. In Japanese.

543. Takao Terano and Z. Muro. On-the-fly knowledge base refinement by a classifier system. *AI Communications*, 4(2), 1994.

544. Takao Terano and Keiki Takadama. An organizational learning model of multiagents with a learning classifier system. In *The 1997 Fall Conference of JASMIN (Japan Society for Management Information)*, pages 128–131, 1997. In Japanese.

545. S. Tokinaga and A. B. Whinston. Applying Adaptive Credit Assignment Algorithm for the Learning Classifier System Based upon the Genetic Algorithm. *IEICE Transactions on Fundamentals of Electronics Communications and Computer Sciences*, VE75A(5):568–577, May 1992.

546. Andy Tomlinson. *Corporate Classifier Systems*. PhD thesis, University of the West of England, 1999.

547. Andy Tomlinson and Larry Bull. A Corporate Classifier System. In A. E. Eiben, T. Bäck, M. Shoenauer, and H.-P Schwefel, editors, *Proceedings of the Fifth International Conference on Parallel Problem Solving From Nature – PPSN V*, number 1498 in LNCS, pages 550–559. Springer Verlag, 1998.

548. Andy Tomlinson and Larry Bull. A Corporate XCS. In Wu [623], pages 298–305.

549. Andy Tomlinson and Larry Bull. On Corporate Classifier Systems: Increasing the Benefits of Rule Linkage. In Banzhaf et al. [18], pages 649–656.

550. Andy Tomlinson and Larry Bull. A zeroth level corporate classifier system. In Wu [623], pages 306–313.

551. Andy Tomlinson and Larry Bull. A Corporate XCS. In Lanzi et al. [364], pages 194–208.

552. Kwok Ching Tsui and Mark Plumbley. A New Hillclimber for Classifier Systems. In *GALESI97*, 1997.

553. Patrick Tufts. Evolution of a Clustering Scheme for Classifier Systems: Beyond the Bucket Brigade. PhD Thesis proposal. http://www.cs.brandeis.edu/~zippy/papers.htm, 1994.

554. Patrick Tufts. Dynamic Classifiers: Genetic Programming and Classifier Systems. In E. V. Siegel and J. R. Koza, editors, *Working Notes for the AAAI Symposium on Genetic Programming*, pages 114–119, MIT, Cambridge, MA, USA, 1995. AAAI. Home page: http://www.cs.brandeis.edu/~zippy/papers.html.

555. Kirk Twardowski. Implementation of a Genetic Algorithm based Associative Classifier System (ACS). In *Proceedings International Conference on Tools for Artificial Intelligence*, 1990.

556. Kirk Twardowski. Credit Assignment for Pole Balancing with Learning Classifier Systems. In Forrest [216], pages 238–245.

557. Kirk Twardowski. An Associative Architecture for Genetic Algorithm-Based Machine Learning. *Computer*, 27(11):27–38, November 1994.

558. J. Urzelai, Dario Floreano, Marco Dorigo, and Marco Colombetti. Incremental Robot Shaping. *Connection Science*, 10(3–4):341–360, 1998.

559. J. Urzelai, Dario Floreano, Marco Dorigo, and Marco Colombetti. Incremental Robot Shaping. In Koza et al. [345], pages 832–840.

560. Manuel Valenzuela-Rendón. Boolean Analysis of Classifier Sets. In Schaffer [463], pages 351–358.

561. Manuel Valenzuela-Rendón. *Two analysis tools to describe the operation of classifier systems*. PhD thesis, University of Alabama, 1989. Also TCGA tech. report 89005.

562. Manuel Valenzuela-Rendón. The Fuzzy Classifier System: a Classifier System for Continuously Varying Variables. In Booker and Belew [59], pages 346–353.

563. Manuel Valenzuela-Rendón. The Fuzzy Classifier System: Motivations and First Results. *Lecture Notes in Computer Science*, 496:338–??, 1991.

564. Manuel Valenzuela-Rendón. Reinforcement learning in the fuzzy classifier system. In *Collected Abstracts for the First International Workshop on Learning Classifier System (IWLCS-92)* [2]. October 6–8, NASA Johnson Space Center, Houston, Texas.

565. Manuel Valenzuela-Rendón and Eduardo Uresti-Charre. A Non-Genetic Algorithm for Multiobjective Optimization. In Bäck [10], pages 658–665.

566. Terry van Belle. A New Approach to Genetic-Based Automatic Feature Discovery. Master's thesis, University of Alberta, 1995. http://www.cs.ualberta.ca/~jonathan/.

567. Gilles Venturini. *Apprentissage Adaptatif et Apprentissage Supervisé par Algorithme Génétique*. PhD thesis, Université de Paris-Sud., 1994.

568. Nickolas Vriend. Self-Organization of Markets: An Example of a Computational Approach. *Computational Economics*, 8(3):205–231, 1995.

569. David Walter and Chilukuri K. Mohan. ClaDia: A Fuzzy Classifier System for Disease Diagnosis. In *Proceedings of the 2000 Congress on Evolutionary Computation (CEC00)* [3], pages 1429–1435.

570. L. A. Wang. Classifier System Learning of the Boolean Multiplexer Function. Master's thesis, Computer Science Department, University of Tennessee, Knoxville, TN, 1990.

571. Gerhard Weiss. Action-oriented learning in classifier systems. Technical Report FKI-158-91, Technical Univ. München (TUM), 1991.

572. Gerhard Weiss. The Action-Oriented Bucket Brigade. Technical Report FKI-156-91, Technical Univ. München (TUM), 1991.

573. Gerhard Weiss. Hierarchical chunking in classifier systems. In *Proceedings of the 12th National Conference on Artificial Intelligence*, pages 1335–1340. AAAI Press/MIT Press, 1994.

574. Gerhard Weiss. Learning by chunking in reactive classifier systems. Technical report, Technical Univ. München (TUM), 1994.

575. Gerhard Weiss. The locality/globality dilemma in classifier systems and an approach to its solution. Technical Report FKI-187-94, Technical Univ. München (TUM), 1994.

576. Gerhard Weiss. An action-oriented perspective of learning in classifier systems. *Journal of Experimental and Theoretical Artificial Intelligence*, 8:43–62, 1996.

577. Thomas H. Westerdale. The bucket brigade is not genetic. In Grefenstette [250], pages 45–59.

578. Thomas H. Westerdale. A Reward Scheme for Production Systems with Overlapping Conflict Sets. *IEEE Transactions on Systems, Man and Cybernetics*, SMC-16(3):369–383, 1986.

579. Thomas H. Westerdale. Altruism in the bucket brigade. In Grefenstette [252], pages 22–26.

580. Thomas H. Westerdale. A Defence of the Bucket Brigade. In Schaffer [463], pages 282–290.

581. Thomas H. Westerdale. Quasimorphisms or Queasymorphisms? Modelling Finite Automaton Environments. In Rawlins [422], pages 128–147.

582. Thomas H. Westerdale. Redundant Classifiers and Prokaryote Genomes. In Booker and Belew [59], pages 354–360.

583. Thomas H. Westerdale. Classifier Systems - No Wonder They Don't Work. In Koza et al. [346], pages 529–537.

584. Thomas H. Westerdale. An Approach to Credit Assignment in Classifier Systems. *Complexity*, 4(2), 1999.

585. Thomas H. Westerdale. Wilson's Error Measurement and the Markov Property – Identifying Detrimental Classifiers. In Wu [623], pages 314–321.

586. Darrell Whitely, David Goldberg, Erick Cantú-Paz, Lee Spector, Ian Parmee, and Hans-Georg Beyer, editors. *Proceedings of the Genetic and Evolutionary Computation Conference (GECCO-2000)*. Morgan Kaufmann: San Francisco, CA, 2000.

587. Jason R. Wilcox. Organizational Learning within a Learning Classifier Systems. Master's thesis, University of Illinois, 1995. Also Tech. Report No. 95003 IlliGAL.

588. Stewart W. Wilson. Aubert processing and intelligent vision. Technical report, Polaroid Corporation, 1981.

589. Stewart W. Wilson. On the retino-cortical mapping. *International Journal of Man-Machine Studies*, 18:361–389, 1983.

590. Stewart W. Wilson. Adaptive "cortical" pattern recognition. In Grefenstette [250], pages 188–196.

591. Stewart W. Wilson. Knowledge Growth in an Artificial Animal. In Grefenstette [250], pages 16–23. Also appeared in Proceedings of the 4th Yale.

592. Stewart W. Wilson. Knowledge Growth in an Artificial Animal. In *Proceedings of the 4th Yale Workshop on Applications of Adaptive Systems Theory*, pages 98–104, 1985.

593. Stewart W. Wilson. Classifier System Learning of a Boolean Function. Technical Report RIS 27r, The Rowland Institute for Science, 1986.

594. Stewart W. Wilson. Knowledge Growth in an Artificial Animal. In K. S. Narenda, editor, *Adaptive and learning systems: Theory and applications*, pages 255–264. Plenum Press: New York, 1986.

595. Stewart W. Wilson. Classifier Systems and the Animat Problem. *Machine Learning*, 2:199–228, 1987. Also Research Memo RIS-36r, the Rowland Institute for Science, Cambridge, MA, 1986.

596. Stewart W. Wilson. Hierarchical Credit Allocation in a Classifier System. In *Proceedings Tenth International Joint Conference on AI (IJCAI-87)*, pages 217–220. Morgan Kaufmann Publishers, 1987. Also Research Memo RIS-37r, the Rowland Institute for Science, Cambridge, MA, 1986.

597. Stewart W. Wilson. Quasi-Darwinian Learning in a Classifier System. In *Proceedings of the Fourth International Workshop on Machine Learning*, pages 59–65. Morgan Kaufmann, 1987.

598. Stewart W. Wilson. The genetic algorithm and biological development. In Grefenstette [252], pages 247–251.

599. Stewart W. Wilson. Bid Competition and Specificity Reconsidered. *Complex Systems*, 2(6):705–723, 1988.

600. Stewart W. Wilson. Hierarchical Credit Assignment in a Classifier System. In M. Elzas, T. Oren, and B. P. Zeigler, editors, *Modelling and Simulation Methodology: Knowledge Systems Paradigms*. North Holland, 1988.

601. Stewart W. Wilson. Hierarchical Credit Allocation in a Classifier System. In Davis [138], pages 104–115.

602. Stewart W. Wilson. Hierarchical credit allocation in a classifier system. In M. S. Elzas, T. I. Oren, and B. P. Zeigler, editors, *Modelling and simulation methodology*, pages 351–357. North-Holland: New York, 1989.

603. Stewart W. Wilson. The Genetic Algorithm and Simulated Evolution. In Chris Langton, editor, *Artificial Life: Proceedings of an Interdisciplinary Workshop on the Synthesis and Simulation of Living Systems*, volume VI of *Santa Fe Institute Studies in the Sciences of Complexity*. Addison-Wesley: Reading, MA, 1989.

604. Stewart W. Wilson. Perceptron redux: Emergence of structure. In *Special issue of Physica D (Vol. 42)* [1], pages 249–256. Republished in Emergent Computation, S. Forrest (ed.), MIT Press/Bradford Books.

605. Stewart W. Wilson. The Animat Path to AI. In Meyer and Wilson [385], pages 15–21. http://prediction-dynamics.com/.

606. Stewart W. Wilson. Classifier System mapping of real vectors. In *Collected Abstracts for the First International Workshop on Learning Classifier System (IWLCS-92)* [2]. October 6–8, NASA Johnson Space Center, Houston, Texas.

607. Stewart W. Wilson. Toward a GA solution of the discovery problem. In *Collected Abstracts for the First International Workshop on Learning Classifier System (IWLCS-92)* [2]. October 6–8, NASA Johnson Space Center, Houston, Texas.

608. Stewart W. Wilson. ZCS: A zeroth level classifier system. *Evolutionary Computation*, 2(1):1–18, 1994. http://prediction-dynamics.com/.

609. Stewart W. Wilson. Classifier Fitness Based on Accuracy. *Evolutionary Computation*, 3(2):149–175, 1995. http://prediction-dynamics.com/.

610. Stewart W. Wilson. Explore/exploit strategies in autonomy. In Maes et al. [377], pages 325–332.

611. Stewart W. Wilson. Generalization in XCS. Unpublished contribution to the ICML '96 Workshop on Evolutionary Computing and Machine Learning. http://prediction-dynamics.com/, 1996.

612. Stewart W. Wilson. Generalization in evolutionary learning. Presented at the Fourth European Conference on Artificial Life (ECAL97), Brighton, UK, July 27-31. http://prediction-dynamics.com/, 1997.

613. Stewart W. Wilson. Generalization in the XCS classifier system. In Koza et al. [345], pages 665–674. http://prediction-dynamics.com/.

614. Stewart W. Wilson. Get real! XCS with continuous-valued inputs. In L. Booker, Stephanie Forrest, M. Mitchell, and Rick L. Riolo, editors, *Festschrift in Honor of John H. Holland*, pages 111–121. Center for the Study of Complex Systems, 1999. http://prediction-dynamics.com/.

615. Stewart W. Wilson. State of XCS classifier system research. In Wu [623], pages 322–334. Also Tech. Report 99.1.1, Prediction Dynamics, Concord MA. http://prediction-dynamics.com/.

616. Stewart W. Wilson. Get Real! XCS with Continuous-Valued Inputs. In Lanzi et al. [364], pages 209–219.

617. Stewart W. Wilson. Mining Oblique Data with XCS. In *Proceedings of the International Workshop on Learning Classifier Systems (IWLCS-2000), in the Joint Workshops of SAB 2000 and PPSN 2000* [4]. Extended abstract.

618. Stewart W. Wilson. Mining Oblique Data with XCS. Technical Report 2000028, University of Illinois at Urbana-Champaign, 2000.

619. Stewart W. Wilson. State of XCS Classifier System Research. In Lanzi et al. [364], pages 63–82.

620. Stewart W. Wilson and David E. Goldberg. A Critical Review of Classifier Systems. In Schaffer [463], pages 244–255. http://prediction-dynamics.com/.

621. Ian Wright. Reinforcement Learning and Animat Emotions. In Maes et al. [377], pages 272–281.

622. Ian Wright. Reinforcement learning and animat emotions. Technical Report CSRP-96-4, School of Computer Science. University of Birmingham, 1996. ftp://ftp.cs.bham.ac.uk/pub/tech-reports/1996/CSRP-96-04.ps.gz.

623. Annie S. Wu, editor. *Proceedings of the 1999 Genetic and Evolutionary Computation Conference Workshop Program*, 1999.

624. Derek F. Yates and Andrew Fairley. An Investigation into Possible Causes of, and Solutions to, Rule Strength Distortion Due to the Bucket Brigade Algorithm. In Forrest [216], pages 246–253.

625. Derek F. Yates and Andrew Fairley. Evolutionary Stability in Simple Classifier Systems. In Fogarty [203], pages 28–37.

626. Takahiro Yoshimi and Toshiharu Taura. Hierarchical Classifier System Based on the Concept of Viewpoint. In Koza et al. [345], pages 675–678.

627. Takahiro Yoshimi and Toshiharu Taura. A Computational Model of a Viewpoint-Forming Process in a Hierarchical Classifier System. In Banzhaf et al. [18], pages 758–766.

628. Zhaohua Zhang, Stan Franklin, and Dipankar Dasgupta. Metacognition in Software Agents Using Classifier Systems. In *AAAI-98. Proceedings of the Fifteenth National Conference on Artificial Intelligence*, pages 83–88, Madison (WI), 1998. AAAI-Press and MIT Press.

629. Hayong Harry Zhou. Classifier systems with long term memory. In Grefenstette [250], pages 178–182.

630. Hayong Harry Zhou. *CSM: A genetic classifier system with memory for learning by analogy*. PhD thesis, Department of Computer Science, Vanderbilt University, Nashville, TN, 1987.

631. Hayong Harry Zhou. CSM: A Computational Model of Cumulative Learning. *Machine Learning*, 5(4):383–406, 1990.

632. Hayong Harry Zhou and John J. Grefenstette. Learning by Analogy in Genetic Classifier Systems. In Schaffer [463], pages 291–297.

633. Raed Abu Zitar and Mohammad H. Hassoun. Regulator Control via Genetic Search Assisted Reinforcement. In Forrest [216], pages 254–263.

Part V

Appendix

An Algorithmic Description of XCS

Martin V. Butz[1] and Stewart W. Wilson[2]

[1] Institute for Psychology III & Department of Computer Science
University of Würzburg, Germany
butz@psychologie.uni-wuerzburg.de
[2] University of Illinois at Urbana-Champaign
Prediction Dynamics, Concord, MA 01742
wilson@prediction-dynamics.com

Abstract. A concise description of the XCS classifier system's parameters, structures, and algorithms is presented as an aid to research. The algorithms are written in modularly structured pseudo code with accompanying explanations.

1 Introduction

XCS is a recently developed learning classifier system (LCS) that differs in several ways from more traditional LCSs. In XCS, classifier fitness is based on the *accuracy* of a classifier's payoff prediction instead of the prediction itself. Second, the genetic algorithm (GA) takes place in the action sets instead of the population as a whole. Finally, unlike the traditional LCS, XCS has no message list and so is only suitable for learning in Markov environments (XCS extensions using an internal-state register have shown promise in non-Markov environments).

XCS's fitness definition and GA locus together result in a strong tendency for the system to evolve accurate, maximally general classifiers that efficiently cover the state-action space of the problem and allow the system's 'knowledge' to be readily seen. As a result of these properties, there has been considerable interest in further investigation and potential extension of XCS and its principles. We therefore thought it would be useful to provide a basic algorithmic description of XCS, both as a core definition of the system and as a common framework from which new variants and research directions could spring.

We first present XCS's relation to the problem environment, followed by the system's structures and parameters. The rest of the paper consists of a top-down modular description of the XCS algorithm, written in pseudo-code accompanied by explanatory notes. We hope the result will be useful, and we encourage researchers to give us feedback regarding potential problems and clarifications. This document should definitely be read in conjunction with some of the basic XCS literature, for example [Wil95], [Kov97], and [Wil98]. Additional papers on XCS and other LCSs, together with a complete LCS bibliography, are found in [LSW00].

P.L. Lanzi, W. Stolzmann, and S.W. Wilson (Eds.): IWLCS 2000, LNAI 1996, pp. 253–272, 2001.
© Springer-Verlag Berlin Heidelberg 2001

2   Environment Interaction, Structures, and Parameters

2.1   Interaction with the Environment

In keeping with the typical LCS model, the environment provides as input to the system a series of sensory situations $\sigma(t) \in \{0,1\}^L$, where L is the number of bits in each situation. In response, the system executes actions $\alpha(t) \in \{a_1, ..., a_n\}$ upon the environment. Each action results in a scalar reward $\rho(t)$ (possibly zero). The interaction is divided into *problems*, which may be either single-step or multi-step. A flag *eop* indicates the end of a problem. While $\sigma(t)$ and $\alpha(t)$ are interactions with the environment itself, the reward $\rho(t)$ and the flag are normally provided by another component which, following [DC98], we term the *reinforcement program rp*. The reinforcement program determines the reward according to the current environmental input and the action that was executed. The separation of environment and reinforcement components is useful and natural because reinforcement is often not an inherent aspect of the environment, but may be due, e.g., to a trainer or to the system's own priorities. Figure 1 illustrates the interaction of the environment and the reinforcement program with XCS.

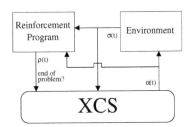

Fig. 1. XCS interacts with an environment and a reinforcement program.

In a single-step problem such as the Boolean multiplexer, the successive situations are not related to each other. After execution of an action the *rp* provides the appropriate reward ρ and signals with the flag *eop* that the problem has ended. In a multi-step problem such as a maze, the successive situations are related to each other. Reward is only provided in certain situations (e.g. the food position(s) in mazes). The point at which a problem ends in a multi-step environment must be defined by the *rp* according to the task that is to be solved.

2.2   A Classifier in XCS

XCS keeps a population of classifiers which represent its knowledge about the problem. Each classifier is a condition–action–prediction rule having the following parts:

- The condition $C \in \{0, 1, \#\}^L$ specifies the input states (sensory situations) in which the classifier can be applied (matches).
- The action $A \in \{a_1, ..., a_n\}$ specifies the action (possibly a classification) that the classifier proposes.
- The prediction p estimates (keeps an average of) the payoff expected if the classifier matches and its action is taken by the system.

Moreover, each classifier keeps certain additional parameters:

- The prediction error ϵ estimates the errors made in the predictions.
- The fitness F denotes the classifier's fitness.
- The experience exp counts the number of times since its creation that the classifier has belonged to an action set.
- The time stamp ts denotes the time-step of the last occurrence of a GA in an action set to which this classifier belonged.
- The action set size as estimates the average size of the action sets this classifier has belonged to.
- The numerosity n reflects the number of micro-classifiers (ordinary classifiers) this classifier – which is technically called a *macroclassifier* – represents.

To refer to one of the attributes of a classifier cl we use the dot notation $cl.x$ where x can be any of the above attributes (i.e. $x \in \{C, A, p, \epsilon, F, exp, ts, as, n\}$).

Important in our notation is the term *payoff*. Due to the Q-learning-like reinforcement learning in XCS, payoff does not refer solely to the expected reward ρ but is a combination of ρ and the payoff prediction of the best possible action in the next state. However, in the case of a single-step problem payoff reduces to the reward produced by the proposed action.

Note that ϵ measures the error of the predictions in units of payoff. The same is true of the parameter ϵ_0 that is defined in Sect. 2.4.

Classifiers in XCS are *macroclassifiers*, i.e., each classifier represents n traditional or *micro-* classifiers having identical conditions and actions. Algorithms covering creation, deletion, and adjustment of the numerosity of macroclassifiers are given in Sect. 3.10, 3.11, and 3.12. In XCS, macroclassifiers are always handled *as though* they consist of n micro-classifiers.

2.3   The Different Sets

There are four different sets that need to be considered in XCS.

- The population $[P]$ consists of all classifiers that exist in XCS at any time t.
- The match set $[M]$ is formed out of the current $[P]$. It includes all classifiers that match the current situation $\sigma(t)$.
- The action set $[A]$ is formed out of the current $[M]$. It includes all classifiers of $[M]$ that propose the executed action.
- The previous action set $[A]_{-1}$ is the action set that was active in the last execution cycle.

2.4 Learning Parameters in XCS

In order to control the learning process in XCS the following parameters are used:

- N specifies the maximum size of the population (in micro-classifiers, i.e., N is the sum of the classifier numerosities).
- β is the learning rate for p, ϵ, f, and as.
- α, ϵ_0, and ν are used in calculating the fitness of a classifier.
- γ is the discount factor used – in multi-step problems – in updating classifier predictions.
- θ_{GA} is the GA threshold. The GA is applied in a set when the average time since the last GA in the set is greater than θ_{GA}.
- χ is the probability of applying crossover in the GA.
- μ specifies the probability of mutating an allele in the offspring.
- θ_{del} is the deletion threshold. If the experience of a classifier is greater than θ_{del}, its fitness may be considered in its probability of deletion.
- δ specifies the fraction of the mean fitness in $[P]$ below which the fitness of a classifier may be considered in its probability of deletion.
- θ_{sub} is the subsumption threshold. The experience of a classifier must be greater than θ_{sub} in order to be able to subsume another classifier.
- $P_{\#}$ is the probability of using a $\#$ in one attribute in C when covering.
- p_I, ϵ_I, and F_I are used as initial values in new classifiers.
- p_{explr} specifies the probability during action selection of choosing the action uniform randomly.
- θ_{mna} specifies the minimal number of actions that must be present in a match set $[M]$, or else covering will occur.
- $doGASubsumption$ is a Boolean parameter that specifies if offspring are to be tested for possible logical subsumption by parents.
- $doActionSetSubsumption$ is a Boolean parameter that specifies if action sets are to be tested for subsuming classifiers.

2.5 Commonly Used Parameter Settings

For parameter settings, it is best to check the literature for a similar experiment. In some cases, the following suggestions could be taken as starting points. The population size, N, should be large enough so that, starting from an empty population, covering occurs only at the very beginning of a run. The learning rate, β, could be in the range 0.1-0.2. The parameter α is normally 0.1. The parameter ϵ_0 is the error below which classifiers are considered to have equal accuracy; a typical value would be about one percent of the maximum value of p, e.g., 10 if the maximum value is 1000. The power parameter ν is typically 5. The discount factor γ has been 0.71 in many problems in the literature, but larger or smaller values could certainly work, depending on the environment. The threshold θ_{GA} is often in the range 25-50. Crossover probabilities χ in the range 0.5-1.0 have been used. Mutation probabilities μ in the range 0.01-0.05 are often used.

The deletion threshold θ_{del} could be about 20. δ is often taken to be 0.1. The subsumption threshold θ_{sub} could be about 20, though larger values (more experience) are important in some problems. $P_\#$ could be around 0.33. Larger values reduce the need for covering, but may make it harder to evolve accurate classifiers. The initialization parameters p_I, ϵ_I, and F_I should be taken very small – essentially zero. The exploration probability p_{explr} could be 0.5, but this depends on the type of experiment contemplated. To cause covering to provide classifiers for every action, choose θ_{mna} equal to the number of available actions.

The setting of *doGASubsumption* and *doActionSetSubsumption* depends on the problem. In general, subsumption is used to eliminate classifiers that clearly add nothing to the system's decision capability. In the case of GA subsumption, these are offspring classifiers whose conditions are logically subsumed by a parent's condition, given that the parent is both accurate and sufficiently experienced. In the case of action set subsumption, a general, accurate, and experienced classifier in an action set eliminates classifiers in the set that its condition logically subsumes. The two subsumption methods are independent and different in their effects. Broadly, action set subsumption appears to be 'stronger': it causes greater 'condensation' of the population. Subsumption is useful in problems where there is a well-defined underlying target function, such as the Boolean multiplexer.

Note, however, that subsumption is *not* necessary for XCS to form accurate maximal generalizations (see [Wil95] for the basic XCS *generalization hypothesis*). Subsumption tends to result in accurate classifiers that are as formally general as possible without being contradicted by any actually occurring input. Without subsumption, the system produces these as well as accurate but more-specific classifiers that match the same inputs as the general ones do [Wil98]. Subsumption produces smaller final populations, but because the more-specific classifiers are not present, the system is more vulnerable to environmental changes – it does not have the more-specific classifiers to "fall back on".

3   An Algorithmic Description of XCS

This section presents the algorithms used in XCS. The description starts from the top level. First, the overall execution cycle is described. The following subsections specify the single parts in more detail. Each specified sub-procedure in this description is written in capital letters. When referring to a module other than XCS (e.g. the environment *env*), a colon is used. However, due to the diverse modifications and extensions of XCS published during the last several years, we first clarify to which 'XCS' we are referring in the subsequent description.

3.1   Which XCS?

Since the introduction of XCS in 1995 several additions and modifications have been reported. Some of them did not result in a change of the name 'XCS', but they were an important step in increasing the robustness of the system. This section describes which changes of the basic XCS [Wil95] are included as well as which ones are omitted herein.

The update of the classifier parameters is modified in several ways from the original publication. First, the order of the update is changed but can easily be switched back to the original one. Second, the calculation of the accuracy measure κ is changed from the original exponential function to a power law function as used in [Wil00]. Finally, the MAM ("moyenne adaptive modifiée") technique is not used in the fitness update of a classifier. This method results in a stronger robustness against inaccurate classifiers.

Moreover, several changes in the discovery component are considered herein. First, the covering criterion is changed. While the original criterion had to consider the mean prediction in the population, the approach herein simply assures that a certain number of actions is present in each match set. The change increases the speed of the program while assuring the original properties of the mechanism. Second, the GA is applied in the action set and subsumption deletion is used as published in [Wil98]. However, the subsumption method is further detailed distinguishing between *action set subsumption* and *GA subsumption*. Next, mutation is modified describing a pure niche mutation. While this mutation style promises a faster convergence later in the run, an unrestricted mutation can help early in the run to solve harder problems. Finally, the deletion method combines the two original methods as proposed in [Kov99].

Despite their importance, we decided not to include Lanzi's modifications of *specify* ([Lan97], [Lan99a]) nor the enhancement for stochastic environments (XCSμ, [Lan99d]). Moreover, no enhancements of the representation of the classifier conditions are considered, e.g., as published in [Lan99b], introducing a messy coding, and in [Lan99c], introducing s-expressions. We also did not incorporate any sort of memory mechanism as recently investigated in detail (see e.g. [LW00]).

Thus, the XCS classifier system described herein includes the most important modifications while staying close to the original work. The modifications are further discussed in the algorithmic description itself.

3.2 Initialization

When XCS is started, the modules must first of all be initialized. The parameters in the environment must be set and, e.g., a maze must be read in. Also, the reinforcement program rp must be initialized. Finally, XCS itself must be initialized. Apart from the parameter settings and the start of the time-step counter referred to as `actual time` t, the population $[P]$ needs to be initialized. The population $[P]$ can either be left empty or can be filled with the maximal number of classifiers N, generating each classifier with a random condition and action and the initial parameters. The two methods differ only slightly in their effect on performance. Thus the simpler way of leaving the population empty in the beginning is commonly used. After the initialization, the main loop is called.

XCS:
```
1 initialize environment env
2 initialize reinforcement program rp
3 initialize XCS
4 RUN EXPERIMENT
```

3.3 The Main Loop

In the main loop *RUN EXPERIMENT*, the current situation is first sensed (received as input). Second, the match set is formed from all classifiers that match the situation. Third, the prediction array PA is formed based on the classifiers in the match set. PA predicts for each possible action a_i the resulting payoff. Based on PA, one action is chosen for execution and the action set $[A]$ is formed, which includes all classifiers of $[M]$ that propose the chosen action. Next, the winning action is executed. Then the previous action set $[A]_{-1}$ (if this is a multi-step problem and there is a previous action set) is modified using the Q-learning-like payoff quantity P which is a combination of the previous reward ρ_{-1} and the largest action prediction in the prediction array PA. Moreover, the GA may be applied to $[A]_{-1}$. If a problem ends on the current time-step (single-step problem or last step of a multi-step problem), $[A]$ is modified according to the current reward ρ and the GA may be applied to $[A]$. The main loop is executed as long as the termination criterion is not met. A termination criterion is, e.g., a certain number of trials or a 100% performance level.

The main loop specifies many sub-procedures essential for learning in XCS. Some of the procedures are more or less trivial while others are complex and themselves call other sub-procedures. The following sections describe all procedures specified in the main loop, covering all relevant processes. Each of them tries to specify the general idea and the overall process and then gives a more detailed description of single parts in successive paragraphs.

3.4 Formation of the Match Set

The *GENERATE MATCH SET* procedure gets as input the current population $[P]$ and the current situation σ. Although the procedure sounds trivial, it has within it a covering process. Covering is called when the number of different actions represented by matching classifiers is less than the parameter θ_{mna}. Thus, *GENERATE MATCH SET* first looks for the classifiers in $[P]$ that match σ and next, checks if covering is required. A classifier generated by covering can be directly added to the population since it must differ from all current classifiers. Note that the while loop at step 2 is executed as long as covering is required.

In the following paragraphs we will describe the sub-procedures included in the *GENERATE MATCH SET* algorithm. The sub-procedure *DELETE FROM POPULATION* however can be found in Sect. 3.11.

RUN EXPERIMENT():

```
 1  ρ_{-1} ← 0
 2  do{
 3      σ ← env: get situation
 4      [M] ← GENERATE MATCH SET out of [P] using σ
 5      PA ← GENERATE PREDICTION ARRAY out of [M]
 6      act ← SELECT ACTION according to PA
 7      [A] ← GENERATE ACTION SET out of [M] according to act
 8      env: execute action act
 9      ρ ← rp: get reward
10      if([A]_{-1} is not empty)
11          P ← ρ_{-1} + γ * max(PA)
12          UPDATE SET [A]_{-1} using P possibly deleting in [P]
13          RUN GA in [A]_{-1} considering σ_{-1} inserting and
                possibly deleting in [P]
14      if(rp: eop)
15          P ← ρ
16          UPDATE SET [A] using P possibly deleting in [P]
17          RUN GA in [A] considering σ inserting and
                possibly deleting in [P]
18          empty [A]_{-1}
19      else
20          [A]_{-1} ← [A]
21          ρ_{-1} ← ρ
22          σ_{-1} ← σ
23  }while(termination criteria are not met)
```

GENERATE MATCH SET([P], σ):

```
 1  initialize empty set [M]
 2  while([M] is empty)
 3      for each classifier cl in [P]
 4          if(DOES MATCH classifier cl in situation σ)
 5              add classifier cl to set [M]
 6      if(the number of different actions in [M] < θ_{mna})
 7          cl_c ← GENERATE COVERING CLASSIFIER considering [M] and σ
 8          add classifier cl_c to set [P]
 9          DELETE FROM POPULATION [P]
10          empty [M]
11  return [M]
```

Classifier Matching. The matching procedure is that commonly used in LCSs. A 'don't care'-symbol # in C matches any symbol in the corresponding position of $σ$. A 'care' or non-# symbol only matches with the exact same symbol at that position. The basic XCS relies on binary coding and thus the care symbols are $\in \{0, 1\}$. Recently, Lanzi ([Lan99b], [Lan99c]) introduced an extension of the conditions in XCS involving messy coding and Lisp s-expressions. Wilson [Wil00] introduced the first XCS extension that is able to handle real coded inputs. However, here we will consider only the basic kind of classifier condition.

The *DOES MATCH* procedure checks each component in the classifier's condition C. If a component is specified (i.e. is not a don't care symbol), it is compared with the corresponding attribute in the current situation σ. Only if all comparisons hold does the classifier match σ and the procedure return *true*.

DOES MATCH(cl, σ):
```
1 for each attribute x in cl.C
2     if(x ≠ # and x ≠ the corresponding attribute in σ)
3         return false
4 return true
```

Covering. Covering occurs if the number of actions present in $[M]$ is $< \theta_{mna}$. A classifier is created whose condition matches $\sigma(t)$ and contains don't cares with probability $P_{\#}$. The classifier's action is chosen randomly from among those not present in $[M]$.

GENERATE COVERING CLASSIFIER($[M]$, σ):
```
 1 initialize classifier cl
 2 initialize condition cl.C with the length of σ
 3 for each attribute x in cl.C
 4     if(RandomNumber[0, 1) < P#)
 5         x ← #
 6     else
 7         x ← the corresponding attribute in σ
 8 cl.A ← random action not present in [M]
 9 cl.p ← pI
10 cl.ε ← εI
11 cl.F ← FI
12 cl.exp ← 0
13 cl.ts ← actual time t
14 cl.as ← 1
15 cl.n ← 1
16 return cl
```

3.5 The Prediction Array

Given an input, XCS makes a "best guess" prediction of the payoff to be expected for each possible action. These *system predictions* are stored in an array called the Prediction Array PA. The system prediction for an action is a fitness-weighted average of the predictions of all classifiers in $[M]$ that advocate that action. If no classifiers in $[M]$ advocate a certain action, its system prediction is not defined, symbolized by *null*.

The *GENERATE PREDICTION ARRAY* procedure considers each classifier in $[M]$ and adds its prediction multiplied by its fitness to the prediction value total for that action. The total for each action is then divided by the sum of the fitnesses for that action to yield the system prediction.

GENERATE PREDICTION ARRAY($[M]$):
```
 1 initialize prediction array PA  to all null
 2 initialize fitness sum array FSA  to all 0.0
 3 for each classifier cl in [M]
 4    if(PA[cl.A] = null)
 5       PA[cl.A] ← cl.p * cl.F
 6    else
 7       PA[cl.A] ← PA[cl.A] + cl.p * cl.F
 8    FSA[cl.A] ← FSA[cl.A] + cl.F
 9 for each possible action A
10    if(FSA[A] is not zero)
11       PA[A] ← PA[A] / FSA[A]
12 return PA
```

3.6   Choosing an Action

XCS does not prescribe any particular action-selection method, and any of a great variety can be employed. For example, actions may be selected randomly, independent of the system predictions, or the selection may be based on those predictions – using, e.g., roulette-wheel selection or simply picking the action with the highest system prediction.

In our *SELECT ACTION* procedure we illustrate a combination of *pure exploration* – choosing the action randomly – and *pure exploitation* – choosing the best one. Lanzi [Lan99a] published first experiments with so-called *biased exploration* where pure exploration is chosen with a probability p_{explr} and otherwise pure exploitation is chosen. This action selection method is known as *ε-greedy* selection in the reinforcement learning literature [SB98] where the ϵ has identical meaning to our p_{explr} parameter. As an aside, it appears better to perform the GA only on exploration steps, especially if most steps are exploitation.

SELECT ACTION(PA):
```
 1 if(RandomNumber[0, 1) < p_explr)
 2    //Do pure exploration here
 3    return a randomly chosen action from those not null in PA
 4 else
 5    //Do pure exploitation here
 6    return the best action in PA
```

3.7   Formation of the Action Set

After the match set $[M]$ is formed and an action is chosen for execution, the *GENERATE ACTION SET* procedure forms the action set out of the match set. It includes all classifiers that propose the chosen action for execution.

GENERATE ACTION SET([M], act):
```
1 initialize empty set [A]
2 for each classifier cl in [M]
3    if(cl.A = act)
4        add classifier cl to set [A]
```

3.8   Updating Classifier Parameters

Although Wilson [Wil95] applied the update procedures as well as the GA originally in $[M]$ and only later [Wil98] was this switched to $[A]$, application in $[A]$ is now commonly used and gives better performance in all cases known to us. Thus we will use the $[A]$ notation in the following procedures although they are basically independent of the classifier set involved.

The reinforcement portion of the update procedure follows the pattern of Q-learning [SB98]. Classifier predictions are updated using the immediate reward and the discounted maximum payoff anticipated on the next time-step. The difference is that in XCS it is the prediction of a possibly general *rule* that is updated, whereas in Q-learning it is the prediction associated with an environmental *state-action* pair. Updates of classifier parameters other than prediction are unique to XCS. Note that in single-step problems, the prediction is updated using the immediate reward alone.

Each time a classifier enters the set $[A]$, its parameters are modified in the order: exp, p, ϵ, as, and F. Variations in the order are possible. The principle one is to exchange the p and ϵ updates. If prediction comes before error, the prediction of a classifier in its very first update immediately predicts the correct payoff and consequently the prediction error is set to zero. This can lead to faster learning in simpler problems but can be misleading in more complex ones. A more conservative strategy which puts the error update first, seems to work better on harder problems. The update of the action set size estimate is independent from the other updates and consequently can be executed at any point in time. While the updates of exp, p, ϵ, and as are straightforward, the update of F is more complex and requires more computational steps. Thus, we refer to another subprocedure. Finally, if the program is using action set subsumption, the procedure calls the *DO ACTION SET SUBSUMPTION* procedure. This procedure is very powerful and is able to eliminate a large number of classifiers in the action set in one step. Section 3.12 describes the procedure in detail.

Fitness Update. The fitness of a classifier in XCS is based on the *accuracy* of its predictions. The *UPDATE FITNESS* procedure first calculates the classifier's

UPDATE SET([A], P, [P]):
```
1 for each classifier cl in [A]
2    cl.exp++
3    //update prediction cl.p
4    if(cl.exp < 1/β)
5       cl.p ← cl.p + (P - cl.p) / cl.exp
6    else
7       cl.p ← cl.p + β * (P - cl.p)
8    //update prediction error cl.ϵ
9    if(cl.exp < 1/β)
10      cl.ϵ ← cl.ϵ + (|P - cl.p| - cl.ϵ) / cl.exp
11   else
12      cl.ϵ ← cl.ϵ + β * (|P - cl.p| - cl.ϵ)
13   //update action set size estimate cl.as
14   if(cl.exp < 1/β)
15      cl.as ← cl.as + (∑_{c∈[A]} c.n - cl.as) / cl.exp
16   else
17      cl.as ← cl.as + β * (∑_{c∈[A]} c.n - cl.as)
18 UPDATE FITNESS in set [A]
19 if(doActionSetSubsumption)
20    DO ACTION SET SUBSUMPTION in [A] updating [P]
```

accuracy κ using the classifier's prediction error ϵ. Then the classifier's fitness is updated using the *normalized accuracy* computed in lines 8-10.

UPDATE FITNESS([A]):
```
1 accuracySum ← 0
2 initialize accuracy vector κ
3 for each classifier cl in [A]
4    if(cl.ϵ < ϵ₀)
5       κ(cl) ← 1
6    else
7       κ(cl) ← α * (cl.ϵ / ϵ₀)^{-ν}
8    accuracySum ← accuracySum + κ(cl) * cl.n
9 for each classifier cl in [A]
10   cl.F ← cl.F + β * (κ(cl) * cl.n / accuracySum - cl.F)
```

3.9   The Genetic Algorithm in XCS

The final sub-procedure in the main loop, *RUN GA*, is also the most complex. First of all, the action set is checked to see if the GA should be applied at all. In order to apply a GA the average time period since the last GA application in the set must be greater than the threshold θ_{GA}. Next, two classifiers (i.e. the parents) are selected by roulette wheel selection based on fitness and the offspring are created out of them. After that, the offspring are possibly crossed and mutated. If the offspring are crossed, their prediction, error, and fitness values are set to the average of the parents' values. Finally, the offspring are inserted in the population, followed by corresponding deletions. However, if GA subsumption is being used, each offspring is first tested to see if it is subsumed by either of its parents; if so, that offspring is not inserted in the population, and the subsuming parent's numerosity is increased. (Besides checking if an offspring is subsumed by a parent, one could also check if it is subsumed by other classifiers in the action set, or even the population as a whole.)

$RUN\ GA([A],\ \sigma,\ [P])$:

```
 1 if(actual time t - ∑_{cl∈[A]} cl.ts * cl.n / ∑_{cl∈[A]} cl.n > θ_GA)
 2    for each classifier cl in [A]
 3        cl.ts ← actual time t
 4        parent₁ ← SELECT OFFSPRING in [A]
 5        parent₂ ← SELECT OFFSPRING in [A]
 6        child₁ ← copy classifier parent₁
 7        child₂ ← copy classifier parent₂
 8        child₁.n = child₂.n ← 1
 9        child₁.exp = child₂.exp ← 0
10        if(RandomNumber[0,1) < χ)
11            APPLY CROSSOVER on child₁ and child₂
12            child₁.p ← (parent₁.p + parent₂.p) / 2
13            child₁.ε ← (parent₁.ε + parent₂.ε) / 2
14            child₁.F ← (parent₁.F + parent₂.F) / 2
15            child₂.p ← child₁.p
16            child₂.ε ← child₁.ε
17            child₂.F ← child₁.F
18        child₁.F ← child₁.F * 0.1
19        child₂.F ← child₂.F * 0.1
20        for both children child
21            APPLY MUTATION on child according to σ
22            if(doGASubsumption)
23                if(DOES SUBSUME parent₁, child)
24                    parent₁.n++
25                else if(DOES SUBSUME parent₂, child)
26                    parent₂.n++
27                else
28                    INSERT child IN POPULATION [P]
29            else
30                INSERT child IN POPULATION [P]
31        DELETE FROM POPULATION [P]
```

While the sub-procedures *INSERT IN POPULATION* and *DELETE FROM POPULATION* are defined in Sects. 3.10 and 3.11, respectively, the others are described in the following paragraphs.

Roulette-Wheel Selection. The Roulette-Wheel Selection chooses a classifier for reproduction proportional to the fitness of the classifiers in set $[A]$. First, the sum of all the fitnesses in the set $[A]$ is computed. Next, the roulette-wheel is spun. Finally, the classifier is chosen according to the roulette-wheel result.

SELECT OFFSPRING($[A]$):

```
1 fitnessSum ← 0
2 for each classifier cl in [A]
3    fitnessSum ← fitnessSum + cl.F
4 choicePoint ← RandomNumber[0, 1) * fitnessSum
5 fitnessSum ← 0
6 for each classifier cl in [A]
7    fitnessSum ← fitnessSum + cl.F
8    if(fitnessSum > choicePoint)
9        return cl
```

Crossover. The crossover procedure is similar to the standard crossover procedure in GAs. Implementations of XCS with one point and two point crossover were tested and resulted in approximately identical results. In the *APPLY CROSSOVER* procedure we show two-point crossover. The actions are not affected by crossover.

APPLY CROSSOVER(cl_1, cl_2):

```
1 x ← RandomNumber[0, 1) * (length of cl₁.C +1)
2 y ← RandomNumber[0, 1) * (length of cl₁.C +1)
3 if(x > y)
4    switch x and y
5 i ← 0
6 do{
7    if(x ≤ i and i < y)
8        switch cl₁.C[i] and cl₂.C[i]
9    i++
10 }while(i < y)
```

A more sophisticated crossover could include assurance that x and y are different. However, even without such special checks the algorithm serves its purpose.

Mutation. While crossover does not affect the action, mutation takes place in both the condition and the action. A mutation in the condition flips the attribute to one of the other possibilities. Mutation in the action changes it equiprobable to one of the other actions. Though more time-efficient methods are possible, we present here the simple one in which a die is flipped for each attribute. Since in XCS most of the time is spent in processes that operate on the whole population such as matching and deletion, the type of algorithm used for mutation only slightly affects efficiency. Note that our mutation is somewhat restricted. Rather than allowing an attribute of the condition to change to any other attribute, we only allow changes either to # or to the specific value that matches the corresponding component of $\sigma(t)$. Thus the resulting condition still matches the current input. The effect (if the action is unchanged) is to search the current action set niche along the axis of specificity vs. generality. Less restricted mutation schemes are of course possible.

APPLY MUTATION(cl, σ):
```
 1  i ← 0
 2  do{
 3      if(RandomNumber[0, 1) < μ)
 4          if(cl.C[i] = #)
 5              cl.C[i] ← σ[i]
 6          else
 7              cl.C[i] ← #
 8      i++
 9  }while(i < length of cl.C)
10  if(RandomNumber[0, 1) < μ)
11      cl.A ← a randomly chosen other possible action
```

3.10   Insertion in the Population

The *INSERT IN POPULATION* procedure checks to see if the classifier to be inserted is identical in condition and action with a classifier already in the population. If so, the latter's numerosity is incremented; if not, the new classifier is added to the population.

INSERT IN POPULATION(cl, [P]):
```
 1  for all c in [P]
 2      if(c is equal to cl in condition and action)
 3          c.n++
 4          return
 5  add cl to set [P]
```

3.11   Deletion from the Population

The deletion procedure realizes two ideas at the same time: (1) it assures an approximately equal number of classifiers in each action set, or environmental 'niche'; (2) it removes low-fitness individuals from the population. The following paragraphs describe the *DELETE FROM POPULATION* procedure and the *DELETION VOTE* sub-procedure.

Roulette-Wheel Deletion. Like the selection procedure, the deletion procedure *DELETE FROM POPULATION* chooses individuals (for deletion) by roulette-wheel selection. But first, the procedure checks to see if the sum of classifier numerosities in $[P]$ is less than or equal to N. If so, the procedure exits, as deletion is unnecessary. Otherwise, the sum of all deletion votes is calculated, and a classifier is chosen for deletion. If the classifier is a macroclassifier and currently represents more than one classifier, then its numerosity is merely decreased by one. Otherwise, the classifier is completely removed from the population.

DELETE FROM POPULATION($[P]$):

```
 1 if (∑_{c∈[P]} c.n ≤ N)
 2     return
 3 avFitnessInPopulation ← ∑_{c∈[P]} c.F / ∑_{c∈[P]} c.n
 4 voteSum ← 0
 5 for each classifier c in [P]
 6     voteSum ← voteSum + DELETION VOTE of c
                          with avFitnessInPopulation
 7 choicePoint ← RandomNumber[0,1) * voteSum
 8 voteSum ← 0
 9 for each classifier c in [P]
10     voteSum ← voteSum + DELETION VOTE of c
                          with avFitnessInPopulation
11     if (voteSum > choicePoint)
12         if (c.n > 1)
13             c.n--
14         else
15             remove classifier c from set [P]
16         return
```

The Deletion Vote. As mentioned above, the deletion vote realizes niching as well as removal of the lowest fitness classifiers. The deletion vote of each classifier is based on the action set size estimate as. Moreover, if the classifier has sufficient experience and its fitness is significantly lower than the average fitness in the population, the vote is increased in inverse proportion to the fitness. In this calculation, since we are deleting one micro-classifier at a time, we need to use as fitness the (macro)classifier's fitness divided by its numerosity. The following *DELETION VOTE* procedure realizes all this.

DELETION VOTE(cl, avFitnessInPopulation):

```
1 vote ← cl.as * cl.n
2 if (cl.exp > θ_del and cl.F / cl.n < δ * avFitnessInPopulation)
3     vote ← vote * avFitnessInPopulation / ( cl.F / cl.n)
4 return vote
```

3.12   Subsumption

Two subsumption procedures were introduced into XCS in [Wil98]. The first, 'GA subsumption', checks an offspring classifier to see if its condition is logically subsumed by the condition of an accurate and sufficiently experienced parent. If so, the offspring is not added to the population, but the parent's numerosity is incremented. The idea is that such an offspring cannot improve the system's performance, since everything it accomplishes is accomplished just as well by the subsuming parent. GA subsumption, if enabled, occurs within the procedure *RUN GA*. It is detailed within that procedure, and is not called as a sub-procedure (though it could be). However, the sub-procedure *DOES SUBSUME* is called, and is described in this section.

The second subsumption procedure, 'action set subsumption', if enabled, takes place in every action set. It has a purpose similar to GA subsumption but is different and independent of it. The action set is searched for the most general classifier that is both accurate and sufficiently experienced. Then all other classifiers in the set are tested against the general one to see if it subsumes them. Any classifiers that are subsumed are eliminated from the population.

DO ACTION SET SUBSUMPTION([A], [P]):
```
 1 initialize cl
 2 for each classifier c in [A]
 3    if(c COULD SUBSUME)
 4       if(cl empty or number of # in c.C > number of # in cl.C
           or (number of # in c.C = number of # in cl.C and
                                    RandomNumber[0,1) < 0.5))
 5          cl ← c
 6 if(cl is not empty)
 7    for each classifier c in [A]
 8       if(cl IS MORE GENERAL than c)
 9          cl.n ← cl.n + c.n
10          remove classifier c from set [A]
11          remove classifier c from set [P]
```

Subsumption of a Classifier. For a classifier to subsume another classifier, it must first be sufficiently accurate and sufficiently experienced. This is tested by the *COULD SUBSUME* function. Then, if a classifier could be a subsumer, it must be tested to see if it has the same action and is really more general than the classifier that is to be subsumed. This is the case if the set of situations matched by the condition of the potentially subsumed classifier form a proper subset of the situations matched by the potential subsumer. The *IS MORE GENERAL* procedure accomplishes this. The *DOES SUBSUME* procedure combines all the requirements.

COULD SUBSUME(cl):
```
1 if(cl.exp > θ_sub)
2    if(cl.ε < ε_0)
3       return true
4 return false
```

IS MORE GENERAL(cl_gen, cl_spec):
```
1 if (the number of # in cl_gen.C ≤ the number of # in cl_spec.C)
2    return false
3 i ← 0
4 do{
5    if(cl_gen.C[i] ≠ # and cl_gen.C[i] ≠ cl_spec.C[i])
6       return false
7    i++
8 }while(i < length of cl_gen.C)
9 return true
```

DOES SUBSUME(cl_sub, cl_tos):
```
1 if(cl_sub.A = cl_tos.A)
2    if(cl_sub COULD SUBSUME)
3       if(cl_sub IS MORE GENERAL than cl_tos)
4          return true
5 return false
```

4   Summary

This paper has revealed the processes inside XCS as well as the problem interaction. We hope that presentation of the algorithm in pseudo code with explanations will lead to deeper understanding of XCS and simplify research. Moreover, the modular structure should enable the reader to program the system in any programming language quite easily. However, our description only includes the basic framework of XCS. Starting from this baseline, we encourage modification as well as enhancement of the system, and welcome feedback on progress and results.

Acknowledgments. The work was sponsored by the Air Force Office of Scientific Research, Air Force Materiel Command, USAF, under grants F49620-97-1-0050 and F49620-00-0163. Research funding for this work was also provided by the National Science Foundation under grant DMI-9908252. Support was also provided by a grant from the U. S. Army Research Laboratory under the Federated Laboratory Program, Cooperative Agreement DAAL01-96-2-0003. The U. S. Government is authorized to reproduce and distribute reprints for Government purposes notwithstanding any copyright notation thereon. The authors acknowledge support from the Automated Learning Group at the National Center for Supercomputer Applications in Urbana-Champaign.

The views and conclusions contained herein are those of the authors and should not be interpreted as necessarily representing the official policies or endorsements, either expressed or implied, of the Air Force Office of Scientific Research, the National Science Foundation, the U. S. Army, or the U. S. Government.

References

[DC98]   Marco Dorigo and Marco Colombetti. *Robot shaping: An experiment in behavior engineering*. Intelligent Robotics and Autonomous Agents. MIT Press, Cambridge, MA, 1998.

[Kov97]   Tim Kovacs. XCS classifier system reliably evolves accurate, complete, and minimal representations for boolean functions. In Roy, Chawdhry, and Pant, editors, *Soft Computing in Engineering Design and Manufacturing*, pages 59–68. Springer-Verlag, 1997.

[Kov99]   Tim Kovacs. Deletion schemes for classifier systems. In Wolfgang Banzhaf, Jason Daida, Agoston E. Eiben, Max H. Garzon, Vasant Honavar, Mark Jakiela, and Robert E. Smith, editors, *Proceedings of the Genetic and Evolutionary Computation Conference (GECCO-99)*, pages 329–336, San Francisco, CA, 1999. Morgan Kaufmann.

[Lan97]   Pier Luca Lanzi. A study of the generalization capabilities of XCS. In T. Baeck, editor, *Proceedings of the Seventh International Conference on Genetic Algorithm*, pages 418–425, San Francisco, California, 1997. Morgan Kaufmann.

[Lan99a]   Pier Luca Lanzi. An analysis of generalization in the XCS classifier system. *Evolutionary Computation*, 7(2):125–149, 1999.

[Lan99b]   Pier Luca Lanzi. Extending the representation of classifier conditions. Part I: From binary to messy coding. In Wolfgang Banzhaf, editor, *Proceedings of the Genetic and Evolutionary Computation Conference (GECCO-99)*, pages 337–344, San Francisco, CA, 1999. Morgan Kaufmann.

[Lan99c]   Pier Luca Lanzi. Extending the representation of classifier conditions. Part II: From messy coding to S-expressions. In Wolfgang Banzhaf, editor, *Proceedings of the Genetic and Evolutionary Computation Conference (GECCO-99)*, pages 345–352, San Francisco, CA, 1999. Morgan Kaufmann.

[Lan99d]   Pier Luca Lanzi. An extension to the XCS classifier system for stochastic environments. In Wolfgang Banzhaf, editor, *Proceedings of the Genetic and Evolutionary Computation Conference (GECCO-99)*, pages 353–360, San Francisco, CA, 1999. Morgan Kaufmann.

[LSW00]   P. L. Lanzi, W. Stolzmann, and S. W. Wilson, editors. *Learning classifier systems: From foundations to applications*. LNAI 1813. Springer-Verlag, Berlin Heidelberg, 2000.

[LW00]   Pier Luca Lanzi and Stewart W. Wilson. Toward optimal classifier system performance in non-markov environments. *Evoultionary Computation*, 8(4):393–418, 2000.

[SB98]   Richard S. Sutton and Andrew G. Barto. *Reinforcement learning: An introduction*. MIT Press, Cambridge, MA, 1998.

[Wil95]   Stewart W. Wilson. Classifier fitness based on accuracy. *Evolutionary Computation*, 3(2):149–175, 1995.

[Wil98] S. W. Wilson. Generalization in the XCS classifier system. In John R. Koza, Wolfgang Banzhaf, Kumar Chellapilla, Kalyanmoy Deb, Marco Dorigo, David B. Fogel, Max H. Garzon, David E. Goldberg, Hitoshi Iba, and Rick Riolo, editors, *Genetic Programming 1998: Proceedings of the Third Annual Conference*, pages 665–674, San Francisco, 1998. Morgan Kaufmann.

[Wil00] Stewart W. Wilson. Get real! XCS with continuous-valued inputs. In P. L. Lanzi, W. Stolzmann, and S. W. Wilson, editors, *Learning Classifier Systems: From Foundations to Applications, LNAI 1813*, pages 209–220, Berlin Heidelberg, 2000. Springer-Verlag.

Author Index

Lecture Notes in Artificial Intelligence (LNAI)

Lecture Notes in Computer Science